Treasury Management, 3rd Edition

Treasury Management

Third Edition

Robert Hudson
Alan Colley
Mark Largan

The Chartered Institute of Bankers

The Chartered Institute of Bankers
Emmanuel House
4-9 Burgate Lane
Canterbury
Kent
CT1 2XJ
United Kingdom

First edition 1986
Second edition 1994
© This edition copyright 1998

ISBN 0-85297-490-6

CONTENTS

Preface to the First Edition

This textbook was commissioned by the Institute of Bankers following the decision of the Council in 1984 to introduce the International Banking Diploma. It is designed expressly to meet the needs of students studying the *International Banking Operations* Syllabus. The words 'Treasury Management' in the title are designed to emphasise the Treasury and Treasury-related functions described in the book. Both authors have many years practical management experience in the Treasury of major international banking groups, and it is their opinion that the book, whilst being written primarily for the international banker, will also be of considerable value to those engaged in the Treasury function of any multi-national enterprise.

For bankers and treasurers alike there is a clearly identified need to be able to understand the various financial instruments and markets, to know how they are handled and how they operate, to recognise and assess exposures and risk, and to control the related dealing and operating procedures concerned. This is of particular importance today with the many developments that are taking place bringing new instruments and techniques into play in the world's international and national markets. The book sets out to meet the needs of students and Treasury staff in this context from a practical rather than a theoretical standpoint.

ALASDAIR WATSON
RON ALTRINGHAM

Preface to the Second Edition

Treasury markets are renowned for being fast-moving and the same applies to the environment in which they operate. In the years since the first edition of this textbook was published there have been many developments in the products, practices and regulation of treasury operations. This edition brings the information up to date, much of the material having been completely revised. This applies particularly to the field of regulation and also to derivative products, which are now given their own sections.

The emphasis on a practical rather than a theoretical approach remains in place from the first edition. As well as providing a reference base for practitioners, the authors hope that such an approach will also meet the needs of a wider audience. The need for management at all levels to understand what happens in treasury operations so as to be able to assess and control the levels of risk being entered into has been repeatedly emphasised by regulators and practitioner bodies alike in recent years. This volume aims to enable readers to understand not only how things are done but also why.

ROBERT HUDSON

Preface to the Third Edition

Continuing developments in the financial markets have forced some substantial changes in the structure of this book but the third edition retains its focus on providing a practical guide for those involved with Treasury businesses. The main changes will again be seen in the sections devoted to derivatives and to regulation.

The growth of derivatives markets continues to astonish even those involved in them with new products and structures appearing frequently. The detailed complexities of the pricing models and risk management structures used in these markets are beyond the scope of a book such as this. We have restricted ourselves to an outline of the general principles involved, together with an identification of possible pitfalls. This is written with the non-specialist Treasury manager in mind. Even those who are not directly involved in the derivatives trading activity will wish to be able to identify the opportunities and risks that have enabled banks to both make and lose fortunes using these instruments.

This edition has been prepared during a period of substantial change in regulatory structures. The Financial Services Authority has taken over the responsibility for the supervision of banks from the Bank of England. Its approach in some areas may differ from what has gone before. In addition, numerous European Union Directives have been implemented which are aimed at harmonising regulation across Europe. The section on regulation has been completely re-written to keep in line with these developments.

A further evolving change that will be of major significance for the financial markets is the introduction of the euro. Again, this edition has been prepared before the final arrangements for the euro become known but we have endeavoured to incorporate material that is as up-to-date as possible. One point that the reader will notice is that whatever 'new' developments take place in the financial markets, certain basic principles remain the same. This book aims to give a clear explanation of those principles.

ROBERT HUDSON

Acknowledgements

A considerable debt remains due to the authors of the first edition of this book, Alasdair Watson and Ron Altringham. Despite the passage of years since their original work, the breadth and depth of their understanding of the markets was such as to mean that much of the present edition remains little changed from their version. Much of Anthony Bradman's work on the second edition has also been retained.

The co-operation of the Bank of England in allowing the reproduction of material first published by them is gratefully acknowledged.

Several individuals contributed to the preparation of particular chapters and their help is acknowledged in the details about the authors.

Finally, the continuing sponsorship of the Chartered Institute of Bankers in taking this work into a third edition is greatly welcomed and the authors are grateful for the opportunity to work with the Institute on this project.

Authors

Robert Hudson MSC BA FCIB is Group Head of Market Risk Management for Standard Chartered Bank. After six years with the Government Economic Service, Robert joined Barclays Bank in 1978. There he worked in futures and options, asset and liability management and on various aspects of risk measurement and control. In 1994 he joined Standard Chartered Bank, working initially on the development of quantitative techniques for the management of bank credit portfolios, before taking up his present position in 1997. Robert was Chief Examiner for the Chartered Institute of Bankers, examination 'Banking Operations: Regulation, Market Practice and Treasury Management' from 1991 to 1994. As well as being the overall editor, Robert has contributed Parts 1, 5 and 6 of the book. Thanks for assistance in the preparation of the material go to Riitta Jeffery, Catherine Hunt, Low Guan Yi and Alastair Wilson.

Alan Colley ACIB DIPFS joined National Westminster Bank in 1972 and has worked in branch banking, credit control, training, marketing and treasury management. He is currently a Corporate Executive in the Treasury dealing room of NatWest Global Financial Markets. He is an evening class lecturer at London Guildhall University where he has taught 'Banking Operations' for ten years. Alan contributed Parts 3 and 4 of the book. Alan is deeply indebted for all the assistance he has received in the preparation of these chapters, in particular from his colleagues in NatWest GFM, from Allan Collings, Clive Davies, John Johnson, Steve Jones and Don Yelland of Greenwich NatWest and from Simon Hills of the British Bankers' Association.

Mark Largan MBA BSC FCIB DIPFS AMSI FRSA is an Associate in the Supervision Directorate of the Financial Services Authority. His background has been in corporate and international banking with various banks including the Industrial Bank of Japan and First National Bank of Chicago. He is also a part-time lecturer with London Guildhall University in Multinational Corporate Finance and an Assistant Examiner for the Chartered Institute of Bankers paper in Corporate Banking Practice and Law. Mark contributed Part 2 of the book.

PART ONE

Treasury Operations

1 An introduction to the treasury functions in international banking

The changing environment

It is easy to forget that the international money markets as we know them today are a relatively recent creation. New entrants to the financial world may find it surprising and salutary to note that the senior managers of their businesses have witnessed the creation of entire markets that did not exist when they themselves were starting their careers. Some of those managers may have done much personally to create the new markets. The pace of financial innovation and the scale and importance of financial transactions is, truly, amazing. A brief economic history of the financial markets is as follows.

Prior to the Second World War, international banking was mostly related to the finance of foreign trade. This activity was conducted by domestic banks in one country using the correspondent banking facilities of other domestic banks in various countries around the world or the branches of international banks that had developed their activities to service these requirements. During the immediate post-war period the international, or more properly the multi-national, character of banks gathered increased momentum as a result of the substantial volumes of trade taking place, post-war aid and reconstruction programmes and the provision of capital for the development of third world countries. Much of this expansion was in response to corporate demand with many banks joining the ranks of international banks through the development of overseas branches and operations to service the expanding international business requirements of their customers.

These developments took place in an environment of relative stability in both interest and exchange rate structures. This background encouraged bankers to accept both types of risk as inherent within the business of banking. Each bank's head office structure tended to reflect this with its main components comprising functional and administrative responsibilities normally carried out by accounting, advances, inspection, secretariat and personnel departments with specialised branches caring for customers' international trade requirements.

Prior to the 1970s, the relationship between different currencies had been governed by a system of fixed parities, albeit subject to occasional realignment. During the late 1950s and early 1960s substantial international payment imbalances developed with both the United Kingdom and the United States running large deficits. It became increasingly apparent that first sterling and later the US dollar (the two major reserve currencies at that time) were substantially overvalued in terms of the basic strength of the respective economies. At the same time, large external holdings of US dollars had developed as a result of the combined effects of the US payments deficit; the post-war outflow of aid from the United States to Europe; and the interest rate restrictions that existed within the United States itself at a time when there was freedom to 'export' the currency. A direct consequence of these factors (amongst others) was the emergence of the eurodollar market. This is essentially a market within which currencies can be borrowed and lent and, through the foreign exchange market, converted into other currencies free of the restrictions that might otherwise operate within the national boundaries for these currencies. The existence of these offshore markets increasingly affected the stability of interest and exchange rates, both as a result of their direct impact upon individual nations' interest rate structures and also via the substantial exchange of funds between currencies for investment purposes, interest arbitrage and speculation against a possible re-alignment of a major currency's fixed parity rates.

The final blow to the fixed exchange parity system came with the collapse of the Smithsonian agreement, which had established fixed rates for the major currencies. On 23rd June 1972, the British government floated the pound and by the Exchange Control Amendment Act effectively disbanded the sterling area in its broader context. Many other countries were forced to introduce measures to stem the substantial movement of capital funds that was taking place. Finally, on 13th February 1973, the United States announced a devaluation by 10% and raised the official gold price from $38 to $42.22. The foreign exchange markets closed briefly and when they re-opened all major currencies were floating against each other.

Since then a number of formal and informal agreements have been established linking various currencies to each other. For example, most of the currencies of the member states of the European Union are linked to each other within specified limits, forming a currency bloc that floats freely against non-member currencies. At the time of writing, it is planned to make this into a formal monetary union with national currencies being replaced by a single common currency, the euro. In other parts of the world, individual currencies may be informally managed so as to maintain an approximately constant rate against the US dollar or some other marker currency.

Within a floating rate structure the rate of exchange of one currency in terms of another should be determined entirely by market forces with official monetary policy or smoothing operations being implemented as necessary through open market intervention mechanisms. Whilst it is often implied in the broadest context that foreign exchange rates are floating this is often far from accurate. Exchange control regulations and other monetary directives; two-tier financial systems; constraints on capital flows; negative interest rates; reserve requirements; withholding taxes; official exchange rate policy; and similar constraints all limit, to some extent, not only the impact of market forces on an individual currency but also individuals' freedom of access to various international currencies on a competitive basis.

The 1970s also witnessed the consequences of the two oil price shocks and the disequilibrium they created within international balance of trade surpluses and deficits. This impacted substantially on the expansion of the eurocurrency markets and the involvement of individual banks as intermediaries in flows of funds to sovereign borrowers, an area which had previously been, in the main, the preserve of private investors, governments and their agencies.

It was during the late 1960s and early 1970s that the european foreign exchange markets, in particular that of London, became increasingly competitive as banks in ever increasing numbers entered those markets. In terms of time zones, the european financial centres are ideally situated to overlap with Far East markets in the morning and the Americas in the afternoon. However, with increasing levels of volatility in both exchange and interest, the lifting of most interest rate restrictions in the

United States and communications systems that facilitated an instant response to world events, commercial requirements or, indeed, rumour, the european centres alone were insufficient to provide for global requirements and other major foreign exchange and eurocurrency markets developed around the world.

The behaviour of interest rates in the late 1970s and early 1980s involved fluctuations that were unprecedented for the major economies at any time in the 20th century. Short term sterling interest rates, which had not exceeded 10% since records began, rose to over 18% and US dollar rates fell from over 20% to under 9% and then rose back to over 21% all in the space of one year.

These dramatic changes in the behaviour of both interest rates and exchange rates were themselves catalysts for the development of new instruments: financial futures and options; interest rate and currency swaps; forward rate agreements and many other derivative products. Skilful operators in these instruments have been able to combine them with the more conventional products to add further levels of innovation. The need for intelligent use of these products as both sources of profitable customer business and tools for managing banks' own exposures, together with increased complexity in the prudent control of dealing activity in them, have been significant factors in the growing importance of treasury management.

Not only were the international banks quickly able to respond to these developments but many traditionally domestic and regional banks also took this opportunity to internationalise themselves to keep pace with, and take part in, these new markets. Although the majority of the larger banks have established a presence in most of the major dealing centres as a matter of choice, the necessity for many banks to develop offshore operations outside their own national boundaries was often prompted by the presence of domestic regulations which either restricted access to these markets or confined the extent to which domestic currencies could be used to finance international corporate requirements. The specific reasons why each bank required or desired access to these markets were varied: protecting existing business; funding domestic or international requirements; deploying surplus deposits; establishing a presence in the growing syndications markets; or simply trading for their own account in the interbank deposit or foreign exchange markets.

Alongside these developments, strategic objectives were heightened and many banks developed international operations not only through branch expansion but also through mergers and acquisitions, thus establishing themselves as major multinational corporations.

These developments were not without associated problems and casualties, for example:

● the secondary banking crisis of the 1970s in the UK;

● the sovereign debt crisis in the early 1980s;

● the Asian financial collapse in the late 1990s;

and other substantial foreign exchange and funding losses incurred by a number of banks due to interest rate and exchange rate exposure in unregulated and volatile markets.

It was within this environment from the mid-1960s that banks evolved specialist head office functions to care for their development and activities within these markets: International Banking Divisions; Treasury Divisions; Eurocurrency Lending and Syndications Departments; and so on. The responsibilities of each type of department will vary from bank to bank and may not be recognisable in any of the above headings. Within the context of this publication, treasury management is better defined as a functional operation rather than a specific division or department of any particular bank.

The treasury function

In a large bank it is likely that the Treasury function and the Financial Control function will be segregated whereas in a smaller bank a combined unit is more common. The centralised Treasury operation is concerned with the following functions:

● Risk exposure management embracing credit, country, liquidity, interest rate and exchange rate risks together with those risks associated with dealing in foreign exchange, deposits, securities, commodities and various financial instruments including futures and options.

● Asset and Liability management which incorporates domestic and foreign currency wholesale and retail funds throughout the world, the funding of assets on the best possible terms, mobilisation of deposits and the utilisation of surplus resources. Within this process, liquidity, interest rate structures and sensitivities together with future maturity profiles are major considerations in addition to the management of day to day funding requirements.

- The co-ordination of local money book management in various centres throughout the world.

- Control and development of dealing operations incorporating cash, forward, futures, options, interest rate and currency swaps and forward rate agreements, etc.

- Responsibility for the judicious use of the bank's name.

- The funding of investments in subsidiaries and affiliates.

- Capital debt raising and loan stock administration.

- Control of investment portfolios and the utilisation of a bank's own liquid resources.

- Fraud protection.

Financial control operations normally embrace the following functions:

- Financial accounts.

- International taxation.

- Management information.

- Budgeting and forecasting.

- Capital appraisal.

The principal functional responsibility of the international treasury of a bank is the funding of the bank's foreign currency business and investments. This embraces not only short term liabilities and working capital raised by way of money market deposits and instruments on the widest possible range of money markets but also the acquisition of long term debt for balance sheet structural purposes. Resorting to any market in a haphazard fashion may reflect adversely on the borrower's name if it is perceived by others in the market that there exists a lack of planning and control in the way in which the borrower operates. To ensure that the bank obtains ready access to all available money markets in order to continue to service its business, it is essential that effective planning and control constantly protect the good quality of the bank's name.

The 1984 banking crisis demonstrated just how fragile the good names of highly respected financial institutions could be. Banks are vulnerable to sudden withdrawal of deposits (frequently prompted by self-prophetic rumours) and unless the liability structure of the bank is sufficiently diversified to withstand a run as confidence evaporates, even the public assurance of a central bank or a public insurance corporation such as the Federal Deposit Insurance Corporation (FDIC) may not necessarily be able to save the bank from liquidation.

Good press coverage and continued payment of healthy dividends can help to conceal fundamental management and structural defects for a while. The size of a company is not a guarantee of its stability. Its structure is all-important. The quality of the debt acquired and the margin over funding costs are key factors in the continued success of a banking business. Growth of loans and investments must also be supported by growth in profits and the capital base.

With diminished margins and increased competition for high quality business there has been a drive for ways to increase profitability. This applies not only to banks but also to most other commercial enterprises and the drive has been directed towards the buyers in industry to improve their sourcing. Likewise in many banks an objective of the treasury function has been to achieve lower costs of funding and various techniques such as interest rate and currency swaps have been introduced which have enabled banks to reduce funding costs.

Large banks which have been created as a result of a number of mergers and acquisitions often have one or more major subsidiary banking or finance companies and therefore tend to have quite different structures. It is not unusual to find autonomous units each maintaining separate treasury and financial control functions and indeed there generally exist good legal and tax reasons for maintaining a completely arms length operation in certain centres abroad. There is also a recognised need for operational units of a large international bank to remain flexible in order to meet local regulations, get the best from local markets and provide a required level of service for customers in a very competitive international banking environment.

Opportunities to streamline and centralise the group treasury function are often inhibited by the need to make fundamental changes to systems, structures, and personnel as well as additional investment for which no immediate return can necessarily be guaranteed and these changes are generally resisted. Extra branches and subsidiaries are tacked on to an existing framework, new business schemes are promoted and new markets developed where a policy of expansion and diversification is apparent. Periodic reviews of the structure may be necessary to ensure that the group's international banking operations remain properly co-ordinated and effectively controlled.

Large banks may aim to compromise between the benefits of decentralised local knowledge and the economies of central co-ordination by establishing a set of internal transfer pricing rules that set the rates at which the central treasury will deal with other bank units. These rates can be adjusted to ensure that the bank makes optimal use of its overall resources whilst still permitting a high degree of local autonomy.

The centralised treasury function of an international bank is essentially one of policy formulation, group control and co-ordination of liabilities and dealing operations. Local treasury functions in branches or subsidiaries are usually responsible for foreign exchange operations, domestic money market operations, eurocurrency money market operations (where applicable) and funding of the branch's or subsidiary's business. The local treasury would maintain a close liaison with the central or group treasury function in respect of group philosophy on risk exposures and the remittance/retention of profits. Local regulations may well be the determining factor regarding the retention of profits and fiscal regulations often have a bearing on the method of distribution. The amount of capital (or quasi-capital in the case of a branch) injected by head office will be governed by the criteria laid down by the host country's regulations and the anticipated level and nature of the branch or subsidiary's business.

The treasury function in local branches and subsidiaries will also maintain close liaison with the internal auditor on the subject of controls and with their local management regarding mandatory and prudential control requirements.

Control of dealing is an essential treasury feature and technical experience by those responsible for this function is imperative. In establishing guidelines, whether by way of a written manual or something less formal, it is necessary to know where to draw the line between sensible and effective controls and those which are merely oppressive and deny dealers the opportunity to function effectively in their market. It is common practice for the central treasury to make surprise visits to various dealing operations throughout the group, in addition to spot checks by the bank's internal audit or inspection teams. It is essential for controllers to be aware of dealers' needs and to be familiar with market conditions. Good dealers are a valuable commodity and they know it! Increasingly, banks are recognising that good risk managers are equally important. Uncontrolled markets are more open to abuse than those which are well regulated - dealers know this too and are sometimes tempted to exploit situations which go apparently unpoliced. The local treasurer, or whoever is responsible for dealing functions, is often an experienced ex-dealer who understands the markets and dealers. It is normal practice for international banks to have arrangements for the local man to have regular and ready access to the central treasury with whom a regular dialogue is maintained.

The segregation of duties is an important principle of treasury control and this has implications for the typical structure. Whereas in the 1970s and even into the 1980s it would have been normal for all treasury functions to be combined, it is now commonplace to distinguish three layers of responsibility. The dealers are responsible for transacting in the market and have accountability for profit and loss. They will be supported by what has come to be known as a 'middle office' function. The term 'middle office' is used to distinguish the role from the transaction processing and recording roles which are often referred to as 'back office'. It is the role of middle office to provide management information and also to review and interpret that data, drawing management's attention to any irregularities. The third layer is provided by a policy and approval unit, which will often have a completely separate reporting line to that of the dealers. This group will not have a profit and loss accountability but will, instead, be charged with ensuring sound risk management.

Management of risk exposure concentrations, including asset exposure in the areas of sovereign and country risk and industrial concentration may also constitute part of the responsibilities of a central treasury.

Profitability is, of course, the principal driving force for an international bank. To this end, banks have tended to focus their thinking on several key areas. These include:

- Improving funding techniques by accessing a more diverse range of markets and entities with liquid funds and so attracting funds as cheaply as possible. The treasury function will be directly involved.

- Tightening advances/investment control policies and spreading the asset portfolio more widely in both geographical and client terms. Only an indirect involvement by treasury would be normal.

- Raising the proportion of income that comes from fees rather than interest income - in particular trade related activities, securities business, new financial instruments and innovative credit lines all of which tend to generate off balance sheet income and perhaps improve the return on capital. Treasury will often take the lead in these developments.

The next chapters of this part of the book describe the nature of the risks inherent in treasury activities and how asset and liability management can provide objective data on which appropriate policy decisions can be based.

Part 2 deals with the regulations that govern the markets within which bank treasuries operate and that define the standards required by regulatory authorities.

Banks involved in international business are often more reliant on money market funds and instruments than on customer deposits to service their loan and investment portfolios. They may also be active as issuers or investors in the securities markets. Part 3 describes the short-term markets whilst Part 4 deals with the longer term or debt capital markets.

Recent years have seen the development of numerous instruments that allow banks to adjust their market risk exposures without the need to employ on-balance sheet assets and liabilities. These items, often called derivatives, are discussed in Part 5.

Two final chapters on accounting principles and correspondent banking complete this outline of the principles and practice of Treasury Management.

2 Exposure management

Chapters 3 to 5 of this publication explain many of the activities a bank might undertake within a wide range of foreign exchange, money, derivative and capital debt markets. Whether the purpose of these operations is related to a bank's own capital or investment requirements, trading for its own account, hedging structural positions, funding purposes or covering underlying commercial business, many elements of risk are involved. Some of these risks are unique to these particular markets, others are not and have in the past been accepted as traditional and inherent risks within the nature of banking. However, they now require increased attention and consideration due to the very volatile nature of interest and exchange rate movements. Other risk considerations arise from the expansion of international banking itself, particularly in its role in the distribution and re-cycling of the substantial disequilibrium in international balance of payments surpluses and deficits. In many instances risk is not only confined to a bank's activities within the international and wholesale domestic markets but also impacts upon the totality of a banking institution's operation.

Part 2 considers the supervisory authorities' approach to the prudential supervision of individual banks together with certain guidelines related to risk exposure which may be applied and within which each bank falling under those authorities' control will be expected to operate. Banking regulation has developed rapidly in recent years and now embodies many of the sound risk management practices that banks should be wishing to put in place themselves, with or without regulatory compulsion. Ultimate responsibility for the management and control of risks and exposure, as with all the other activities a bank may undertake, rests with the board and management of each individual banking institution. It is their responsibility to consider and review the totality of that institution's exposure to each risk. In discharging this responsibility it is necessary to identify all the various areas of risk to which the particular institution is exposed, assessing and evaluating the possible impact each type of risk could have upon its capital structure and the continued success of its operations. Thereafter it should quantify, through approved limits and policy documents, the levels of exposure that the institution is prepared to accept relative to each type of activity and with each individual counterparty, taking into account any official guidelines or statutory restrictions. Management should also establish a suitable system of internal controls and reporting requirements to ensure compliance with these objectives and should monitor actual exposure on a regular basis. The whole of this process comprises Exposure Management. These responsibilities extend not only to the activities of the parent but also to those of its overseas branches, subsidiaries and associate companies.

Each individual bank's management should not only be concerned with its own internal risk and exposure considerations but also should ensure that their decisions are consistent with, and contribute to, the continued development of orderly and sound markets. In addition, management must be conscious of the impact of market forces upon their decisions. For example in reviewing credit risk exposures the effect of exchange rate movements must be considered. For a UK bank to give a credit line to a borrower in US dollars when the $ rate is 2.40 implies an entirely different credit risk than if the $ rate falls to 1.20, for if the customer was unable to repay then the cost to the bank in its own reported currency would be twice as much. This chapter considers the implications of some of the various types of special risk associated with a bank's dealing and treasury operations together with the related exposure management issues, elements of control, and internal reporting requirements.

Credit risk

Credit risk relates to the risk that individual counterparties or other creditors will be unable to meet their obligations. This risk is as important in the context of a bank's operations in the international financial markets as it is in traditional retail operations and no business should be permitted with any counterparty bank or other debtor unless it is within an approved credit limit for that type of business. The subject of basic credit analysis, which is already well documented, falls outside the scope of this book and therefore comment is confined to credit risk issues specifically related to counterparty limits within the interbank markets, including criteria for assessing acceptable exposure levels on individual banks together with the format of counterparty limits which may be applicable to market related activities.

The largest volume of counterparty limits within the context of the interbank markets is established on an unadvised basis, in other words there is no underlying commitment to undertake business. Without additional information that is probably only known to each individual bank's management, it is difficult to undertake a meaningful appraisal of a bank's true financial strength merely based upon the information available in published accounts. This is in no small measure due to the growth of dealing in 'off-balance sheet' instruments such as those described in Part 5, details of which are seldom disclosed in banks' published accounts. However, counterparty risk assessments are undertaken and unadvised limits established often without any direct discussion or contact with a counterparty but merely on the knowledge that the name in question is active in the markets. Consequently, within each bank it is important that management approve the parameters of approach and criteria upon which interbank credit assessment is to be based within its own institution. Whatever additional factors are taken into consideration the prime issues will be those related to published accounts, eg capital resources and capital/asset (gearing) ratios. Other factors considered may incorporate overall size and world ranking, the standing of a bank in its own country, the quality of official supervision to which the counterparty is subject and its central bank's possible attitude to support and/or lender of last resort issues.

Reputation within the international financial markets is also very important. Trading markets are extremely sensitive to rumour and word soon spreads regarding banks that may be facing any kind of difficulty. Caution should be exercised where a bank is considered to be over-trading or expanding the size of its operations without prudential consideration of its capital base. The most recently published financial results are reviewed in detail. Substantial losses or other adverse figures will impact upon the size of limit one bank is prepared to approve in favour of another. Known strengths and reputations of management are a further factor together with a bank's spread of activities. The overriding measurement as to the maximum level of exposure provided to any one name will also be a function of the approving institution's own capital risk ratios, which will influence the institution's appetite for risk.

Within the context of unadvised facilities it is important to emphasise that lines can be instantly withdrawn, subject to the proviso that current exposure will only be expected to be eliminated within the terms of each specific contract. Whilst this procedure may provide some internal comfort particularly in considering liquidity and country risk exposure issues, each bank's management must be aware of their own responsibility towards facilitating the continuance of orderly markets when they consider how to use this capability. Whilst prime considerations must be a bank's own interests, and prudence must prevail, many instances have been seen where unsubstantiated rumour relating to a particular bank has resulted in the indiscriminate withdrawal of unadvised facilities to that bank without due recognition or consideration being given as to whether there was in fact a real problem. In some of these situations the action of cancelling lines has in itself precipitated a major liquidity crisis for the bank concerned.

For credit control purposes, limits in favour of another bank's subsidiaries or associate companies should normally be considered in isolation of the parent, based on the strength of the subsidiary or associate as a separate entity. A basic assumption of ultimate parental responsibility will not normally be given undue weighting within the assessment unless guarantees or other formal support are established. Subject to the considerations of local regulations or restrictions overseas branch operations are normally considered on the basis of the parent institution. However, this is not always the case and for judicious reasons individual banks may not be prepared to extend facilities to specific branches of an international bank's operations so freely particularly where claused confirmations, restricting repayment terms are in evidence or where there is particular concern in relation to primary country risk. It should also be remembered that a parent bank's support for its associates depends not only on its expressed willingness to stand behind them but also its ability to do so. In the event of the subsidiary getting into difficulties, the parent may find that there are legal impediments to its ability to provide support, especially if ownership is less than 100 per cent. For this reason, limits will usually be set at both group and individual company level.

Each bank will have an established policy for the level of internal authority required for the approval of limits, frequency of review, report and ratification by a bank's management or, as appropriate, board. A bank may vary these policies for facilities that fall within its own established credit assessment criteria for banks and those that do not comply with such criteria. Some banks have in the past drawn differentials between requirements for banks in a selected top stratum of world rankings and other institutions. However experience now proves that even some of the largest of banks can run into serious financial difficulties, which makes it questionable as to whether this procedure has merit.

Rating agencies play an important role in credit appraisal. These are independent organisations that publish their own assessments of the credit quality of debt issues made in the major public markets. Details of the procedures adopted by these agencies are contained in Chapter 18. It is useful to note here, however, that the ratings given to a bank can have a significant impact on the willingness of other banks to do business with it and hence on the price it needs to pay in order to attract funds. Recognition of this fact means that banks are often willing to give the agencies much greater access to information regarding performance and future plans than would normally be available to another bank's credit department. This reinforces the significance of the agencies' credit ratings.

Types of credit limit

The type of credit limit which management have to consider applying to any particular counterparty, be it bank, corporate or other market participant with whom the bank deals, will be dependent upon the nature of the underlying business it envisages undertaking; the manner in which it will be transacted; and the related market practice and settlement procedures.

Credit exposure manifests itself in a variety of ways. Within both the interbank deposit and foreign exchange markets it is customary for each contract to be settled in full at maturity or value dates. However, in the commodity and precious metals markets, counterparties normally only settle the net difference of all contracts maturing with each other on any particular value or settlement date. Within futures markets, it is usual for a clearing house to stand at the centre of all trades thus relieving counterparties of credit risk issues on each other but replacing it with exposure to the clearing house. Upon granting an option the receipt of the premium may be the only credit issue which a grantor has to consider but with the purchase of an option there is a credit exposure on the grantor during the life of the contract. Within the secondary markets, where delivery of a security is required, a bank will not only be concerned with credit risk considerations relating to the issuer of the underlying security but will also have to consider risks associated with the counterparty with whom the trade is transacted.

Within the deposit markets, both international and domestic, the major credit risk consideration is the ability of the counterparty to repay at maturity. Approved lending limits will clearly define loans that may be made available to a particular name and will usually incorporate time constraints. Larger limits will be given for shorter dated facilities and banks will differentiate between various periods when approving limits, eg overnight, call, up to one month, up to three months, up to six months, and will, as appropriate, specify longer dated facilities which may be provided. Unadvised facilities that allow for loans beyond a six month period tend to be the exception rather than the rule. Loan approvals will also normally identify the types of business which may be written in a particular name eg money market facilities, CDs, acceptances etc and in the absence of any inner constraint, limits will relate to total exposure whether transacted through the primary or secondary markets.

Credit risk considerations for foreign exchange limits differ from those for lending where a bank is concerned with the creditworthiness of a counterparty during the total period of a loan. A foreign exchange contract involves the receipt of one currency against the payment of another on the agreed value date, at which point each counterparty has a delivery risk which is the risk that it may pay away good value funds subsequently to find that it has not received the corresponding settlement. A delivery or settlement limit is usually established to cover this exposure. Secondly, a counterparty position risk is to be considered in that prior to value date a counterparty may become unable to meet future obligations. In this event actual exposure would be restricted to the possible cost related to closing out the counterparty's contracts at current exchange rate levels. Therefore in addition to a delivery risk limit, a limit will be placed on the total aggregate of outstanding purchases and sales. However, in recognition that the real value of this latter risk is far less than the face value of the contracts, it is customary in most banks to apply only a percentage of this total limit and utilisation when reviewing the actual credit exposure to a particular name.

Various mechanisms, with greater or lesser degrees of sophistication, exist to do this. A simple approach is to use a rule of thumb such as estimating the exposure to be a fixed percentage of the notional principal. This is commonly used as a starting point or in areas of business where the aggregate risks are not material. More advanced methods will take account of the tenor of the instrument and may apply statistical estimates of the likely exposure based on observation of historical volatilities and price distributions. Where markets are particularly volatile, and/or the sums involved are very large, further enhancements may be made to take account of the overall portfolio of transactions with the counterparty and the direction of rate movement that could be most damaging. Banks may choose to undertake scenario analyses, revaluing their counterparty exposure according to a range of plausible movements in exchange and interest rates so as to identify any particular vulnerabilities.

Within several primary, secondary and security markets arrangements frequently exist to exchange the underlying security for good value payment simultaneously, either through a wire (electronic) or physical clearing facility or over the counter. In these circumstances delivery limits are not normally established for counterparties. However, in other securities markets over the counter delivery may be made against anticipated receipt of good value funds or against an uncleared payment instruction. In these circumstances appropriate delivery limits will have to be established.

Netting

The scale of payments that need to be made between regular counterparties has prompted the growth of interest in legal mechanisms which permit the netting of payments due rather than having the full gross principal amount on each deal treated separately. In the gold and other commodity markets it has long been customary to net purchases and sales due between counterparties on any particular value date. In these circumstances ultimate delivery exposure continues to be an important consideration and suitable limits are established to cover this risk. It is also common practice in these markets for a principal to establish the right to net a counterparty's long and short positions irrespective of value dates.

This approach is now being adopted in other markets. It is quite common, for example, in the foreign exchange markets for Bank A to have a large volume of forward contracts outstanding with Bank B, the net value of which is quite small but the gross values of pays and receives is large. A number of schemes have been set up to try to establish that the real exposure of the counterparties can be assessed as the net value only.

It is now quite common for banks to sign bilateral agreements with each other that provide for netting to take place. A further step towards reducing risk exposures can be made by using a multilateral netting system. Several attempts have been made to establish systems for multilateral netting with the leading system, which now has widespread support within the banking industry, being that provided by Exchange Clearing House Limited (ECHO). ECHO was established by a London based group of banks and is now owned by Continuous Linked Settlement Services (CLSS), which itself was established by major American banks. ECHO provides a service whereby all foreign exchange payments between its users are settled with ECHO on a net basis by currency on the appropriate value date. In other words, if Bank A is due to receive $25 million from each of Banks B, C, D and E but due to pay $25 million to each of Banks V, W, X, Y, and Z, it will settle all these transactions with a single payment of the net amount ($25 million) to ECHO. Further details of the operation of ECHO are contained in Chapter 14.

Use of collateral

Margin trading, whereby a customer is required to make an initial deposit of, say, ten per cent of the face value of a forward foreign exchange contract, is one way to minimise the need for extensive credit checks when dealing with smaller customers. Thereafter, if the value of the customer's contract declines by, say, five per cent he will be required to top up his margin again to ten per cent. If he fails to meet the margin call, the bank will close out the position.

It is not just small customers who may find collateralised dealing attractive. Major derivatives houses may also have similar agreements between themselves, although the margin requirements tend to be low. The purpose of such deals is largely to prevent the accumulation of large mark-to-market exposures in long dated deals (which would require regulatory capital support) rather than to guarantee basic credit-worthiness.

Whilst collateralised trading can ease credit concerns, it brings its own problem in terms of operational risks. Banks' monitoring areas need to be capable of monitoring when margin calls are required and also to act promptly if requested payments are not received if the credit benefits are to be realised.

Country risk

Country risk refers to the possibility that sovereign borrowers of a particular country may be unable or unwilling, and other borrowers unable, to fulfil their foreign currency obligations for reasons beyond the usual risks which arise in relation to all lending. Sovereign risk arises from the special risk associated with a sovereign loan, which is a loan to, or one guaranteed by, a government. The special significance of sovereign risk lies in the risk that it might prove impossible to secure redress through legal action, ie the borrower might claim immunity from process or might not abide by a judgment. For country risk purposes, sovereign lending is treated as constituting part of a bank's total exposure and, although the subjects of sovereign and country risk are closely related, sovereign risk is ultimately a credit risk.

Following the third world debt crisis, the subject of the management of country risk and exposure has assumed increased importance and attracted greater attention. An individual bank or banking group's country exposure is its total external claims on borrowers in individual foreign countries and it is incumbent upon a bank's management to ensure that it does not become disproportionately at risk if a particular country with whom it has exposure runs into economic difficulties. Each bank normally has a process of country risk assessment which, as with bank risk assessment, will require management to define the parameters of approach to this task. First considerations will evolve upon whatever statistical information is available. Current or recent history of a debt moratorium or reschedulings will obviously be of major significance. A country's current external debt, official reserves, balance of payments, exchange, interest and inflation rate trends will also be considered. Economic developments and potential social and political stability, the possible impact of external factors such as world recessions, conflict or natural disasters together with the impact of movement in basic commodity prices, particularly oil, will all play a role. Where there is a secondary market for the country's debt, the prices at which it is traded will be of relevance. These assessments will be considered in conjunction with the individual bank's own prudential considerations relating to capital etc and a bank's management will establish maximum levels of exposure it is prepared to accept for each country. This will normally differentiate between short and medium term risk and perhaps incorporate various sub-divisions relating to its mix of business. Whilst country limits themselves will constitute part of the normal credit approval process, consolidated reports reflecting country limits, total commitments and utilisation will be frequently prepared and reviewed by management.

Country risk exposure is a complex subject which requires an examination of the totality of a bank's assets which cross national boundaries. Each parent bank will require to consider its treatment of the activities of, and its own relationship with, its overseas branches, subsidiaries and affiliates. Additionally, it will consider its own criteria in reviewing its exposure on the overseas branches, subsidiaries and affiliates of other institutions. Within the context of country risk it is necessary to consider both primary and transfer (or secondary) risk. The primary risk allocation is determined by the location of a borrowing entity. However, where the borrowing entity is itself an overseas branch, subsidiary or affiliate of a parent to whom the creditor bank could reasonably, in case of need, assume parental responsibility for a debt, there is also a transfer risk to be considered on the country of domicile of the parent. Conversely, where a parent bank accepts parental responsibility for the obligations of its branches, subsidiaries or associates, it will require to consider a primary risk against the country of domicile of that branch, subsidiary or affiliate. For example, if the Panama-based subsidiary of a London bank borrowed US dollars from a Japanese Bank in Tokyo against the London parent's guarantee, the Japanese bank would have a primary risk on Panama and a transfer risk on the United Kingdom. The London based bank would have created a primary risk on Panama. A bank's management will, when reviewing country exposure, consider figures in relation to both primary and transfer risk.

There are extensive legal, economic and prudential implications concerning transfer risk and therefore the management of each bank needs to consider its own circumstances individually. It has in the past been common practice to assume a parental transfer risk in relation to country risk issues associated with lending to overseas branches of a bank. However, the refusal of a major US bank with a branch in the Philippines to meet this assumed obligation has resulted in individual banks reviewing their stance and whilst continuing to assume a transfer risk, it is quite common for banks to differentiate between other banks' overseas branches on primary country risk considerations. It may also be the case that banks apply a restrictive clause when taking deposits in foreign branches to the effect that repayment will only be made in the specified country and subject to any government restrictions that may be imposed, thus denying any responsibility for ensuring the transferability of funds.

The position of subsidiaries and associate companies is more definitive. In law a shareholder is only primarily liable to the extent of his capital commitment to a company, be it subsidiary or affiliate, except where any legally binding additional facilities have been extended or agreed to. Therefore when considering country risk as with credit risk a creditor of another bank's overseas subsidiary or associate should not assume a transfer risk and, similarly, the parent may not consider itself to have any legal obligations.

Whilst for prudential reasons banks are frequently required to consider the cross border liabilities of subsidiary and associate companies on a consolidated basis, this should not be taken to imply parental responsibility. Many subsidiaries of a large international bank may in their own right be substantial banks within the country of their operations. Negotiating advised facilities with another bank's subsidiary without any reference or advice to the parent institution of such discussions or arrangements, or alternatively, undertaking transactions within unadvised lines should be taken to imply that parental responsibility was not sought or expected.

It is usual, when considering both commitments and exposure in relation to country risk, to consider all balance sheet and off-balance sheet items, eg acceptances, commitments under a bank's own letters of credit, confirmations of other banks' credits, liabilities under guarantees and letters of comfort. Transfer risk can arise where no primary risk exists eg lending to a branch of an overseas parent in domestic money markets.

Whilst the treatment of many items is readily apparent special attention requires to be given to unadvised lending limits, overdraft facilities and foreign exchange and other trading limits. It is reasonable to assume that for unadvised facilities commitment and current utilisation are the same. Inclusion of a commitment figure for overdraft facilities may range from current utilisation up to a total of all limits plus any excesses dependent upon internal policy and, where appropriate, agreement with supervisory authorities. Similarly, the exposure under foreign exchange lines is contingent on rate movements which may themselves be related to the likelihood of a cross-border problem arising. Banks will have varying views on what proportion of foreign exchange lines should be regarded as constituting country risk.

In June 1982 the Basle Committee issued a paper entitled 'Management of Banks' International Lending: country risk analysis and country exposure measurement and control' which set out for banks a number of considerations, recommendations and guidelines which the Committee considered banks should bear in mind when establishing or reviewing country risk assessment and control systems. The purpose of the report was also to encourage the development of a standardisation of approach by banks when considering these subjects, the advantages of which would be:

- To give banks some assurance that their system of measurement conforms at least to some minimum standards.

- To allow aggregation in summary form for banking groups nationally and globally for the statistical reference of all participants in the market.

- To enable individual banks to assess their own exposure in comparison with others - information which will be of value to both senior management and supervisors.

Market risk

Credit, country and sovereign risk considerations are all specifically related to exposure with individual counterparties. Other areas of risk which require to be considered within a bank's exposure management concern those internal elements of risk created by, or inherent within a bank's asset/liability portfolio and its dealing and trading activities. These subjects are associated with the impact of interest rate risk, maturity mismatch risk, liquidity risk, open position risk and currency risk, to which a bank is exposed in its day to day activities.

Whilst a bank is unable independently to control or influence the extent of price movements which give rise to some of these risks, it is able to quantify in absolute terms the total amount of assets/liabilities upon which it is prepared to accept this type of exposure. The main considerations in establishing such parameters are the relationship and possible adverse impact of each type of risk upon the bank's free capital base.

Increased volatility in both exchange rate movements and more recently, interest rate levels have, on several occasions, precipitated substantial losses, and at times irretrievable situations for several banks. These movements have also resulted in increased attention being placed both upon asset/liability management and group strategy to contain these exposures. It is now quite common for banks with an extensive branch network to centralise (as far as possible) the management and control of asset/liability exposures at strategically placed treasury divisions and dealing centres, thereby following a policy within which all but very short-dated interest rate risks and mismatched positions, together with a small element of foreign exchange business to cover customer requirements, are the responsibility of a specialist market-orientated unit.

Interest rate risk is the risk associated with applying different bases of interest rates to assets and corresponding liabilities, for example, lending or borrowing medium or long term funds at fixed rates of interest and funding such assets or utilising such liabilities against short-dated interest rate structures which will fluctuate throughout the period of the loan. Despite the maxim of banks not lending long and borrowing short, in an environment of controlled interest rate structures many banks in the past were able to develop substantial interest rate exposures within their advances/deposit portfolios without incurring losses. Appreciation of this risk was only recognised when some of these markets moved to floating rate structures. The demise of many Savings and Loans Associations in the United States was as a result of mismatched exposure to interest rate risks and some German banks have found themselves encountering a problem related to the same exposure with fixed rate medium and long term investment portfolios being funded with short-term and even overnight moneys in an environment of rising interest rates.

In the context of its activities within the international financial markets, a bank as a matter of course would not accept this type of interest rate exposure as part of its day-to-day activities. Any risk of this nature would normally require the specific authority of senior management. Although an element of longer dated fixed rate lending is evident within the markets, this is normally funded by similar period, fixed rate liabilities or hedged with other financial instruments, eg futures. However, this does not mean the banks do not raise capital, invest and trade in, medium and long-term fixed rate instruments as part of their investment, trading or business strategies.

Banks frequently make substantial fixed rate capital issues and substantial portfolios of fixed rate bonds may be held. However, whilst banks may accept the interest rate risk on capital issues, particularly where there is a capital expenditure project directly related thereto, there is an increasing tendency to exchange such funds (if merely raised for capital gearing) for floating rate liabilities through the swap markets so that they should relate more closely to the yield of the underlying assets being funded. Portfolios may be developed through the management and investment of a bank's free capital and reserves where the management criterion is to maximise rates of return, the success of which is measured against opportunity cost criteria. In this context the subject of interest rate risk is not necessarily a prime consideration. Many banks operate fund management schemes at arm's length in subsidiary companies and some relate to fixed rate instruments. However, the return to the investor is represented by the rate of return achieved by the fund managers and therefore the bank itself is not directly exposed to an interest rate risk. Another area of operation in fixed rate assets is within trading and underwriting portfolios. The assets will for the purposes of exposure management be traded as an outright position in bonds, securities or other instruments in the same manner as foreign exchange or any other open position exposure.

There are also many areas of the world in which international banks operate where statutory requirements are such that banks require to have minimum holdings of specified investments, some of which are fixed rate medium or long dated stock in a quantity related to their overall assets or liability position or their total statutory assets. As with other exposure of this nature, senior management within banks will require to be advised of these situations and, as appropriate, they will authorise appropriate risk limits thus controlling in absolute terms the totality of that bank's exposure.

Maturity mismatch or gapping risk is the risk associated with the movement in interest rates and interest rate differentials between assets and liabilities which are priced on the same basis, eg interbank or prime, but are mismatched in time. As part of a dealing operation, it is normally accepted policy to provide treasury areas with authority to establish mismatched positions to enable them to structure their various currency portfolios in anticipation of interest rate movements, allow an element of flexibility in managing short dated liquidity positions and avoid pressure on balance sheet footings being created through excessive entry into the interbank markets for the purpose of maturity matching. Management will normally establish limits by currency within which these mismatches are to be contained. Each limit will incorporate constraints as to the periods for which such mismatches can be established and will normally include a net, by currency or aggregate, progressive figure which must not be exceeded. Other types of limit structure, including the now popular value-at-risk approach are discussed in the next chapter.

As discussed in detail later in this book it is also common practice to run managed maturity mismatches within a bank's spot and forward exchange positions. Whilst taking nostro, one day value, spot and forward positions together, a bank may have a square overall position, mismatches in the value dates of individual contracts making up the forward portfolio will be permitted within established limits. This will enable positions to be structured to take advantage of interest rate movements as reflected by the differentials in the swap prices and facilitate the management of short-dated liquidity positions. The format of these limits will be similar to those for placings and deposits.

Open position dealing or trading risk is the risk associated with a bank being long or short for its own account, on an outright basis, of a foreign currency, bullion, commodity, stock, bond or other security in the physical or futures markets at any point in time in the course of its day to day operations. This exposure remains open until an opposite deal is undertaken to square or hedge the position. Within the international financial markets, even the briefest period can be sufficient time to transform a potential profitable outright position into a substantial loss. An open or outright position is the resultant net difference of an actual asset or liability position in a particular instrument adjusted by the total commitment to buy and sell that currency, security or commodity in the future.

Within its consideration of open position risk, a bank is not concerned with the time mismatch between purchases and sales or the implied cost of carry as reflected by forward premiums and discounts, but with the absolute gross impact of subsequent price movements on a net long (over bought), or net short (over sold) outright position.

To control dealing risk exposure the management of each bank will establish appropriate limits within which the outright open positions are to be contained in each type of instrument or currency traded. Separate limits will normally be approved for end of day positions and intra-day or daylight positions. The size of limits will differ considerably between banks dependent upon their size, the levels of risk they are prepared to accept together with their overall strategy towards trading activities. Many banks adopt a prudent and conservative stance towards these risks, preferring to rely on profitability from intra-day jobbing or spread trading expertise. Whilst accepting a reasonable level of outright exposure during the day, these banks will expect dealers to revert to end of day limits at levels which are square to near square.

Other banks take a more aggressive stance and will allow open positions to reflect short-dated views on exchange rate and other price movements, frequently in very sizeable amounts. This will be reflected within the end of day limits established but will also normally specify a senior officer or officers who approve each position taken.

Limits established for intra-day trading are generally much larger than those allowed for overnight positions and will frequently distinguish between the size of dealing positions that may be created in the normal course of a bank's own account trading and larger temporary positions which may be required to accommodate underlying customer interests. Some banks prefer not to establish intra-day dealing limits but to control outright exposure by placing limits on the maximum size of transactions permitted which must then be closed down within a specific time constraint. It is also increasingly common for management to place individual stop-loss limits on positions to ensure dealers close out a loss-making position rather than incur the risk that a position will further deteriorate.

Within the context of foreign currency exposure risk, a bank will also consider the impact of future exchange rate movements on both its foreign currency income flow and any corporate structural positions maintained. Until such time as foreign currency income, whether resultant from direct business activities, profit or dividend remittances, is sold or hedged, any exchange rate movement against the reported currency will impact upon profit and loss figures. Management will therefore formulate policy and strategy in relation to covering or hedging this risk with the objective of maximising its reported profits.

Corporate structural positions are normally of a longer-term nature than dealing or income flow positions and usually relate to a bank's fixed and long-term currency asset and liability positions. A bank will not normally during the course of its daily activities borrow in one currency and lend in another without covering the exchange risk. However, outright structural positions may of necessity have to be established or created for a variety of reasons for example:

- Net capital investments in branch, subsidiary and affiliate companies.
- The utilisation of excess liquidity in another currency where a bank is unable satisfactorily to deploy resources within the appropriate domestic currency due to local laws or market conditions, and a forward swap market of sufficient depth is not available to cover the exchange risk.
- Reserves or provisions maintained in currencies appropriate to the risk against which they are held.

Structural foreign exchange positions related to these and other special situations will normally be considered and approved by senior management on a case by case basis and be outside the day to day control of the dealing room. Within this process, management will consider the underlying reasons for the positions being created, evaluate as far as it can be determined the extent of the impact of exchange rate risk upon its reserves and consider whether or if, this could be minimised through a hedging strategy which may involve cash, future, forward or option positions, or by holding one particular currency with a close correlation to the base currency or through the deployment of a basket of currencies.

The revaluation and accounting principles for dealing, investment and structural positions are developed in Chapter 30. However, at this juncture it is pertinent to reflect briefly upon the impact of translation exposure. Translation exposure arises from the influence of exchange rate fluctuation on the consolidated balance sheet when incorporating the figures of foreign branches and subsidiary companies which maintain their assets and liabilities in foreign currencies. This exposure can impact considerably upon the free capital base, ultimate balance sheet size and consequently the gearing ratios of a bank, particularly where a high percentage of a bank's free capital resources are maintained in the reported currency albeit the main asset/liability constituents of the balance sheet are in various currencies. The possibility of such distortions make it necessary for management to consider the viability of the establishment of structural positions by raising or transferring capital resources between currencies to equate approximately with the currency mix of the underlying asset base or otherwise hedge against these movements.

Futures and options

There are also other special exposure risks to be considered in relation to futures and option activities. In futures trading (whether for hedging or trading purposes) the adverse impact of cash flow volatility through variation margin calls must not be overlooked. During periods of high volatility in price movements these can be substantial and limits in absolute terms should be formulated within which variation margin requirements are to be contained. The granting of call options on an uncovered basis exposes a bank to unlimited risk on a rising market while the granting of put options gives rise to a quantifiable but nevertheless substantial risk of a falling market.

Unless a bank is operating within the parameters of a proven pricing and hedging module (a subject which is discussed in further detail in Chapter 28), all options granted should be considered in terms of potential outright exposures. Additionally, as with futures, the impact of any negative margin requirements must also be quantified if the option is exchange traded.

Liquidity risk

Liquidity risk is the risk related to a bank being unable to continue to obtain funds to meet its commitments, or having to pay a substantial premium to do so, and is considered in conjunction with Asset and Liability Management in Chapter 3. This risk is usually associated with the problems that a bank, through its activities, has incurred and which have detracted from its ability to continue to obtain deposits. However, in terms of the international markets, liquidity risk also has other implications not always relevant to the standing of a particular bank. These are more particularly concerned with the ability of the market to be able or willing to continue to meet the increasing demands being placed upon it for funding purposes especially by banks lacking a substantial base in a particular currency. The extent of maturity transformation which takes place within the euro and other offshore markets continues to escalate. This results from banks extending medium and long-term facilities to customers upon the basis of floating interest rate structures related to, and often dependent upon their continuing ability to obtain relatively short dated market funds to cover these commitments. The euromarkets do not have any formal lender of last resort facilities available to them and are interest rate sensitive markets in which the level of liquidity may be erratic.

A bank's ability to obtain funds at the finest rates and indeed to retain the confidence of its depositors will depend to a large extent on management ensuring that its capital adequacy, balance sheet ratios and exposure to loss are maintained at acceptable levels. Cognisance must also be given to external forces. In particular to the perception formed by investors and market participants of its country of domicile and major activities, together with the implications of its reliance upon the continuing liquidity of specific markets. These objectives all constitute part of the exposure management process. In addition, a bank recognises the need to retain or improve the market's perception of the quality of its name since this is essential to ensure a healthy and continued access to its sources of funds.

Adverse credit exposure decisions will be reflected in increased debt provisions. Adverse dealing, maturity mismatches, interest rate, currency and other exposure will lead to losses which will adversely impact upon either current profit and loss or reserves and can be very serious if they are allowed to occur. All of these factors will affect free capital ratios, diminish the return available on shareholders funds and restrict the expansion of a bank's business. These events will also influence other banks' perception of appropriate credit risk limits and this could precipitate liquidity problems. Although in the short-term a bank may be able to sustain the impact of running losses, an inability to repay deposits would immediately put it out of business. Management will continually review consolidated figures to ensure that acceptable ratios are maintained and, if appropriate, strategies will be formulated to direct activities to achieve this objective by ensuring the retention of sufficient profits or raising additional debt or equity capital.

3   Asset and liability management

The standard accounting schedules that detail the nature of a bank's assets and liabilities reveal relatively little about the risks that banks are running in their exposure to movements in rates and prices in the international money markets. It is the function of the asset and liability management unit to analyse these hidden exposures and ensure that the level of risk that is being taken is consistent with the profitable survival of the bank. In doing so, they will consider not only the on-balance sheet items but also relevant exposures arising from guarantees, commitments and all activities in off-balance sheet instruments.

Many banks control their market exposures through their Asset and Liability Management Committee (ALCO). The ALCO should involve representatives of Treasury, who will supply much of the analysis and recommendations, but must also involve senior representatives of the main business lines (eg retail banking, corporate banking, money market trading) so that the impact of individual decisions on the bank's overall structure can be properly discussed and understood. It is common for the ALCO to be chaired by the bank's Chief Executive Officer and for it to have considerable authority in vetting or initiating business proposals.

ALCO will be concerned with the following main issues:

- Portfolio mix.
- Liquidity management.
- Maturity transformation.
- Interest rate sensitivity.
- Foreign exchange exposure.
- Judicious use of the bank's name.
- Product pricing.

Portfolio mix

Within any portfolio of assets and liabilities there will be some concentrations of business. Some banks may make a particular specialisation of lending to, say, vehicle distributors or may have a particularly strong branch network in one region of a country. Such specialisations can bring benefits if the bank establishes a good reputation in that area but may also be a source of weakness if not planned and monitored carefully.

For example, a bank which has a high proportion of its lending book committed to one industry will find that its fortunes are closely tied to those of the industry concerned. A downturn in that industry will then give rise to problems for the bank. Most industries exhibit some form of cyclical behaviour and banks can easily fall victim to over optimism about the prospects for their customers when times are easy. A classic example of this is the property market, where excessive lending on the back of unrealistic business projections was the cause of a number of bank failures in the UK in the 1970s; Texas in the 1980s; and is again giving problems in many countries in the 1990s as a slow down in general economic activity leads to an inability of property owners to let their properties and so results in default on bank loans.

Equally, over reliance on a particular region will mean that a bank will have great difficulty in performing well if the regional economy is weak. US banks have been subject to constraints on their ability to set up branches in other parts of the country, although these are gradually being eased. The legacy of these constraints has inhibited them from spreading their portfolios internally and has been one driving force in their movement into the international arena.

Banks can avoid the damaging cyclical effects of such industrial and geographical concentrations by spreading their portfolios more widely. A serious problem affecting one industry or region will then affect only a small part of the bank's business and successful operations in other areas will be able to compensate for any losses incurred here. A bank ALCO may choose to establish limits on the maximum proportion of its portfolio that can be committed to any one industry, group of industries or geographical area so as to ensure that it can take advantage of such offsetting fluctuations.

These considerations apply just as much to the source of deposits as to the loan book. If the bank's source of funds is heavily concentrated, then removal of deposits by a group of large customers could have a disastrous impact on the ability of the bank to continue in business. The collapse of Continental Illinois in the 1980s was at least partly due to a heavy dependence on short term interbank funding. Once rumours of difficulties at Continental Illinois began, other banks rapidly withdrew their deposits forcing the rescue of the bank by the US authorities.

A broad spread of deposits is therefore desirable in itself, quite apart from the advantages it can bring in terms of pricing strategy. ALCOs may again set targets for the minimum proportion of deposits that comes from retail sources, these being typically much more stable and reliable than the more volatile wholesale and interbank markets. They will also have views on the appropriate currency mix of deposits, a subject that is developed in more detail in the next chapter.

Liquidity management

All banks should have a clearly stated policy for the management of their liquidity. It will normally deal with five main topics:

- Control of cash flow.
- Monitoring of undrawn commitments.
- Control of short term borrowing capacity.
- Management of a portfolio of liquid assets.
- Contingency plans.

A bank's first source of liquidity is the natural cash flow that is generated by its day-to-day banking operations. Those banks which operate principally in the wholesale markets, where loans and deposits are given and taken for fixed periods of time, should be able to forecast and control their cash flow quite accurately, in the absence of default by the counterparty. This will not be so simple in the case of a bank with a substantial amount of retail business.

A common characteristic of retail business is that the exact maturity of the loan or deposit is vague. Short term funding lines for small corporate customers, such as the overdraft in the UK, may be granted subject to review on an annual basis but contain a clause stating that they are repayable whenever the bank requests it. In practice, this does not make the facility either a one year or an overnight transaction for purposes of predicting cash flow. It will, instead fluctuate from day to day as the needs of the business vary and, if the bank did call it in at short notice, would quite probably result in the collapse of the customer and a bad debt for the bank!

Equally, retail deposits usually offer the customer immediate or very short notice access to the funds but do not need to be treated as overnight deposits for cash flow purposes. In practice, although some deposits will be withdrawn every day, other new deposits may be attracted and many of the deposits will be untouched. In projecting its need for cash, the bank should make allowance for the likely behaviour of its retail business, based on established patterns of seasonal variation and so on, building in a conservative estimate of the irregular variations that can occur.

We should also not overlook the need for cash arising from the settlement of foreign exchange transactions. Although they involve an exchange of what are probably roughly equal values of currencies, the bank must be able to supply the full amount of the currency which it has sold and should beware of finding itself in a position where it needs particularly large amounts of, say, mexican pesos to settle foreign exchange deals at the same time as it has to refinance a lot of maturing mexican peso deposits.

Similarly, an estimate should be made of likely drawings under committed facilities. Banks commonly have far more facilities agreed than are drawn at any one time. If there are reasons to expect particularly heavy drawings, perhaps for seasonal reasons or because a single very large transaction is about to be completed, these should be taken into account. In any case, banks should allow for a conservative margin of error in estimating the cash flow impact of undrawn commitments.

Banks will typically monitor their cash flow by means of a table such as that shown in figure 3.1. For each currency, assets and liabilities are tabulated according to their maturity. It may be useful to tabulate both the contractual maturity, assuming that everything behaves according to its legal form, and the expected maturity, which would adjust the contractual maturities according to the bank's experience of the actual behaviour of items such as retail deposit accounts. The table should also incorporate allowances for off-balance sheet transactions and potential drawings under committed facilities.

Figure 3.1 Liquidity Analysis

a)   Contractual Maturity (in £ million)

	Next day	2-8 days	8 days – 1 month	1 – 3 months	3 – 6 months	Over 6 months
Assets						
Marketable assets	10	30	30	50	20	5
Interbank placings	100	50	50	50	10	5
Commercial loans	20	30	30	40	100	300
Investments	5	5	10	10	10	50
Other assets	30	30	5	5	5	50
Total assets	165	145	125	155	145	410
Liabilities						
Retail deposits	450	100	20	15	5	0
Interbank deposits	80	30	20	20	5	5
Commercial deposits	40	65	45	10	5	0
Bond issues	0	0	0	0	0	75
Other liabilities	40	20	5	5	5	80
Total liabilities	610	215	90	50	20	160
Net foreign exchange	(5)	15	(5)	0	(5)	0
Net cash flow	(450)	(55)	30	105	120	250

b)   Expected maturity (in £ million)

	Next day	2-8 days	8 days – 1 month	1 – 3 months	3 – 6 months	Over 6 months
Assets						
Marketable assets	100	40	5	0	0	0
Interbank placings	100	50	50	50	10	5
Commercial loans	10	10	15	20	50	415
Investments	0	0	5	5	5	75
Other assets	5	15	5	5	5	90
Total assets	215	115	80	80	70	585
Liabilities						
Retail deposits	50	25	10	10	50	445
Interbank deposits	80	30	20	20	5	5
Commercial deposits	30	40	30	30	25	10
Bond issues	0	0	0	0	0	75
Other liabilities	5	10	5	5	5	125
Total liabilities	165	105	65	65	85	660
Net foreign exchange	(5)	15	(5)	0	(5)	0
Commitments	(20)	(20)	(5)	(5)	(5)	
Net cash flow	25	5	5	10	(25)	(75)

In countries where there is a well-developed interbank market for loans and deposits, borrowing from other wholesale market counterparties will be a regular source of funds. Access to potentially large amounts of money for short periods gives considerable flexibility to a bank to adjust its short-term cash flow. If a bank expects to have a shortage of funds today but a surplus tomorrow the simplest solution is to borrow to cover today's shortage in the overnight market. Banks must beware of becoming over reliant upon this source of funds, however, since there is a limit to the amount of funds a bank can expect to raise quickly without giving the impression that it is facing some sort of difficulty.

Furthermore, lenders in the interbank market are effectively competitors and may not always be prepared to lend money when it is needed. There is also the danger of a general shortage of liquidity hitting the market so that no bank had surplus cash to lend. In the case of such systemic problems, it is reasonable to expect that support would be forthcoming from the central bank but individual banks should not rely on such support being available if they alone get into cash flow difficulties.

The bank should also pay heed to the natural depth of the market in which it is dealing. Whilst very large amounts of US dollars or sterling can be raised at short notice, the same amount could not be raised in, say, rand or baht.

As an insurance policy against being unable to cover an expected shortage of cash flow in the interbank market, a bank should hold a portfolio of marketable assets that can be quickly sold for cash in case of need. Central banks may specify certain assets that are acceptable as collateral for short-term borrowings to meet exactly this kind of situation. In the absence of official guidance, the bank should choose assets that are regularly traded in deep and liquid markets and which carry minimal credit risk. This will typically be domestic government securities but may also include prime name bank or corporate paper in well-developed markets.

Stand-by lines negotiated with other banks may provide some comfort as a last resort facility. It is not uncommon for small foreign banks to negotiate a facility with a major domestic bank where, in return for a fee, the domestic bank guarantees to supply funds to the foreign bank in case of need. Not all banks are prepared to enter into stand-bys, however, since they are most likely to be needed when there is a general shortage of liquidity in the market. If that is so, then the stand-by provider may not be able to supply the funds called for no matter how willing it is to do so. Stand-bys are therefore of dubious reliability.

Finally, the bank should have a clear contingency plan in case it should run into difficulties. It should specify who is responsible for the management of liquidity in a crisis; what action is to be taken and at what point (for example, how late in the day can a shortage be left uncovered in the hope of borrowing in the interbank market before marketable assets must be sold); what arrangements exist with 'last resort' lenders, be they stand-by providers or central banks; and so on. With a properly run liquidity policy, it may never be needed, but liquidity problems can arise very quickly from unforeseen areas and are perhaps the major cause of bank failure.

Maturity transformation

One of the main functions of a bank is to take short-term deposits and transform them into long term deposits. This can only be sustained by the maintenance of depositors' confidence. The bank must be able to rely on depositors leaving their sight deposits in place or rolling over their short term fixed deposits in order to fund long term loans to customers. Partly this is a matter of remaining profitable and well regarded in the community. It is also, however, a question of prudence in deciding to what extent the bank is prepared to be mismatched in the maturity of its assets and liabilities.

Typically, a substantial proportion of banks' loans will be for periods in excess of one year but few of its liabilities will be. It will have its capital and reserves but there will be very few natural deposits. Banks can access the capital markets by issuing notes and bonds, some of which may serve the dual purpose of providing long term funding and qualifying as regulatory capital (see chapter 10).

Some loans that are apparently short term in nature may, in reality, be long term as the borrowers are relying on being able to roll the loan forward. This is also likely to be the case with short term funding of subsidiaries who themselves are making long term loans.

In deciding the extent to which it is prepared to extend the maturity of its assets, the bank must also bear in mind that it loses flexibility by committing its balance sheet capacity into the medium term. A bank which needs to rely on 50 per cent of its short term deposits being rolled over to fund medium term loans is in a weaker position to respond to changes in market conditions than one with only 20 per cent of its deposits so committed.

Interest sensitivity

The high volatility of interest rates in recent years has made banks much more aware of the impact that changes in rates can have on their profitability. A trading operation which is taking mismatched positions, for example borrowing six months money and lending it for one month in the hope that interest rates will rise, will clearly have a direct exposure to interest rate changes. Such dealing positions should be controlled by position limits imposed in accordance with one or more of the methods described below. In addition, normal banking business may give rise to interest rate exposure in ways that are not immediately obvious, but nevertheless pose difficulties for the profitable management of the bank and must be monitored and controlled by the treasury.

Perhaps the most dramatic example of the importance of interest rate management for bank treasuries is supplied by the US Savings and Loans industry which was badly damaged in the 1980s by exposure to interest rate movements. It was normal for S&Ls to grant fixed rate mortgages for periods of up to 30 years. Rates for customers had typically been around ten per cent and the deals had been financed with cheap retail deposits or by short term borrowing in the money markets at rates of five per cent or six per cent. During the 1980s, short term money market rates rose above ten per cent (and above 20 per cent at times!) destroying the profitability of the business.

Mismatch tables

At its simplest level, interest rate sensitivity can be measured by drawing up a table such as that shown in figure 3.2 which lists various classes of asset and liability according to the time at which their interest rate changes. Note the difference between figure 3.2 and figure 3.1 where, for example, medium-term loans may be granted for a maturity of 5 years but bear interest rates related to Libor which change every 3 months. The table shows the periods when the bank has more assets repricing than liabilities (over lent) and those when more liabilities reprice than assets (over borrowed). If the bank is over lent in the short time bands and over borrowed in the long time bands, then a fall in interest rates will reduce its profitability since its assets will begin to earn the lower rate before it begins to pay the lower rate on its liabilities.

Figure 3.2 Interest mismatch analysis (in £ million)

	Under 1 month	1 – 3 months	3 – 6 months	6 – 9 months	9 – 12 months	Over 1 year
Assets						
Marketable assets	70	60	15	0	0	0
Interbank placings	200	50	10	5	0	0
Commercial loans	330	90	50	30	20	0
Investments	20	10	10	10	10	30
Other assets	65	5	5	5	5	40
Total assets	685	215	90	50	35	70
Liabilities						
Retail deposits	570	15	5	0	0	0
Interbank deposits	130	20	5	5	0	0
Commercial deposits	150	10	5	0	0	0
Bond issues	0	0	75	0	0	0
Other liabilities	65	5	5	5	0	75
Total liabilities	915	50	95	10	0	75
Off balance sheet	270	(160)	(25)	(50)	(40)	5
Net mismatch	40	5	(30)	(10)	(5)	0

Interest rate mismatch tables such as this provide a quick overview of the bank's exposures but can be difficult to interpret. It is easy enough to see that the position illustrated in figure 3.2 is over lent at the short end and hence exposed to a decline in rates. The exposure presented by a more complicated set of perhaps alternating over lent and over borrowed time bands would be much more difficult to establish. Most importantly, a mismatch table does not provide a direct quantification of risk, ie it tells the bank no more than that it will lose money if rates fall, it does not tell it how much. For this reason, several alternative techniques are commonly used in bank treasuries. Amongst the more popular are duration analysis, value at risk and simulation analysis.

Duration analysis

Duration analysis is a mathematical technique that was developed in the bond markets. The technique takes account of all cash flows that are expected from a particular transaction, calculates their present values and then uses those present values as weights in calculating the average life of the transaction. A five-year bond, trading at par and paying semi-annual coupons at a rate of ten per cent per annum would have a duration of a little over four years, for example. It is beyond the scope of this book to explain the mechanics of duration analysis and, indeed, its pitfalls as it is far from being a simple technique to apply. It does have a major advantage over the simple mismatch table, however, in that it can be used to calculate the sensitivity of individual transactions or whole portfolios to a given movement in interest rates. A portfolio with an appropriately defined duration of 2.5 years, for example, would change in value by 1.25 per cent for a movement in interest rates of one half of a percentage point. This provides the quantification of risk that the simpler form of analysis could not supply.

Duration analysis can be difficult to apply in some circumstances. Many retail products in banks have interest rates that are not very sensitive to changes in market rates. They remain fixed within quite broad ranges of market rates and then jump to a new level once a particular boundary is reached. Base rate in the UK and Prime rate in the USA are examples, tending to move in 0.5 per cent or even one per cent steps or not at all. Similarly, the shareholders' funds of the bank are effectively a long term, fixed rate liability but they are of indeterminate maturity and hence of unknown duration. Furthermore, duration calculates the sensitivity of the present value of the bank's portfolio to interest rate changes and not the running profit and loss that may accrue. This may be ideal for a bond portfolio that is traded on the basis of buying and selling items at market value but it may not suit a banking book with loans and deposits that are accounted for on an accruals basis.

Value at risk

Value at Risk (VaR) takes the duration approach one stage further. Whilst duration analysis will tell a bank what its profit or loss might be if interest rates were to rise by one percentage point, it does not give any indication of how likely such a movement might be. VaR models aim to combine the impact of rate movements with the probability of their occurrence, thus permitting the bank to build a statistical distribution of possible profit and loss movements and so estimate, with a specified degree of confidence, its exposure to loss.

VaR models can be based on mathematical pricing models or on direct observation of actual rate movements in the past. Advances in computing power now mean, for example that a bank could revalue its entire trading portfolio under hundreds of different price assumptions in a matter of hours, if not minutes. The complexity of VaR models has grown in line with this enhanced technology so that they can now explicitly take account of any correlations that exist between interest rates in dozens of currencies and time periods.

VaR models tend to be based heavily on historical experience, which, of course, is not an infallible guide to the future. In particular, a VaR model calibrated on the basis of a historical period of stable rates will, correctly, indicate a very low probability of a sudden sharp change. However, as banks active in Asian currencies will know well, a history of stable exchange rates does not mean that significant movements cannot occur. Their probability may be low, but it is not zero. To cater for the possibility, albeit remote, of particularly damaging extreme movements, banks may supplement their VaR analysis with specific scenario or 'stress' tests based on simulation analysis.

Simulation analysis

Simulation analysis has also developed with the expansion of computing facilities able to process large amounts of information quickly and efficiently. A model is constructed containing details of the structure of the bank's balance sheet (maturities, interest rate characteristics, etc) and interest income and expense streams can then be generated from the model under various different assumptions about interest rates, growth of balances, competitor behaviour and so on. This is the most general form of interest rate sensitivity analysis since it can be used to demonstrate not only what might happen if rates in general rise by 0.5% but also the implications of 3 month rates rising by 0.25% whilst one year rates rise by 0.75% and so on. It can also identify whether the bank has a serious exposure to specific low probability events.

Simulation can be of particular value in dealing with some of the more complex problems in retail bank interest rate management such as early repayment risks. Many retail products are priced at fixed rates for periods that may be as long as 30 years but which can be repaid at the customer's option with little penalty. Examples can be found in consumer credit, leasing and especially mortgages. These features are referred to as embedded options and the management of the risks to which they give rise can be greatly assisted by simulating the likely behaviour of customers under different interest rate regimes. A considerable industry has grown up around the management and packaging of repayment risk in the mortgage market as detailed in the later chapter on securitisation.

A further type of interest rate risk that is not well handled by techniques other than simulation is basis risk. This arises from the funding of an asset whose interest rate relates to one benchmark rate, say treasury bill yields, with a liability that is priced in relation to another benchmark, say interbank rates. Although both may reprice according to the three month rate, any change in the differential between treasury bill and interbank rates will cause a change in the bank's interest margin. This is again a common problem in retail banking where customer rates are often quite unresponsive to the changes in interbank funding costs. A full simulation model of the structure of the bank's business will enable the treasury to identify basis risk and take appropriate action to offset it.

Foreign exchange exposure

The ALCO will be concerned with the continuing structural exposures to movements in foreign currency rates that arises from the differing currency mix of assets and liabilities in the balance sheet. This may arise within the portfolio of a bank based solely in one country, if it undertakes a range of international business, but is particularly relevant in the case of banks which have subsidiaries operating in several countries.

The principal choice to be made in deciding on how such operations should be funded is whether to fund the investment in the bank's base currency or the local currency of the subsidiary. If the base currency is chosen, fluctuations in exchange rates will lead to a variation in the reported value of the investment when recorded in the parent company's accounts. This is known as translation exposure and was alluded to briefly in Chapter 2.

If we designate the base currency of the parent as currency A and the local currency of the subsidiary as currency B, then the parent is taking on an asset whose value is dependent on currency B. If it funds this asset with a currency A liability, then a strengthening of currency A against currency B will result in a shortfall of assets expressed in currency A terms necessitating a write off from reserves in the parent bank.

It is possible that the bank might judge the exposure of funding a currency B asset in currency A as a desirable risk. This would be the case, for example, if the bank were confident that currency B was going to strengthen (by more than the forward interest differential implies) against currency A, or if taking on this exposure would help to offset another exposure already in the balance sheet. The decision must be taken in the light of the bank's overall funding policy which may include considerations of maturity structure, capital requirements, preference for certain markets, etc. The bank will also need to consider exchange control, legal and taxation matters which may dictate where, and in the name of which company, the funding is best raised.

The currency structure of the subsidiary's natural business must also be considered. This may give rise to natural hedges of the funding exposure or might, indeed, produce an exposure to a third currency that also needs to be managed.

Finally, the bank's attitude to risk as a whole must be considered. Some companies consider translation exposure to be no more than an accounting issue which has no real impact on the company's long term value. In that case, the funding of the subsidiary would simply be undertaken in currency A with no hedging. Likewise, the bank and its shareholders may be actively seeking to diversify the currency exposure of their assets.

The opposite extreme would be match funding of subsidiaries in all cases, minimising currency risk. Most banks will probably take a middle course, judging each case on its merits.

Structural foreign exchange exposures should be reviewed from time to time and not be regarded as immutable once the initial investment has been made. If the bank wishes to change its exposure, it can adopt one of a number of courses of action:

• Repay borrowings in one currency as they mature and replace them with borrowings in another.

- Enter into a long-term currency swap.
- Continue to borrow in the currency it wishes to switch out of, but use a series of short-term forward foreign exchange contracts or, indeed, options to change the effective currency exposure.

Use of the bank's name

The development of markets for syndicated and securitised deals is in one sense a threat to the position of banks as the intermediary between lenders and borrowers. However, it has also offered business opportunities to banks as providers of guarantees or other forms of credit support. Commercial paper lines, for example, will often require credit enhancement in the form of a letter of credit provided by a well-known bank. This gives comfort to the purchasers of the commercial paper that not only does the issuer stand behind the paper but also, in the event that the issuer defaults, the bank will cover its obligations.

Banks will undertake this kind of business in return for a fee and may protect themselves by requiring collateral or some other form of security. There is, nevertheless, a limit to the extent to which a bank can expect to be able to lend its name in support of other people's business. The commercial paper purchaser, for example, might have its own internal limit for how much exposure it was prepared to take to Bank X. If Bank X has guaranteed the commercial paper, then the purchaser may have used up all its available capacity for Bank X risk in buying that commercial paper and be unwilling to buy a direct issue by Bank X or to place funds with it by way of deposit.

The treasury should monitor the extent to which the bank's name is used and ensure that where it is franchised to other issuers, a suitable return is earned to compensate for other business opportunities that may have to be foregone.

Pricing

The final area that will be considered by treasury as part of the ALCO process is pricing. This can be divided into two parts: the pricing of products and individual transactions in order to earn a satisfactory return and internal transfer pricing.

The bank's sales force, whether they are front-end dealers or corporate account executives, have a natural inclination to get deals done. This is perfectly fine so long as the price at which they agree to do the deal is enough to produce a satisfactory level of profit after taking account of all the risks involved. These include not only credit risk, i.e. the chance that the counterparty will fail to fulfil his side of the bargain, but also all the other risks described above. A borrowing for 8 months and 15 days, for example, cannot be perfectly matched in the interbank markets but will need to be covered with either 6 months or 9 months money. This gives rise to interest rate risk and, if 6 months money is chosen, liquidity risk. Such exposures should be priced by the treasury and included in the cost of the deal.

Nowadays, pricing is often related to the return on capital generated. Capital is a scarce resource in most banks and requiring deals to meet a minimum expected return on the capital committed to them can ration its use. This capital may be calculated either by applying the central bank rules as described in chapter 10, or by some internally devised mechanism of risk adjusted capital allocation.

Banks that are not short of capital may price their business in relation to its use of whatever is their most scarce resource. This might be credit quality, liquidity, management expertise, etc.

Transfer pricing is concerned with the efficient allocation of funds to different business units. As banks increase in size, it becomes more difficult to ensure that a central treasury can keep track of all the business opportunities available and so optimise the bank's funding. When negotiating transactions, the bank's sales force cannot be expected to be able to envisage exactly how each deal will be funded. The most efficient mechanism is to aggregate all deals centrally and then fund them as a portfolio. In order to do this, there must be an agreed set of standard prices at which transactions agreed by the business lines can be sold on, internally, to treasury. These are referred to as transfer prices.

It is generally accepted that the most appropriate basis for transfer pricing is to use the principle of marginal cost. Each deal is assumed to be an independent addition to an otherwise matched portfolio so that a new loan, for example, forces treasury to raise a new deposit, the cost of which will be related to rates in the most active and liquid local market (normally the interbank market) plus the cost of whatever reserve requirements have to be met. Funds to cover the loan will therefore be priced to the business line at this marginal cost and the rate charged to the customer must be sufficient to cover the transfer price plus risk margins before the deal can be seen to be profitable.

The same principle applies in determining the reward due to those business lines that raise deposits. If the bank would otherwise need to raise funds in the interbank market, then the value to the bank of a retail deposit is the interbank rate. By rewarding deposit raising divisions at market rates, the bank provides an incentive for the sales force to search for low cost deposits.

Frequently, treasury will post a set of transfer prices reflecting prevailing market interest rates at different points on the yield curve. This means that the sales force can transact business with a certain knowledge of its own margin and treasury can be left to exercise its own expertise in maximising the efficient use of funding opportunities.

4 Funding operations in a multicurrency book

A bank's mix of current liabilities for funding its ordinary banking business will depend on the scale of its operations in each currency and each country. The degree to which it can attract retail deposits or indeed wishes to attract retail deposits has traditionally been dependent on the scale and geographical spread of its branch banking operations. Such deposits are an important source of domestic currency funding for both the major indigenous banks and those international banks with a wide spread of retail branch banking operations in various countries. Additionally, in those countries that are free from exchange control, a branch banking operation usually attracts substantial deposits of a retail nature in a variety of foreign currencies.

Banks with only a limited number of branches within a country will, however, tend to rely more on being able to raise wholesale funds. This may be an active choice, in order to avoid becoming labour intensive, but in addition may reflect market trends. As private and corporate investors have become more aware of alternative homes for their money, there is now a greater reliance on market related funds than on customer deposits in the form of current, savings and fixed deposit accounts received at advertised rates through retail operations. The overseas branch operations of many large international banks are often heavily dependent upon interbank money sources. To supplement this, issues of Certificates of Deposit, commercial paper programmes and other similar funding instruments (which are discussed in Section 3) are commonplace.

The bank treasury will aim to ensure that all assets are funded efficiently and that all liabilities are employed profitably. These aims can conveniently be considered together under the heading of cash management and the next part of this chapter considers various aspects of this function. The concluding section of the chapter considers some of the obstacles to fully effective funding management that can exist in the form of exchange controls.

Cash management

During each day a bank's treasury operation will analyse the bank's daily actual and projected cash position in each of the currencies in which it operates. A bank's payments in various currencies on any one day may well comprise, among other things, drawdowns on overdrafts and loans, drawings on current accounts, repayment of deposits, the purchase value of any assets bought, interest payments, fees and commissions, operating expenses, taxation and dividends. Receipts may be represented by new deposits; repayment of loans or reductions in overdrafts; cleared credits to current accounts; the gross proceeds of any marketable assets sold; together with any fee, commission, interest or dividend income. Additionally, both assets and liabilities in each currency will be affected by the net amount of any foreign currency exchange deals that are for settlement that day.

A bank's real end of day position is represented by cleared funds on its nostro accounts. For clearing banks in the United Kingdom, major money centre banks in the United States and large domestic operations in other countries, nostro balances in domestic currency will normally constitute their accounts held with, respectively, the Bank of England, the Federal Reserve or other central monetary authority. Other banks' domestic and each bank's foreign currency nostro balance will usually comprise the net cleared balance on their clearing or overseas correspondent bank account in each currency. Where more than one nostro account is held in each currency, the bank's true net cash position in that currency will be represented by the net of the balances on each account.

Each day the treasury will record and revise the assessed balances and for the major currencies of operation agreed cleared balances on each of its nostro accounts. These balances will be adjusted by any uncleared items anticipated to come into value that day, then, within the confines of agreed reporting lines and other internal procedures for trading, the treasury will monitor and control the deployment and funding of these accounts in each currency.

The objective of this exercise is to ensure that the bank's day to day cash positions are employed to the maximum advantage and that any shortfall positions are covered. At the end of each day the balance of each account will be expected to be maintained at the lowest possible levels within the agreed criteria for the establishment of the account.

Such criteria will normally be clearly defined.

Nostro account balances

Nostro accounts are occasionally interest bearing although by and large they are non-interest earning currency accounts and may in many cases require compensating balances to be maintained. A large or excessive balance left on a nostro account is generally a sign of bad husbandry rather than a planned treasury operation. Conversely, it is equally important that there is sufficient balance maintained on the account to service the business transacted across the account.

Nostro accounts maintained with correspondent banks or a bank's own overseas operations may be charged solely on a fee basis related to transactions processed or may require a specific level of compensating or other form of credit balance to be maintained. Some accounts will encourage credit balances by paying interest. The majority require interest to be paid on debit balances, often at penal rates of interest. Where regulations or agreements permit overdrafts on nostro accounts, any utilisation will normally be related to the highest or closing overnight money market rate for a particular day. This procedure is to discourage banks from using such facilities as a convenience in periods of day-to-day liquidity shortages in the money markets.

An essential function in an international bank is the reconciliation of its nostro accounts and the daily identification of balances held on it. Time differences in various centres around the world, coupled with the different practices of banks and dissimilar computer systems used by them, mean that the management of nostro accounts is a less than perfect science. Payments received as a result of, say, UK exporters' open account business may not be advised to the account holding bank before one or more days have elapsed. Many payments issued or authorised by a bank may not be debited to its nostro account for a while and the debit date cannot be determined at the time the transaction is originated.

Within a climate of relatively high and volatile interest rates the internal day to day management of a bank's cash position has become a specialised subject with major banks developing systems of instant internal communication to monitor movements. Also many banks have developed advanced computer and communications systems related to money transfer and balance reporting systems for the use of both their bank and commercial clients.

Throughout any particular day a bank can only estimate its cash position as at the end of that day on the basis of anticipated cash movements. During the day the actual accounts will reflect substantial swings from debit to credit as various payments and receipts are recorded. It is not until the end of the business day at the place where the account is maintained that the actual balance is apparent. The non-receipt of anticipated funds or receipt of funds that were not expected will result in lower or higher closing balances on the accounts than forecast. Within the financial markets it is normal practice to incorporate a value date on each payment order, which instructs the correspondent of the exact date upon which a payment is to be made in cleared funds. Additionally many correspondent banks will accept value dated "receive instructions" and are prepared to monitor receipt of funds on behalf of the beneficiary bank and, as appropriate, investigate non-receipt. However, irrespective of these procedures funds frequently are not received or paid on the appropriate value date and in these circumstances it is normally accepted practice to request or make payment with good value or to claim for compensating interest directly from the bank's counterparty or client.

Where funds are being paid or received by mail or other form of paper transfer such as cheques, traveler's cheques, mail transfers, bills for collection, negotiations, etc, it is not always possible to determine accurately when good value funds will be received or paid away from a nostro account. This is a particular feature where large retail foreign trade related operations are concerned. Usually in these circumstances the day to day cash management exercise will estimate an ultimate cash position based upon assessed mail and clearing collection periods but this may still result in large surpluses or shortfalls over anticipated positions. Where possible, arrangements will be made to compensate for these discrepancies. Many correspondent banks will now provide facilities whereby surplus resources at the end of each day will be employed within the local money markets and appropriate interest rates applied to these balances.

From the above it is evident that the day to day cash movements of one bank can impact upon the daily cash flow of another and a similar situation exists with regard to large corporate clients. Therefore, in practice, so long as no specific advice to the contrary is received, note will be taken of anticipated receipts and payments to cover individual client banks' positions and, whilst closely monitoring such movements, no action will be taken until an actual end of day net position becomes apparent. Additionally a regular dialogue is frequently maintained between bank officers responsible for these controls and their respective clients to determine ultimate end of day positions as accurately as possible.

In managing the daily cash position, certain products give rise to special difficulties. All overdraft facilities, for example, can be drawn down at the customer's option up to the agreed overdraft limit. Overdraft facilities are sometimes used by corporate clients as standbys and are most likely to be drawn at the least convenient time when there is a shortage of liquidity in a particular currency. The cumulative size of outstanding overdraft facilities should be closely monitored, particularly if the money base in the currency of the facility is thin, and funding sources are limited.

There are various interest rate formulae that may be applied to overdraft facilities and some offer alternative formulae for charging overdraft interest in certain currencies. The formulae bases include overnight euro-rates, base rate, prime rate and a variety of composite or other short term money rates. The ability of customers to repay an overdraft at their own option as well as drawing funds when they want makes this type of facility a particularly flexible method of borrowing. However, without a similarly priced liability base being available or achievable within the drawn currencies, it is not always possible for a bank to realise its full profit potential and this factor is taken into account when pricing overdraft facilities. In other words the flexibility of an overdraft is usually reflected by the relatively high margin over the base, prime or other formula cost.

Where insufficient retail funds are available in the liability base by way of current, demand or short call liabilities it will be necessary for the treasury to obtain market related funds at current rates to meet both current and anticipated obligations. In practice a mixture of both these strategies may be adopted. However, for the purposes of interest rate risk and liquidity issues, such liabilities will normally be relatively short dated obligations and will incorporate a spread of maturities for the bank's own day to day liquidity purposes. This also avoids excessive exposure to the vagaries of the substantial interest rate movements which may take place within the markets for funds in the very short dated periods, due to liquidity shortages.

Within the above strategy any subsequent increase in overdraft rates would improve margins whereas conversely decreases would diminish margins. The results of 'round tripping' (ie arbitrage activity by customers) is also a risk of funding overdraft facilities from market and fixed rate funds as opportunities will be taken when money market rates are in excess of the effective base related or composite lending rate for customers. They can then draw down on agreed overdraft facilities for the purpose of short term investment at market related rates, often with other banks. This practice increases a bank's funding requirements at a time of liquidity shortages and, immediately market rates return to below effective lending levels, overdrafts will be repaid and the bank whipsawed by its funding strategy unless express action has been taken within facility letters to exclude such practices.

Even loans granted for fixed terms can give rise to funding difficulties as their interest rates may relate to a variety of bases, for example, 7 day call, 3 month interbank, etc. As with overdrafts, a bank will endeavour to fund its loan portfolio with liabilities of a similar period and interest rate structure and, where deemed appropriate, a bank will access the wholesale money markets to facilitate matched funding of part of these portfolios. The extent to which matched funding is desired will be dependent upon the depth and spread of its liability base, liquidity issues related to the funding of other assets and the bank's current dealing strategy. The level to which matched funding can be achieved is dependent on the extent to which market related funds or suitable hedging instruments are obtainable for the period concerned.

Where fixed rate term lending is undertaken for periods in excess of those for which liabilities are either available or obtainable from retail or market sources (for example in consumer credit or hire purchase activities), a bank will endeavour to achieve a spread of liabilities at the lowest attainable cost, taking into consideration anticipated cash flows created by repayments and anticipated increased activity. With the development of the interest rate swap market, it has become possible to unbundle the funding and rate risks so that short term funding coupled with a long term interest rate swap can match the interest rate exposure of a long term fixed rate loan.

Negotiation facilities involve a payment with recourse usually to the drawer of a trade bill drawn on an overseas importer. The exact period of finance is indeterminable at the time of negotiation due to the vagaries of collection periods. Proceeds of a three month negotiated term bill would not be received in three months' time but three months plus the collection period. On the assumption that the drawee pays promptly and that the collecting bank abroad can and does remit the funds without delay, it will be a matter of several days before the negotiating bank can expect to receive notice that the funds have been credited to a nostro account, either in the collecting bank's country or elsewhere, or authority is given to debit the collecting bank's account in reimbursement. When considering the funding of such items the negotiating bank can only rely upon its experience to estimate the likely collection period and arrange funding accordingly.

Bills presented for negotiation may be drawn in either domestic or foreign currency. Domestic bills negotiated are usually priced on the basis of domestic fixed rates whereas foreign currency bill rates generally are determined by the respective eurocurrency rates for the underlying period for which it is anticipated that the bank will be short of these funds. The beneficiary of a foreign currency bill, usually an exporter of goods or services, may require the negotiated proceeds in foreign currency credited to a foreign currency account, but more likely will require the foreign currency to be exchanged immediately for domestic currency.

In the first instance, the modus operandi is similar to that for domestic negotiations to the extent that there is no exchange involvement. Within the negotiation the cost of the perceived funding requirements plus a margin will be deducted from the gross proceeds. However, should the negotiated bill be subsequently unpaid, a bank will expect to receive from its client the face value of the underlying instrument in the currency of the negotiation. If an exporter has subsequently sold the underlying currency for his base currency, any resultant exchange loss would be for his account, as the currency would have to be purchased at the then spot rate to reimburse the bank.

Trading portfolios

Funding decisions related to a securities trading portfolio are different from those applied to fixed rate loan or investment portfolios because the assets are marketable instruments which will be traded on a day-to-day basis rather than being held to maturity.

Within a trading portfolio it is essential that flexibility exists to trade in the underlying instruments and therefore funding applied for this purpose will normally be of much shorter term than that of the underlying assets comprising the portfolio. Such funds ideally will comprise a mix of liabilities from both retail and wholesale sources with the period of such funding being dictated in the main by considerations related to the time for which it is anticipated that the various elements of the trading portfolio will be held prior to their sale. Many banks fund such trading positions on a mix of short period liabilities with maturities often peaking below three months. The assets (in theory) are marketable securities although a hard core of positions held can be identified and funded for longer periods if interest rates are expected to rise.

Investment portfolios

It is inevitable within a bank's investment portfolio, funded from retail or wholesale sources, that the average life of the assets will normally be substantially in excess of the funding cover. Within this type of operation funding issues are an integral part of the portfolio management and therefore the fund manager will dictate requirements with the treasury operation *per se* responding to his requirements.

Exchange control

Controls are restrictive and any form of exchange control, by its very nature, will not only tend to have an inhibiting effect on free international trade but also upon a bank's access to international markets. Controls, however, are often considered necessary in order to maintain economic and/or exchange rate stability, although such measures will often prohibit new markets from developing or artificially restrict growth and development of international business and investment. During periods of contracting imports, weak export markets, substantial increase in debt servicing costs and a general development of adverse terms of trade, many developing countries adopt, or intensify, restrictive exchange and trade practices. Whilst there has been something of a trend away from exchange controls and towards freer markets, the widespread collapse of Asian currencies in 1997 did prompt some tightening of exchange controls in those countries. Exchange control in the United Kingdom was suspended in 1979, although the Act remains on the Statute Book and can be reintroduced if considered necessary without a great deal of legislation.

Banking operations conducted in an environment governed by exchange control regulations are, of course, quite different from those in an exchange control free environment. Bankers in the UK who experienced the post-1979 changes were confronted with new business opportunities when the long established regulations were swept away. As new markets and international banking operations and services developed in London there was a greater awareness by bankers of other types of control and regulations, in particular tax and accounting matters.

Exchange control may be described as the limitation of free dealings in the exchanges or of free transfers of funds into other currencies and other countries. The effect of exchange controls on an international business is a restriction on the free movement of funds between subsidiaries and between currencies. As a result, funds may accumulate at a profit centre where they are not required or reinvestment opportunities are strictly limited and from which it is impossible to transfer them. On the other hand, it may be impossible to make additional investments in a particular subsidiary because the country's exchange controls prevent capital inflows. Constraints may also be imposed on the provision of additional funding to branch operations from external sources.

The treasurer of a multinational bank needs to monitor the distribution of funds so that imposition of foreign exchange controls will have a minimum effect on its operations.

In an environment of exchange control regulations many countries distinguish between resident and non-resident funds with the latter being freely convertible. Such regulations will define the forms of permitted transactions. These invariably include accounts with banks authorised by the exchange control regulations. It is usual that only funds emanating from external sources, approved investments or other non-resident accounts in the normal course of business can be credited to non-resident accounts. Any funds that are required to be transferred from any other domestic source to non-resident accounts must comply with or be approved by the authorised institution(s) established for this purpose. This usually applies even where such funds originally emanated from a non-resident source.

The impact on domestic economies of "non-resident" funds, whether recognised through exchange control regulations or emanating from a freely convertible source, has, in the past, made it necessary for separate controls to be introduced. For example, in the 1970s specific controls were imposed to guard strong currencies such as Swiss francs or D-marks against unwanted inflows of non-resident domestic funds resultant from the sale of foreign currencies, particularly US dollars. Such controls typically are forerunners of currency revaluations and devaluations. They are often used by governments attempting to alleviate the need for currency realignment. In addition, they may be used to strengthen the effects of a parity change. The economic and other factors that indicate the need for parity changes, also indicate the possible imposition of exchange controls.

Exchange control regulations are an important tool in regulating the monetary affairs of a country with balance of payments problems. Whilst the regulations are generally designed to contain the potential outflow of investment funds without impeding the country's trading capabilities or foreign exchange earning capabilities, controls tend to restrict world trade and restrict access to the international capital market.

The central bank is normally charged with the management of exchange control regulations but usually delegates much of the administration to the commercial banks of its country.

It is not intended within the scope of this book to cover specifically, even in outline, the various systems in force throughout the world. The changes in this field are fairly frequent and many loose-leaf volumes would be needed. The areas that may be addressed specifically or generally by such regulations can include various combinations of the following:

- Matters of administration regarding authorised banks' deposit activities and methods of applying for permissions.
- The import and export of financial paper such as bank notes, bills of exchange, securities and insurance policies.
- Loans to resident companies controlled by non-residents.
- Permissions needed for transactions in foreign currency securities.

- Permission needed for securities denominated in the home currency.
- Disposal of estates, wills, trusts and other settlements.
- The issue and recording of securities by registrars, payments of interest, dividend and capital repayments on securities.
- Travel and education facilities, including allowances for travelers' emergency funds, accounts abroad for travelers, study grants and correspondence courses.
- Inward and outward direct investment.
- The way in which residential status must be determined and the action to be taken when a person changes status.
- Emigration of residents and treatment of assets, which may be restricted.
- Banking transactions on behalf of non-residents, in particular the type of accounts that may be maintained.
- Residents' holding of foreign currency, accounts held abroad, foreign currency accounts with local banks and blocked funds.
- Requirements concerning payment for imports and exports.
- Dealing in foreign notes and coin.
- Requirements for both spot and forward foreign currency dealing.
- Transactions in precious metals and other commodities.
- Permissions for documentary credits, contract guarantees, loans and overdrafts to non-residents.
- Local currency payments to non-residents.
- Types of insurance and freight payments.
- Payments due for various services by residents to non-residents and to residents temporarily employed abroad.
- Transactions concerning countries with whom major political disputes or differences exist.
- Property owned by residents abroad for private use.

The restrictive nature of exchange and trade controls is widely accepted as fact and, in recognition, the International Monetary Fund was established in 1945 as an independent organisation whose headquarters are based in Washington D.C. Its functions embrace the promotion of the following six criteria for its member countries (which number over 150) and it should be noted that the abolition of exchange restrictions was by no means the paramount reason for the formation of the IMF.

- Exchange rate stability.

- Removal of exchange restrictions.

- International monetary co-operation.

- Growth and acceleration of world trade.

- High levels of employment and improving standards of living.

- Development of national productive resources.

The IMF's Articles of Agreement prohibit member countries engaging in (directly or indirectly) multiple currency practices or any discriminatory currency arrangements without the Fund's approval.

Quantitative control techniques

Quantitative controls imposed on imports physically limit goods and services that a country may import from abroad. These controls are usually imposed in order to protect local industry from severe competition from one or more foreign countries. This is an area of extreme national sensitivity and protectionist pressures on governments have multiplied since the Tokyo Round, a Gatt (General Agreement on Tariffs and Trade) meeting at ministerial level in 1973. The ministers met again in 1982 and agreed to make a determined effort to ensure that Gatt principles were adhered to and to avoid taking measures that would restrict or distort international trade. These discussions have been extended to cover impediments to free trade in services as part of the Uruguay Round of Gatt talks that began in 1986. This resulted in the General Agreement on Trade in Services, which provides an umbrella framework for further liberalisation of trade in services going forward.

Relaxation of quantitative controls is often achieved by degrees in the form of the negotiation of bilateral agreements on a country-by-country basis rather than by the country that had imposed the control abolishing it altogether for the industry or product concerned. Within the European Union, the establishment of a single internal market has speeded up progress towards the abolition of controls between member states, although differing tax and other local regulations still inhibit completely free movement of goods and services.

Fiscal controls

Import surcharges, import duty and taxation also place economic or commercial barriers to the free movement of goods and services across frontiers. Measures adopted include the imposition of an extra ad valorem duty on all goods imported subject to VAT; stamp duty on imports and financial services; import surcharges on all goods or specific classes of product; and selective import and excise taxes. Fiscal measures are also adopted in order to stimulate exports from a particular industry or specific products. Examples include tax rebate schemes for exports, export tax credit arrangements, reduced level income or corporation taxes for profits arising from export sales and specific types of financial and banking services. Some countries employ such fiscal levies merely to increase government revenues rather than for domestic supply purposes.

It is quite common to find that countries impose a withholding tax on interest payments made to foreign residents in respect of securities held or loans made. Whilst there are often exemptions made regarding payments between banks or double taxation treaties in place between the country of the payer and the country of the recipient of the interest payment, it is nevertheless important to check that interest expected to be received from another country will not effectively be taxed twice as a result of withholding tax being applied without the benefit of a tax deduction at home.

Fiscal/payment controls

Advance import deposit schemes act as a very severe disincentive to trade, particularly if the percentage of the value of the goods to be imported which is required to be deposited is high. In some countries an advance exchange licence deposit is also required which necessarily means that the importer has to submit up to 100% of the local currency required for payment of the import, in advance of the foreign exchange permit or licence being issued, which is needed to enable him to buy the foreign currency for remittance abroad in settlement.

Controls by mandatory payment terms

Mandatory deferred payment terms may be imposed for the settlement of goods imported. Documentary credits may be required specifically by the authorities in the buyer's country. Forward purchases of foreign currencies may be prohibited or limited to within a few days prior to the due payment date. Official and unofficial protracted delays may be experienced at various times.

For exports, preferential finance schemes and credit terms that reduce the final cost of goods exported act as inducements to overseas buyers to prefer the products so subsidised. Various export credit guarantee schemes in the form of insurance cover and/or financial support arrangements are modified from time to time and tend to stimulate trade rather than restrict it.

Retention of foreign currency earnings is often prohibited under exchange control regulations and these have to be surrendered either at the official rate to the central bank or at the market rate. There exist variations of the percentages to be surrendered at each rate and likewise the period for which exporters may retain foreign currency receipts is sometimes adjusted according to the perceived national economic requirements of the country.

Countries experiencing difficulties in foreign exchange management may often promote counter trade or barter transactions. Such transactions are more frequently seen when exchange restrictions and other restrictive trade practices are intensified.

Convertibility and multiple currency practices

A currency is said to be convertible if the holder (irrespective of his own domicile) may exchange it freely into the currencies of other countries. Certain currencies are fully convertible where no restriction exists on the nature of the transaction giving rise to the required exchange or of the residence qualification of the holder. Examples of freely convertible currencies include the US dollar, sterling, and Swiss franc.

A large number of countries apply exchange restrictions to their own residents and therefore recognise external (non-resident) convertibility only. It was at one time common to have a two-tier exchange rate for a currency as a result of drawing a distinction between the types of transaction involved. Financial transfers as opposed to commercial transfers in respect of goods and services was the most common distinction. The last major country to apply such a distinction was South Africa, which abandoned its distinction between the commercial and financial rand in March 1995.

5   Control of dealing

It has always been a concern of banks' senior management that the scale of dealing activity is such that a few mistakes or inaccuracies could cause substantial loss to the bank. For many years, cases of this happening were few in number, the instance of Lloyds Bank Lugano branch (where a foreign exchange dealer kept losses hidden from his superiors) being the stock example. In recent years, however, spectacular examples of multi-million dollar losses caused by the activities of 'rogue' dealers have become almost common with institutions such as Merrill Lynch, Kidder Peabody, Sumitomo and National Westminster all suffering damaging losses. Most famous of all is the case of Barings, an old established group forced into collapse by the unauthorised activities of a single trader. The proper control of dealers' activities is now, therefore, a very high priority for bank managements.

Requirements for dealing control have also begun to be incorporated in regulation. Chapters 7 to 9 include details of some of the codes of conduct now in force. Within a dealing environment it is generally recognised that a specialist audit function is required to review control systems to ensure that their design is adequate and that they are being correctly applied. This chapter covers the basic principles of control which should be in place whether or not they are required by law and considers the fundamental requirements for a Treasury audit unit to ensure that adequate internal controls over dealing operations exist.

The UK auditing standards and guidelines define an internal control system as:

> "the whole system of controls, financial and otherwise, established by management in order to carry on the business of the enterprise in an orderly and efficient manner, ensure adherence to management policies, safeguard the assets and secure as far as possible the completeness and accuracy of the records."

The necessity for effective controls in dealing areas was stressed as early as 1974 in a letter from the Governor of the Bank of England to all authorised banks. This followed a number of losses suffered as a result of imprudent or unauthorised foreign exchange operations in a number of countries. The Bank suggested that each bank should undertake a thorough review of its internal controls, paying particular attention to the following:

- Some general managements seem to have placed their dealers in an exposed position by looking well beyond the service element of the dealing function and imposing ambitious profit targets upon them.

- In some overseas offices, managements do not appear to have paid sufficient attention to the relations between dealers and brokers.

- Dealers should never write their own outgoing confirmations nor receive incoming confirmations.

- Forward deals should always be confirmed at once: in particular, confirmations should not be delayed until instructions are passed just prior to maturity.

- There should be unannounced snap checks of dealing activities between regular internal audits or inspections.

- Central management should from time to time, on a random basis, seek from correspondent banks independent second confirmations of outstanding forward contracts.

- A bank should check with its correspondent's Head Office or main dealing office, if it notices that a branch of that bank has suddenly or unaccountably significantly expanded its operations in the forward market.

These concerns resurfaced in the early 1990s with regard to derivative products. The President of the Federal Reserve Bank of New York stressed in a much publicised speech that activities in products such as interest rate swaps *"have a role, but they must be managed and controlled carefully, and they must be understood by top management, as well as by traders and rocket scientists."*

Within a dealing environment the prime control objectives must be to safeguard the assets of a bank and at the same time ensure adherence to management policies. Many of the international and domestic financial markets are not sited in one building as formal exchanges. They are dealer-to-dealer telephone markets. During trading there is no independent supervisor or arbitrator available, a dealer does not have to substantiate the existence of his authority to trade and therefore can commit the bank to unlimited risk if not properly controlled. Many of the large losses that have been sustained by banks have arisen from dealers acting either without or outside delegated authority. Inadequate controls and lack of suitable division of responsibility have enabled adverse positions to be maintained without management knowledge or detection. Such situations do not always involve an abuse of position for personal gain but are often the consequence of misplaced zeal and judgement and subsequently a desire to conceal from management the true extent of a loss.

Within the structure of any dealing environment it is essential to provide for appropriate divisions of responsibility between dealing, processing and accounting staff with the senior officer responsible for each area reporting independently to senior management. Thereafter responsibilities and, as appropriate, authorities or limits must be formally and precisely communicated and acknowledged by each member of staff.

Trading limits

There are clear risks arising where dealers are dealing with their counterparts on the end of a telephone where commitments can be made with limited reference to supervisors. These will be controlled by the allocation of delegated authority to dealers defining their ability to act. Not only are delegated authority levels the basis of well managed operations, the monitoring of how this delegated authority is being used or abused is just as important for the security of the bank. Where a dealer has operated outside his delegated authority, it might be wrong to assume that this was done in order to defraud the bank or make material gain from the unauthorised intervention. In many cases the situation may arise because of the enthusiasm, commitment and exuberance of the individual rather than any attempt to profit personally. Given that these are traits that, if suppressed, could damage the performance of the individual, it is in the bank's interest to clearly define the appropriate delegated authority and monitor the situation.

In effect, there is a chain of delegated authority beginning with that set by the bank's board and extending down through each treasury operation to dealer level. Each dealer's authority to take positions must be clearly defined by appropriate limits (notional principal, mismatch, value-at-risk, etc) differentiating between intra-day (or daylight) exposure and end of day positions.

Where dealing books are separately defined (eg currency deposits, spot foreign exchange, interest rate options, etc) each dealer's authority to act for that book and the types of instrument that may be included must be defined.

Stop loss limits or the necessity to report adverse dealing positions at a particular level of loss must also be clearly defined and established.

Predefined bank and other counterparty limits must be established.

Where other forms of control over trading exposure are imposed these must be clearly communicated.

Senior management will normally approve limits by type, period and currency, and where appropriate indicate maximum aggregate positions for each dealing centre or group of centres if positions are transferred from centre to centre. These authorities will be vested in a specified person, usually the treasury manager or chief dealer who, whilst retaining responsibility for ensuring compliance therewith, will, within the overall authority delegated to him, provide specific sub-limits to each dealer dependent upon his experience and the item being traded. Thereafter each dealer should be solely responsible and accountable for positions maintained.

Trading policy

Outright open positions for daytime trading must at all times be contained within the limit specifically delegated in writing to each dealer.

Dealers may be allowed, through specific authority delegated to them, to maintain close of business outright open positions. In the absence of such authority, square positions should be achieved.

Mis-matched positions by period for loans, deposits, foreign exchange and all other trading items must be contained within the specific authority delegated in writing. Likely excesses over trading limits should be reported promptly and approved in advance.

Dealers may only undertake transactions with other market participants within approved counterparty credit limits for the principal name. Where transactions are undertaken in respect of a customer it is the responsibility of the dealer concerned to ensure that an appropriate limit is available to accommodate such business.

Each dealer must ensure profitable use/covering of surplus/deficit overnight cash balances as projected (on the basis of deals transacted and past experience on the nostro account balances in the currencies under his control.

Dealers should not enter into deals where the agreed rate is substantially different from current market levels. Requests for such deals can occur for valid reasons, for example where the customer's accounting procedures make it preferable to roll over a foreign exchange swap at the historic spot rate rather than the current one or where an interest rate swap is being structured to match cash flows on a bond issue. However, it is quite possible that the counterparty's request for an off-market rate is due to an attempt to hide losses or a deliberate fraud. For this reason, deals at rates other than current market levels should require specific approval on each occasion. It may also be advisable to check with senior staff in the counterparty organisation that the deal has their approval.

Customer dealers must only base quotations on rates obtained from the market dealers. Such quotations and rates applied must not be finer than those quoted by the market dealers.

It should be noted that the United Kingdom's Financial Services Act makes a distinction between wholesale and retail counterparties, the former being those who habitually deal in large amounts (exact figures are specified in the regulations relating to the Act). Special legal protection is afforded to retail counterparties, imposing an additional duty of care upon the bank dealing with them. Whether or not such a distinction has legal backing in the jurisdiction concerned, it is nevertheless good practice to take special care when dealing with occasional operators in the international markets since they cannot be expected to have the same degree of understanding as professional players. It is incumbent upon banks to ensure that their clients are fully aware of the exposures into which they are entering.

In undertaking trading activity, dealers must act prudently at all times and in particular be wary of structuring positions and portfolios where extraneous circumstances such as the introduction of penal, restrictive or exchange control regulations, could adversely impact upon their trading decisions.

'Put through' business to accommodate a particular bank name at the behest of brokers, jobbers or other parties should not be arranged.

Any deviation from the above policy must receive the specific approval of the manager responsible for the dealing operation or other appropriately delegated officers on a deal by deal basis.

Operational policy

The roles of all parties involved in the transacting, processing, recording, checking and monitoring of transactions must be clearly defined and well understood by those concerned. The list of duties should be complete and clear so that there is no scope for important tasks to be omitted because the person responsible believed it was someone else's job.

Within the authority delegated to him each dealer is solely responsible and accountable for positions maintained by him. All deals transacted must be properly recorded in the dealer's own position record and subsequently agreed at the close of business each day with the settlement records or other such position record maintained. All transactions should be properly recorded on dealing slips and submitted to the operations area for processing at the time the deal is concluded. Some dealing systems automatically update the dealer's position on a real time basis and process confirmations without the necessity of raising dealing slips. Where dealing slips are used, a system of time stamping and numbering each deal should be used as it will assist in ensuring all deals are promptly recorded and undertaken within the market spread.

Although still said to be illegal in some countries, it is common for all telephone lines used in dealing and the immediate back-up functions to be recorded. UK regulators strongly favour such voice logging. This facility is normally only used to resolve discrepancies or mis-understandings of trades undertaken and both parties to the deal would normally be invited to be present when the tape was reviewed. When installing recording equipment, banks should take steps to inform other market participants that conversations will be recorded. Access to the recording equipment should be controlled.

The accuracy of information recorded on dealing slips and its legibility are important in ensuring that misunderstandings do not occur in the processing and accounting areas. Where unusual or complicated deals are concerned, a brief note providing an audit trail to the transaction should be attached.

Dealers must take care to annotate on dealing slips the correct rates at which the deals were concluded. Fictitious rates should not be recorded on dealing slips for any reason. Many banks have programmed their computers which process deals to ensure that there is a daily tolerance for spot movements based upon anticipated volatility. The computer will reject any transaction that is outside the tolerance.

Moral and ethical policy

To avoid any misunderstanding, it is important that dealers are made aware of the code of moral and ethical conduct that the bank desires them to follow.

Dealers are expected to act prudently and in the best interests of their bank at all times. In addition to internal requirements, they must be conscious of, and work within, the requirements of any local statutory regulations, exchange controls, etc and codes of conduct issued by regulatory bodies. Likewise, a firm is deemed to be responsible for the actions of its dealers and should ensure that they conform to best practice at all times.

The highest level of confidentiality must be maintained and the anonymity of the markets respected at all times.

Should a dealer receive a request to transact a deal outside of current market rates, notice a willingness by dealers in other banks to deal outside market rates or consider that another bank or counterparty is trading at an unusually large volume, the matter should be brought to the attention of management immediately. Similarly, if a dealer hears through the market any suggestion of a problem in relation to any counterparty, management should be informed immediately.

Whilst the importance of personal contact with counterparties, customers, banks, brokers, etc is recognised, dealers must act prudently in accepting entertainment. Prior approval should be obtained within the bank to any entertainment offered outside the dealer's normal working hours. Gifts or favours must not be accepted without similar prior approval.

High-pressure environments such as dealing rooms may also be prone to the abuse of drugs or alcohol. Management should take reasonable steps to identify staff who may become dependent on abused substances as they could in due course become vulnerable to outside inducements to take action detrimental to the interests of the bank.

It is also necessary to place the following restrictions within a dealer's terms of reference:

- Under no circumstances should dealers become involved either directly or indirectly in processing and accounting issues, in particular confirmations, brokers' notes and pay and receive procedures. Any computer facilities made available to dealers must be on a restricted access basis.

- Dealers should normally only be permitted to transact business with brokers, jobbers, banks or other counterparties from their (the dealer's) place of work. A principal's dealer shall at no time deal within the offices of a broker or vice versa. The transacting of business by dealers from locations outside the office or exchange should require the specific authority of senior management. With the extension of markets across global time zones, many banks will permit selected staff discretion to deal outside normal hours for their particular time zone. Where this is permitted, great care should be taken to ensure that standard procedures are followed and that deals are recorded within the bank's main systems as soon as possible. Confirmations, etc should be sent as normal.

The dealer's own account refers to the individual's own personal interests in markets being pursued on a direct basis. If dealers wish to trade in the markets they must do this through another dealer. A dealer is party to a lot of information which could be put to use for personal gain and clearly this breaks any moral code. Even operating through another dealer the individual is in danger of sailing very close to the insider dealer regulations. Bank management are likely to be very nervous of dealers being active in the markets on their own account under any circumstances, and would explicitly forbid them to use specific knowledge gained from being on the inside.

Attention should be paid to the avoidance of conflicts of interest which could arise where dealers have responsibility for both the bank's own proprietary positions and customer deals. This opens up the opportunity for 'front running' (ie taking a proprietary position knowing that the subsequent customer deal may move the market in the bank's favour); misallocation of deals with losing trades being placed in customer accounts; or concealed personal account dealing.

In some markets, dealers must be licensed, in which case the bank must obtain and retain on file a copy of the licence.

The subject of segregation of duties should not be overlooked when defining the authority and responsibility of the processing and accounting areas. It is equally important to ensure that staff other than dealers do not have access to the dealers' equipment: direct lines, Reuters dealing facilities, etc. It is normal practice for the dealing room to be a secure and restricted area at all times.

Remuneration

Dealers are highly paid individuals and it is common for a large part of their annual income to come in the form of a performance-related bonus. If dealers' compensation packages are not carefully structured, a significant divergence between the interests of the dealer and the interest of the firm could arise. For example, a dealer who is underperforming and fears he will not achieve his bonus target is likely to become more adventurous in his position taking, feeling that he has nothing to lose. Equally, the prospect of making large profits, which will result in an increased bonus, whilst large losses will impact only the firm is likely to skew a dealer's preferences towards taking greater risks.

Often, dealers are in high demand in the market and even the possibility of dismissal following persistent losses may not be a real deterrent to risk taking as the dealer may expect to be able to find another job elsewhere. Firms should consider ways to reward and incentivise their dealers other than simple profit related bonuses. This could include deferred bonuses that are only payable after several years of satisfactory performance with the firm and the coupling of bonuses to team, rather than individual, performance.

Attention should be paid to the influence of individuals on determining others' bonuses. If, for example, the Chief Dealer has a significant influence on the bonus of an internal auditor, the latter's willingness to challenge the actions of the former may be substantially reduced.

The firm's monitoring systems should also be designed to ensure that they capture any attempt to manipulate recorded performance. The 'hedging' of deals between books one of which is marked-to-market and the other of which is accrual accounted is a way for an apparent profit to be generated out of nothing when it suits traders to do so.

Confirmations

In telephone markets, the importance of confirmations and their verification cannot be over stressed, as they are normally the first formal notification of a trade having been undertaken. This is particularly so where forward value dates are concerned. Same day, one day and spot value transactions will frequently be settled before a confirmation is received. Confirmations for all deals should, however, be dispatched immediately the deal is concluded and all details should be verified on incoming confirmations. In the event of delay in the receipt of confirmations from counterparties, prompt remedial action should be taken to obtain the necessary confirmation. Many confirmations are now issued by automated systems and care should be taken to ensure that they have not been overridden by subsequent manual correction.

Immediate attention must be given to confirmations received that cannot be identified with a recorded transaction. Where differences are noticed, management should be advised and steps taken to identify the reason. Special care should be taken to ensure that inward confirmations do not contain any qualifying clause that may prohibit the fulfillment of the underlying contract on the value or maturity date. Such clauses should be brought to the attention of senior management. It is a general principle that any variation from standard market practice must be stated at the point of dealing and not introduced at the stage of confirmation.

All confirmation procedures and controls must be undertaken by staff who are not connected with, or do not have access to, the dealers or dealing room. Under no circumstances should dealers be involved in procedures relating to incoming and outgoing confirmations.

Brokers' notes

The same regulations for dealing staff's non-involvement in

confirmations should equally apply to brokers' notes. All detail on incoming brokers' notes must be reconciled with the bank's records of the transaction and should any discrepancies be apparent these should be taken up directly with the broker involved by staff not involved in dealing.

After details have been verified, brokerage or commission rates and the individual charges should be checked. In due course, when the relative statements are received, commissions and charges are agreed prior to payment.

All brokerage and commission payments should be analysed on a monthly basis and special attention paid to any evidence of excessive activity, large fluctuations or partiality towards any individual broker. Ethical codes of conduct usually exist for the relationship between brokers and dealers but instances still occur of these relationships being abused for the benefit of the individuals concerned and hence the detriment of their employers.

Nostro reconciliations

Correspondent statements of account should be efficiently reconciled on a regular basis to ensure that all outstandings are identified, investigated and agreed. Accounts should be reconciled whenever the account has worked and at least monthly. Large, active accounts should be balanced daily. More importantly, upon receipt of statements, the items should be 'marked off' against the in-house nostro record thereby identifying any outstandings, which can be immediately investigated.

In many cases, particularly same day, one day and spot value transactions, discrepancies can be highlighted before a confirmation has been received. The receipt of unanticipated amounts will be identified, investigated and, as appropriate, corrected. Swift identification of errors in payment minimises the cost of correcting them. If funds are not received on the value date a claim for compensating value will need to be submitted to the counterparty.

Revaluation 'mark-to-market' and profit calculations

Procedures for revaluation must be established with attention being focused on where precisely the rates used for this purpose originate. They should be provided, or at least checked, independently of the dealing room. If undertaken properly, revaluation will highlight any substantial underlying trading losses that have not been reported or identified. It is normal for dealers to maintain a running position of profits as they estimate them to be. These should be compared with the result of a revaluation of the accounting records and any significant discrepancies investigated and reconciled.

Positions that are accounted for on an accruals basis may not immediately show the impact of trading decisions in instruments that take a long time to mature. Revaluing long dated positions using current market rates for the maturity concerned ('marking-to-market') can highlight any future problems that may occur as a result of wrong trading decisions made in long dated instruments. Even if the bank's accounts treat a particular book on an accruals basis, it is still good practice to mark-to-market for risk management purposes so as to highlight any embedded exposures which are not apparent from the daily accruals.

With the increasing complexity of financial instruments, specially designed pricing models may be used by banks to calculate the fair market value of existing positions. The validity of these models should be verified by qualified staff independent of the traders responsible for the positions.

All accounting and memorandum records must be properly and accurately maintained to ensure accurate and timely reporting of all profit and loss figures at the desired frequencies and in accordance with each bank's accepted accounting principles.

Formal arrangements should be established for the production of accurate and timely accounting records to conform with the bank's accounting policy and local legislation on the subject. Information must be prepared to meet dealer, management, audit and external reporting requirements. Amongst other things, such information will include:

- Outright positions updating, reporting and agreement.
- Forward maturity profiles.
- Clearing and cash control.
- The settlement of deals at maturity.
- Facilities to monitor utilisation against counterparty limits.

All deals transacted on any particular day should be properly accounted for or recorded in the formal records of the bank on the same day. Where for any reason this is not possible, approval to defer must be obtained from the manager responsible for the dealing centre. Irrespective of any ancillary detail of positions or other information maintained, the accounted records are the prime record of account to which all other information must be related and agreed.

Security issues

Other aspects of security that must be considered in the context of a dealing environment, bearing in mind the high value of the transactions and documents that are handled, are:

- There is a need to create a clearly defined authority for authenticating and authorising incoming payment or release/ delivery instructions, together with authority to originate and approve outward payment instructions. Extreme care should be taken to control all outward payments especially those in favour of third parties. Delivery procedures for securities, commodities and bullion should ensure that delivery only takes place when good value funds have been credited to the bank's account, unless an approved delivery risk limit exists within which the transaction may be effected.

- Procedures and responsibilities for the control of items of security and other items of value including test key data and equipment should be clearly defined. Under no circumstances should dealing staff be allowed access to such items.

- Procedures to ensure appropriate documentation and mandates for customers should be established especially when unsigned instructions by telex, telephone or customer terminals are received. Within the interbank market it is common practice to establish trades without any formal documentation apart from confirmations and a list of authorised signatories. This is normally considered to be an acceptable practice. However, in all other cases, the bank's full account opening procedures must be completed for the type of account involved. Signing authorities must be established and verified. If appropriate, Memorandum and Articles, board resolutions, powers of attorney etc must be obtained and verified. Where necessary, any security formalities should be completed prior to business being undertaken and records of any liens or other charges against deposits properly recorded.

- Security arrangements for computer and communication systems should also be established and defined. Dealing areas are generally dependent upon the degree of sophistication of these systems. Levels of access to computer facilities need to be considered and systems designed so as to ensure that audit trails are available and appropriate levels of computer security are maintained with adequate back-up arrangements. It is increasingly common within banks for there to be a specialised unit that considers issues related to computer security risk.

- Errors made in processing, reconciliation, payment, receipt or delivery procedures can be costly in terms of subsequent claims and therefore concise procedural manuals should exist to cover every aspect of the support functions related to a dealing operation.

- There is often an unfortunate tendency for some specialist areas to believe that they operate outside a bank's normal control procedures. This should not be the case unless specific senior management authority, preferably in writing, has been obtained. It is also essential that banks do not become involved in trading new instruments until adequate control, recording and reporting systems are in place.

Audit

All of the above topics are prerequisite to establishing and maintaining effective control of a dealing operation. Additionally, formally established policies, procedures and systems provide the necessary environment within which an effective audit control function can operate. This latter activity will comprise both preventative and detective action, ie prevention of errors and irregularities and also the detection of irregularities that have occurred. This will be achieved through the implementation of formal audit programmes, which will be fully documented with formal reports being prepared and submitted to management on the auditor's findings. These programmes will ensure *inter alia* that:

- Appropriate divisions of responsibility are maintained between dealing, processing, accounting and control functions.

- Counterparty limits are established and the system caters for the judicious apportionment of such limits to different dealing rooms within the group. If systems provide for limits to be temporarily borrowed/reallocated between different sections of a dealing room or bank, then there must be a clearly defined procedure for arranging, approving and recording such allocation.

- Dealing positions are maintained within established limits and that all other regulations imposed on trading are observed.

- Line dealing management assesses or reviews positions throughout the day.

- Any excesses created over either counterparty or dealing position limits are reported to senior management.

- Dealing is only transacted by persons authorised to do so within the authority delegated to them individually and in the interests of the bank, in accordance with its dealing policy.

- All deals undertaken are promptly and accurately recorded.

- Confirmations are exchanged and agreed.

- An appropriate contingency plan is in place to cater for disruptions to normal communication and dealing facilities.

The frequency and depth of audit projects will be established and regularly reviewed in the light of these findings. Where weaknesses are identified, frequency and depth of testing should be increased. Conversely, where areas are operating efficiently, it may be acceptable to decrease the frequency and depth of examination to devote more time to other areas. The audit programme should be supplemented by regular studies of specific areas and should cover all aspects of operation, including workflow efficiency, identifying and subsequently making recommendation for the necessary correction in any areas of risk.

The way in which audit control is implemented is all-important. An audit function based merely upon the numerical verification of data serves little purpose. A full appreciation of the underlying nature of all transactions, particularly new products and their risk implications, are absolutely essential, together with an awareness of potential risks. It is also important to remember that a control system that appears sound on paper may fail in practice when strong and determined individuals are able to coerce weak operatives into over-riding appropriate controls.

Normally the audit control function will also have responsibility for preparing, developing and scrutinising reports on exposure, excesses, budgets, profit performance, management accounts, dealing limit reviews, dealing policy issues and other management information relating to dealing activities.

The method by which these responsibilities are discharged will be dependent upon the dealing structure of each bank. For example, for excess reporting a bank with a small number of dealing centres and an effective communication and reporting system may operate from centralised limits with any excesses being reported to the controlling centre. Alternatively, where a larger network is concerned, control will be achieved through exception reporting ie each centre will be provided with maximum exposure limits for both trading and counterparty purposes, with any excesses over these limits being reported immediately. Within this latter procedure, the parent's control unit will be aware of its total potential exposure and can quickly identify actual positions.

Where a bank has several dealing operations, the parent institution's control unit will also have overall responsibility for these other operations. It is important that reporting lines recognise this even if only by dotted-line responsibility. This relates not only to audit but frequently extends to other senior executives who have a line responsibility for specialised dealing activities, albeit that various dealing centres are part of a regional area for which direct responsibility rests elsewhere.

In these situations, the parent control unit will ensure that an effective internal audit capability is established within each area incorporating all the criteria discussed above. Thereafter it will:

- Establish and maintain a regular reporting system to facilitate continued monitoring and control together with providing a base of information from which management reports may be prepared, such as:
  - Advice of all excesses over limits;
  - Details of outright positions;

- Forward purchases and sales together with loans and deposits;
- Mismatched positions;
- Sensitivity analysis for derivative products;
- Profit and loss;
- Brokerage and commission;
- Balance sheet details relating to liquidity, margins, portfolio mix, etc.

• Obtain local management confirmation that specific controls and dealing policies are being observed.

Additionally, the central control function will undertake both regular and surprise audit inspections of these operations. During such visits they will ensure that acceptable levels of technically competent senior staff and management are available to safeguard the interests of the bank. A warning sign that all may not be well is to find that only one individual seems to be able to answer questions about particular positions. Surprise visits are frequently carried out by senior ex-dealers from Head Office who spend a considerable time in the dealing room 'sniffing the atmosphere' and seeing how their dealing colleagues behave generally.

It is essential that internal control functions retain at all times their independence and integrity. They must be responsible to a member of senior management who is not involved with day to day trading activities or other areas that they examine. This independence will frequently extend right up to board level with the audit function reporting to a different director to the one responsible for Treasury performance.

Fraud

The subject of the control of dealing and risk exposures would be incomplete without reference to fraud. Whilst the diligent implementation of control procedures will afford an element of protection against this risk it is also essential that all members of staff are fully aware of potential fraudulent approaches.

Fraud in its variety of forms tends to keep pace with technical developments in banking and regrettably these activities are not accompanied by any common identifying characteristic of the practitioners. In law, fraud means dishonesty and is defined in *Derry v Peek* (1889) as being proven when it is shown that false representation has been made knowingly or without belief in its truth or recklessly or carelessly (whether it be true or false).

There is no doubt that a banker must exercise reasonable care and he is legally bound to follow up any suspicion of fraud to satisfy himself that it is unfounded before developing a proposition. It is essential, therefore, for bankers to be able to identify whether a proposition is spurious or not and the best way of achieving this is with a working knowledge of the international markets and how transactions are structured. Many potential fraudulent approaches are naive, patently obvious and hence quite easy to identify. These include proposals with amounts that are quite unrealistic in terms of the market or the bank or customer's balance sheet. Some transactions are referred to as mega-deals and involve tons of gold, vast quantities of oil or huge deposits of money. Frequently, such proposals are introduced by a friend of a friend and the real source of wealth is kept at arm's length on the pretext of required confidentiality. However, in practice it may not always be easy to discover if a fraud has been perpetrated or is being attempted, as a grey area exists between a bad banking proposition and fraud.

Vigilance should also be maintained so as to avoid the bank becoming involved in transactions which assist criminals to disguise their financial dealings. Such deals are referred to as 'money laundering' which is defined by a European Union Directive issued in 1990 as:

> *"The conversion or transfer of property, knowing that such property is derived from a serious crime, for the purpose of concealing or disguising the illicit origin of the property or of assisting any person who is involved in committing such an offence or offence to evade the legal consequences of his action, and the concealment or disguise of the true nature, source, location, disposition, movement, rights with respect to, or ownership of property, knowing that such property is derived from a serious crime."*

Concern over money laundering grew out of its use by drug traffickers and gave rise to international agreements to implement concerted action, including recommendations of the Financial Action Task Force on money laundering established pursuant to the Paris summit of the Group of

Seven in 1989. The European Union Directive calls for each member state to implement legislation requiring their banks to co-operate with their law enforcement authorities by informing them, on the bank's own initiative, of any facts that could be related to a money laundering offence and by supplying all information requested in the case of a criminal inquiry related to money laundering. This overrides any duty of confidentiality towards customers to which banks would normally adhere.

The case of money laundering is an extreme illustration of the importance of a bank knowing its customer. Deals should not be undertaken where there is any suspicion that the counterparty may be bogus or may not be acting in a proper way.

There has undoubtedly been a development in the sophistication of fraudulent propositions as well as the variety and skill of confidence tricksters in approaching bankers. Many bankers on hearing a proposition that they do not understand will immediately recall that they do not know everything and wrongly assume that the reason why a proposition does not make sense to them is their lack of technical knowledge. A banker is trained to be polite and helpful and a legacy of this excellent training is that when faced with a proposition that sounds wrong he will suggest alternative ideas or provide introductions to someone who might be able to help. This can be dangerous as it trains the opposition. As a basic rule, when a potential fraud is suspected the bank should:

- Immediately terminate all discussions on the subject.
- Convey nothing in writing or on a telex.
- Consider severing any banking connection it may have with the parties concerned.

As a result of becoming involved, however unwittingly, a bank may lose its money and reputation. The more sophisticated approaches involve propositions introduced via a highly respected and reputable source. Introductions through bankers, lawyers, accountants, major corporate entities and one's own board of directors naturally lend credibility to an approach and are generally sufficient to ensure that the bankers at least listen carefully to the proposition. In some cases names of reputable individuals or organisations have been used without their authority, false proof of representation having been made. It is essential that potentially fraudulent propositions are not passed round. Bankers should not introduce the parties concerned to anyone else as by doing so they will give unwarranted credibility to the proposition by adding the bank's name as an informal reference. Even a letter formally refusing a proposition can be used to good advantage by the fraudster if it has the right bank's name at the top!

The successful practitioner of the spurious deal is said to be gifted with an instinctive understanding of human psychology. He will, for example, be unlikely to introduce himself as a principal and in his alleged role as representative or agent he will not disclose the identity of his principals except in the most general terms. One American lawyer, when describing the approaches made by these professional confidence tricksters, said that 'aside from love, no human emotion is so useful in unseating sound judgement as greed.' Whenever someone is offering something for nothing, suspect it at once and remember that no one gives away money. Indeed, great care should be exercised when any of the following features occur in a proposition being offered:

- If the transaction involves amounts which are substantially larger than are normally experienced for a particular customer or market, especially if the client has no previous experience of the industry or commodity involved.

- If there is any undue haste to complete a transaction, particularly a complicated one, where large amounts of money are involved.

- If there is an over-emphasis on maintaining secrecy. Remember that it should be quite unnecessary for anyone to request a banker to keep confidential any matters of a financial nature brought to him professionally. Only in the most exceptional circumstances should a bank disclose information to third parties and such circumstances might, of course, include those when it is deemed to be in the bank's interest to do so. If additional assurance that the proposition will be kept confidential is demanded, this should be suspected. There may be good reason to be careful.

Beware of any technical double talk, particularly if it comes out with total confidence and the proposer, whom you may be meeting for the first time, is clearly at ease with large figures. This is often accompanied by impressive name dropping (companies, directors, etc).

Avoid the temptation to pass messages that have no banking significance, particularly if the content is not understood. The passing of messages through a bank may be designed to create an apparent and totally unmerited involvement of the bank in the proposition itself. Such messages have been known to be forged and correspondence with such individuals is undesirable. Cases exist where, for example, the original of a document that was sent by the bank to the proposer stated that the bank was not interested in the proposition. The copy had the word 'not' deleted! People who are involved in fraud may also be involved in other forms of crime.

The newspapers often bear stories of substantial transactions or events happening somewhere in the world. These can be followed by look-alike propositions, which should be treated with great care, particularly where requests for fiduciary or trust services are requested. Experience has shown that such events have been taken as a relatively plausible excuse to obtain correspondence from banks, lawyers and accountants which is then used to defraud gullible investors, usually in some other country, of fees paid in advance for loans which never materialise.

When fraud is suspected it is imperative that the appropriate designated senior management is advised immediately and that the bank's internal rules regarding communication with anyone are strictly observed.

Whilst retaining an awareness of spurious propositions, it is essential that an appropriate perspective is maintained towards new business offered to the bank. There is no doubt that there has been a growth, both in volume and sophistication, of potentially fraudulent approaches but this should not colour a banker's judgement to the extent that worthwhile and profitable business is turned aside. The most important things to remember are the need to understand exactly what the client requires, why he is doing it, how it works and to ensure that it is in accordance with legal and statutory requirements and established market practices, principles and terms.

PART TWO

Regulation

6 The international framework of regulation

Amongst the most pressing issues confronting financial services regulators is the need to develop practical arrangements to supervise an increasingly global industry. Unsurprisingly, regulators are involved in a game of catch up, trying to impose effective regulation on firms who already have global groups, branches and above all global risks.

In 1974 the Basle Committee on Banking Supervision was established by the G10 central banks with the initial focus of its work being to define the role and responsibilities of home and host country supervisors of internationally active banks. Its key success has been in the development of capital adequacy rules that set down minimum internationally acceptable requirements. The securities industry has the International Organisation of Securities Commissions (IOSCO) of which the regulators of some 70 countries are members. More recently the world's derivatives regulators have agreed to co-operate in the sharing of information through the Windsor Declaration and the Boca Raton agreement. These initiatives are the basis of international information sharing and standards setting, a process being actively supported by G7 nations.

Within Europe, the single market in financial services became a reality on 31st December 1995, the date when a number of European Union Directives finally came into force. These enforce common standards on financial institutions throughout the member states of the EU.

Banking has for many years been an international business, not least as a result of its role in financing international trade. But where there are opportunities for profit there is always risk as has been aptly demonstrated by Barings. The example of Barings has clearly shown that where subsidiaries have been established, events in one part of a group can damage other parts of the group, reinforcing the need for active collaboration between financial regulators to supervise financial business at a consolidated level.

On a global scale there can be little doubt that the regulators' ability to supervise internationally active firms is deficient. The existence of different accountancy standards, insolvency laws and hugely variable standards amongst many national regulators create a far from ideal background. Coupled with this the spread of financial markets into the less financially sophisticated parts of the world and the emergence of information systems such as the Internet, mean that interdependence, and thus systemic risk, grows bigger daily.

The spread of international consultation on regulatory matters is much to be welcomed but it would be foolish to imagine an overnight harmonisation of controls on financial services. Politics, protectionism and national pride will continue to slow this process down.

The Basle Committee on Banking Supervision

The Basle Committee was established at the end of 1974, following serious disturbances in international currency and banking markets, including the failure of a German bank, Bankhaus Herstatt, part way through the trading day. The committee is comprised of members from Belgium, Canada, France, Germany, Italy, Japan, Luxembourg, the Netherlands, Sweden, Switzerland, the UK and the USA. The authoritative nature of the Committee means that its recommendations are followed not only in all member countries, but also in virtually all other counties with internationally active banks.

Basle Concordat

The principle of consolidated supervision was agreed internationally as early as 1975 by the Basle group with the publication of what became known as the 'Concordat'. This has since been supplemented by a number of further papers including, in 1992, one entitled Minimum Standards for the Supervision of International Banking Groups and Their Cross-border Establishments. These papers are aimed at ensuring that no bank escapes effective supervision. They define the respective responsibilities of home and host country regulators, also placing a responsibility upon each regulatory authority to co-operate with its counterpart in the exchange of information.

Whilst the Concordat itself has no legal force, the 1992 paper stresses that the members of the Basle group expect each other to apply the stated minimum standards and urges other countries to do so as well. Four minimum conditions for effective supervision are stated:

- All international banking groups and international banks should be supervised by a home country authority that capably performs consolidated supervision.

- The creation of a cross-border banking establishment should receive the prior consent of both the host country supervisor and the home country supervisor of the bank or banking group.

- Supervisors should possess the right to gather information from the cross-border banking establishments of the banks or banking groups for which they are the home country supervisor.

- If a host country supervisor determines that one of these standards is not met to its satisfaction, it may apply restrictive measures so as to satisfy its prudential concerns, including the prohibition of the creation of banking establishments.

The Concordat places primary responsibility for the supervision of the solvency of cross-border banking establishments with the home authority and that for liquidity with the host authority. The supervision of foreign exchange is a joint responsibility, this being a primary area where co-operation between authorities to ensure a consolidated view is highly important.

Collaboration between regulators within a single country is also necessary where banking groups include insurance, investment management or other securities businesses. Without co-operation and consistency of treatment, there is a danger that banks (particularly unscrupulous ones) will structure their business in such a way as to at least minimise the regulatory impact and possibly frustrate it altogether.

Capital adequacy

The Committee is best known for its work on common standards of capital adequacy. These are referred to as the Basle Accord and were adopted in July 1988. This work established internationally agreed standards for what could be regarded as capital and also for the measurement of credit risks.

This was followed up in 1996 by the publication of recommended rules for the allocation of capital to market risks. These have now been adopted through the EU Capital Adequacy Directive.

Details of the capital regulations are contained in Chapter 10.

The Committee's success in leading the development of international capital standards has been followed up with several further agreed papers on issues of common interest to regulators.

Interest rate risk

The paper 'Principles for the Management of Interest Rate Risk' published in 1997 listed eleven criteria for good practice in this area. In summary, these are:

- Strategies and policies for interest rate risk management should be approved at board level and monitoring reports should be reviewed by the board.

- Senior management should ensure that policies, procedures and resources are in place to manage the risk.

- There should be clear segregation of duties between those individuals responsible for taking positions and those responsible for risk management.

- Policies should be clearly defined and consistent with the nature of the bank's business.

- Risks inherent in new products should be identified in advance.

- Information systems should capture all material sources of risk.

- Risk limits should be established and enforced.

- Banks should measure their potential vulnerability to stress conditions including possible model breakdown and take the result into consideration when setting policies and limits.

- Information systems should provide timely reports.

- Banks should undertake regular independent reviews of the adequacy of their interest rate risk management processes and systems.

- Supervisors should obtain information from banks that is adequate for them to evaluate their level of interest rate risk.

Effective supervision

'Core Principles for Effective Banking Supervision', also published in 1997, lists twenty-five criteria by which a supervisory system can be judged. These include the following recommendations:

- An effective legal framework is a precondition for an effective system of banking supervision.
- Permissible activities of banks must be clearly defined.
- The licensing authority must have the right to set standards in particular relating to ownership structures and financial condition.
- Supervisors should have the authority to review proposed changes of ownership and major acquisitions or investments.
- Supervisors should enforce policies with regard to capital adequacy, management of loan portfolios, concentrations and connected lending, country risk and market risk.
- Supervisors should ensure that banks' internal control systems and information systems are adequate for the nature and the scale of their business.
- Banks should be encouraged to follow high ethical and professional standards.
- Supervisory methods should include both on-site and off-site reviews. Prudential and statistical reports should be required and be subject to independent validation.
- There should be regular contact with banks' managements.
- Supervision should be conducted on a consolidated basis, including cross-border consolidation where relevant.
- Supervisors should have powers to enforce corrective action where needed.
- Contact should be established and maintained with supervisors in other countries where local banks operate or which are the home state of branches of foreign banks.

Internal Controls

Framework for the Evaluation of Internal Control Systems, published in 1998, notes that control breakdowns typically seen in problem bank cases can be grouped into five broad categories:

- Lack of adequate management oversight and accountability, and failure to develop a strong control culture within the bank;
- Inadequate assessment of the risk of certain banking activities, whether on- or off-balance sheet;
- The absence or failure of key control activities, such as segregation of duties, approvals, verifications, reconciliations, and reviews of operating performance;
- Inadequate communication of information between levels of management within the bank, especially in the upward communication of problems;
- Inadequate or ineffective audit programs and other monitoring activities.

The paper notes that many recent problem cases highlight the fact that control systems that function well for traditional or simple products are unable to handle more sophisticated or complex situations.

Fourteen principles for the assessment of internal control systems are defined in the paper under the categories: management oversight and the control culture; risk assessment; control activities; information and communication; monitoring; evaluation of internal control systems by supervisory authorities. Under each principle there is discussion of key issues. In addition, there is a useful appendix entitled 'Supervisory lessons learned from internal control failures'.

The document is consistent with the implementation of the RATE model developed by the Bank of England which is discussed in further detail in Chapter 8, and also with the recent re-iteration by UK regulators as to the responsibilities of directors.

The International Organisation of Securities Commissions (IOSCO)

IOSCO was established in 1974. Its members comprise the chief statutory or governmental authorities responsible for the regulation of securities and derivatives markets in more than 70 countries. The key role of IOSCO is to facilitate international communication and co-operation between regulators, which it achieves through its various committees and working parties. As with the Basle Committee the conclusions reached by IOSCO are not legally binding but represent standards that may be reflected in the national regimes and practices of individual countries. The agreed objectives of IOSCO include:

- to co-operate together to promote standards of regulation, in order to maintain just, efficient and sound securities markets;
- to unite efforts to establish standards and effective surveillance of international securities transactions;
- to provide mutual assistance to promote the integrity of markets by rigorous application of the standards and effective enforcement against offences.

Specific issues that have working parties include multinational disclosure and accounting, the regulation of secondary markets, the regulation of intermediaries and capital adequacy, enforcement and exchange of information, and investment management.

IOSCO and the Basle Committee announced in June 1996 a joint initiative to strengthen co-operation between the regulators of diversified financial groups. Basle and IOSCO will look at whether additional co-ordinating arrangements to facilitate information exchange, in both normal and emergency situations, should be set out, and the extent to which existing provisions of national law may need to be amended to support this objective.

EU directives

To understand the impact of the EU directives it is important to understand some of the background. Under EU rules financial services business is deemed to be conducted by two principal groups: banks and investment firms. For the banks (or credit institutions) the major changes necessitated in preparation for the single market were included in the Second Banking Co-ordination Directive enforced in 1993 (2BCD). For investment firms the key piece of legislation, which led to the creation of a single market, was the Investment Services Directive (ISD), which came into force on 31st December 1995.

The purpose of both Directives was to create a business environment in which European financial institutions of whatever type may operate throughout the region without the burden of having to be separately authorised in each member state and without being bound by different capital adequacy regimes. They form part of a programme of Directives to develop a single market in financial services, the main ones of which are listed in Figure 6.1.

Figure 6.1 Main EU Directives relating to financial services

SUMMARY OF EUROPEAN DIRECTIVES TO DATE
1989 Undertakings in collective investments in transferable securities has enabled certain collective investment schemes to be sold throughout Europe.
1993 Second Banking Co-ordination Directive which created a single market for banks throughout the European Economic Area (EEA is EU states plus Norway, Iceland and Liechtenstein).
1994 Insurance Directive created a single market for insurance.
1996 Investment Services Directive created a single market for investment firms throughout the EEA, although to date only the UK, Eire, Netherlands, Spain, Norway, Sweden, Belgium, Finland, France, Italy, Denmark and Germany have implemented the ISD.
1996 Capital Adequacy Directive created a uniform set of financial requirements for banks, securities and investment firms.

It should be noted that the various directives, which have introduced the idea of passporting, do not do away with the ability of the various member states to have different laws from one another. However, if a state chooses to have different and more demanding regulations, these regulations must satisfy the so-called "general good" criteria. Broadly, these criteria outlaw rules or laws that discriminate against businesses from other member states and that are overly restrictive. Furthermore, where differences exist, such differences should be justifiable in the public interest.

The Second Banking Co-Ordination Directive (2BCD)

The Second Banking Co-ordination Directive was implemented in the United Kingdom on 1 January 1993. It allows, among other things, a bank incorporated and authorised in one EEA country (the 'home' country) to provide certain banking and financial services in another EEA country (the 'host' country) without needing prior authorisation from the host country supervisor. This can be done either on a cross-border basis or through opening a branch in the host country. Banks that have used the 2BCD passport to provide such services in the United Kingdom are known as European Authorised Institutions (EAIs). Banks authorised in any one EEA country are subject to a range of EU directives which provide a common regulatory framework for their prudential supervision throughout the EEA. In the United Kingdom there are at present 115 branches of EAIs, which, with their 14 UK subsidiaries account for about a quarter of the UK's banking sector balance sheet. The largest 10 EAIs in London account for around half of this figure.

Under the 2BCD, responsibility for the prudential supervision of UK branches of EAIs was, with the exception of that for the supervision of liquidity, passed from the UK regulator to that institution's home supervisory authority. This means that, for example, the prudential supervision of the UK branches of French banks is the responsibility of the Commission Bancaire: similarly, that of the UK branches of Italian banks is the responsibility of the Banca D'Italia. Conversely, the FSA is now solely responsible for the prudential supervision of branches of UK incorporated banks in other EEA countries.

As a result of these changes the FSA has very limited supervisory powers and responsibilities for EAIs. In particular, the FSA has virtually none of the legal powers over UK branches of EAIs that it has over institutions authorised under the Banking Act 1987. For example, the FSA has no authorisation powers; no powers to set capital requirements; and no powers to require information on large exposures, provisioning or profitability. No 'fit and proper' tests are carried out by the FSA on EAIs or their shareholders, controllers and management; no significant prudential information systematically passes from a UK branch of an EAI to the FSA; no reports on systems and controls from reporting accountants are received; and no Review Team Visits are undertaken.

Under 2BCD the supervision of liquidity remains a responsibility shared between the home and host supervisor. Where the EAI manages its liquidity on a global basis (and is monitored as such by its home supervisor), the FSA's policy is to look to Head Office to ensure that the UK branch has appropriate liquidity. To achieve its limited supervisory responsibility for liquidity, the FSA generally holds one meeting a year with UK branches of EAIs. This meeting typically consists of a very general discussion of strategy, business environment, and the liquidity of its UK operations.

There is a danger that the clarity of responsibility, which the home/host country principles bring, could have a perverse effect if the home country regulators do not meet the standard of supervision previously exercised by the host country. The FSA has signed formal agreements - 'Memoranda of Understanding' - with other EEA supervisors. These Memoranda provide a framework for the exchange of information between home and host supervisors. They also make clear the home country responsibility for prudential supervision.

This passport is only available to credit institutions and to financial institutions as defined in the directive. The limitations on the definitions in the directive led in part to the ISD. Many firms in direct competition with the passported banks would not themselves fall within the definition of credit or financial institutions and would therefore not be able to obtain the passport. With the introduction of the ISD investment firms are now able to compete on the same basis as the banks.

The EU Capital Adequacy Directive (CAD)

The CAD is part of the single market regime and sets out the minimum standards of capital adequacy with which both investment firms and banks doing investment business must comply. The purpose of the CAD is to develop common rules of capital adequacy in respect of both credit institutions and investment firms when they engage in direct competition with one another. Since the directive applies to both banks and investment firms the regulations differentiate between the trading book and the non-trading book. The items that comprise the non-trading book will include those concerned with traditional banking such as lending, whilst trading book items will be those that involve positions in financial instruments for short term trading purposes.

As well as the impact on capital standards (described more fully in Chapter 10) the CAD introduced several other significant changes to the EU regulatory regime.

Consolidated supervision

Consolidated supervision, which had long been established as a principle for banks under the Basle Concordat, now extends to other financial institutions. Previously UK Self Regulatory Organisations (SROs) such as IMRO and the SFA supervised only UK domiciled investment businesses. If this business were part of a larger group with international activities and exposures, the SROs would not have knowledge of the larger financial situation. This could clearly lead to an inaccurate understanding of the risks being run and thus potentially an inappropriate resources requirement being calculated. Under CAD financial supervision is applied on a consolidated basis, thereby providing regulators with a complete picture.

Financial resources

The CAD applies two measures to a firm's capital, which are the Initial and Further Capital Requirements. Investment firms at all times must meet a level of initial capital of one of three levels. These are as follows:

- ECU 50,000 providing that the firm does not hold client money or securities and does not deal on its own account or underwrite;
- ECU 125,000 provided the firm does not deal on its own account or underwrite;
- ECU 730,000 for all other investment firms.

Already authorised firms that do not satisfy these requirements are eligible for transitional arrangements - 'grandfathering' - that will allow them to remain in business.

Further Capital Requirements include the following items:

- Financial resources equivalent to 13 weeks fixed overheads to cover various basic risks to which a firm is exposed.
- Financial resources sufficient to cover any of the following quantifiable risks to which firms may be exposed:
  - position risk in transferable securities and derivatives including underwriting risks;
  - counterparty/settlement risks;
  - foreign exchange risks;
  - concentrated exposures.

The financial resources requirement has been modified to include two new items: LER (Large Exposure Requirement) and FER (Foreign Exchange Requirement). These two will be added to the existing Position Risk Return and Counterparty Risk Return numbers.

Super equivalence

Home states are entitled to enforce regulations that exceed the minimum standards established by the CAD. This is referred to as super equivalence. The various UK regulators have adopted a super equivalent stance on a number of issues, illustrating the difficulty of harmonising regulation even with Europe, let alone the rest of the world.

Investment Services Directive (ISD)

The Investment Services Directive is an important part of the European Union's single market programme and became effective on 1 January 1996. The directive gives a "common passport" to all securities firms within the community (with a limitation on Greece, Spain and Portugal where the directive is planned to come into effect on or after 1 January 1999). The guarantee of investor protection will lie in a license to trade, which will be granted by the local regulator. The ISD is however silent on a number of important issues such as solicitation and marketing. Consequently, passported firms may need to market in accordance with a plethora of domestic laws.

A firm may obtain authorisation in its home state, for example Denmark, and then wish to open a branch or cross-border sell in the UK. They will then apply for membership of the appropriate UK regulator. The UK regulator will not be able to refuse them membership since they are already deemed to be fit and proper elsewhere in the EEA. Once authorised by the local regulator the firm will be bound by the local conduct of business rules. This will be a major advantage for those firms which have a network of European offices or which conduct cross-border business. Figure 6.2 outlines the basic split of responsibilities.

Figure 6.2 Home and Host country responsibilities under ISD

HOME	HOST
• AUTHORISATION • FITNESS AND PROPRIETY • CAPITAL ADEQUACY • CLIENT MONEY • CONDUCT OF BUSINESS (within home state)	• CONDUCT OF BUSINESS (in host state)

There are a number of important issues to stem from this directive; not least amongst them being the fact that the client money rules will comprise part of the prudential regulation conducted by the "Home" regulator. An earlier worry was one of regulatory arbitrage in which firms might set up in the easiest jurisdiction within the EEA and then outwardly passport. This as yet does not appear to be happening.

A further concern relates to the ability to discipline "passported" business. At present the ultimate sanction is the withdrawal of authorisation, thereby removing the ability of the firm to trade. The use of such a sanction by a host state would implicitly be questioning the fitness and propriety of the firm and thus the competence of the home state regulator. This is not a step that host regulators are likely to take lightly.

The Money Laundering Directive

Money laundering is the conversion of illicit funds from any criminal activity (but in particular drug trafficking and terrorist activities) into what appears to be clean money. Although earlier legislation to combat money laundering enabled the courts to trace, freeze and confiscate assets in the UK, there were no requirements for specific control systems within financial institutions.

In 1991, the European Union adopted Council Directive 91/308 on prevention of the use of the financial system for the purpose of money laundering. This Directive must be implemented by all member states. In part, the impetus for the directive was the removal of obstacles to free movement of capital and freedom to supply financial services, which was to come about upon completion of the European internal market.

The Directive provides that European Union member states should ensure that all financial and credit institutions located within the national member states should implement certain internal procedures and controls.

The aim of those internal procedures is threefold:

- Deterrence. To prevent credit and financial institutions being used for money laundering purposes.

- Co-operation. To ensure that there is co-operation between credit and financial institutions and law enforcement agencies.

- Detection. To establish customer identification and record-keeping procedures within all financial and credit institutions which will assist the law enforcement agencies in detecting, tracing and prosecuting money launderers.

The Directive and subsequent UK legislation apply to all firms and individuals authorised to conduct investment business under the Financial Services Act 1986, as well as to other financial institutions.

The Directive envisages that these provisions will enable the financial sector to play a powerful role in combating money laundering and consequently, criminal activity. Additionally, it foresees that regulation of this kind will maintain public confidence in the soundness and stability of the European financial system.

For some years, there has been UK legislation dealing with the laundering of terrorist funds and the proceeds of drug trafficking. In the implementation of the European Council Directive, the UK has extended the existing legislation to cover the laundering of proceeds of any criminal conduct. In addition, obligations have been imposed upon the financial sector to ensure that it fulfils the provisions of the Directive.

The Criminal Justice Act 1993

The Criminal Justice Act 1993 implemented into UK legislation the Money Laundering Directive. Under the Criminal Justice Act 1993 financial institutions became responsible for establishing systems and controls to prevent money laundering and are liable to prosecution if they fail to do so. Systems are needed to identify clients, record transactions, allow disclosure and train employees. The Joint Money Laundering Steering Group issues guidance notes for institutions such as banks and life companies on how to implement the requirements of the Criminal Justice Act 1993 and later legislative amendment.

Under the Criminal Justice Act 1993, staff can be liable for prosecution, including fines and custodial sentences if:

- they knowingly become involved in money laundering for which the punishment is a maximum of 14 years imprisonment and/or fine;
- they are not knowingly involved but fail to disclose suspicious transactions for which the punishment is a maximum of five years imprisonment and/or fine;
- they alert clients under investigation for which the punishment is a maximum of five years imprisonment and/or fine.

Although this duty of care falls outside the conduct of business rules an adviser must be aware of the implications of the Criminal Justice Act in his job. Any breach could result in legal proceedings.

7 The regulation of financial services in the UK

The UK regulatory framework has traditionally leaned more towards informal supervision than formal regulation. A degree of regulatory flexibility is a great asset for a financial centre but the traditional banking principles, based on trust and honesty, are not of themselves sufficient to prevent fraud and failure.

The first Financial Services Act (FSAct) followed the recommendations of an inquiry led by Professor Gower, reviewing the regulatory requirements of a market that was undergoing a lot of changes, particularly in its commercial approach. The protection required by both individuals and institutions was considered, as was the need for regulatory control of dealers, investment managers and investment advisors. The final Gower report published in 1984 was consolidated into a white paper from the DTI entitled 'Financial Services in the United Kingdom'. The particular emphasis was on protection against fraud or hiding the risk, not on reducing the obvious risks involved in any type of investment. It drew attention to the need not to stifle enterprise by over-regulating the industry but saw the need to make transactions transparent by encouraging disclosure of information. It was on the basis of Gower's recommendations that the Financial Services Act of 1986 was put on the statute books.

A further major change in the regulatory structure of banking and investment business in the UK began with a government announcement on the 20th May 1997 stating that it was their intention to unify most aspects of financial services regulation within a single statutory regulator. This single body is the Financial Services Authority (FSA). Given the increased blurring of divisions between different types of financial institutions, the government's aim was to establish a single statutory regulator to deliver more effective and efficient supervision of all financial business. This process will take place in two phases. First, the Bank of England's responsibility for banking supervision passed to the Financial Services on the 1 June 1998. The second phase will consist of a reformed Financial Services Act, which will take place "at an early opportunity" and will, amongst other things, transfer the function of the Self Regulatory Organisations (SROs) to the FSA. Prior to a reformed FSA, the government expects the FSA, the Bank of England and the SROs to co-operate and embark on the transition.

The Financial Services Authority

The FSA is a company set up as the designated agency in order to take on the responsibilities of the Financial Services Act. As the Securities and Investments Board (SIB), it was formed in 1985 and has a constitution like any other company. It is, though, a company limited by guarantee and as such it is entitled to drop the word 'limited' from its name. It should be remembered that the employees of the FSA are not civil servants, nor are they Crown Agents immune from prosecution. However, the FSAct does give them and the employees of the SROs an equivalent degree of immunity from prosecution so long as they were acting in good faith.

The FSA will be responsible for the direct supervision of banks and other financial services sector entities as well as the supervision of financial markets and of clearing and settlement systems. It will be responsible for regulatory policy and will advise on the regulatory implications of market developments and of initiatives such as domestic legislation and EU directives. The Bank of England retains its responsibility for the overall stability of the financial system as a whole. This will include achieving monetary stability and seeking to minimise systemic risk through close involvement in developing and strengthening the financial system.

The establishment of a banking supervisory body separate from the central bank is a departure from tradition in the UK. The responsibility for the supervision of the banking system can fall with the central bank, as in Italy and the Netherlands or with a separate body. For example, in Germany the supervisory body is the Federal Banking Supervisory Office, not the Bundesbank, and it is in fact more common to find a separate supervisory body. In France there is a Banking Commission, the same in Belgium, and there is a Federal Banking Commission in Switzerland. In Japan the Ministry of Finance controls supervision, whilst in the US there is a more complex picture. Different roles are played by the Federal Reserve, the Federal Deposit Insurance Corporation (FDIC) and the Comptroller of the Currency. In addition, the separate state authorities have some supervisory influence. However, in most countries day to day supervision and collection of information tends to take place through the central banks even where there is a separate supervisory body.

The legislative background

The FSA will acquire its full range of responsibilities in two stages, following the enactment of the necessary two pieces of legislation.

As noted above, the FSA now has responsibility for supervising banks, listed money market institutions and related clearing houses. Further steps await the proposed financial regulatory reform bill, which will create a new statutory regime under which the FSA will, in broad terms, acquire the regulatory and registration functions currently exercised by the SROs, the DTI Insurance Directorate, the Building Societies Commission, the Friendly Societies Commission, and the Registry of Friendly Societies. The FSA will also be given responsibility for the authorisation of firms currently authorised to do investment business by virtue of their membership of a Recognised Professional Body (RPB). The Government has indicated its intention to publish this Bill in draft, for consultation, in the summer of 1998. Early introduction of the Bill in Parliament might lead to enactment in 1999. The date on which the FSA acquires the full range of powers under the financial regulatory reform bill to regulate this wider constituency is referred to as 'N2' - perhaps late 1999 or early in the year 2000.

It is intended that the financial regulatory reform bill will give the FSA responsibility for the authorisation of members of professional bodies carrying on investment business (for example, accountants and solicitors). The Treasury is currently consulting the bodies concerned and the FSA on the possibility of amending the relevant provisions in the FSAct, in order to remove any requirement for unnecessary authorisation of such firms. Ministers are also considering providing the FSA with powers to refrain from making specified rules or categories of rules where it considers those of the relevant professional body to be adequate and providing the FSA with the powers to engage a professional body to carry out specified functions (eg monitoring) on its behalf. The FSA will publish details on this aspect in due course.

Until the N2 date, the various bodies that will eventually constitute the FSA will continue to have legal responsibility for regulating their firms under the existing statutory or contractual arrangements. For example, the SROs will continue to take decisions on authorisation and enforcement in relation to their firms. The SRO Boards will continue to be responsible for setting regulatory standards and for ensuring for example, that there are adequate and effective arrangements in place for monitoring and enforcing compliance with those standards.

In the interests of making as much progress as possible towards operational integration and practical co-operation before N2 date, the constituent bodies have agreed a number of matters, which include common terms and conditions for staff. Also detailed contracts will be put in place between the FSA and the SROs setting out the services which the FSA will provide to them in the interim period. In particular, the SROs will use FSA staff, working under the relevant SROs direction, to carry out their regulatory work.

The self-regulating organisations

The SROs represent the front-line of regulation. Whilst the FSA exerts the strategic influence over regulation it is the SROs that are involved in the day to day monitoring of the market.

Formed out of the old trade associations, or created from new where no association existed before, it is the SROs that bring with them the experience of practitioners that the FSAct relies upon. It was the process of recognition of the SROs, along with the drafting of the rule books, which necessitated the delay between the passage of the FSAct and its implementation in 1988.

The FSAct did not pass the legal responsibilities (and powers) down to the SROs to enforce. In essence the obligation still rests with the FSA which simply allows the SROs to fulfil this role on its behalf.

The relationship between the SRO and its members is a contractual one, whereby each member commits itself to the rules. Failure to abide by the rules will result in the ultimate sanction of expulsion from the SRO. Since the SRO is the means by which the firm is authorised this, therefore, removes their authority to conduct investment business.

Requirements for recognition of an SRO

The current SROs will continue to exist until at least the end of 1999 when it is expected that the new financial services reform bill will be passed. It is the responsibility of FSA to ensure that each SRO is able to fulfil the obligations imposed upon it by Schedule 2 of the Act. These obligations relate to:

- *Members to be fit and proper persons.* The rules and practices of the organisation must be such as to ensure that any members authorised by it are "fit and proper" to conduct investment business.

- *Admission, expulsion and discipline.* The rules on admission, expulsion and discipline must be fair and reasonable with adequate provision for appeal.

- *Safeguards for investors.* The rules of the organisation must provide an adequate level of protection for investors. The initial text of the Act required an equivalent level of protection to the rules of FSA. This was amended by the Companies Act 1989 to the test of adequacy in order to allow the revision and simplification of the rulebooks.

- *Monitoring and enforcement.* These must be sufficient to ensure compliance with the rules as laid down.

- *The governing body.* In line with the governing body of FSA each SRO must have a board which is comprised of a variety of participants, thereby ensuring a proper balance between the interests of the different members of the organisation and the public.

- *Investigation of complaints.* The organisation must have effective arrangements for the investigation of complaints.

- *Promotion and maintenance of standards.* The organisation must be able and willing to promote high standards of integrity and fair dealing in the carrying on of investment business.

The three SROs each has its own defined scope, although each SRO will have some degree of overlap with the others.

The Securities and Futures Authority (SFA)

The SFA has responsibility for regulating those firms that deal in investments. SFA is not one of the original SROs and resulted from the merger of two of the original SROs, The Securities Association (TSA) and the Association of Futures Brokers and Dealers (AFBD).

SFA member firms are able to conduct any form of investment business as laid out in schedule one of the Act other than:

- Acting as a trustee in relation to a regulated collective investment scheme;
- Acting as the operator of a regulated collective investment scheme other than one dedicated to:
  - Options, futures or contracts for differences;
  - Land and other property related assets;
  - Warrants to subscribe or purchase securities; whether or not the scheme holds other investments.

Whilst this initially seems a wide brief there is further guidance given in the appendices to the rules which significantly narrows this scope down. On application to SFA each firm will have to provide a profile of the type of business with which they are going to be involved. This profile is an ongoing document and must be abided by at all times. The fit and proper tests are all driven by the profile and whilst a firm may be considered fit to conduct some types of business they may not possess the skills required to take on a new area. If any firm wishes to expand its activities beyond the scope of its current profile then they must apply to SFA before any new business is commenced.

On receipt of a new applicant's business profile the membership department of SFA will consider whether the applicant is more appropriately authorised under the auspices of another SRO. In many cases the decision will not be clear cut and the choice will be resolved by negotiations between the firm, SFA and other SROs.

The Investment Management Regulatory Organisation (IMRO)

IMRO's prime area of responsibility is the regulation of fund managers, covering pension funds, investment trusts, unit trusts and individual management for investors.

IMRO regulates those firms whose main business falls within the scope of the following headings:

- Managing investments.
- Managing Occupational Pension Schemes (OPS) assets as an OPS member of IMRO
- Acting as manager or trustee of authorised unit trust schemes.
- Managing or operating other collective investment schemes.
- Investment advice to non-private customers.

The Personal Investment Authority (PIA)

As its name implies, PIA is concerned with the retail investment market. Its areas of responsibility are the control of the retailing and distribution of packaged investment products and the control of independent financial advisers.

PIA regulates all types of investment business within the meaning of the Act where carried on in relation to the following types of investment:

- Securities.
- Units or shares in collective investment schemes.
- Investments falling within paragraph 10 of Schedule 1 to the Act (long-term insurance contracts).
- Derivatives, but only where used for the purposes of efficiently managing a portfolio of securities or, in other circumstances, where the derivative is a traded option.

Objectives and structure of the FSA

The FSA will consolidate the work of the SROs as well as the supervisory side of the Bank of England. The aims of the FSA are:

- To protect consumers of financial services.
- To promote clean and orderly markets.
- To maintain, in conjunction with the Bank of England, confidence in the financial system.

The style of regulation is envisaged to be "a flexible and differentiated risk based approach ... reflecting the nature of the business activities concerned".

The organisation structure will be largely based on regulatory functions: policy; authorisation; enforcement; consumer relations; and supervision. However, the supervision function will be sub-divided by type of business.

FSA's board members will represent a mix of those with a consumer, industry and professional background. All will be appointed in the public interest and not as representatives of any particular interest group. Practitioner involvement will be maintained, but it is recommended that they should never have a majority voice.

The FSA will be accountable to Government and Parliament.

The FSA Rulebook

According to a consultation paper issued by the FSA, changes would be made only where regulations needed to be brought into line with the new legislation. The FSA will have the power to make rules covering everything from broad principles to conduct of business and the design of products. The government's intention, however, is not to extend conduct of business regulation to industries which are not currently subject to such rules (deposit-taking and general insurance, for instance) for the time being.

The new handbook will be divided into six modules:

- High level standards, including the criteria for fitness and propriety which will be applied to senior managers.
- Business standards, including basic rules for conduct of business and prudential standards.
- Regulatory process, including manuals for authorisation, training, supervision and discipline.
- Financial consumers, involving complaints codes and compensation guides.
- Specialist sourcebooks, such as rules for collective investment schemes or credit unions.
- Special guides for independent financial advisers, professional firms and small friendly societies.

Statements of Principle issued by FSA

In September 1998, the FSA issued a statement of principles to apply throughout the financial services industry. These built upon previous statements issued by the SIB and are as follows:

Integrity

A firm must conduct its business with integrity.

Skill, care and diligence

A firm must conduct its business and organise its affairs with due skill, care and diligence. This will include arranging adequate protection for customers' assets when the firm is responsible for them.

Management and control

A firm must organise and control its affairs effectively. This will include:

- having directors and senior managers who are all fit and proper for their roles and operating adequate arrangments for securing the suitability of persons who carry out functions on its behalf;
- apportioning responsibilities among its senior managers and directors in such a way that their individual responsibilities are clear and the business and affairs of the firm are adequately monitored and controlled at senior management and board level;
- operating robust arrangements for meeting the standards and requirements of the regulatory system and for guarding against involvement in market abuse or financial crime (including the detection and prevention of money laundering);
- keeping adequate and orderly records of its business and internal organisation.

Prudence

A firm must conduct its business and organise its affairs with prudence. This will include maintaining adequate financial resources, including adequate liquidity, and maintaining adequate risk management systems.

Market conduct

A firm must observe proper standards of market conduct.

Customers: general

A firm must pay due regard to the interests of its customers and treat them fairly. This will include paying due regard to their information needs; communicating information in a way that is fair and not misleading; and managing conflicts of interest fairly.

Customers: relationships of trust

A firm must keep faith with any customer who is entitled to rely upon its judgment. This will include taking reasonable care to ensure the suitability of its advice and discretionary decisions.

Relations with regulators

A firm must deal with its regulators in an open and cooperative way. This will include telling the FSA promptly anything about the firm of which the FSA would reasonably expect prompt notice.

Authorisation of banks

Most countries apply certain minimum standards that must be met before a bank can open for business. Within the European Union, these standards are governed by the First and Second Banking Co-ordination Directives. These directives have established the principle that member states of the European Union must pass legislation, which guarantees a certain minimum level of regulation. If they wish to do so, states may opt for higher standards of regulation than the minimum for their own banks. However, once all member states have minimum standards in place, any bank meeting authorisation standards in one member state is automatically entitled to open a branch in any other member state. Supervision of the branch's activities is the primary responsibility of the home state of the bank with the host state authorities having responsibility for liquidity and monetary policy matters only. This mutual recognition of home country regulation is commonly referred to as the 'European passport' for banks.

Authorisation within the UK is governed by the provisions of Schedule 3 of the 1987 Banking Act as amended by the Bank of England Act 1998 and is a necessary requirement before an institution may conduct a deposit taking business. The Bank of England Act 1998 transferred this responsibility to the FSA. The FSA is empowered to grant authorisation and its main criteria are as follows:

- **Directors should be fit and proper persons**

A questionnaire on the background, business record and experience of the controllers of the company must be filled in. The FSA will consider whether their experience and skills are adequate and, in addition, the individuals' history of dealings under the various codes of practice and any criminal record. Persons responsible for the conduct of the business of a deposit-taking institution must be of the highest integrity.

- **'Four-eyes' principle**

No single individual may direct a business and the FSA expects to see at least two active executives in the making of business decisions. Both persons must have sufficient experience, knowledge and authority to be able to detect and deal with any irregularities in the institution.

- **Composition of board of directors**

The FSA encourages the presence of non-executive directors on the board and, in particular, likes to see an audit committee defined as a sub-committee of the board and chaired by a non-executive director. This should be responsible for seeing that management performs satisfactorily with respect to accounts, records and internal controls in general.

- **Business to be conducted in a prudent manner**

The institution should submit a programme of operations setting out the nature and scale of intended operations. The FSA will consider the implications of the proposed customer base and exposures to such things as foreign exchange movements. They will consider specifically the size of net assets; liquidity; depreciation provision; accounting systems, records and controls.

- **Minimum net assets**

At the time of application, the net assets of the Institution must be at least £1 million.

Authorisation of investment business

There are four main routes to authorisation in the UK.

Membership of an appropriate SRO or SROs. As we have seen, each SRO has a specific target market or scope of responsibility. A firm wishing to obtain authorisation should select the SRO that most closely matches its operations. It may well be the case that the firm's operations are so wide and general that membership of more than one SRO will be necessary in order to give full regulatory coverage.

Membership of a Recognised Professional Body (RPB). Certain professional groups have been giving investment advice for many years. As long as giving such advice does not constitute a major proportion of their business, they will be able to continue doing so covered by the professional bodies to which they belong.

For example, accountants who are members of the Institute of Chartered Accountants in England and Wales are able to provide services relating to investments to their clients. However, in all cases, the right to give investment advice is not automatic, and once again, approval to do so must be sought from the appropriate professional body.

As with the SROs, the RPBs are obliged to seek recognition from FSA. In accordance with schedule three of the Act they are obliged to fulfil broadly similar requirements to those expected of an SRO.

Under the ISD this will be a more restricted regime. The ISD permits authorisation to be granted by a professional body, responsible for maintaining ethical standards, only where such service is provided in an incidental manner to the main trade. Therefore, for those professionals conducting ISD services in a non incidental manner, they will now be obliged to seek authorisation from one of the SROs.

Direct authorisation by the FSA. For some firms there is no one SRO or combination of SROs which is truly satisfactory. At present, these firms have the ability to seek direct authorisation from the FSA.

ISD 'Passport'. The Directive allows firms providing 'investment services', once authorised in the country in which their registered office is established to provide their services throughout the EEA.

Outside the scope of the FSAct are a number of institutions plus the wholesale markets which are supervised under the terms of the 'Grey Book', which is discussed in Chapter 9. In terms of institutions, the Stock Exchange, the Bank of England, Lloyds insurance market, Recognised Investment Exchanges, Recognised Clearing Houses and trustees fall outside the FSAct, as do listed money market institutions. These organisations are dealing in large numbers and dealing only with other commercial clients and counterparties and, as such, it was deemed that the FSAct would be difficult to implement. This became the logic behind regulation in the wholesale market via the London Code of Conduct and the 'Grey Book'. However, it is expected that the exchanges together with Lloyds will be brought into the scope of the FSA as investment business in future by way of a Financial Services Reform Act in 1999.

8   Objectives, standards and processes of regulation & supervision

Governments' objectives in imposing controls are related to three concerns. First, there is a desire to protect depositors in banks against the danger of losing their money. Without a high degree of confidence in its ability to repay deposits, a bank will not be able to continue in business and it is part of the regulators' role to ensure that confidence is merited. Second, a sound banking system is essential for the healthy functioning of the economy as a whole. It acts as the mechanism for facilitating payment for goods and services as well as being one of the means by which savings are channelled into productive investment. Third, regulation of the banking system is often used as a means of monetary control with a view to influencing the levels of growth and inflation in the economy as a whole.

Each country has developed its own techniques of control which will entail varying degrees of 'regulation' (that is, detailed rules) and 'supervision' (general guidance). The topics of concern to central banks in ensuring that their banks and the banking system as a whole remain sound are, however, common and can be listed as follows:

- authorisation;
- deposit protection;
- capital adequacy;
- liquidity;
- foreign exchange exposure;
- position risk;

- large exposures;
- monitoring and inspection.

In the UK, the FSA seeks to achieve this through the discharge of its responsibilities, as set out in the Banking Act of 1987, relating to the safety and soundness of individual authorised banks. The Act accepts the possibility of bank failures and is not aimed at delivering an unlimited guarantee of banks' deposit liabilities. To attempt to avoid any bank failing would be unhealthy for the economy (as it would involve limits on competition, innovation and the taking of risk, and increase the costs imposed by supervision); it would also be virtually impossible to achieve. Rather, the intention of the Act is that effective supervision should sufficiently reduce the risk of capital loss to depositors that strong depositor confidence in authorised banks is maintained. In carrying out its supervisory function, the FSA is required to act in the interest of depositors.

Monitoring and inspection

In terms of reporting, banks in all countries with developed financial centres make detailed reports to the central bank or to a supervisory body. The frequency of the report will depend on local requirements and the nature of the review area. Normally the reports required relate to liquidity, large exposures, capital adequacy, balance sheets and profit and loss, assets and liabilities by currency, and foreign exchange exposures. The FSA must be in a position to assess the accounting position on an ongoing basis and so requires accounting records to be up to date and financial soundness to be assessed on a daily basis

Authorities differ in their approach to the control of banks. The FSA calls for regular standard reports to assist it in its role, for example on the maturity structure of the bank's assets and liabilities, the foreign currency composition of its business, exposure to particular industrial sectors and so on. In addition to these reports, the FSA relies heavily upon auditors and reporting accountants to provide it with guidance and information on the financial health of banks.

The US authorities, which include not only the Federal Reserve but also the Federal Deposit Insurance Corporation and the Office of the Comptroller of the Currency, take more direct action themselves to investigate the state of their banks. They employ large teams of examiners who visit banks on a regular basis. The assessment of a bank's health is based on what is often referred to as the CAMEL test from the initial letters of the following factors:

- Capital strength;
- Asset quality;
- Management ability;
- Earnings;
- Liquidity.

These factors are assessed in accordance with standard quantifiable ratios backed up with the examiner's own views.

The assessment of banks' health can be undertaken at various levels. Large banking groups will include several subsidiaries within them, each of whom may be subject to regulation in some form or other. This is referred to as the solus position. In addition, however, the health of the group as a whole is an important consideration and there is an increasing tendency towards consolidated supervision. This is both more realistic, in that it allows for offsetting exposures within the group, and also more thorough, preventing frauds which might be perpetrated by showing different regulators in different countries only part of the whole picture.

Standards

The FSA's approach to supervision starts from the recognition that bank management is responsible for its business but that the Banking Act, augmented by the Guide to Banking Supervisory Policy issued in June 1998 and other supervisory Notices, creates a framework within which supervision of banks is carried out. In order to achieve its objectives, the FSA has set itself a number of standards, which are summarised below:

- To discharge its legal responsibilities;
- To discharge its policy objectives:
  - defining and disseminating appropriate supervisory policies and guidelines as a basis for consistent supervisory action;
  - working to raise international standards of banking supervision and developing effective relations with other

regulators, supervisors and market authorities in the United
Kingdom and overseas;

- Institution-specific responsibilities:
  - assessing banks' businesses, their risk profiles and the
    macroeconomic context;
  - designing effective supervisory plans and making
    appropriate use of supervisory tools;
  - ensuring appropriate reliance is placed on other regulators;
  - applying policies and taking appropriate supervisory action
    promptly and consistently;
- Management and communication issues:
  - ensuring the optimal allocation of supervisory resources
    based on the risk assessment of individual institutions;
  - communicating the supervisory framework, approach,
    policy and decisions.

Risk based supervision

The UK approach to supervision, begun by the Bank of England and
now carried on by the FSA, is characterised as the RATE model. RATE
is an acronym for the three stages of the process: Risk Assessment,
Tools of Supervision and Evaluation.

The approach introduced the concept of a supervisory period, which
is the length of time between undertaking formal risk assessments on a
particular bank. This period will usually be a year, but may vary
according to the risk profile of the bank concerned, from six months for
a bank whose risk profile is classified as very high or for a bank
undergoing major change; up to two years, or possibly longer, for a
bank whose risk profile is low and whose business and control
framework is stable. In each supervisory period, the FSA will perform a
risk assessment, take appropriate supervisory action, apply the tools of
supervision and undertake a formal evaluation.

The FSA will undertake the risk assessment using nine evaluation
factors. Six are quantitative: Capital, Assets, Market Risk, Earnings,
Liabilities, Business. Three are qualitative: Controls, Organisation and
Management. This extends the CAMEL acronym to become CAMEL-B-
COM.

The objective will be to identify the business or inherent risks of a bank and to assess the adequacy and effectiveness of its controls, organisation and management in a systematic manner.

The FSA includes in its risk assessment control functions, such as internal audit and risk management departments, and other areas of support, including IT and human resource departments.

Where the FSA identifies significant concerns, either from the risk assessment or at any time during the supervisory period, it will seek appropriate remedial action. In addition, after each risk assessment, the FSA will feed back its views on the FSA's risk profile to the FSA's Board of Directors. The FSA will also outline any remedial action it is seeking or intends to take, and a supervisory programme. This will set out the tools of supervision it intends to use, such as reporting accountants' reports on internal controls, Traded Markets Team visits and Review Team visits and the likely timing of their application. The tools will be targeted at areas considered to be of higher risk or to follow up issues identified during the risk assessment. The results coming from use of the tools will be examined as they become available, which may require the FSA to reassess the risk profile of the bank or take appropriate supervisory action.

During the course of the supervisory period the FSA will constantly evaluate the information it receives. In addition, at the end of the period, the FSA will undertake a formal evaluation to ensure that it has completed its original work plan, to check that it has acted appropriately on the results of the supervisory tools and generally to assess how effectively it has supervised the bank in question. The conclusions from the evaluation will be a key input into the next risk assessment.

The objective is to link the supervisory role more closely with the organisation being supervised, so that regulators have a more informed view of operations and procedures and can therefore bring more value and precision to their overall assessment of the business. This is a top down approach including a significant amount of fieldwork.

The development of the RATE model reflects an increasingly sophisticated understanding of the interaction of risk and reward in financial institutions, and in particular the way that risks across an organisation's operations aggregate to give a distinctive picture of an institution's business health.

Looking ahead, the creation of a more systematic regulatory model is an important element in ensuring and developing the transparency of regulation, which is itself strongly linked to the demands of the markets, analysts and investors. London as a marketplace commands many advantages, but faces strong competition in future from within Europe and globally. Having regulatory standards that are open, predictable in implementation and effective in operation is absolutely essential to protect London's reputation as a financial centre.

Regulators cannot and should not second-guess management but must have the tools to ensure that their assessment of a particular institution incorporates a sufficiently detailed picture of key risk areas and how they are managed. The ideal is a framework which enables the regulator both to see the business through management's eyes, without being in management's shoes, and to assess it using a framework of tools and techniques which identify the effectiveness with which risk is being managed. Some of these tools grow out of developments in the international regulatory arena, but the real motivator in developing these measures is to build greater precision into the supervisory process in the areas where such precision forms a useful complement to the skill of the regulator's experienced assessment.

The way management exercises executive power is at the head of an effective control framework. The management culture, the tone set at the top of an institution, establishes the tone for the whole organisation's operational style. A management culture centred on discipline, honesty, openness and integrity, both in the conduct of the business and the operation of controls, sets value standards that cascade down the entire organisational matrix. Conversely, a management culture, which is secretive and willing to allow controls to be breached without punishment can undermine even the most well structured control framework.

A sound management culture should establish standards, principles and ways of doing business so that problems are identified promptly and resolved quickly, while at the same time encouraging creativity and determination in pursuing profitable market opportunities. Balancing empowerment and control in fast-moving businesses is a complex task, but care must be taken that the creative tensions between an institution's deal makers, entrepreneurs and controllers does not become unconstructive anarchy.

It is in this area that the regulator, in assessing whether management is fit, proper and prudent in managing the business under its control, must necessarily rely on qualitative as much as quantitative assessment. These will include factors such as strong management culture, as well as the comprehensiveness of the internal control and risk framework. Qualitative and quantitative measures in assessing management performance are mutually supportive. The RATE framework acknowledges this by giving regulators the chance to develop a much closer understanding of the interaction of management and the business at both an operational and strategic level.

Complex groups provide a challenge for regulators as to how they can supervise institutions whose operations may encompass sizeable business units outside of their remit. Complex businesses with conflicting regulators are a risk management nightmare. Turning this into a satisfactory regulatory solution will involve close co-ordination both in the UK and overseas. It is for these very reasons that the FSA has set up a complex groups division to supervise those banks that are financial conglomerates.

Risk based supervision for investment businesses

Both IMRO and SFA use models, which are similar to RATE being the Relative Risk Assessment for IMRO firms and FIBSPAM for SFA firms.

Each factor must, wherever possible, be objective and able to be verified. These models have a number of broadly similar components as follows:

- Reconciliations. Stock/cash reconciliations are done on a timely basis.
- Financial Viability. The firm can pay/settle with the market/ clients.
- Company Structure. The firm has a well defined chain of command and duties are clearly specified. People with authority to commit the firm should be clearly identified.
- Key individuals. The firm's dependence upon key individuals to generate revenue/supply capital.
- Regulatory history. The compliance history of the firm and whether there have been any disciplinary cases.
- New products. The firm should have procedures to introduce

and authorise new products. These procedures should cover limits and settlement.

- Management reports. These reports should reflect accurately the business of the firm and should cover the relevant business activities within the firm.

The fundamental purpose of the models is to establish what makes one firm riskier than another and the reasons for arriving at these conclusions. Risk profiling is an important discipline for any regulator to undertake. Regulators should not be blinded by the apparently absolute measures that figures offer. The SFA and IMRO models deal in relative measures, which are at best an approximation given a particular array of data and intelligence. Risk profiling is a dynamic process. Perceptions of a firm's profile are, correctly, always subject to change in the light of new information.

Liquidity .

Although a bank's capital ratio is a clear indicator of its long-term health, it is a shortage of liquidity that is the most common immediate cause of bank failure. There is, however, little agreement between different supervisors as to how liquidity can best be regulated. There are three main approaches: reserve requirements, mandatory liquid assets and cash flow monitoring.

Historically, it has been quite common for monetary authorities to require banks to hold a certain proportion of their deposits in non-interest-bearing balances with the central bank. The main reason for these was as a way of controlling growth in the money supply by discouraging banks from expanding their balance sheets. The effect of requiring non-interest-bearing deposits is to increase the cost of funds to banks and hence make it more expensive to borrow. Reserves are, consequently, a hidden tax on intermediation.

Greater efficiency for all concerned can be achieved by requiring banks to hold interest-bearing liquid assets rather than non-interest-bearing deposits. In the UK, banks negotiate liquidity requirements individually with the Bank of England, one requirement being that they hold an agreed level of high-quality liquid assets, this level usually being related to the size and structure of their deposit base. Qualifying assets include treasury bills and other short-term government stock, eligible bills, and secured placings with discount houses, gilt-edged market makers and Stock Exchange money brokers. Other types of asset, such as certificates of deposit may also be included by negotiation.

In many countries, the level of reserves varies with the type of deposit. In Germany, for example, transaction deposits attract reserve requirements of between 6.6 per cent and 12.1 per cent whilst time deposits attract 4.95 per cent and savings deposits only 4.15 per cent. This is intended to relate reserves to the liquidity of the relevant deposits so that the banks concerned would be able to call reserves back from the central bank to meet withdrawals in the event of a run.

The trend in recent years has been towards dismantling reserve requirements. Their validity as a monetary control mechanism has been eroded by the development of alternative means of finance, which by-pass banks' balance sheets such as commercial paper or acceptance credits. As a liquidity buffer, there are also more efficient techniques, as explained below. In the UK, there is a requirement for 0.35 per cent of eligible liabilities to be placed in a non-interest-bearing deposit with the Bank of England. The stated purpose of this deposit is solely to provide funds for the running of the Bank of England itself. In the USA, reserves are only required now for transaction accounts, although they are levied at the rather high rate of 12 per cent. The European Central Bank has announced its intention of maintaining reserve requirements but at a fairly low level of 1.5 per cent to 2.5 per cent.

The advantage which a mandatory liquid assets approach has over simple non-interest bearing reserve requirements is that it allows the bank to manage its liquidity position actively and at minimum cost, since its liquidity portfolio will yield a return, albeit a low one because of the very low risk of the assets involved. Given this low risk, however, and the ready marketability of many of these assets, supervisors can still be assured that the bank will be able to raise funds rapidly by selling its liquid assets should the need for quick liquidity arise.

Supervisors will also be interested in monitoring a bank's cash flow position. It is better to ensure that a liquidity shortage does not occur than to try to cope with one through realising assets. This can be done by drawing up a table showing the maturity of the bank's assets and liabilities, which will highlight possible periods of cash shortage and allow the bank to take remedial action. The FSA's Q6 and S5 returns which UK banks are required to submit regularly are maturity ladders. The use of such tables was discussed in chapter 3.

Whilst most aspects of bank supervision are deemed to be the responsibility of home country regulators, liquidity is, under both the Basle Concordat and the European Union Banking Directives, a host country issue as explained in chapter 6. This emphasises both the responsibility of a country for maintaining orderly market conditions in its own currency and also the fact that liquidity problems can arise very rapidly, making it difficult for home country authorities who are not on the spot to diagnose and react to a problem fast enough.

Foreign exchange

The foreign exchange exposure of banks in the UK is controlled in accordance with two chapters on Foreign Currency Exposure and Foreign Currency Options, which are contained in the FSA Guide to Banking Supervisory Policy. This stresses that banks should pay attention to all exposures arising from any uncovered foreign exchange position and those incurred through the writing of options business in any currency. Monthly returns are required showing:

- the net spot long or short positions in each currency at the close of business on the reporting day;
- the net forward long or short positions in each currency at the close of business on the reporting day.

The sum of spot and forward positions, without discounting, is taken to be the overall net position in each currency.

Banks which are inexperienced in the trading of foreign currency options have to include exposures arising from options trading under 'worst case' assumptions for the outcome of each transaction. This will mean that full allowance is made for the possibility of customers exercising options against the bank but no credit is given for options taken, the grounds for these extreme assumptions being that, in the absence of full details of periods and exercise prices and so on, an extremely conservative view is required.

Such treatment would be very restrictive on a bank that trades actively in currency options. Banks which can satisfy the FSA that they are competent to handle the mathematics of an options pricing model and who can demonstrate adequate operating systems for controlling the business may be permitted to use estimates of the exposure arising from options which have been derived from an approved pricing model. The delta values would be a suitable measure of the true exposure.

The FSA agrees guidelines with each bank as to the maximum size of open position that it may run. In doing so, it takes into account the institution's expertise in foreign exchange operations and suggests that experienced banks may expect to agree limits along the following lines:

- net open position in any one currency not more than 10 per cent of the institution's capital base as defined for capital adequacy purposes;

- net short open position in all currencies taken together not more than 15 per cent of the capital base.

These guidelines are applied to dealing positions of banks. Structural positions arising from long-term assets and liabilities, including loan capital, premises and investments in subsidiaries and associates, may, by agreement with FSA, be excluded from the calculation. Structural positions can also arise from holding reserves or provisions in specific currencies to match the banking risks against which they are held. These positions are not without risk, and will be considered by the FSA in its general supervision of the institution concerned. Being long-term in nature, it is convenient to leave them out of the position calculated for dealing control purposes.

Large exposures

The capital adequacy requirements are aimed primarily at protecting banks and their depositors against the consequences of default by counterparties. This is, however, backed up by limits on the extent to which a bank can commit its capacity to a single borrower. This is typically expressed in terms of the bank's capital base.

UK banks are required to report to the FSA their 20 largest exposures and to limit exposures to any one counterparty to not more than 10 per cent of their capital base although in exceptional circumstances permission may be granted to go up to 25 per cent.

Discussions on enhancing the sophistication of this type of control have considered two main variations. First, it has been suggested that exposures should be risk-weighted using the same weights as for capital adequacy purposes. The idea of risk-weighting is valid but the broad-brush nature of the risk asset weights makes it questionable whether they are appropriate. Exposures to a weak bank should not be considered safer than those to a strong corporate customer. Second, it has been proposed that limits should not be 'hard' in that they could never be exceeded but that they should be 'soft' permitting banks to exceed them provided that they allocated extra capital specifically to partial coverage of that exposure.

With the diversity of customers that any bank has, it is difficult to draw up regulations that will have general applicability. The existing FSA approach, whereby specific permission is needed to exceed certain modest levels on a case-by-case basis, has much to recommend it.

Deposit protection

A primary objective of bank regulation is to protect depositors against the risk of losing their deposits. Most countries have formal deposit protection schemes, which guarantee to repay depositors if the bank concerned cannot do so. It is normal for the amount covered to be limited on the grounds that large-scale depositors should have enough financial knowledge to be able to take credit judgements themselves and will also have the scope to spread their deposits across several institutions thus limiting their own risk rather than relying on a protection scheme. The objective is to protect small retail depositors who may suffer particular hardship in the event of a bank failure.

Some schemes limit not only the amount that is covered but also the proportion of the deposit that may be reclaimed. The Deposit Protection Fund in the UK was established under the Banking Act 1979 and upgraded in the 1987 Act. Deposits made with an authorised bank's offices in the European Economic Area (EEA), denominated in the currency of the member state of the EEA, are eligible for compensation. In the event of a bank becoming insolvent this fund pays 90% of the deposit, including accrued interest, subject to a maximum of the greater of £18,000 or the sterling equivalent of Ecu 20,000.

The purpose of the maximum percentage cover is to encourage an element of co-responsibility on behalf of the depositor who would otherwise be able to place his funds with whichever institution offered the highest rate irrespective of the risk involved, as he would be sure of repayment from the deposit protection scheme if the bank failed. This is sometimes referred to as the moral hazard problem, which has given rise to considerable debate in the USA where the whole of deposits up to $100,000 are covered.

The Investor's Compensation Scheme

The investor's compensation scheme was set up by FSA to provide investors with compensation in the event of financial loss on the insolvency of an authorised firm. The claims are dealt with by the relevant SRO and funded by a levy on the members of the SROs. An investor can claim up to 100% of the first £30,000 and 90% of the next £20,000 for any one loss, giving a maximum of £48,000. There are provisions for interest to be added to the amount of compensation, which may take the total amount paid over the limit expressed above. Conversely, the compensation may be reduced if the investor is deemed to be largely to blame for the loss he has suffered.

9 Regulation of the wholesale markets in the UK

The Financial Services Act (1986) was aimed primarily at the protection of the interests of retail investors. It contains many provisions that would be onerous for regular wholesale operators in the financial markets to observe and that are, in any case, of little relevance to the protection of their interests. For this reason, institutions that qualify as wholesale are exempted from some of the provisions of the Act. In return, they must comply with the wholesale market regulations as published by the Bank of England and the FSA.

These regulations are embedded in two papers. These are 'The Regulation of the Wholesale Cash and OTC Derivatives Markets' first published in 1988 (otherwise known as the 'Grey Book') and the London Code of Conduct of 1992. These have been revised since their first issue, not least to incorporate the requirements of EU Directives.

Listed institutions

Central to the wholesale market regulatory framework is a list of institutions that act in the market as either principal or broker and are recognised as wholesale operators. The FSA maintains this list. In order to qualify for a listing, the following conditions must be met:

- The institution can demonstrate that it is financially secure and has an appropriate ownership and management structure. There should be no conflicts of interest or source of potential weakness. Capital adequacy requirements must be met.
- Directors, managers and controllers must be suitable for their positions and not prejudice prudent control within the institution.

- It must have the necessary operational resources. Systems controls and record keeping must be of a high standard.
- It can show that its activities are wholesale in nature, whether its activities are as a core principal or principal acting for an institution.
- Its standards of conduct are high, being recognised as such within the financial markets.

Removal of listing

Should an institution fail to comply with the conditions for remaining a listed institution the FSA may exercise its power to remove the offending firm from the list, restrict its activities or publicly or privately reprimand its management. Reasons why this might be necessary include the following:

- The institution has provided false or misleading information to the FSA.
- Dishonest means have been used to gain or retain a listing.
- Wholesale business is being carried out beyond its permitted scope.
- The listed institution fails to fulfil an undertaking it has been required to make.
- Another supervisory body terminates authorisation.
- A supervisory authority in the institution's home state reports that there has been a failure to comply with its requirements.
- Listing conditions have not been met.

The Grey Book

The Grey Book defines the scope of wholesale market regulation in terms of the list of approved institutions, the products traded and the size of the transaction. The products covered are primarily short term in nature, traded over-the-counter and serve the treasury requirements of participants. Products listed include:

- wholesale deposits in sterling, foreign currency and gold or silver bullion;

- spot and forward foreign exchange or bullion contracts;
- certificates of deposit;
- bank bills;
- other debentures with an original maturity of not more than one year;
- medium term notes;
- UK local authority debt with an original maturity of not more than five years;
- other public sector debt with an original maturity of not more than one year;
- OTC options or futures on any of the above;
- interest rate and currency swaps, FRAs and other contracts for difference on any of the above;
- sale and repurchase agreements that mature within twelve months.

Wholesale transactions normally involve large amounts. The Grey Book defines wholesale transactions sizes as follows:

- For debentures, bonds, loan stock and repos the minimum size is £100,000.
- For swaps, options, futures and forward rate agreements (FRAs) the minimum underlying notional value is £500,000.

Smaller transactions are also exempt from the FSAct if they meet at least one of the following conditions:

- Both parties to the transaction are listed institutions.
- One party is listed and the other is a 'wholesale counterparty'. Wholesale counterparties are non-listed counterparties who have transacted a deal above the specified limits in the past eighteen months with, or by arrangement with, a listed institution. The exemption only exists for future deals between the two parties.
- Both parties are counterparties of a listed broker involved in setting up the transaction.

London Code of Conduct

The Code, the full title of which is 'The London Code of Conduct for principals and broking firms in the wholesale markets' was last revised in July 1995, replacing the previous version of May 1992. The purpose of the Code is to ensure that the UK money markets are operating within the highest standards in terms of ethics and business conduct. It is in the interests of the market and the institutions themselves to demonstrate their worthiness of a reputation for good practice. The code of conduct provides both a regulatory framework and a basis for the internal control operations of firms to function. The document can claim further credibility from the fact that it was produced in conjunction with practitioners from the banks. It has been designed to be a close companion of the 'Grey Book' with the two publications forming the nucleus of the regulation of wholesale markets. The main points covered by the Code are considered in the following paragraphs.

Scope

The level of competence and integrity in the London financial markets is an important part of retaining London's status as a leading financial centre. It is in the best interests of all those operating in the City to make their individual contribution for upholding a reputation for both commercial excellence and for probity.

The purpose of the Code is to establish the controls and standards applicable to core principals (banks, building societies and financial institutions authorised under the FSA), and for brokers operating in the same markets. The core principals then have the responsibility to ensure that parties with whom they are dealing have a copy of the code and are aware of its requirements. Overseas based firms are also encouraged to use the Code and the FSA will endeavour to ensure that they are aware of it, as well as encouraging UK based firms to make them aware.

The FSA seeks the highest standards of fairness and integrity through the Code and any breaches will be taken very seriously. Any institution feeling that there have been breaches of the Code by another party should attempt to settle the issues between themselves. Should this not be possible then the Code encourages firms to bring the matter to the attention of the FSA Banking Supervision Division. All complaints are then investigated and digressions addressed appropriately. In such cases there may be a public reprimand or some restriction in the activities of the offending institution's activities. Redress, in terms of compensation, is not provided for in statute, but the Code places an obligation on institutions to give recognition of their shortcomings

Roles and responsibilities of principals and brokers
Role of principals

- To assess the creditworthiness of counterparties.
- To consider any information given by the broker.
- Agents for connected or other companies should be clear about their capacity and declare for whom they are acting. All confirmations must be clear when the deal is done on an agency basis.

Role of brokers

- To act as arrangers of deals between parties on mutually acceptable terms, in return for a fee.
- Brokers are expressly disallowed to act as a principal.
- Brokers must respect confidentiality but can discuss information that is in the public domain.

Responsibilities of principals and brokers

- Those firms dealing with private individuals must have procedures in place demonstrating how the individual will be treated as a retail customer or a wholesale customer.
- All staff must be familiar with the code.
- Staff must be adequately trained.
- Firms must take full responsibility for the actions of their staff.
- Management must ensure that staff are kept up to date with any FSA requirements.
- Firms dealing with new counterparties should make them aware of the liabilities involved.
- The limited role of brokers should be explained.
- Conflicts of interests should be identified when transacting deals and measures taken to eliminate them.

- Full assessments should be made of counterparties' abilities to meet their commitments.
- All steps must be taken to prevent money laundering.
- All counterparties must accept full responsibility for the risks of entering into wholesale transactions.
- Parties should follow good practice in taking independent legal advice.
- Management of broking firms must advise employees that any attempt to mislead is not acceptable.

Responsibilities of the employee

- Misrepresentation of the transaction must not be allowed to happen and identities and roles of firms for whom the employee is acting must be clear, as should the products. The facts relating to the deal must be disclosed.
- Employees of broker firms must not unfairly favour one client in any deal.

Knowledge of the counterparty

Checks must take place before transactions are undertaken with a counterparty. There should be, according to the Code, a clearly articulated approval process. This would need to include, for example, reference to legal issues and to potential conflicts of interest between the firm's interests and those of the customer. Procedures are also required to ensure that product information is reviewed and analysed prior to dealing taking place. Finally, the Code extends a cautionary note on the extent to which institutions should get involved in over the counter deals with small investors. In particular, dealing in products outside the provisions of the FSAct with small investors should always carry the warning that they do not have the protection of the FSAct.

The Code refers to the growing use of mandates in order to clarify the terms of reference between the counterparties. Both parties should agree the content of the mandate, but they can receive guidance on this from the British Bankers Association and from the Association of Corporate Treasurers.

A fairly recent development has been the use of discretionary management companies to front deals where an institution does not wish to have their names revealed. The problems associated with this practice revolve around the inability to assess the real principal. The FSA, in the latest edition of the Code express their wish to take up this matter with other supervisors in Basle. In the meantime the FSA suggests that the basis for decisions under such circumstances should be fully documented and referred to senior management.

Confidentiality

The Code says that the issue of maintaining confidentiality is the equal responsibility of principals and brokers. No information should be disclosed without explicit permission. It is up to management to make employees aware of the general confidentiality issues and those related to specific deals. Examples of possible breaches are quoted in the Code. These might include the indiscreet use of loudspeakers in dealing rooms or individual dealers visiting the dealing rooms of the other party. In fact, the Code stresses that normally this should not happen and if it does it must be with permission from the management of both sides.

Segregation of functions

The FSA is prepared to accept that back office functions might be physically located with dealing functions provided there is clear segregation of duties. Equally they are prepared to allow back office functions at another physical site, even in another country. The proviso is that there is still someone to whom problems and queries can be referred at a local level.

Taping

The FSA strongly recommends the use of tape recording in order to settle misinterpretations and disputes. The FSA recommends that tapes should be kept for at least two months.

Dealing at non-market rates

The Code clearly states that deals at non-market rates should not be undertaken. Senior management should have procedures in place to identify such proposals. On the other hand, the FSA accepts that there may, on occasions, be structural reasons for doing a deal outside current rates. In these circumstances, the Code insists that full documentation is put in place and reviewed by senior management. Specific attention is drawn to an area that is not considered acceptable in any circumstances, that is, the temptation not to fix spot foreign exchange rates immediately at market price. This practice is considered unethical and inappropriate for UK based institutions and spot rates should be determined immediately after completion of the transaction.

After hours dealing

This section of the Code stresses that though after hours trading has become acceptable practice, particularly in foreign exchange markets, there need to be clear management guidelines on types of deal that can be transacted and the limits within which these deals may be done. All deals must be confirmed promptly to avoid the risk of one side denying a deal has been done.

Stop loss orders

A stop loss order is an instruction, most likely to be given to a broker, that a security or a currency should be bought or sold if it reaches a certain level. The FSA wishes that all stop loss orders be explicitly identified and management of the counterparty be aware of their obligations.

Conflicts of interest

Should management allow employees to deal on their own account in the markets covered by the Code, then they must take full responsibility for any problems that ensue.

Brokers should provide written notification if a material connection exists between themselves and any parties involved in a transaction, where that transaction could be affected by the connection. For example the FSA considers a shareholding in a broker to be material if it is greater than ten per cent, but there may be circumstances where even a lower shareholding is considered material.

Marketing and incentives

Marketing efforts by listed firms should be directed towards market professionals. This principle is very loose but the FSA considers that specific rules are not appropriate for large institutions in professional markets. Under this heading, they do uphold the view that incentives must be tightly controlled and above all, brokers should not make payments to banks for using their services.

Entertainment, gifts and gambling

The Code stresses that management must have a clearly articulated policy towards gifts, at the same time being sure that these do not constitute inducements to do business. It is hard to draw a distinction that can be applied in all circumstances between inducements and entertainment given during the normal course of business. The FSA prefers to see a policy made and upheld within the institution. Periodic control reports should be produced and made available to internal control staff, senior management, and if necessary by the bank. Authorisation and control procedures must be clearly defined making it clear where accountability lies.

Abused substances

Management must understand the signs where drugs and alcohol might be taken by employees, particularly dealers and brokers whose judgement can be impaired, distorted or corrupted by the use of these substances. Given the large amounts of money involved in wholesale money market transactions, together with the high occupational pressure and availability of drugs, this has the potential to become a real problem.

Dealing principles - Statement of best practice

The Code's stated best procedural practice for dealing activity includes the following items.

Preliminary negotiation of terms

Firms should clearly state at the outset, prior to a transaction being executed, any qualifying conditions to which it will be subject.

Undertaking derivative transactions with end-users, ie 'customers' of the market

It is important, before derivative transactions are undertaken with a customer, that dealers are satisfied that appropriate 'know your counterparty' procedures have been implemented for the product under consideration.

Firmness of quotation

All firms, whether acting as principal, agent or broker, have a duty to make absolutely clear whether the prices they are quoting are firm or merely indicative. Prices quoted by brokers should be taken to be firm.

Concluding a deal

Principals should regard themselves as bound to a deal once the price and any other key commercial terms have been agreed. Oral agreements are considered binding. However, holding brokers unreasonably to a price is viewed as unprofessional and should be discouraged by management.

Passing of names by brokers

Brokers should not divulge the names of principals prematurely, and certainly not until satisfied that both sides display a serious intention to transact. Principals and brokers should at all times treat the details of transactions as absolutely confidential to the parties involved.

Use of intermediaries

Brokers must not involve a further intermediary in any deal that could take place without its introduction.

Confirmation procedures

Prompt passing, recording and careful checking of confirmations is vital to minimise the possibility of errors and misunderstanding whether direct or through brokers. Details should be passed as soon as practicable after deals have been done and checked upon receipt. The passing of details in batches is not recommended. For markets where standard terms are applicable, it is recommended that confirmations conform to the formats specified for the market or instrument concerned.

An increasing number of practitioners find it helpful to undertake oral deal checks at least once a day, especially when using a broker.

Payment/settlement instructions

Instructions should be passed as quickly as possible to facilitate prompt settlement. The FSA strongly recommends the use of standard settlement instructions. Their use can make a significant contribution to reducing both the incidence and size of differences arising from the mistaken settlement of funds.

Fraud

There is a need for greater vigilance by all staff against attempted fraud. This is particularly so where calls are received on an ordinary telephone line.

Terms and documentation

It is now common for wholesale market deals to be subject to some form of legal documentation binding the two parties to certain standard conditions and undertakings. The FSA endorses the use, wherever possible, of such documentation (which typically will take the form of signed Master Agreements exchanged between two parties or can take the form of standard terms).

Assignments or transfers

Assignments should not generally be undertaken without the consent of the parties concerned.

Settlement of differences

Provided that all the procedures above are followed then the size and incidence of differences should be reduced and remaining differences should be rectified easily. Any differences that do exist should be settled in cash.

Arbitration procedure

Where there is a dispute relating to the application of the London Code of Conduct, the FSA is prepared to arbitrate. It will expect the two parties involved to have considered all the options and applied judgment in good faith.

Commission/brokerage

Brokers' charges are freely negotiable and principals should pay broker bills promptly. The lack of prompt payment among some firms is explicitly described as bad practice.

Market convention and terminology

The Code emphasises the need to use clear, unambiguous terminology. The search for plain English provides the concise terminology that reduces the risk of misunderstanding and makes for a more fluid market based on clear definitions, integrity and mutual trust

Market disruption/Bank Holidays

Interruptions to settlement happen infrequently but from time to time require that interest rates be set to compensate for late payment. The

Joint Standing Committee has agreed that in such unexpected circumstances the Bank of England should determine the interest rate to be applied.

Relationships with brokers

The issue of confidentiality and anonymity has already been touched on and these principles must be followed in dealings with brokers. Not only must bank secrets be kept but brokers should not be pushed to reveal information that should remain confidential. Where confidential information must be shared between the two parties then great care must be taken to ensure that communication between them goes no further.

It is not considered appropriate for dealers to conduct business with a broker in order to obtain the name of a counterparty with whom they will then try to establish a direct dealing relationship.

Although brokers have a secondary role in the markets it is incumbent upon them to live by similar codes of conduct to those followed by the banks themselves. Equally they are expected to conform to established market practices. Staff should be adequately trained in these practices and expected to work according to a set of standards.

Brokers should not be encouraged or allowed to use gifts or other offerings in order to gain favours from dealers or any bank personnel. Entertainment of any kind should be offered and accepted with due care to the reputation and standing of the brokers and dealers concerned. Ultimately it can be the reputation of their employer that suffers. In a business that relies so much on maintaining confidence the reputation of brokers and in particular banks should not be placed at risk.

Insider trading

The main objective of insider trading laws is to protect corporate confidences and to prevent persons with inside information from gaining an unfair advantage when they deal. Insider dealing can be defined as trading on the basis of unpublished price-sensitive information obtained as part of an individual's employment. It involves exploiting information obtained through a privileged relationship when dealing in securities.

It is a criminal offence under the Criminal Justice Act 1993 to do any of the following:

- Deal in price-affected securities on the basis of inside information;
- Encourage another person to deal, whether or not he subsequently deals;
- Disclose the inside information to another person.

The penalties depend on the court used. Through the Magistrates Court, the maximum penalty is six months' imprisonment and £5,000 fine. Through the Crown Court, the maximum imprisonment is seven years and the fine is unlimited.

Duty of a firm

A firm must not effect (either in the United Kingdom or elsewhere) an own account transaction when it knows of circumstances that mean it is prohibited from effecting that transaction by the statutory restrictions on insider dealing. This applies to the firm and any of its associates or employees.

Every firm has a duty to ensure that it does not knowingly make a transaction for a customer if it knows it would be an offence under the insider dealing legislation. There are three exceptions where this does not apply:

- If the prohibition only applies because of knowledge of the firm's own intentions.

- If the firm is a recognised market maker with obligations to deal in the investment.

- If the firm is a trustee or personal representative who acts on the advice of a third party appearing to be an appropriate adviser who is not so prohibited.

Duty of an individual

Any individual with inside information:

- cannot deal for himself, or on behalf of his firm or a client;
- should not procure or encourage another person to deal in the price affected securities (regardless of whether the other party knows the information is price sensitive);
- should not pass on the information to another person unless it is a normal part of his employment.

An individual will not be regarded as being guilty of insider dealing in the following circumstances:

- he uses information where he did not intend anyone to profit;
- a new issue is stabilised under the strict terms of the FSA stabilisation rules;
- a market maker has inside information in the course of his business but acts *bona fide* for that business;
- where the information that a person dealing has is only that certain securities are to be or have been issued, acquired or disposed of and that it is reasonable to deal.

The Criminal Justice Act applies to all securities traded on a regulated market and to all warrants and derivatives (including index options and futures) relating to those securities.

10 Capital adequacy

Capital adequacy has played a central part in banking regulation for many years. The main purpose of capital is as a buffer to absorb losses. If banks were to fund all their assets with deposits, then a default on any loan would mean that there would no longer be enough funds left to repay depositors. A strong capital base is important in maintaining the confidence of not only depositors but also counterparties to any market transaction, guarantee, and so on, into which the bank enters. Its importance to regulators is therefore clear.

Until recently, each country's regulatory authority had developed capital adequacy regulations in isolation. This had resulted in substantial differences in the overall level of capitalisation of banks and also in the treatment of particular classes of asset. In 1987, the Basle Committee on Banking Supervision published proposals that were aimed firstly at a general increase in the levels of bank capital but also at establishing a common system of capital adequacy throughout the main financial markets. By harmonising regulation, this initiative meant that banks in all countries would be faced with more or less the same level of capital requirements for the same type of business thus establishing a 'level playing field'.

The general principles governing capital adequacy are now common not only in the countries represented on the Basle group but also in many other countries that have chosen to base their procedures on that agreement. The following description is mostly based on the implementation of the proposals by the FSA in accordance with the Solvency, Own Funds and Capital Adequacy Directives of the European Union.

The original Basle Accord concentrated on capital to support credit risks. Banks are also vulnerable to losses arising from market (or position) risk and subsequent papers from both the Basle Committee and the EU have introduced this into the capital adequacy framework too.

The absence of explicit measurement of the capital required for position risk became a particular problem when comparing the capital regimes for banks with those for other types of investment institution. The EU Capital Adequacy Directive was intended to cover both banks and investment firms and so needed to provide rules that integrated both types of operation. The concepts of position risk differ in that banks tend to hold loans and deposits to maturity whereas investment businesses will buy and sell, operating for short-term gain. The CAD achieves compromise by introducing a distinction between the trading book and the banking book.

The trading book is defined according to whether transactions are in specified financial instruments and also whether they are held with the intent to profit from short term price movements or to hedge other exposures. The banking book is defined, by exclusion, to cover everything else. It is particularly important to note that loans and deposits do not fall within the definition of financial instruments for trading book purposes. Banking book exposures remain subject to the earlier Basle rules for capital purposes whereas exposures in the trading book fall under CAD.

The approach to assessing overall capital adequacy is to express the bank's capital as a percentage of the risks as measured by the weighting process described below. This produces the 'risk asset ratio'. The international agreement called for all banks to have a risk asset ratio of no less than 8 per cent by 1 January 1993 at the latest. National supervisors may choose to apply higher ratios to some or all of their banks, the FSA being one authority that does indeed apply higher levels.

The various building blocks used in measuring a bank's capital adequacy under the UK approach are described in the following sections.

Regulatory capital

Capital, for regulatory purposes, is defined in terms of three tiers. Tier 1, or core capital, is regarded as the most secure form of capital, being comprised mainly of shareholder's funds. Tier 2, or supplementary capital, is primarily comprised of debt whilst Tier 3, or ancillary capital, is limited to use in support of market risk exposures.

Tier 1 capital

Tier 1 takes two forms namely issued capital, such as share capital, and internally generated capital, which arises from accruing profit to reserves, or by capitalising dividends.

Tier 1 capital consists of:

- Permanent shareholders' equity:

    - Allotted, called up and fully paid share capital/common stock.

    - Perpetual, irredeemable non-cumulative preferred shares and perpetual non-cumulative preferred shares convertible at the issuer's option into common shares.

- Disclosed reserves in the form of general or other reserves created or increased by appropriations of retained earnings, share premiums or other surplus.

- Published interim retained profit verified by external auditors.

- Minority interests arising on consolidation from interests in permanent shareholders' equity.

Tier 2 capital

Tier 2 capital is itself split into upper and lower tiers. All dated subordinated debt should be included in Lower Tier 2 capital, while perpetual debt instruments may be eligible for inclusion in Upper Tier 2.

Like Tier 1, Upper Tier 2 can be split between issued and internally generated capital. Issued Upper Tier 2 capital includes hybrid capital instruments (eg perpetual subordinated debt that is able to absorb losses, and cumulative preference shares). Issued Upper Tier 2 capital is perpetual but it is generally cumulative in that dividend or interest payments may be deferred, but not cancelled. Internally generated Upper Tier 2 capital includes general provisions and certain revaluation reserves.

Lower Tier 2 capital typically has a maturity date but must have a minimum maturity of over five years and interest should be paid as it falls due. It takes the form of term subordinated debt. Such debt is classed as a lower form of capital because its availability to absorb loss only comes into effect in the event of insolvency, and in general there is less funding flexibility, since a deferral of an interest payment can itself be an event of default.

Tier 2 Capital may therefore consist of:

- Reserves arising from the revaluation of tangible fixed assets and fixed asset investments.
- General provisions.
- Hybrid capital instruments:
  - Perpetual cumulative preferred shares redeemable at the option of the issuer but with the prior consent of the FSA.
  - Perpetual subordinated debt including such debt convertible into equity.
- Subordinated term debt:
  - Dated preferred shares.
  - Convertible subordinated bonds not included above.
  - Subordinated term loan capital with a minimum original maturity of over five years, subject to straight-line amortisation in the last five years.
- Minority interests arising on consolidation from interests in Tier 2 capital items.

Tier 3 capital

Tier 3 capital was introduced by the Capital Adequacy Directive and may be used only in support of market risk activity in the trading book (see below). It may be more short term than Lower Tier 2 capital having a minimum maturity of two years.

Tier 3 capital may consist of:

- Short term subordinated debt meeting the qualifying conditions and subject to the following restrictions:
  - The debt must have a minimum original maturity of two years.
  - The FSA may require that the interest and principal payments be deferred on Tier 3 debt if capital falls below the target capital requirement.
- Daily trading book profits net of any foreseeable charges or dividends, subject to FSA being satisfied that they have been

calculated using appropriate techniques.

- Minority interests in Tier 3 capital.

Deductions from capital

Certain deductions are made from the sum of the various tiers of capital including:

- Goodwill and other intangible assets.
- Current year's unpublished losses.
- Investments in unconsolidated subsidiaries and associates.
- Connected lending of a capital nature, including guarantees of a capital nature.
- All holdings of capital instruments issued by credit institutions and investment firms that are subject to CAD or an equivalent regime (except holdings by market makers).

Limits and restrictions

In order to ensure that banks maintain a strong capital base certain restrictions are placed on the amount of Tier 2 and Tier 3 capital that can be included in a bank's capital base. They are expressed in relation to Tier 1 capital and on the types of activity that each tier of capital can be used to support. These are as follows:

- The total of Tier 2 may not exceed the total of Tier 1.
- Subordinated term debt (lower Tier 2 capital) may not exceed 50 per cent of Tier 1.
- The sum of Tier 2 and Tier 3 capital used to meet trading book requirements must not exceed 200 per cent of the Tier 1 capital used to meet those requirements.
- General provisions may not exceed 1.25 per cent of weighted risk assets.

In order to avoid a sudden diminution of capital available to a bank, Tier 2 dated capital is amortised on a straight-line basis in its final five years to maturity. Where a bank has an option to repay subordinated loan capital early, the FSA does not normally assume early repayment for the purposes of amortisation, unless failure to exercise the option incurs a significant increase in the interest paid on the debt.

Assessing capital for credit risks

The assessment of the level of credit risk present in a bank's business is made by reference to Weighted Risk Assets. The Basle Accord introduced this concept, reflecting differing degrees of credit risk arising from dealing with different counterparties. These are summarised as follows.

Weighted risk assets: on balance sheet

0 per cent weighting

Cash and claims collateralised by cash.

Gold and other bullion held in own vaults or on an allocated basis.

Claims on, or guaranteed by, Zone A central governments and central banks.

Claims on, or guaranteed by, Zone B central governments or central banks where denominated and funded in local currency.

Certificates of tax deposit.

Notes: Zone A is defined as those countries that are members of the OECD or have concluded special lending agreements with the IMF.
Zone B is defined by exclusion to be anywhere not in Zone A.
Central government securities attract a risk weight as listed below.

10 per cent weighting

Holdings of Zone A central government securities with a residual maturity of one year or less or bearing a floating interest rate or index-linked.

Claims collateralised by Zone A central government securities with a residual maturity of one year or less or bearing a floating rate.

Holdings of Zone B central government securities with a residual maturity of one year or less denominated and funded in local currency.

Note: Most countries, including the USA, apply a zero weight to all Zone A central government debt. The FSA apply a weighting to government securities held in the banking book as a proxy for market risk.

20 per cent weighting

Holdings of Zone A central government fixed interest securities with a residual maturity of over one year and claims collateralised by such securities.

Holdings of Zone B central government securities with a residual maturity of over one year denominated and funded in local currency.

Claims on multilateral development banks and claims guaranteed by them or collateralised by their securities.

Claims on banks incorporated in Zone A or guaranteed by them.

Claims on banks incorporated in Zone B with a residual maturity of one year or less and claims of the same maturity guaranteed by them.

Claims on Zone A public sector entities and claims guaranteed by them.

Claims on investment firms subject to the CAD.

Claims on recognised clearing houses and exchanges.

50 per cent weighting

Loans to individuals fully secured by a first priority charge on residential property that is (or is to be) occupied by the borrower or is rented.

Loans to registered housing associations.

Mortgage backed securities (subject to certain conditions).

100 per cent weighting

Claims on the non-bank private sector.

Claims on Zone B banks with a residual maturity of over one year.

Claims on, or guaranteed by, Zone B central governments and central banks unless included above.

Claims on commercial entities owned by the public sector.

Premises, plant and equipment.

Real estate and trade investments.

Weighted risk assets: off balance sheet

The principle adopted with all off balance sheet items is to apply a credit conversion factor which produces the equivalent exposure to that of a loan and then multiply this by the weight applicable to the category of counterparty as defined above. Categories of instrument are as follows:

100 per cent credit conversion factor

Direct credit substitutes such as stand-by letters of credit.
Sale and repurchase agreements where the credit risk remains with the bank.
Forward asset purchases and any other commitments with certain drawdown.

50 per cent credit conversion factor

Transaction related contingent items such as performance bonds, bid bonds, and so on.
Note issuance facilities and revolving underwriting facilities.
Other commitments with an original maturity of over one year.

20 per cent credit conversion factor

Short term self-liquidating trade related contingent items such as documentary credits collateralised by the underlying shipments.

0 per cent credit conversion factor

Endorsements of bills that have previously been accepted by a bank.
Other commitments with an original maturity of up to one year or which can be unconditionally cancelled at any time.

Credit exposure to foreign exchange and interest rate related items

The Basle agreement offered two alternative approaches to assessing the credit risk which attaches to transactions in interest rate and exchange rate related items such as swaps or forward exchange. The intention of both methods is to approximate the cost to the bank of replacing the cash flow arising from such instruments if the counterparty defaults. The two methods are as follows:

Original exposure method

To obtain the credit equivalent amount, the notional principal amount should be multiplied by a conversion factor according to the table in Figure 10.1.

Figure 10.1 Credit equivalent conversion factors: original exposure

Original Maturity	Interest Rate Contracts	Exchange Rate Contracts
1 year or less	0.5%	2.0%
1 – 2 years	1.0%	5.0%
Each extra year	1.0%	3.0%

Replacement cost method

The method favoured by the FSA is more complicated to administer but more likely to reflect the true exposures accurately. The credit equivalent amount is found by summing the current replacement cost of all contracts having a positive value to the bank (obtained by marking-to-market) together with an add-on for potential future exposure calculated according to the table in Figure 10.2.

Figure 10.2 Credit equivalent conversion factors: replacement cost

Residual Maturity	Interest Rate Contracts	Exchange Rate Contracts
1 year or less	0.0%	1.0%
1 to 5 years	0.5%	5.0%
Over 5 years	1.5%	7.5%

Assessing capital for position risks

As mentioned earlier, a requirement for capital to be held against position risks was introduced by the EU Capital Adequacy Directive in 1996. This was amended in 1998. The Basle Committee has also published similar recommendations for handling market risk capital and the FSA has released new regulations to implement an approach consistent with both these initiatives. These are referred to here as CAD2.

CAD2 defines a standard approach to the measurement of market risk capital but encourages banks to develop internal models for that purpose. Under the standard approach, foreign exchange capital is measured as 8 per cent of the net open position. Capital for interest rate risk is assessed according to a mismatch ladder type of approach with the impact of a variety of specified interest rate shocks being measured. Capital for equity position risk is assessed at either 4 per cent or 8 per cent of the positions in individual equities depending on their degree of liquidity, plus an element for general exposure to an individual country's stock market. The simplified approach to measuring capital for position risk in commodities takes 15 per cent of the open position by commodity.

Internal models approach

The standard approach is designed to be conservative. Banks that are particularly active in trading are likely to find the standard approach penal. They may, therefore, opt to develop internal models to assess their capital requirements. Banks will be allowed to quantify their exposures to major sources of risk by using their own internal models and then aggregate these into a single value at risk (VaR) number to be used as the basis of their regulatory capital charge. This process will be complemented by a feedback loop in that firms will be expected to compare their risk assessment with profit and loss fluctuations. Should it transpire that a firm is understating its risk, its capital charges will be ratcheted up. If the problem persists, the reporting privilege may be withdrawn.

Internal models must be approved by the FSA and must meet a number of specified criteria.

CAD 2 does not specify the algorithms that must be used to calculate a bank's VaR. Importantly, it is the bank's responsibility to assess, quantify and aggregate its risk in the most appropriate manner. Nonetheless there are required quantitative criteria to consider and these state minimum standards for model calibration.

- For the purposes of capital calculations, the bank should produce VaR based upon a 99 per cent one-tailed confidence interval, over a holding period of ten days and assuming its portfolio remains unchanged over that time.
- Banks will be required to consider at least one year's market information in calibrating their models. The data set must be updated at least every three months.
- VaR models may recognise correlations between a wide variety of risk factors but banks must justify to their regulators the appropriateness of their assumptions.

- A bank's VaR figure should capture the material risk of its positions, While it is inevitable that any model will only be an approximation of reality (and further simplifying assumptions are likely to be made in the process of aggregation), it is important that significant exposures are adequately captured.

Unquestionably, there is a lot of science involved in the quantifying of risks associated with investment business. Clearly though, managing these risks involves far more than the output of a few models, important though this information may be. In addition, there is what we might call the art of risk management. In allowing firms to use their own models to assess risk for regulatory purposes, CAD 2 will also require them to demonstrate that they understand and can control risk at all levels in the firm's front office, operations and management areas. In particular:

- Banks will be required to use their internal models as an integral part of their risk management process. The models should have a track record of reasonable accuracy and should be used as part of the daily risk reporting process.

- Banks should have a risk control unit, independent of the business units, which produces reports and analyses risk information. It should report into a tier of management senior enough to have the authority to alter the risk profile of both the firm as a whole and individual traders.

- In all areas of the organisation there should be suitable numbers of staff - from traders to independent risk managers, internal audit to back office - who are experienced in the use of sophisticated models.

- Banks must have documented their processes and procedures for the operation of the risk measurement system.

- Banks should have stress testing in place to identify vulnerability to extreme circumstances. Results should be reviewed by senior management.

- In an environment where internal models are being used to determine regulatory capital, internal auditors must review the robustness of the model and the appropriateness of the processes and procedures surrounding it.

Counterparty risk positions in the trading book are subject to similar capital rules to those for the banking book but with some variation in the weighting categories.

The future of capital regulation

Whilst the original Basle recommendations were a major step forward, their limitations are now well recognised. These include the lack of recognition of either insolvency probability or relative risk management competencies and the use of a limited number of risk weighting categories. Industry groups have argued that the Basle Accord requires banks to hold more capital than they really need to cushion them against the risks they run.

The regulators believe that simplicity and imprecision will always be needed to achieve and maintain a common global prudential standard. They are, however, concerned that where regulatory capital becomes much more expensive than economic capital (as determined by internal risk management systems) regulatory capital arbitrage, primarily through securitisation, will flourish.

There are lobbies within the banking industry that are calling for replacement of the Accord by the use of internal models for credit risks as well as for market risk. Some concerns must be met before it will be possible to extend the internal models approach to encompass credit risk. These include the dependency on two-state (default/non-default) rather than multi-state models; the shortage of empirical data and supportable correlations; and the lack of either back testing or stress testing.

Notwithstanding these reservations, the regulators think an internal models approach for credit risk may hold promise in the long run and this is likely to provide the next step forward in capital regulation.

11 Offshore banking centres

Offshore banking markets have arisen as a result of anomalies in regulatory regimes and a quite natural desire on the part of financial institutions to conduct their business on the most favourable terms. In the most general sense of the term, the euromarkets are offshore markets where deposits are made outside the regulations and constraints that might apply in the local economy. Despite its geographical connotation, 'euromarket' has become the term used to describe the collective international offshore banking market.

The markets became significantly active in the 1950s. Many Eastern European countries used offshore facilities in order to avoid, on the one hand, the political embarrassment of lodging dollar deposits in the US, and on the other, the expensive regulation under the US Banking Act of 1933. By not having to follow regulatory conditions, banks could make themselves very competitive in the lending markets and in the interest bearing deposit markets. Various regulatory restrictions on the ability of American banks to pay interest on deposits paved the way for the euromarkets to plug the gap without the shackles of restrictive supervision and control. Whilst these markets might involve more risk, the risks are known and limited as the banks operating in these markets tend to be well known and generally reputable. It has become so lucrative and competitive that reputations have become as important as those in regulated markets. Many banks in this sector take great pride in their prudential control based on their own set of internal standards.

Encouraged by regulatory anomalies, banks have expanded their operations by establishing 'offshore' branches, subsidiary and associated companies to gain access to the eurocurrency market. Within this development, other features emerged which included the establishment of consortium banks and syndicated lending through which banks were able to share the credit and country risks as increased demands were made for substantial facilities by individual companies and countries. American and Japanese banks were quick to enter this market. A particular attraction to US banks was the existence of a further regulatory anomaly whereby US dollar funds deposited with US domiciled banks by their foreign branches were, until 1969, exempted from the reserve requirements imposed through Regulation D. Therefore, many US banks used the international currency market as a substantial funding source for their domestic operations, an activity which was also encouraged through constraints imposed upon the development of more conventional funding bases by restriction on interstate domestic banking and some individual states' control over the branching activities of banks. For Japanese banks the euromarkets provide a funding source for both Japanese trade finance and overseas investment, most of which is arranged in US dollars.

The eurocurrency deposit markets are international markets in which freely convertible currencies are deposited and lent outside of the regulations, restrictions and constraints that may normally apply within the national boundaries of the country of issue of those currencies. 'Euro' and 'Asian' currencies have no separate existence from currencies without those prefixes but are simply ordinary deposits, the right to which is vested and retained in external hands until such time as they are transferred to official or resident ownership within their country of issue. The terms 'euro' and 'Asian' have no special significance other than to identify the geographical regions in which the banks that transact business in these external funds are domiciled. Indeed, the term 'euro' is now in common use for such deposits wherever they are based and it is used in this way throughout the rest of this chapter.

The euromarkets are effectively part of one substantial international offshore currency market through which banks domiciled in several countries around the world take and make foreign currency deposits and which creates chains of financial transactions. Only the net impact of these transactions is reflected as part of each bank's nostro accounts maintained with banks domiciled within the domestic deposit market of the respective countries of issue of the currency (for example, a US dollar nostro account in New York).

Controls

Although offshore currencies function outside the regulatory controls applicable to those currencies' country of issue, the banks which operate within this market are subject to the regulations of their respective country of operation, be it host or parent authority. Therefore a bank's ability to be competitively active in this market will be dependent upon that country's policy as to whether it wishes to discourage, encourage or be indifferent to the development of eurocurrency activity. This policy will be reflected through each country's regulatory, monetary and fiscal policies and will, in the main, involve similar matters to those discussed in earlier chapters, but applied to each country's treatment of banks' foreign currency assets and liabilities rather than those imposed on domestic currency. Three key issues in the successful development of eurocurrency centres are:

- The ability to maintain foreign currency accounts on a freely convertible basis.
- The treatment of foreign currency deposits for mandatory reserve purposes.
- The treatment of withholding tax on foreign currency deposits.

Exchange control regulations may also prohibit banks from accepting foreign currency deposits from residents and/or non-residents. These are discussed in more detail elsewhere in this book.

A bank's taxation position may have a bearing on the decision as to where to locate business. Benefits may be derived through bilateral tax agreements or a fiscal authority's treatment of particular types of transaction. The imposition of such taxes as stamp duty on certain transactions in one country may lead to a bank booking its business elsewhere.

Functions of offshore currency markets

Those regulatory, monetary and fiscal differences already discussed have not been the only incentives for the developments of offshore operations, nor is London the only centre involved. Opportunity existed for tax havens such as those found in the Channel Islands and the Caribbean, which had become substantial deposit centres, to extend their banking industry and encourage the establishment of offshore banks. Several countries, for a variety of reasons, introduced specific legislation to license and encourage their development as offshore banking centres. These included Singapore, the Philippines, Bahrain, the Cayman Islands, the Bahamas and the International Banking Facilities (IBFs) within the United States. These areas and their regulation are discussed in the next section of this chapter. To increase and retain a market share of commercial business it was frequently considered necessary for many international banks to establish and maintain a presence in most, if not all, of these areas.

Additionally, with the development of the instant electronic communication systems which are now available, some countries encouraged the growth of 'brass plate' or 'shell' booking centres whereby banks arrange and transact business in one country but record and book it in another. Consequently, international banks not only have the opportunity to develop activities within the international currency deposit market in one or several countries, but are also able to attract certain transactions towards a particular domicile. These decisions will be dictated by each individual bank's perceived policy objectives and fiscal considerations. For example, where a bank's gearing or lending capabilities are constrained in one centre, the level of business carried out in its offshore subsidiaries may be developed in those countries which permit higher levels of activity, although scope to do this is being reduced by international moves towards the consolidated supervision of banks.

Some countries will place lending or gearing constraints on banks whilst others provide the means to operate outside such tight guidelines. The effect from the bank's point of view is that it can reduce its costs and provide lower cost funding and higher returns on deposits.

Individuals working overseas will often find it advantageous to conduct their financial affairs through offshore centres. Such centres have developed expertise in providing the types of financial services that expatriates require, as well as offering attractive tax regimes.

The lure of offshore banks as tax havens provides one of the strongest attractions to depositors. Those using the services of these financial centres will value the confidential framework within which they operate. Clearly trustworthiness is also a key consideration.

Offshore banking centres

A distinction can be drawn between international financial centres, such as London, Tokyo and New York, which are highly active in a wide variety of currencies and banking activities, and offshore banking centres, which tend to specialise in particular types of business and to focus on non-domestic currencies. The latter often enjoy special tax and regulatory advantages granted by their governments to encourage the development of financial business.

Offshore centres can be considered either as operational centres or booking centres. Singapore is an active operational centre with a well developed financial structure, whereas the Cayman Islands is a booking centre. A booking centre is where there are few actual banking activities, but where transactions are recorded to take advantage of secrecy and low tax rates.

The main features of offshore banking can be illustrated by considering the arrangements available in some of the major centres.

Bahrain

The Bahrain Monetary Agency (BMA) has actively promoted offshore banking by issuing approvals for branches, subsidiaries and affiliates, and for commercial banks established in Bahrain, to become OBUs or offshore banking units.

The operators within these markets have to meet local capital requirements and to have a physical presence in Bahrain. They can provide a full range of banking services to non-residents, but are not allowed under regulatory rules to deal with nationals and local enterprises, unless the BMA gives its consent.

The BMA, as the regulatory body, requires the submission of regular returns including data reflecting assets and liabilities by currency, class of customer, maturity profile and country analysis - and audited accounts. It will also carry out reviews from time to time.

Bahrain has recently been experiencing some political difficulties, which the government hopes, will not affect confidence in its financial stability. The concern for Bahrain is that its offshore banking sector is heavily reliant on short dated foreign wholesale deposits, so may be vulnerable to disruptions affecting their ability to fund their operations. However, the BMA is considered a strong asset being regarded as a rigorous yet commercially aware regulator. Having survived the regional problems associated with the Kuwait invasion and the Iran-Iraq war, the financial centre of Bahrain is unlikely to give up its Middle Eastern role in the international money markets easily.

Bahamas

The Bahamas facilitates banks operating on either a direct or an indirect representative basis. In the case of the former, a physical presence is established as an operating unit; in the latter, a bank does not have any physical presence within the Bahamas, except a registered place of business and a list of named appointed officials which can be provided through a resident trust company or other body.

The Central Bank issues two types of banking licence: restricted and unrestricted. The former limits operations only to those parties specified in the licence, and the latter provides for full banking operations to be undertaken. A distinction between domestic banking and offshore operations is provided through the exchange control regulations under which banks may apply to be designated either resident or non-resident. Resident and non-resident applies to the type of business a bank undertakes and not to the domicile of its business activities. Non-resident banks are only permitted to deal in foreign currencies and otherwise in general operate outside of local exchange control requirements, inclusive of profit and dividend remittances. Resident banks may transact business with residents in Bahamian dollars. Banks wishing to partake in both domestic and foreign currency business are, within the context of the exchange control regulations, required to be appointed authorised dealers.

Operations can be established as branches, subsidiaries or affiliates. Upon application, references are required and the Central Bank will wish to ensure that a foreign bank's head office supervisory authority supports the application for a licence in Nassau. The Bahamas provide a tax-free environment for offshore banking operations and upon approval the only formal regulatory requirement is the submission on an annual basis of audited financial statements within four months of the end of the licensed bank's financial year end.

Nassau operations have provided an attractive point of entry into the international currency markets for many US-domiciled banks. The US authorities have accepted the principle of US banks establishing 'brass plate' operations in Nassau and running Nassau desks from their US branch operations.

The Bahamas had suffered a decline in importance in the 1980s as the result of competition from the Cayman Islands and suspicion that the centre was being used for money laundering. Even so, nearly 200 banks still have a physical presence in the Bahamas. The government has now introduced legislation to inhibit money laundering and is supportive of the renewed development of the financial sector.

Cayman Islands

The offshore facilities in the Cayman Islands are similar to those in the Bahamas, with many banks being registered there but not being operational on the islands, thus taking advantage of its tax-free status. The major difference between the Bahamas and the Cayman Islands is that the Cayman authorities distinguish between domestic and offshore banking operations through licensing procedures and not by exchange control designations. A system of licensing uses two categories.

Category A licences permit domestic and offshore activities, whilst Category B licences are limited to offshore operations. As with the Bahamas, a physical presence is not required. Cayman Islands operations may be used as 'shell' booking centres and reporting requirements are limited. Over 500 banks have some form of representation.

The Cayman Islands have had something of a cavalier reputation in terms of financial regulation. However, the Cayman Monetary Authority was established in 1997 with responsibility for the oversight of the financial system in the islands. Whilst the islands have tight banking secrecy laws, there are anti-money laundering regulations in place that take precedence over other considerations of customer confidentiality.

Singapore

The Singapore government has encouraged the development of Singapore as the centre of the Asian currency market since 1968. Offshore banking in Singapore is normally conducted through a bank's Asian Currency Unit (ACU). An ACU is an integral part of a licensed banking operation conducted in Singapore. Other than the separation of its activities for accounting, fiscal and reporting purposes, together with the exemption of certain of its activities for regulatory and fiscal requirements, an ACU has no separate identity from the bank within which it is situated.

The Monetary Authority of Singapore (MAS) can issue full banking licences, restricted licences and offshore licences, all of which enable banks to operate in the offshore markets. Banks may operate both domestic and ACU business with the ACU being an integral part of the bank, but with separate offshore accounting and regulatory procedures. The characteristics of the different types of licensed banks are as follows:

- Full banking licenses entitle banks to conduct the full range of commercial banking business. No monetary limit is imposed on Singapore dollar lending activities.

- Restricted banking licenses restrict banks from having more than one main branch each and from operating general savings accounts. There is a minimum sum of S$250,000 per time deposit from non-bank customers. There are no restrictions on foreign currency-denominated banking business.

- Offshore banking licenses are now effectively the only option remaining to new entrants to the commercial banking sector in Singapore. Holders are limited to operating out of single branches, providing wholesale banking services to non-residents and banking services to residents in foreign currency. Acceptance of interest-bearing Singapore dollar deposits from non-bank residents is disallowed, but licensing restrictions on lending to residents in Singapore dollars have been relaxed. The ceiling for this "resident funding limit" has been raised from S$50 million in 1988 to S$150 million in 1996.

ACUs are exempt from statutory liquidity requirements and enjoy a concessionary tax rate of 10% on revenue from transactions with non-residents. Non-residents are exempt from withholding tax on interest income earned on foreign currency deposits placed with ACUs. There is no stamp duty on ACU offshore loan agreements and Asian dollar bonds. ACU transactions with domestic banking units or residents, however, are subject to tax at the normal corporate rate.

To encourage the trading of foreign securities in Singapore, income derived by ACUs from transactions in foreign securities with non-residents are exempted from tax. In addition, transactions in foreign securities with non-residents are exempted from contract note stamp duty.

New York IBFs

The rise of offshore centres was indirectly encouraged by restrictive regulations in the US, particularly in respect of reserve requirements and interest rate ceilings. In 1981 IBFs (or international banking facilities) were made exempt from US Regulations D and Q, making it possible for banks of New York State to introduce offshore units. Whilst the main restrictive regulations no longer apply, there are continuing tax advantages as income attributable to IBF transactions is exempt from state and local taxes.

IBFs are an integral part of a banking operation, and as such are subject to regulatory control applied as part of normal review processes. In general, an IBF is authorised to undertake banking business in US dollars and other currencies with non-residents and other IBFs. They may not accept individual deposits below the equivalent of US$100,000, accept any deposits (other than interbank funds) repayable on less than two days demand, raise deposits through the issue of bearer instruments or lend to non-residents to finance operations within the US.

As a result of the development of IBFs in New York State, it is usual to find individual banks simultaneously undertaking activities related to domestic, Nassau and IBF operations, the three being segregated for accounting and recording purposes. The major difference between IBF and Nassau activities is that the former may only transact business with non-residents, whereas the latter may undertake business with US residents.

The Philippines

In the Philippines the formal supervisory and regulatory body for banks is the Monetary Board but much of the supervisory process is undertaken by the Central Bank. Offshore banking facilities are provided through two types of operation:

- offshore banking units (OBUs);
- foreign currency deposit units (FCDUs).

OBUs are authorised under presidential decree number 1034 and FCDUs under presidential decree number 1035 issued in September 1976.

Decree 1034 facilitates the establishment of foreign currency operating units by branches, subsidiaries or affiliates of foreign banks without any other presence in the Philippines. Decree 1035 provides for banks, both local and foreign with domestic operations in the Philippines, to obtain authority to accept foreign currency deposits and undertake similar activities as OBUs. Both operations require a full banking presence within the Philippines and are subject to the full supervisory requirements and arrangements of the Central Bank of the Philippines.

PART THREE

Financial Markets

12 Introduction to financial markets

Markets are meeting places for the purpose of buying and selling goods. The markets discussed in this and the next two parts of this book perform a similar function. However, the underlying transactions in financial markets relate not only to buying and selling but also include markets for investing, borrowing, swapping and establishing future and forward prices. Financial markets also provide the mechanism for:

- The transfer of funds between original suppliers and end users in domestic and foreign currencies.

- The transfer of risks between those who require protection and those who are prepared to accept them.

- Current and future price determination through the process of bid and offered prices.

Although markets are meeting places, they need not necessarily be physical meeting places. The dispersed markets of foreign exchange, interbank deposit and securities trading are telephone or electronic markets. Each comprises many principals, investors and borrowers throughout the world being represented by many hundreds of dealers and brokers who are linked through a network of telephone lines and a variety of electronic dealing services. Most domestic securities markets and futures exchanges began as central meeting places with transactions being undertaken on the floor of an exchange and, in some cases, off-floor trading strictly prohibited. Many still retain a central trading floor but there is an increasing tendency to electronic trading as communications technology improves.

Direct access as principal to various markets is frequently restricted or selective. The international currency deposit and foreign exchange markets are the preserve of banks. On futures exchanges, direct access is restricted to members. The current regulatory environment in most countries allows financial institutions to undertake most types of activity provided they can convince their regulator that they are 'fit and proper' and will adhere to the local code of conduct for doing business. The advent of screen based trading in the foreign exchange and other markets extends the possibilities for trading on a global basis, subject to appropriate authorisation, and diminishes the role of traditional brokers.

Markets function on bid and offered prices. A bid price is the price at which participants are prepared to borrow or purchase. The offered price is the price at which they are prepared to sell, lend or grant. There are many factors that influence these prices as well as the concept of supply and demand. The influences of technical and fundamental analysis are discussed at the end of this chapter.

Brokers and banks communicate their rates by contributing to Reuters, Telerate, Bloomberg, Knight-Ridder or other similar screen information services. Generally these rates can only be taken as indication rates and firm rates can only be obtained by contacting a quoting bank by telephone, through an electronic dealing service or through brokers. Although the screen information services are important sources of data, the dealer's primary forms of communication for keeping in touch with markets are still direct telephone lines to brokers, banks' internal group dealing centres and other major users and suppliers of money. Most major dealing rooms have loudspeaker systems that are fed from brokers' offices and facilitate instant awareness of prices.

Dealers and traders in any market should be able to assume safely that the persons executing trades with them have the necessary authority and do not require any formal evidence thereof. Mandates are required from other users and participants in the market, for example, corporate customers. These should not contain any restrictions on the powers of anyone authorised to conclude transactions. Each dealer and trader will be aware of the authorities governing his activities and with which counterparties he is authorised to conduct business.

Within the context of these markets, each transaction is an individual deal and each constitutes an individual contract. There are usually two principals to each trade, the buyer and the seller, the borrower and lender, or the swappers. Each principal refers to the other as his counterparty. Together they are the counterparties to the contract. A contract is established immediately two counterparties agree terms, which may be done orally or by responding to a price on an electronic screen. The contract rules may be implied by market custom and practice, be governed by rules and regulations, follow the terms of a master agreement or be the subject of unique detailed terms between the counterparties for each transaction.

In each market all settlements and payments are normally required to be made in the appropriate immediately available form with good title and good value, to be freely transferable and to be made without deduction. Settlement can only be made on a business day in the place where settlement is due to be made. When a value date is agreed which is not a business day, market custom and practice or specific agreement will determine the business day on which settlement is to be effected. Where settlement or delivery crosses international borders, good value dates will be business days in each of the centres where delivery is required to take place. Although a bank in London may require to settle in US dollars with a bank in Zurich and it is a business day in both these centres, settlement can only be made if it is also a business day in New York.

Transaction types

Cash, forward, futures, option contracts and swaps are different types of transaction within financial markets. Each transaction type has its own characteristics and may form the basis of separate and distinct markets in the same underlying subject matter. For example, deposits, foreign exchange and securities may be traded as cash, forward, future or option contracts. Additionally, one instrument may be based on another, for example, options on foreign exchange.

'Cash' contracts refer to those transactions that are due for settlement and/or delivery on the day of the transaction or a set number of business days ahead. This may be 'spot' (two working days ahead), as with foreign exchange, or 'trade plus three working days', as with eurobond secondary market transactions. Forward contracts are contingent assets and liabilities that are due for settlement on an agreed date or within an agreed period in the future. Both cash and forward contracts require settlement for the contracted amount between the counterparties. Many arrangements are being put in place to provide for payment of net amounts due between counterparties to reduce settlement risk. Cash and forward contracts may only be cancelled or amended with the mutual consent of the counterparties concerned and this will usually involve settlement of any financial differential.

Liquidity

Although the fundamental purposes behind the activities of traders, dealers, investors, hedgers, arbitrageurs, speculators and brokers are entirely different, they are complementary in that the presence of all provides liquidity to the market. Liquidity is an essential ingredient for the success and effectiveness of a market as it facilitates business being executed easily and in substantial quantities.

Each market can be measured in terms of both its size and its depth. The size of a market is measured in terms of turnover. The depth, or more properly, the liquidity of a market is related to supply and demand, the number of players and the size of individual transactions that can be done without moving the price. Liquidity impacts on the ease with which business can be transacted. Liquidity is affected by several other factors and even the larger markets can have liquidity problems. This is particularly so in periods of highly volatile conditions or when sizeable movements of foreign exchange or interest rates are experienced or anticipated. In situations of high volatility, when the market is moving erratically in both directions, both supply and demand often evaporate as dealers widen spreads to protect their positions. When a large movement is anticipated in one direction, supply or demand will disappear according to the anticipated direction.

The marketability and therefore the realisable value of liquefiable assets are determined first by their negotiability and second by the availability and depth of a secondary market in which each type of instrument is traded. This differs from instrument to instrument.

London as a financial centre

London is one of the world's three main financial centres and is the leading financial centre in Europe. New York and Tokyo are more influential in terms of the size of their domestic economies whereas London's success can be attributed to its international wholesale business. The UK is the largest centre for cross border bank lending, with $1,464 billion of assets outstanding at the end of December 1996. London is the leading centre for foreign exchange business and average daily net turnover amounts to $464 billion, some 30 per cent of global foreign exchange business, according to the BIS survey conducted in April 1995. It is estimated that 60 per cent of primary international bond syndication and 75 per cent of secondary market trading is centred in London. There are over 550 foreign bank branches, subsidiaries and representative offices authorised to operate in the UK, one third coming from EU countries. Most of these entities have a presence in the City and its various markets, particularly the currency deposit and foreign exchange markets.

London is the leading centre for OTC derivatives business with a market share of 27 per cent as at April 1995. The London International Financial Futures and Options Exchange is the largest financial futures exchange outside Chicago and together with the other derivatives exchanges in London accounts for 16 per cent of global exchange-traded derivatives contracts turnover.

There are many hundreds of individual financial markets throughout the world. Each market has its own customs and practices, rules and regulations and codes of conduct that are usually documented, particularly in the major centres. Clearly, it would be impossible to comment on each individual market without running to great length. This book takes the London market as the main focus of the following chapters.

Participants in financial markets

Each market comprises a mix of principals and brokers. Principals will include traders, dealers, investors, hedgers, arbitrageurs and speculators. Traders, in this context, are defined as commercial users and suppliers, with the exception of floor traders on a futures exchange. Dealers are market makers who quote concurrently bid and offered prices at which they are prepared to buy and sell, borrow or lend. Dealers provide a service to other market members and endeavour to take advantage, for profit, of the spread between buying and selling prices. Investors seek a return on a capital investment and they enter the markets for income generation and security of capital. Hedgers are transferors of risk. They enter the market to cover perceived risk exposure and will undertake contracts with a view to:

- offsetting possible changes in the value of, return on or cost of underlying assets and liabilities;
- protecting the cost of anticipated purchases or the proceeds of sale of assets at some future date;
- hedging underlying structural positions or net investment exposure.

Arbitrageurs take advantage of any rate or pricing differential that they perceive to exist between markets. The activities of arbitrageurs add efficiency to each market by closing price distortions that become apparent. Speculators are risk takers within a market. Speculators are prepared to assume a capital risk associated with maintaining 'open' positions, being either long or short of assets or liabilities.

There is a perception that within a market environment there is a winner and loser to each transaction. This is incorrect. Each participant enters these markets for a perceived objective and specific purpose, the achievement of which represents success. Other than for speculators, the fact that a price, exchange rate or interest rate subsequently increases or decreases is not of primary concern to that participant, albeit perhaps representing a lost opportunity. Speculation is also frequently confused with gambling. There is a slight but important difference. Speculation is the assumption of an already existing risk for its perceived profit potential. Gambling is the creation of chances on which one places wagers. In this sense, there is no place for winners, losers and gamblers in the financial markets.

It is noteworthy, indeed, that the avoidance of unnecessary risk is of considerable importance to market participants. The reduction of counterparty and settlement risk is a major preoccupation in these markets. The repo market, for example, is a market based on the use of collateral, and clearing houses and settlement systems exist to facilitate rapid, secure settlement.

The role of banks

The reasons for, and the extent of, each bank's participation in these markets will vary from bank to bank according to the spread and depth of its underlying commercial business and its trading and dealing objectives. A bank's ability to access these markets will be subject not only to the regulations of each market, but also to the controls and regulations of the country of the bank's domicile. Subject to these considerations, a bank may enter these markets as market-maker or participant; to cover underlying commercial transactions; to cover its own internal funding; to hedge perceived exposure or net investment positions; as an investor; or to participate as a dealer, trader or speculator for its own account. The latter activity is known as proprietary dealing. Although an individual bank may undertake any one, a number, or all of these roles it is important to distinguish between them as each has a separate and distinct function involving different risk/reward relationships and requiring different monitoring and control procedures.

The role of brokers

Brokers act as intermediaries, ie they do not take positions themselves but instead introduce principals who will deal on opposite sides of the market. Brokers (whether telephone brokers or electronic systems) are an integral and essential part of many markets. Within dispersed markets they provide, as intermediaries, a common market place in which buyers and sellers are brought together on a principal to principal basis.

Brokers, whether voice or electronic broking systems, provide facilities for any individual bank to support either side of the market, with brokers making prices, on the basis of a mix of individual quotations from several different principal banks. Although there are two segments of the various interbank markets (the market-making banks and the broker market), they are complementary to each other with market-making banks frequently buying and selling through, and supporting prices in, the broker market. In a highly liquid and volatile market, time is of the essence in conducting business and it is time-consuming to obtain the best rates available. The intermediation of brokers is an essential ingredient to the success of dispersed markets, providing a central marketplace for price determination in which principals can negotiate and arrange to transact business.

The role of brokers differs from market to market. In the interbank deposit and foreign exchange markets, the broker's role is entirely one of an intermediary, but in the futures markets floor brokers frequently have direct responsibility as principals. In futures markets, brokers are usually the only medium of access to the market by non-members of an exchange. Brokers charge set or negotiated fees for their services.

Investors

Different types of investors have widely differing investment parameters and, whilst it is not possible to quantify all the types of instruments which may be of interest to each classification of investor, it is useful to identify some types of investor and their likely investment criteria.

Managed funds

Managed funds are established to attract a particular sector of investor requirements and their continued ability to attract funds often depends on managers' proven and published performance compared to competitors. Some funds are specifically structured to attract small retail investors, as are unit trusts, while others are designed for major institutional investors such as pension funds. The level of their success is as varied as the specialised composition of the various funds. Portfolio specialisation can include varying combinations of capital growth and income objectives; highest quality government securities and AAA rated debt to lower quality risk investments; property; currencies; precious metals and 'soft' commodities; and any mix of these. Geographic specialisation is also commonplace, including European, American, Asian and emerging markets funds.

Hedge funds

So-called 'hedge' funds are in fact major speculative participants in the financial markets. Whilst most managed funds will invest no more than the subscriptions they receive, a characteristic of hedge funds is that they will, in addition, use borrowed funds to increase their leverage and so raise the potential gains to investors. They are typically short term traders who aim to move in and out of trading positions frequently. This, coupled with the large size of trades that they may conduct, has led to hedge funds becoming a significant influence on short term market behaviour.

Insurance and pension companies

Insurance companies' investment requirements range from life, marine and product underwriters, who tend to seek long term investments with high duration, to motor, accident and general underwriters, where the need for liquid assets and shorter maturities is higher. Pension funds are likely to seek mainly high duration and index-linked assets but will also have some requirement for short term investments as part of their own liquidity management.

Trustees

Insurance companies and banks act as trustees for trust funds, which are maintained under independent management from the trustee. They also manage substantial individual discretionary portfolios for private and corporate clients who frequently require flexibility and liquidity. The terms of trusts and regulations covering trusts may limit the range of investments permissible for trust portfolios. Trustees are often required to seek high quality, low risk instruments with a limited geographic spread.

High net worth individuals

These may be resident anywhere in the world. They often seek bearer investments, which provide anonymity, liquidity and no immediate liability to withholding tax. The quality of assets is usually of high importance to this group of investor, which generally seeks investment opportunities in currencies that have potential relative strength. The financial strength and credit rating of issuers are of prime importance as is the economic and political strength of the issuer's country. Investors will shun any country where fiscal or monetary regulations might be imposed which would adversely affect the value or realisability of their investments. The private investor tends to be conservative in his investment objectives, however ill defined they may be. Often he lacks financial expertise and time to devote to his investments and may rely on the investment services offered by institutions. This leads to substantial funds being lodged with investment houses and managed trusts.

Government agencies

Government agencies, corporations and supranational institutions are often major borrowers in financial markets. However, they may have substantial but irregular surplus cash flows that give rise to a cautious approach to investment. They tend to keep relatively liquid portfolios of short term funds and securities with a spread of maturities. Some countries hold significant foreign exchange reserves and will look to invest them profitably. Security of capital is likely to be of much more importance than yield in this case.

Central banks

Central banks and their equivalents are the providers to the indigenous banking system of short term funding, directly or indirectly. Rediscount (outright purchase) and repo facilities are methods used to supply liquidity to the banking system.

Commercial and investment banks

Banks are required to maintain adequate liquidity and therefore need a portfolio of short term money market assets. These include various forms of short term government paper, bank bills and certificates of deposit. Banks are well placed to take advantage of arbitrage opportunities through swaps to fund assets profitably whilst matching their asset and liability portfolios.

In every institution, the amount of liquidity that is available for investment purposes is liable to fluctuate over time and often specifically depends on the investor's business climate as well as the general economic and political scenarios in which he operates. An investor's appetite for a given asset (be it a CD, a long term bond, a money market deposit or whatever else) will depend upon whether he has sufficient liquidity to make a new investment, how long he expects such liquidity to continue and what influences him so far as 'risk versus return' on the investment is concerned.

Trading and settlements

Typically, the process of trading consists of a number of distinct stages, with the duties of front and settlement offices being clearly defined and segregated, as follows:

- Either the dealer is approached by another dealer or an order is taken from a client by a salesperson and is passed to the dealer for execution.

- The dealer makes a price determined by his own dealing position or by obtaining a price from the market or a broker. Appropriate limits are checked.

- The counterparty agrees to (or declines) the terms proposed.

- Details of agreed trades are keyed and passed electronically to the back office or are written onto a trade ticket for processing.
- Where the dealer executes a trade to match the client's deal or fund his book, a second set of entries is passed.
- The back office takes the information from the system or ticket and keys it into one or more systems for confirmations, payments and securities deliveries to be made or received and for position keeping and accounting purposes.

A legally binding contract is established at the point when the parties agree terms, whether this is by phone or screen dealing. An exchange of confirmations is made which evidence the particulars of the contract already established but they do not constitute the contract itself. It is a function of the settlement offices to exchange and verify the formal confirmations. Initial verbal confirmations may be made. Confirmations are then sent either electronically or in writing, by fax or telex. Cross-border transactions between financial institutions are most likely to be confirmed using the S.W.I.F.T. system and correspondent banks for money and foreign exchange deals, and Trax for eurobond trades. The accounting system will generate records for checking counterparty and trading limits, balance sheet and profit calculations and for account reconciliation purposes. Payments relating to trades are settled with counterparties on value dates using Standard Settlement Instructions (between banks) or 'usual' settlement instructions (companies and other counterparties). One of the netting systems may be used for interbank foreign exchange. Euroclear or Cedel Bank will most likely be used for settlement of eurobond transactions.

A 'middle office' is often linked to the front office for risk management purposes. The middle office is able to collate deal information from all dealing positions in all products in order to provide consolidated trading reports on risk exposures. Ideally these are real time and provide mark-to-market calculations and valuations.

The resulting combination of paper and technology within a bank or investment house has many pitfalls, particularly if information is entered into different systems for one deal. Many banks are addressing this problem by the introduction of 'straight through processing' (STP). In STP, the dealer enters the deal information into a front office trade capture system. This creates an electronic ticket that is automatically routed to the back office processing system. The front office system will feed the middle office position keeping records. This means that keyed-in data is uniform across all systems. STP can be extended so that relevant payment and settlement messages are automatically created in a format which will input directly into the respective payment system. However, because of the segregation of dealing and settlement, a strong layer of trade approval is needed to prevent a dealer making unauthorised or incorrect payments.

The use of electronic means in exchanging confirmations is recommended in view of the short time between trades being made and settlement. Confirmations for same day value trades can be exchanged electronically or by fax within an hour or two of the trade. Non-receipt of confirmations from counterparties should always be followed up. Automated systems for matching confirmations and reconciling payments and nostro accounts are now the standard in back offices to achieve the required accuracy and speed in balancing the institutions' records and minimising manual errors.

In some markets, including the repo and derivatives markets, the counterparties rely on the terms of master agreements which the regulator or market association has introduced so that the confirmation of individual deals is relatively simple. Institutions in the financial sector can assume that these master agreements are the basis of contracts. Other counterparties will be expected to sign a specific master agreement to establish the basic terms of subsequent transactions.

Settlement systems

CHAPS and Real Time Gross Settlement

Sterling interbank payments in London for same day value are remitted through CHAPS, the Clearing House Automated Payment System. Payments are currently in sterling only. A euro payment facility, CHAPS euro, is being developed for use from 1 January 1999.

The clearing system in London from 1854 to 1996 involved end-of-day net settlement of balances across accounts at the Bank of England. CHAPS was introduced in 1984 as an electronic, same-day large-value credit transfer system to complement the Town Clearing (last used in 1996 for same-day large-value debit clearing). There is now no minimum transaction size for CHAPS although charges may make it uneconomic to transfer small sums.

As the size of exposures within the financial system and the interdependence of financial intermediaries increased, so too did the risk that a payments or settlement failure by one institution could bring down another and ultimately disrupt the whole financial system. While the receiving or collecting banker would typically make the relevant funds available to his customer when the CHAPS advice was received, it did not receive value from the paying banker until the relevant net settlement was completed at the end of the day. This exposed banks to unquantified risks towards each other. In practice, if a bank found itself unexpectedly short of immediate liquidity at the end of the day, it was able to borrow from the other clearing banks or from the Bank of England at a penalty cost. In the event of a settlement failure, however, it would have ranked simply as an unsecured creditor.

An interim step to reduce settlement risk was to impose intra-day limits on the extent to which a CHAPS settlement bank could build up a net sender position with another CHAPS settlement member. This meant that banks knew the extent of their exposures within the system; were able to impose limits on their counterparties; and could actively manage these limits to avoid payment delays.

However, concerns over net settlement continued and in April 1996 the Bank of England introduced Real Time Gross Settlement (RTGS). Individual sterling payments are now paid gross across accounts at the Bank of England in real time during the course of the business day with finality, paid for and backed with balances and collateral pledged by the banks to the Bank of England. Before a bank can make an outward payment, it must have primed its RTGS account at the Bank of England. As a result, receiving banks can confidently credit payees' accounts in instantly available funds when CHAPS credits arrive, eliminating settlement exposures which banks would otherwise build up between each other during the day.

There are some 17 Settlement Members and some 400 Participants of CHAPS. Peak daily volumes through CHAPS in 1997 were 135,000 payments worth around £240 billion with an average daily throughput of 60,000 payments valued at around £150 billion. To send a payment message, a Member transmits it to its CHAPS Gateway to the Bank of England for settlement. Once settlement has been achieved, a confirmation is sent to the sender's Gateway and the entire message is forwarded to the receiving bank giving advice of a pre-settled payment.

Within a RTGS system, intraday liquidity from a central bank is needed when a commercial bank is to make a required payment on behalf of a customer immediately to a customer of another bank and it does not have sufficient funds itself at that precise moment. A bank that wants to be sure that it completes its payments within the business day should have no difficulty using RTGS systems, without any intraday credit. It would merely need, through its normal treasury operations, to ensure that it received sufficient funds during the day to match its outgoing payments. Outgoing payments are simply queued and are executed as and when incoming payments arrive to match them. However, such queuing does not make for an efficient system and the provision of intraday liquidity is desirable. It is possible to provide liquidity in the following ways:

- Banks can hold positive balances at the central bank which are available to be drawn down intraday and on which interest is payable for overnight usage.

- The central bank may make credit available during the business day for which banks may provide collateral by way of intra-day repo. The Bank of England provides intra-day repo facilities without limit and without charge, but always against first-class security or collateral.

- Credits received from other settlement banks naturally form part of the RTGS collateral pool.

The potential risk of spillover from intraday liquidity is addressed in two ways. First, by applying an earlier cut-off after which no customer payments are accepted. Second, by applying a scale of penalty rates for any intra-day advances which become overnight credit.

Charges for the maintenance of overnight repo applied by the Bank of England depend on the circumstances in which the overdraft arises. If the Bank has under-supplied the necessary liquidity, perhaps because of a fault in the forecast, which misleads the banks about the day's overall liquidity shortage, the overdraft attracts non-penal rates. If the market, or the CHAPS banks collectively could have obtained enough liquidity in normal operations to avoid an overdraft, the penalty is Base Rate plus one per cent (or the highest overnight rate, whichever is higher), with an additional one half of one per cent for each time a particular bank has incurred an overdraft over the previous three months.

CHAPS euro and TARGET

CHAPS euro was developed by the CHAPS company and the Bank of England to handle the real-time transmission of euro-denominated payments. Since the UK government opted not to participate in EMU in 1999, CHAPS euro will operate alongside the sterling RTGS system, in parallel. CHAPS euro enables euro payments to be made both domestically between its members within the UK, and with members of other RTGS systems elsewhere in the EU through TARGET. TARGET is the 'Trans-European Automated Real-time Gross settlement Express Transfer system' for payments in euro. TARGET links together national RTGS payment systems denominated in euro so that large-value payments are made or received throughout the European Economic Area, with finality and in real time. Response times for cross-border payments within TARGET depend on the performance of the other RTGS systems involved in receiving and sending payments. CHAPS euro is open on every day that TARGET is open, that is, every week day except Christmas Day and New Year's Day. The operating hours for TARGET are 7:00 am to 6:00 pm (Frankfurt time). As with CHAPS sterling, access to CHAPS euro is on a two-tier basis, with settlement members and participants, but there are likely to be more direct participants in CHAPS euro.

If all countries are to benefit by using TARGET, intra-day liquidity will need to be provided to participants by the central banks, whether or not their respective country is a member of the euro-area itself. It is expected that 'out' national central banks will have the same unlimited access to intraday credit as 'in' national central banks. If this is not the case, 'out' banks will need to minimise the need for euro credit by making payments from positive balances only. There will, in any case, be an earlier cut-off time for 'out' banks to make payments if liquidity is not available.

All the current arrangements for making payments will continue to be available, including correspondent banks and the Euro Banking Association's (EBA) net end of day clearing, which is the successor to its ECU net end-of-day clearing. CHAPS euro allows connection by

S.W.I.F.T. so that members can use the same interface for their international traffic and their CHAPS euro traffic.

Payment systems in the USA

Within New York, overseas banks will normally make US dollar payments using the CHIPS system (Clearing House Interbank Payment System). Payments outside New York are made using the Federal Reserve Banks and associated 'ABA' (American Bankers' Association) codes. Both are RTGS systems.

S.W.I.F.T.

S.W.I.F.T., the 'Society for Worldwide Interbank Financial Tele-communication', was founded in 1973 and provides communication services across all financial markets through member banks. It has over 3,000 members and provides services for over 5,600 financial institutions in 151 countries. Sub-members and participants include brokers, investment managers, securities deposit and clearing organisations and stock exchanges. In 1997, 812 million messages were processed through the system. At peak times, it processes more than 4,000,000 messages in a day. Around 70 per cent of these are payments messages.

S.W.I.F.T. provides or is involved with several national real-time gross settlement systems (eg in Belgium, Ireland and France) and netting systems (eg ECHO). Examples of S.W.I.F.T. messages are the MT 202 - General Financial Institution Transfer, MT 100 - Customer Transfer and MT 950 Statement message. An MT 100 – Customer Transfer can be used in two ways: either the sending bank instructs the receiving bank to make a payment in favour of a beneficiary customer's account, using their bilateral account relationship; or the sending bank instructs the receiving bank to make a payment in favour of a beneficiary customer's account, telling the receiver that cover will be sent to their correspondent(s). Two of these message formats are illustrated in figures 12.1 and 12.2.

Figure 12.1 MT 202 - General Financial Institution Transfer

(Bank A, Zurich, is remitting USD100,000.00 to Bank B, Berlin value 22 January 1998, using different correspondent banks in New York, for the account of beneficiary Bank C).

Explanation	Field No.	Format
Sender		S.W.I.F.T. Code Bank A, Zurich
Receiver		S.W.I.F.T. Code Bank B, Berlin
Message Type		202
Transaction Reference	:20	:
Value Date-CCY-Amount	:32A	:19980122 USD 100000,00
Sender's Correspondent	:53A	:S.W.I.F.T. Code, Bank A's New York correspondent
Receiver's Correspondent	:54A	:S.W.I.F.T. Code, Bank B's New York correspondent
Beneficiary Institution	:58A	:S.W.I.F.T. Code, Bank C
Sender-Receiver Information	:72	:

Source: Based on format from S.W.I.F.T. User Handbook, reproduced with permission.

Figure 12.2 MT 100 Customer Transfer

(London Bank A is instructing London Bank B to make a transfer, value 23 April 1998, of Australian dollars 1,000,000 for the account of customer C with Bank B's London Branch. A cover payment will be made through their respective correspondent banks in favour of Bank B).

Explanation	Field No.	Format
Sender		S.W.I.F.T Code Bank A, London
Receiver		S.W.I.F.T Code Bank, B London
Message Type		100
Transaction Reference	:20	:
Value Date-CCY-Amount	:32A	:980423 AUD 1000000,
Ordering Customer	:50	:General Company Ltd
Sender's Correspondent	:53A	:S.W.I.F.T. Code, Bank A's Sydney correspondent
Receiver's Correspondent	:54A	:S.W.I.F.T. Code, Bank B's Sydney correspondent
'Acct With' Intermediary	:57B	:Bank B London Branch
Beneficiary Customer	:59	:Customer C
Details of Charges	:71a	:

Source: Based on format from S.W.I.F.T. User Handbook, reproduced with permission.

The central moneymarket office (CMO)

The CMO was opened by the Bank of England in October 1990 to provide a central depository and electronic book entry transfer system for sterling non-fungible money market instruments. Non-fungible means that each instrument retains its separate identity. It eliminates the handling of paper between members and thus provides a quick, efficient and secure way of transferring money market instruments and for producing the associated payment instructions. A euro CMO service is being developed as a separate 'clone' from the sterling CMO. This is to ensure that, if and when the UK joins EMU, a dedicated euro CMO system will already be operational allowing a straightforward transition to settling euro only instruments.

Instruments eligible for settlement

The CMO service provides an electronic book entry transfer system. All instruments are stored in safe custody at the CMO and must be payable at maturity by a CMO member with no interim interest payments prior to redemption. The CMO covers the following sterling bearer instruments:

- bank and building society certificates of deposit;
- treasury bills, local authority bills;
- eligible bank bills, ineligible bank bills, trade bills;
- commercial paper.

Participation in the CMO

There are two ways of participation in the CMO service:

- *Direct membership*: A direct member has a book entry account in the CMO in his own name, inputs and receives instrument deliveries via a terminal linked directly to the CMO. Members arrange for their settlement bank to make and receive payments on their behalf for instruments transferred from and to other member of the service.

- *Indirect participation*: Settlement is conducted on behalf of indirect participants by a nominee which is itself a direct member of the service.

CMO accounts

Each CMO member is allocated a CMO Instruments Account on which his inventory of instruments is held. The inventory is sorted first by issue type (Treasury bills, CDs, etc) and sub-sorted in order of form held (outright, collateral, repo), maturity date and nominal value. All instruments held within the CMO system must be payable at maturity by a CMO member. Cash Memorandum Accounts and 'pledged in' and 'pledged out' inventories are also held by each member. These record payment instructions created for deliveries of instruments between members and instruments pledged as collateral between members. Security measures ensure that only authorised operators can verify and authorise transactions.

Lodgement of new issues

Members lodging instruments first input both the issue and the lodgement details on their terminals, including the CMO number of the member for whose account the instrument should be held. New issues are delivered into the CMO by the member who is the issuer/ acceptor of those instruments or the authorised agent of the issuer/ acceptor, accompanied by a lodgement slip. The lodging member guarantees the validity of the paper instruments being lodged into the CMO. A unique identifier number is allocated to each instrument lodged. A member has the option of lodging instruments:

- direct for his own CMO account for retention there;
- to his own account for onward delivery to another CMO member against consideration (which may be nil), by creating an automatic member to member delivery from his own CMO account to the counterparty;
- direct to another CMO member's account without generation of a payment instruction.

Parcelling

Parcelling is a way of batching instruments in the CMO to make it easier to transfer them in the system. In order to create batches, a member uses his terminal to display a list of instruments that he holds which are not already in a parcel or earmarked for other purposes. From the screen display, he selects no more than 99 instruments to be amalgamated into a parcel. The system allocates a unique identifier to each parcel created and each parcel also carries a parcel note to describe its contents to future holders. The content of any parcel may be amended by the holding member, at which point a new parcel identifier is created. The parcel may be unbundled and the contents returned to the member's Instruments Available Inventory.

Member to member delivery

The member offering the instruments/parcels enters the appropriate details into his terminal either by selecting items from the full list of instruments held for his account or by inputting the instrument/parcel identifiers directly. One delivery can be for a maximum of 16 parcels and/or 970 instruments. The transfer does not take place until after an offer of instruments has been positively accepted via the system by the taking member. The settlement process transfers instruments/parcels from the account of the giver to the account of the taker and generates the payment instruction for the amount of the consideration to the member's cash memorandum account at the CMO.

Collateral

A member initiates a pledge of collateral to another CMO member using the normal member to member delivery procedure. A pledged-out memorandum account is available to pledgors recording instruments pledged to other CMO members. Collateral may subsequently be substituted or returned. For substitutions, the instrument/parcel identifiers of the substitute collateral are keyed. In order to obtain the return of collateral, the pledgor inputs via his terminal the instrument/parcel identifiers to be returned from the pledgee. The positive acceptance of the second party is required for the transfer to take place.

Payment

The CMO provides a payments facility. The latest time for the input of deliveries incorporating a payment instruction is 4:00 pm, with positive acceptance needed by 4:10 pm and the payments run being made at 4:15 pm. These payments are not assured, that is, they are not irrevocable and unconditional. Each member must have an agreement with a settlement bank that is a settlement member of CHAPS. The cash memorandum accounts start each day with the balance set at zero and record the debits and credits of individual transactions and the running balance during the day. The records of members' payment instructions are available for enquiry by the settlement banks at 4:20 pm for the postings to their customers' accounts that day. Transfers against nil consideration may be input up to 4:30 pm with positive acceptance needed by 4:45 pm.

Withdrawal

An instrument may be withdrawn from the system, eg for sale to a non-member who does not have nominee arrangements with a direct member. The CMO member inputs the relative instrument identifier and completes a withdrawal slip for presentation at the CMO counter where the instrument is made available for collection. The member is then responsible for any subsequent delivery and settlement.

Maturity

All instruments held as 'outright' are automatically presented within the CMO system to the CMO member payer on the maturity date for payment over the CMO cash memorandum accounts. At the same time, they are deleted from the CMO instruments accounts.

Technical and fundamental analysis

Traders in financial markets use various means to try to predict how prices might move. As well as their experience and market 'feel' many will use some forms of technical or fundamental analysis.

Technical analysis is an approach to forecasting prices in a market by identifying and projecting past patterns of market behaviour. It comprises a wide range of specific techniques, the main one being charting. Charts are used to analyse patterns of price movements and price trends from which buying and selling signals may be identified. The market is also examined in terms of volumes and open positions. Technical analysis is based on the propositions that market action embodies everything that there is to know about the instrument being traded and that patterns of market activity repeat themselves. Price action then reflects shifts in supply and demand and the study of these price patterns gives an indication of the way future prices are likely to move. Technical analysis is used in the foreign exchange, bond and futures markets, particularly in tracking short term trading.

Types of charts are:

- Line charts, which produce a solid line by connecting only closing prices.

- Bar charts, which have vertical bars connecting each day's high and low price, together with a mark for the closing price.

- Point and figure charts (where alternating columns of x's and o's show rising and falling prices).

- Candlestick charts, which use colours for opening and closing prices to indicate days when prices rise or fall.

Technical analysts are seeking to identify, among other things:

- Established trend lines that may represent long term ('major'), intermediary or short term trends.

- Support and resistance levels beyond where buying pressures overcome selling pressures and vice versa.

- Patterns such as a 'double top', 'double bottom', or 'head and shoulders' which indicate reversals of price trends.

- Flags, wedges and pennants which are often seen before prices break upwards or downwards and may give an indication of the direction of the change.

There are arguments against technical analysis. It may be seen as over-simplistic in attempting to see trends and patterns as they form. Prices are, of course, driven by unpredictable market sentiment and new information as well as by the reactions of buyers and sellers to previous price movements. The fact that it embodies no explanation of why prices move is seen as a weakness. Nevertheless, if enough market participants believe in technical analysis, and act on its predictions, it is likely to at least be a significant influence on price movements and may, indeed, become self-fulfilling.

Fundamental analysis focuses on the factors which are thought to determine supply, demand and prices: monetary policy; economic theory; statistics; political considerations; events affecting a country's stability, balance of payments and economic development; and capital flows. The many factors to consider can mean that followers of fundamental analysis come to conflicting conclusions. In addition, fundamental analysis may provide a view that is too long to provide practical targets for the markets to identify. Traders' time horizons tend to be measured in days (if not hours) and economic forces take much longer to come to dominance.

The markets focus on figures or economic indicators as they are released at pre-determined times. In an efficient market, all the information necessary to track the supply of and demand for a commodity is already incorporated in the market price. Forecasts for the figures to be released are 'discounted' in prices. There will be reactions and adjustments if the out-turn is different from the forecast. This sometimes results in apparently perverse behaviour when, for example, the market improves after the announcement of a 'bad' set of figures. The market may have been expecting the figures to be even worse than they really were and so have been pleasantly surprised.

The main indicators relate to:

- Inflation: Consumer price index, wholesale price rises and wage rise (in particular, the non-farm payroll figures in the US).
- Manufacturing orders, industrial production, factory prices and consumer spending.
- Unemployment and jobless claims.
- Trade figures and balance of payments.
- Changes to official interest rates following Monetary Policy Committee meetings in the UK, Federal Market Open Committee meetings in the US or European Central Bank meetings for the euro.
- Public sector borrowing requirement and money supply statistics.

Dealers and managers in trading rooms must be aware of their exposures, sift the mass of information that might affect rates and take on board the comments of their technical analysts as a start to trading successfully.

13 Money markets

A bank's funding base has four major components:

- Equity and debt capital.
- So-called 'free funds', which comprise non-interest bearing accounts where the cost of funds is related solely to operating expenses.
- Retail deposits taken at advertised rates, which may include interest-bearing current account balances, call, notice, savings and fixed rate deposits.
- Market-related deposits, which comprise all those deposits taken at money market rates and at related rates, including funds raised from the issue of short term money market instruments.

The latter class of deposits is referred to as 'wholesale' deposits and is the main subject of this chapter. The funds, which may come from private clients, commercial entities, banks and other financial institutions, are usually the direct responsibility of a bank's treasury operations. The volatility of interest rates has resulted in a shift from free or advertised rate deposits to deposits at market-related rates and other forms of direct investment. Market-related deposits now often make up the largest proportion of many individual banks overall liability base, particularly for banks which have no access to a retail deposit base.

The characteristics of money markets are that they are short term, wholesale and liquid. Short term means from overnight to twelve months with most activity being in the overnight to seven day range. In general, periods beyond twelve months are regarded as capital markets activity but this is not a cut and dried distinction. Money markets are wholesale in that they are dominated by financial intermediaries dealing in large cashflows. For short periods, it is only economic to deal in large amounts. The markets are liquid because of the short term nature and high volumes of cash flows in the markets.

Interbank markets

The interbank markets are, as the name implies, principally bank-to-bank markets. The interbank deposit markets are dispersed markets with business being transacted by dealers, situated in their own bank's dealing room, conducting business with each other as principals. Trading is conducted direct by phone with counterparties, through brokers or using conversational screen dealing systems such as Reuters 2000-1. The primary and historical purpose for which the interbank markets exist is to enable banks with negative cash flows to borrow from banks with positive cash flows on a day to day basis, providing a conduit between the primary suppliers of funds and the ultimate users of funds. This is a market to which banks may resort for a variety of purposes. These may include the generation of funding requirements, utilisation of surplus deposits or internal resources, acquiring assets and liabilities for trading purposes or fulfilling liquidity requirements. Major banks in the market quote two-way prices as market makers running a portfolio of deals rather than match-funding individual trades.

In the market there is a chain of financial transactions that link the initial supplier and the ultimate user of funds as maturity transformation takes place and funds pass from bank to bank. A substantial amount of double counting needs to be taken into consideration in order to assess the actual size of the market itself. Interbank funds do not create additional funds, they merely redistribute funds which are already in the system between the supplier and user. The only factor that will affect the supply of funds is the official movement of funds between the private and public sector of an economy. This may result from central bank open market operations, official monetary policy requiring more reserves or through official fixed funding requirements. However, large amounts of money do move between domestic and international markets and also between the short-dated money markets and capital investment markets.

There are many factors that influence the direction of interest rates. Dealers must be aware of all events that may impact on rates immediately they happen or as soon as the information becomes available. Each dealing room is normally equipped with the latest automated and electronic technology to facilitate such communication. A constant flow of data and key monetary indicators are provided to dealers through these facilities.

Where the market anticipates a rise in interest rates, the majority of players within the market will keep funds in short-dated periods so that they can benefit from placing funds for longer periods after rates have risen. This causes short term rates to fall because of the over supply of funds for these periods. Where the market anticipates a fall in interest rates, the majority of players within the market will place funds for as long as possible at the current higher rates available. This causes the overnight and short term rates to rise because of the shortage of funds for these periods.

A dealer's success and expertise can be measured by his ability to anticipate events and their results rather than reacting to them. Within the deposit markets, the primary consideration, on a day-to-day basis, is supply and demand, as each bank must balance its end-of-day cash positions. Where there is a shortage in the markets, the lenders will control the movement of rates in an upward direction by their supply of funds to the market. The market will work in the opposite way when the supply of funds exceeds demand.

In normal conditions, the interbank spread between bid and offered rates is around 0.125% per annum. In times of substantial surplus, shortage or volatility, spreads can move much wider. There may be 'no bids' or 'no offers' in the market. There is always an element of tiering within these markets with lesser names required to pay a premium on market rates when borrowing funds. This may apply to an individual name or affect all banks in a country due to adverse country risk factors. Lending or placing limits will apply to interbank exposures in the same way as any other credit risk exposure.

Customer deposit and loan operations

For competitive reasons, banks may be prepared to pay interbank market rates to commercial and private clients for deposits and also provide facilities at fine margins over interbank market rates, on the basis of normal bank/customer relationships. The main difference between these contracts is the method of access to the bank. Access may be directly into the sales area of the treasury, through a bank's retail operations or through the intermediary services of a money broker.

On loan transactions, a margin will be applied reflecting the client's credit status and other terms of the facility. The credit sanction will have been obtained by the marketing area responsible for the client through the credit sanctioning office. The margin will accrue to the marketing unit through a system of transfer pricing, leaving the treasury to fund the loan at interbank lending rates and giving the treasury the opportunity to make a profit on its portfolio of trades.

When dealing with customers in these bank deposit and bank credit markets, it is expected that formal documentation and mandates or board resolutions will be obtained prior to transacting business. It is usually the responsibility of the area originating the business to complete these requirements, particularly for loan documentation.

Domestic v Eurocurrencies

Money market operations may involve domestic or eurocurrencies. Domestic money market operations are deals in the country of the 'home' currency. A eurocurrency deposit is a deposit traded outside the country of origin of the currency.

Eurocurrencies originated as external deposits of dollars, being domiciled in European banks after the Second World War originally as a result of the Marshall Plan for the reconstruction of Europe. Restrictive regulations in the USA, together with political factors, encouraged the continued growth of these offshore markets, which have expanded to include all convertible currencies. The currencies in question are bank balances in the country of the currency concerned. They become eurocurencies because they are controlled outside the country of origin of the currency. They are held in the nostro accounts of foreign banks. The ultimate owner of the funds is not evident to the regulatory authorities in the financial centre of the currency. Net trading positions are settled over bank accounts in the country of the currency in question which mirror the nostro account entries that are passed in the centre where the trades are made.

Reserve requirements

Historically it has been quite common for monetary authorities to require banks to hold a certain proportion of their domestic currency deposits in non-interest bearing accounts with the central bank. The purpose is to control growth in the money supply, by discouraging banks from expanding their balance sheets, and to ensure that they maintain a minimum level of liquidity. In recent years, the validity of reserve requirements as a monetary control mechanism has been eroded by the development of other means of finance which by-pass banks' balance sheets. Capital adequacy requirements have been much more effective in discouraging banks from expanding their balance sheets.

A second element of reserves is a requirement for banks to hold interest bearing liquid assets such as Treasury or eligible bills. For large banks in the UK this requirement has been based, since 1996, on the bank's cash flow over 5 working days whereas other banks' liquidity requirements are based on the mismatch approach using maturity ladders. Some other countries continue to have very high reserve requirements (liquid assets equal to 25 per cent or more of deposits, for example), this being at least partly in order to guarantee a demand for issues of government securities. It is accepted practice in many countries for banks to pass on the cost of maintaining reserve assets to commercial customers by means of a specific formula.

London money markets - trading practices and procedures

Characteristics of trading in the London Money Markets

Loan and deposit contracts arranged in the interbank market have characteristics relating to currencies traded, market amounts, periods, quotations, Libors, interest basis, value dates, trading practice and settlement.

Over 40 currencies are traded in the London money markets although most activity is in domestic sterling, US dollars and (from 1999) euros. Liquidity in many of the less actively traded currencies is thin. Brokers' screens show rates in the manner of Figure 13.1, in this case showing a negative yield curve. A positive yield curve is more usual, reflecting a positive time value of money and greater credit risk in longer periods.

Brokers' rates quoted on information vendor screens are indication rates for market amounts. Market practice determines what is regarded as a market amount. For domestic sterling, this may be between £5 million and £50 million pounds. Below £5 million may be considered small; above £50 million may be considered large; and rates may be shaded (the spread widened). For US dollars, market amounts are, say, $10 million to $50 million. In the dealing environment, the dealer is not aware when a quote is requested whether a bank requesting rates is a borrower or lender. He could ask for an indication of the size of the intended transaction by asking 'in what size?' Based on the response, and his position, the dealer will give a two-way quote.

Figure 13.1 Example of a money market broker's screen rates

STERLING DEPOSITS		
OVERNIGHT	7 3/8	7 5/16
WEEK	7 3/8	7 5/16
1 MONTH	7 5/16	7 1/4
2 MONTHS	7 1 /4	7 3/16
3 MONTHS	7 1/8	7 1/16
6 MONTHS	7 1/16	7 0/0
12 MONTHS	7 0/0	6 15/16

The interest rates quoted are expressed as simple interest per annum on a principal amount for the period of loan and deposit contracts. Rates are quoted on an offer and bid basis, eg 7.125% - 7.000%. The offer rate is the rate at which the trader is prepared to lend money. The bid rate is the rate at which he is prepared to take deposits. In the London Market the offered price is quoted first. The difference is the 'spread' but this is not an in-built profit for the dealer. It is only profit if other counterparties approach him and deal on the other side at his rates in matching amounts and periods. A single deal merely gives him the opportunity to make a profit. There is no set spread between offer and bid rates. Rates are still quoted in fractions of up to 1/64th of one per cent but can also be quoted in basis points. One basis point (bp) is one hundredth of one percent ie 0.01%.

The lending rate is generally called Libor, or the London interbank offered rate. The Libor for a given currency and period may change during the day. Banks 'fix' their Libors at 11 o'clock each day and these rates are displayed on information vendor screens. 11:00 am Libors are used where there is a contractual agreement to lend or fix rates in this way as in syndicated loan or interest rate swap agreements.

British Bankers' Association Interest Settlement Rates (BBAISRs) are an average of 11.00 am fixings published for 13 currencies, calculated and published on information screens by the British Bankers' Association (BBA). US dollars, sterling, D-Marks, Swiss francs, Japanese yen, and ECU (euro from 1999) are on Telerate page 3750. Australian dollars, French francs, Canadian dollars, Italian lira, Spanish pesetas and Dutch guilder are on Telerate page 3740 and Portuguese escudos on Telerate page 3770. These rates are also displayed on Reuters' pages LIBOR01 and LIBOR02 and on Bloomberg. The rates for one week and one month through to twelve months (thirteen periods) are given. The weekly rate fixing was introduced on 1 December 1997. The following is the definition of the BBA Interest Settlement Rates (BBAISRs):

> *BBAISRs are based on rates quoted by 8 or 16 BBA designated banks as being, in their view, the offered rate at which deposits are being quoted to prime banks in the London Interbank Market at 11.00 am London time (16 banks for USD, DEM, STG, ECU (Euro from 1999), ITL and JPY, 8 banks for the other currencies). For 8 contributors, the 2 highest/ lowest rates are eliminated. For 16 contributors, the 4 highest/ lowest rates are eliminated and an average of the remaining 4 or 8 are taken. The results (the fixing) are rounded up to 5 decimal places where the sixth decimal place is 5 or more. The value date for the GBP fixing is the date on which the rate was actually fixed and for all other currencies, the value date is two London working days after the fixing.*
> Source: British Bankers' Association

When the euro is introduced, the BBA will cease to fix Libor for the ECU and replace it with a euro Libor, fixed for spot value. A panel of 16 banks will be selected on the basis of market activity and perceived reputation in the euro market. A cash (ie same day settlement) euro fixing will be provided if there is sufficient demand. If and when sterling becomes a participating currency, sterling Libor will be re-based on a spot basis. Rate fixings for currencies participating in the euro for which Libor is currently calculated will continue to be set during the transition period and the rates published will be the same as the euro Libor rates.

In Europe, when the national currencies disappear, price sources covering several jurisdictions, rather than being particular to one centre, will be needed to create a Euribor price. The methodology for setting

Euribor has not been set at the time of writing. It is expected that rates from 59 banks, including at least one bank from each participating member state within the euro area, and a small number banks from outside the euro area will be averaged on a weighted basis.

Interest in sterling is calculated on the basis of the actual number of days elapsed and a 365 day year, as is interest for South African rand, Hong Kong and Singapore dollars and Malaysian ringgits. Portuguese escudos, Irish punts and Belgian francs are currently quoted on a 365 day basis but these will based on a 360 day year from 1999. Interest on all other eurocurencies is calculated on the basis of the actual number of days elapsed and a 360 day year. Interest on the euro will be calculated on this basis. In the interbank market, interest is payable at the end of the fixture and annually if loans or deposits are traded over twelve months. It is market custom for corporates to pay interest semi-annually on loans or fixtures of over six months.

The value date of a transaction is determined by the currency traded. Sterling in London is normally traded for same day value. Movements on call and notice accounts should be given by 12 o'clock. Eurocurrencies are traded for 'spot' value with settlement two business days after the trade date. These business days will take account of holidays in London, the country of the currency in question and, for most currencies, New York. Currency dealers generally balance their books at the beginning of the day after spot, which is known as 'tom' (for value tomorrow). For some currencies, for example yen, dealers may trade until late morning on the 'tom' date. The exceptions are US dollars and Canadian dollars where most dealing is for same day value because the trades can be settled in New York or Toronto which are open to settle the deals until after London closes. Sterling deals can be concluded for value tom or spot. Loans and deposits are repayable with interest on their maturity date with good value.

Trades for standard periods, eg one month, will mature on the corresponding date in the month of maturity or on the next business day if that day is a weekend or a holiday. There is an exception to this, the 'end-end' rule. When a trade is completed on the last business day of a month for, say, a one month period, it will mature on the last business day of the next month. For example, a deal for one month value 31 January will mature on 28 February or earlier if the 28 February is a holiday. Although rates on screens are displayed for standard periods, most currencies are traded by dealers on a portfolio basis and it is possible for counterparties to deal for any period or 'odd date'. Interest rates on call accounts are subject to change by the accepting bank with interest payable at agreed periods, usually quarterly or semi-annually.

Trading practice and procedures

The procedures for negotiating, and subsequently processing, a deposit transaction are set out below. The procedures are similar for all types of traded instruments and so are not repeated in full in subsequent chapters.

Prior to agreeing a transaction, a dealer will ensure that all necessary credit approvals are available and also that any trade undertaken will not exceed sanctioned trading limits. Trading between bank counterparties may be conducted with voice brokers, via electronic dealing (eg Reuters 2000-1 conversation-based dealing service) or telephone. There is no trade matching system in the money markets yet. Loudspeakers between dealing rooms and brokers offices are for brokers to convey current prices to the market. Deals with brokers are completed by telephone. When dealing through a broker, the name of the lender will only be disclosed when the borrower's name has been accepted by the lender but the broker is committed to the price once this has been accepted by the lending bank. If the counterparty is not acceptable to the lending bank, the broker must provide another name.

Reuters 2000-1 dealing screens are the modern version of exchanging telex messages. A dealer can call up another bank on his screen using that bank's code and request a price. A trade can be confirmed if the price is acceptable. Cryptic messages are the norm, for example as in this Swedish krona trade:

```
-HIHI WHERE IS YOUR SEK ONE MONTH  IN ABOUT 100 MIO
-5.25 - 5.00
-MINE 100 MIO AT 5.25 WE TAKE AT SE BANK
-OK  DONE  USUAL INSTRCTIONS FOR US  BIBIFN
```

The calling bank has borrowed Swedish krona 100 million for one month at 5.25 per cent. *'BIBIFN'* is shorthand for 'Good-bye for now'. As each trade is completed, the deal will be keyed onto a screen or a dealing ticket will be prepared. Keying allows the deal to be recorded directly in the dealer's position. The positions clerk records all money coming in and all payments out on the current value date(s). The dealer will note the deal in his maturity ladder and profit records. His aim is, first, to match all inflows and outflows during the day and then to ensure that the interest rate mismatch or gap position is within the pre-defined limits where individual deals are not matched.

Deposits received tend to be for shorter periods than loans and these mismatches may be maintained deliberately to take advantage of the yield curve (longer term rates normally being higher than short term rates). Where action has to be taken to reduce the interest rate gap, other markets or instruments may be used to achieve this, eg financial futures, repos, certificates of deposit or interest rate swaps.

In less liquid currencies, it is quite usual to match deposits and loans through deposit arbitrage deals. For example, a deposit is received in South African rand where the dealer does not run a book and there are no other banks with whom the funds may be profitably placed. The rand are sold for dollars, which are invested for the period in question. A forward swap is done to sell the dollars received at maturity in return for the rand, which are then returned to the original depositor. The calculations for this type of swap are given at the end of this chapter. Swaps can be used to arbitrage from any currency into another. If the dollar dealer is short and the sterling dealer long during a dealing day, an overnight or longer term swap may enable them both to square their positions.

If terms and conditions differ from normal market custom, the dealer should annotate such information on the deal slip and this should be recorded in the support area. The dealer may also exchange payment instructions. It is normal practice in the interbank market for the support areas in the respective banks to confirm settlement instructions. At the end of the day, each dealer will verify that all transactions undertaken have been processed correctly by checking his trades against hard copies of system-produced records. Assuming all deals have been recorded correctly and the day's cash position covered within agreed criteria, a dealer should have no further involvement with a transaction. Brokerage will subsequently be paid on a set fee or negotiated basis.

Settlement

The relative dealing slips or computer data will pass immediately to the processing area that is responsible for making payment and monitoring receipt of funds, confirmations and recording each deal in the accounting system of the bank.

Payments in sterling will be made using the CHAPS system and receipts can be monitored during the day to ensure they match the anticipated amounts. When the transaction is in other currencies, payment instructions will be dispatched by the lending bank to its correspondent bank on or prior to the value date to effect payment to the borrower's correspondent bank, with good value on the value date. Payments in foreign currencies will be made using the services of the bank's correspondent bank abroad and the S.W.I.F.T. system. Banks rely on the use of Standard Settlement Instructions (SSIs) and other counterparties should be encouraged to provide these. The wholesale markets are not intended to provide a money transmission service. Payments are made only to accounts in the counterparty's name and not to third parties.

Smaller corporate customers dealing in currencies who maintain foreign currency accounts at a local branch are sometimes unaware of the full instructions that must be given for payments. 'Pay USD to Barclays London' is insufficient. The full instruction might be 'Pay USD to Barclays New York, for account Barclays London, account Barclays Fleet Street branch, account XYZ Ltd number 12304560'. As well as requesting its correspondent bank to transfer funds to Barclays Bank New York by means of a S.W.I.F.T. MT202, the settlements area will send a S.W.I.F.T. MT100 instructing Barclays to make a payment in favour of XYZ Ltd, telling Barclays that cover will be sent to their correspondent.

During the course of each business day, confirmations will be produced and dispatched by each principal to each principal with whom trades have been undertaken. Production of confirmations is triggered automatically once the deal details are input into the bank's main accounting system. A confirmation will identify the parties to the deal including brokers (if used); the currency and amount; the trade, value and maturity dates; the interest rate and amount; and payment instructions. If the trade is undertaken through a broker, the broker will also confirm the deal to both parties. It is now common practice for banks to confirm deals undertaken with other banks electronically, either using S.W.I.F.T., telex or a local market confirmation system with a separate confirmation to the broker if needed. For commercial counterparties not linked to an electronic system, it is usual practice to fax confirmations so that they are received, if possible, on the trade day. Unsigned computer produced confirmations are generally used.

Upon receipt of each other's confirmation and that of the broker, each bank will immediately verify the details with its accounting records. The incoming confirmation from the counterparty bank should not incorporate any clauses that are contrary to market practice. Many banks have automated the process of reconciling trades against incoming confirmations that are received from counterparties. The system will report by exception deals that are not matched in all details. These unmatched confirmations are referred back to the dealing room. Where confirmations are not received, systems should be in place to chase receipt after short periods of time.

Figure 13.2 Specimen computer generated confirmation for interbank placing

	Bank name and address
Counterparty name and address	
	Trade date 19.10.99
	Basis 360
	Our Reference 90102-71

Confirmation of our deposit with you

Currency/amount	Value date	Maturity date	Days	Rate	Interest at maturity
USD10,000,000.00	21.10.1999	21.11.1999	31	5.5%	USD 47,361.11

Settlement instructions

Value 21.10.1999	Value 21.11.1999
we remit USD10,000,000.00	please remit USD 10,047,361.11
to XXXX Bank, New York	to ABBA Bank, New York
CHIPS 049291 account 0013891	CHIPS 021102 account 001011 128109

CONFIRMATION ONLY. THIS CONFIRMATION IS NOT NEGOTIABLE OR TRANSFERABLE AND DOES NOT OPERATE AS A DOCUMENT OF TITLE. THIS CONFIRMATION DOES NOT REQUIRE A SIGNATURE

It is an essential task of the nostro reconciliations section to check statements received from banks abroad, usually daily via the S.W.I.F.T. system, in order to reconcile payments, monitor receipts and investigate any discrepancy from the bank's own records.

Recording the deals in the main books of the banks will ensure that interest accruals are recorded in accordance with accounting practice. Reports are generated for gap positions and profit records to be checked against dealers' own records and by senior dealing management. Treasury, Financial Control and Audit units will also have an interest in the trading exposures, balance sheet assets and liabilities and profits records.

Money markets in New York

Within the New York money markets, the main sub-market is that for Federal Funds (Fed Funds). A bank holding balances at the Federal Reserve can settle claims on it through same day transfer. Banks are required by the Fed to maintain average balances in their reserve account over fortnightly periods from Wednesday to Wednesday. For this reason, alternate Wednesdays are known as 'make-up' day when overnight rates are frequently firmer. The interest rate payable on Fed Funds is a key indicator of U.S. financial policy. Dollar interest rates are also firmer at year end and quarter end dates because of the role of the dollar in the global financial markets.

The Bank of England's operations in the sterling money markets

On 3 March 1997, the Bank of England (the Bank) reformed its daily operations in the sterling money markets. These are sometimes referred to as open market operations. The Bank extended the range of instruments in which it conducts its daily open market operations to include gilt repo. It broadened the range of counterparties able to participate directly in these operations to include market participants active in the gilt repo and bill markets. It made changes to the way it provides liquidity at the end of the trading day.

The changes related to the mechanics of its day-to-day operations and did not alter its basic approach to implementing monetary policy, which is to manage short term interest rates through open market operations. The Bank's aims in its daily operations are:

- To steer short term interest rates to the levels required by monetary policy.
- To help the banking system manage its liquidity effectively.

The Bank satisfies the marginal liquidity demand of the banking system on a transparent basis using prime quality market instruments.

- To foster the development of efficient and competitive sterling markets.

The market's need for financing depends on transactions between three sets of players: the Bank itself, the government (the Bank is banker to the government) and all other players including commercial banks and their customers. There is a steady demand for liquidity from the Bank by the market for the following reasons:

- The main liability on the Bank's balance sheet is the note issue. Any increase in notes held by banks or their customers has to be paid for either by running down deposits with the Bank or by seeking refinance from the Bank.
- The Bank manages its balance sheet in such a way that the market is normally required to go to it for refinancing. The Bank acquires assets in its money market operations, for example bills of exchange, which must be redeemed by the banks. A proportion matures each day in the Bank's hands and repayment drains money from the system to the Bank.
- The government's account at the bank reflects inflows, eg tax receipts and the proceeds of borrowing, which drain money from the system and mean that the market has additional need of financing from the Bank. To ensure that there is a steady demand for liquidity, the Bank drains liquidity from the market by issuing Treasury bills each week, which involves payment to the government's account at the Bank. Government expenditure, on the other hand, puts money into the system.
- The settlement banks, which hold accounts at the Bank, have to maintain positive balances at the end of each day. Final daily settlement within the commercial banking system and between the banking system and the Bank occurs over the settlement accounts of these banks at the Bank.

The settlement banks, at June 1998, are NatWest, Barclays, Lloyds-TSB, Midland, Royal Bank of Scotland, Bank of Scotland, Clydesdale, Coop, Girobank, Citibank, Standard Chartered, Credit Lyonnais, Deutsche Bank and ABN-AMRO.

Daily operations

Each morning at 9:45 am the Bank publishes the official forecast of the daily shortage on the screen services. The forecast gives details of the main influences affecting the position of the money market, including Government transactions, changes in the note issue, the amount of maturing finance to be repaid to the Bank and the deviation from target of the settlement banks' accounts. If the size of the shortage warrants it, the Bank will offer assistance at this time.

The forecast is kept up-to-date throughout the day and, when necessary, an update is published at 2.30pm, when a second round of open market operations takes place. The first two rounds of operations are open to all the Bank's money market counterparties. The normal maturity of liquidity provided in the first two rounds of operations is broadly two weeks. The noon round of operations was discontinued in June 1998. A final round of open market operations may take place at 3.30pm, normally on an overnight repo basis at a rate of 1% over the Bank's repo rate. The facility is intended only to enable counterparties to square off unforeseen variations in their positions.

After the market has closed, a late facility will be available to the settlement banks between 4.20pm and 4.30pm, normally on an overnight repo basis and at rates determined by the Bank. This facility recognises that the settlement banks provide wholesale market services to the rest of the market and need to balance their settlement accounts at the Bank of England.

The Bank undertakes open market operations through repo of gilts, marketable HM government foreign currency debt and eligible bills (Treasury bills, eligible local authority bills and eligible bank bills), requiring a margin over their face value, and through outright purchase of bills. The instruments must be of prime credit quality; be actively traded in a continuous, liquid market; be widely held across the financial system for the management of sterling liquidity; and be available in adequate supply. The Bank's operations are broadcast on Reuter's pages beginning from BOE/MONEYOPS1. A typical day's report is shown in figure 13.3. Publication of the daily forecasts and updates, together with publication of the amount of liquidity supplied to the market, helps promote transparency of the markets.

Counterparties

The Bank deals with a wide variety of financial institutions in its daily operations. These institutions must satisfy a number of functional criteria to ensure that the daily operations run smoothly. The Bank will sign legal agreements with counterparties (banks, building societies and securities firms) who can satisfy the Bank that they:

- are subject to appropriate prudential supervision;
- have the technical capability to respond quickly and efficiently to the Bank's operations;
- maintain an active presence in the gilt repo and/or bill markets, thus contributing to the distribution of liquidity around the system;
- participate regularly in the bank's operations;
- provide the Bank with useful information on market conditions and developments.

There is no formal commitment to underwrite the weekly Treasury bill tender but the Bank looks to its counterparties to participate actively in the tender.

Calculations

Six calculations follow: simple interest; yield; annualised cost; annual to semi-annual interest and semi-annual to annual interest; the cost of breaking a fixture; and interest arbitrage swaps.

Simple interest

The formula is: $\dfrac{\text{Principal} \times \text{Rate} \times \text{Term}}{100 \times \text{basis days (365 or 360)}}$

Example: A bank places $10,000,000 from 15 January to 15 February at 5.50 per cent.

Figure 13.3 Bank of England's daily operations in the Sterling Money Markets

13JUL98	BANK OF ENGLAND

9.45 am Initial liquidity forecast Stg 450 mn shortage
A round of fixed rate operations is invited. The Bank's repo rate is 7.5%.
The operations will comprise repos to 27 July and outright offers of bills maturing on or before 27 July
Principal factors in the forecast
Treasury bills & maturing outright purchases - 168
Maturing bill / gilt repo -1556
Bank / Exchequer transactions - 80
Fall in note circulation + 1360
Bankers balances below target - 10
9.54 am Total amount allotted – Stg 250 mn
of which – outright Stg 38 mn, repo Stg 212 mn

2.30pm Liquidity forecast revision–Stg 400mn, Residual shortage–Stg 150mn
A round of fixed rate operations is invited. The Bank's repo rate is 7.5%.
The operations will comprise repos to 27 July and outright offers of bills maturing on or before 27 July
2.38 pm Total amount allotted – Stg 150 mn
of which – outright Stg 92 mn, repo Stg 58 mn

3.30 pm No residual shortage
No further operations are invited

$$\frac{\$10,000,000 \times 5.50 \times 31}{100 \times 360} = \$47,361.11$$

You could say that the future value of $10,000,000 is $10,047,361.11. The calculation to give you the future value directly is:

$$\$10,000,000 \times \left(1 + \frac{(5.50 \times 31)}{36000}\right) = \$10,047,361.11$$

Yield

Given an interest amount, a period and a principal amount, calculate the rate of interest.

Formula: Interest x 36000 (or 36500)
                        Principal x Term

Using the interest amount above:

Calculation: $\dfrac{\$47,361.11 \times 36000}{\$10,000,000 \times 31}$ = 5.50%

Annualised yield

Interest paid on a 360 day basis is more expensive than interest payable on a 365 day basis. To see by how much, simply multiply the rate of interest (eg 5.50 per cent) by 365/360 to obtain an annualised yield:

$$5.50 \times \frac{365}{360} = 5.5764\%$$

Converting annual interest to semi annual interest

$10,000,000 at 5.50 per cent pa gives annual interest of $557,638.89. If the interest is paid semi-annually, what rate can be paid to give the same return? An approximate calculation (since it assumes exact half years and reinvestment of the half yearly interest at 5.50 per cent) is the following:

Formula: $\sqrt{(1 + \text{annual rate}/100)} - 1 \times 200$ = semi annual rate

$\sqrt{(1 + 5.50/100)} - 1 \times 200 = 5.4264\%$

If interest is being paid semi-annually at a rate of 5.50 per cent, what is this worth on an annual basis?

Formula: $\left(\left(1 + \dfrac{\text{semi-annual rate}}{200}\right)^2 - 1\right) \times 100$ = annual rate

Calculation: $\left(\left(1 + \dfrac{5.50}{200}\right)^2 - 1\right) \times 100 = 5.5756\%$

Breaking a fixture

Money market deposits are non-negotiable and interbank deposits always go to maturity. However, commercial customers may ask for deposits or loans to be repaid early.

In the case of a loan fixture, the bank will seek to be compensated for any lower return on reinvesting the funds paid back early for the remaining term of the fixture. For example, a borrower asks to repay a 183 day loan of £5,000,000 at 10 per cent after 140 days. The bank can only reinvest the funds at the current 43 day bid rate of 9.5 per cent. The cost of 0.5 per cent of £2,945.21 is added to the interest payable by the customer.

$$£5,000,000 \times \frac{0.5 \times 43}{36500} = £2,945.21$$

The compensation is usually paid when the fixture is broken rather than at the maturity of the original loan. Where the compensation is significant, it may be discounted to present day value in the following manner:

$$£2,945.21 \times \frac{1}{1 + \left(\dfrac{9.5 \times 43}{36500}\right)} = £2,912.61$$

Interest arbitrage swaps

A common technique within a bank's dealing operation is the swap deposit, which is also referred to as a foreign exchange swap or currency switch. The purpose of this technique is to employ funds received in one currency usefully by switching them into another currency or to fund a lending in one currency with deposits from another currency. The exchange rate risk is covered through the forward foreign exchange market.

Suppose a money market dealer has received a deposit of South African rand 10,000,000 for 122 days and does not run a book in rand. The rand deposit market is thin, so he checks the forward swap rates. The US dollar dealer will pay 5.75 per cent for the period. The spot mid rate is USD = ZAR 5.4000 and the forward points are 1500 - 1550. The money market dealer will 'sell and buy' rand (left hand side of the forward rate). The forward points indicate that rand are at a discount, ie rand interest rates are higher than US dollar rates. What is the yield available on the rand? This is determined by calculating:

(a)   The amount of US dollars purchased and available to lend, using spot FX rate.
(b)   The amount of US dollars repayable at maturity from the placing with the dollar dealer.
(c)   The rand forward rate and the rand forward amount.
(d)   The rand interest rate, using the yield formula above.

In tabular form, the calculations are:

	Rand		US dollars
Today	Receive deposit 10,000,000.00 →	sell at 5.4000 →	1,851,851.85 Invest ↓
			Add interest 36,085.39 ↓
At maturity	10,478,051.68	← sell at 5.5500	←1,887,937.24

Implied rand rate $= \dfrac{10,478,051.68 - 10,000,000}{10,000,000} \times \dfrac{36500}{122}$

$= \dfrac{478,051.68}{10,000,000.00} \times \dfrac{36500}{\times 122} = 14.3024\%$

The money market dealer would round the rate he pays on the rand down to allow for costs and a profit margin. In this type of swap, there is a mismatch in the spot and forward amounts. Forward dealers trade in constant round amounts for one currency of the swap. If the money market dealer is dealing with the forward dealer in his own bank, the spot dealer may take the mismatch into his position. If dealing with another bank, the money market dealer will have to cover the mismatch separately.

14 Foreign exchange markets

Collectively the foreign exchange markets constitute the largest markets in the world by turnover value. Daily global turnover in all currencies has been estimated at $1.3 trillion. Typical wholesale deals are for amounts of $1m to $10m though transactions can be much larger. The foreign exchange markets have no single location. They comprise hundreds of foreign exchange dealers throughout the world trading through brokers, telephone lines, conversational electronic dealing systems and automated dealing systems. Apart from official holidays and weekends it is possible, with the aid of modern technology, for a dealing room to trade actively around the clock. In practice, liquidity for trading is affected by time overlaps in the three main regional zones of the world. London opens before the Far East markets close and is operational at the same time as other European centres. There is usually substantial liquidity in the London market throughout the day for the major traded currencies. Activity increases as New York opens for business and the market in New York is active until London and the other European centres close. Trading by American west coast banks will overlap with Tokyo and the other Far East centres before the market comes full circle back to Europe when the Far East closes.

The foreign exchange (forex or FX) markets are principally interbank markets in which banks trade with each other to cover and anticipate the foreign exchange requirements of their customers and also to trade for their own account. Many major banks function as market makers in the main financial centres of the world and are prepared to make prices continuously for the major traded currencies. Within each financial centre the main currency traded is usually the currency of domicile against the US dollar. The exception is London where the US dollar/D-mark is the most actively traded currency pair. This is likely to change to euro/US dollar following the introduction of the single currency in 1999.

In spite of the level of turnover, the foreign exchange market is now mature. It is subject to rationalisation in terms of the number of dealing rooms, currencies traded, methods of trading (the introduction of automated screen based trading systems) and settlement efficiencies. With modern communications, a single settlements area can process the work of a number of dealing rooms, for example covering a bank's foreign exchange and money market trading for all its European operations.

The foreign exchange markets are much more volatile than money market where rates may not change during the day. Changes in base rates, for example, are often made at predictable times, even if the nature and scale of the movement cannot be predicted. Foreign exchange rates, however, are constantly changing. Whilst the media in each financial centre will quote closing prices, these are merely a reflection of exchange rates at a single point in time. What characterises these markets, besides their size and the dealing jargon used, is the speed at which rates change and at which trades are transacted.

History

The Smithsonian Agreement of 1946 introduced a fixed parity system for exchange rates, subject to occasional realignment. In the 1950s and 1960s, substantial international payment imbalances developed with the two major reserve currencies, the US dollar and sterling, being overvalued and both countries running large balance of payments deficits. As discussed in Chapter 1, this led to the abandonment of the fixed rate system in 1972/73.

Within a floating exchange rate structure, the rate of exchange of one currency in terms of another should be determined entirely by market forces. Governments, both collectively following G7 agreements and using individual initiatives, occasionally seek to influence the level of exchange rates through open market intervention. Although foreign exchange trading in London is free from restrictions, regulations in other countries may affect exchange rates of those currencies and also affect individuals' freedom to access international currencies on a competitive basis. Regulations can include exchange controls and other monetary directives; constraints on capital flows; reserve requirements; official exchange rate policy; and similar constraints.

Size of the market

A three-yearly survey is conducted by the Bank for International Settlements (BIS) / central banks on the foreign exchange markets. The results of the 1995 survey showed the estimated daily global turnover was $1.3 trillion. Turnover in the three main centres was London $464 billion, New York $244 billion and Tokyo $161 billion.

In London, turnover for spot trading was $186 billion and forward trading $278 billion, of which 90 per cent was swap business. The main currency pairs traded were: US dollar/D-mark, with 22 per cent share of trading; US dollar/yen 17 per cent; and sterling/ US dollar 11 per cent. Around 75 per cent of business was between financial institutions and the remaining 25 per cent was with non-financial institutions. 35 per cent of interbank business was conducted through brokers. (Now over 50 per cent of interbank spot trading is conducted through electronic broking systems.) The top 20 firms accounted for 68 per cent of the market.

Participants

Broadly speaking, there are four types of participant in the markets. Central banks are a special type, using the markets to manage their foreign exchange positions and to intervene in the market to influence exchange rates. The other types are banks, brokers and customers. Banks participate as market makers. That is, their dealers will at all times quote buying and selling prices for currencies. Other banks or corporations seek rates from the market makers and may then buy or sell, giving the market maker the opportunity to make a profit from the difference between the buying and the selling rate. Dealers have to be ready to change their prices very quickly so that they avoid holding onto a depreciating currency or being short of a rising currency, since exchange rates are constantly moving.

Voice brokers act as intermediaries with telephone lines to banks throughout the world so that at any time they know which bank has the highest bid and offered rates. By telephoning a broker or listening to voice boxes it should be possible for banks to find the best dealing rate currently available. The broker does not deal on its own account but charges a commission for its services. Brokers' commission rates are negotiable. Electronic broking is discussed in the next section of this chapter.

Customers, such as multinational corporations, are in the market because they require foreign currency in the course of their cross border trade or investment business. The foreign exchange markets enable companies, fund managers, banks and others to buy and sell foreign currencies, if necessary in large amounts. Capital flows arising from trade in goods and services, international investment and loans together create this demand for foreign currency.

Trading practice and procedures

Foreign exchange comprises both cash and forward transactions. The date upon which a foreign exchange transaction is agreed is referred to as the trade date and the date upon which settlement is to be made is the value date. A good value date must be a date upon which banks are open for business in both countries of the underlying currencies for payment of cleared funds.

The principal rate of exchange for any currency in terms of another is the spot rate. The spot rate relates to deals transacted for an actual exchange of currencies (delivery and settlement) with a value date two business days after the trade date.

Forward rates apply to transactions with a value date after the spot value date. Same day rates are where the trade and value dates are the same and 'tom' (ie tomorrow) deals are where the value date is the business day following the deal day. These rates are calculated by reference to the spot rate and the interest rate differentials between the currencies for the period from the spot date. Outright forwards involve a delivery date further into the future, normally for periods up to one year but on some occasions over 12 months ahead. By buying or selling in the forward market a bank can, on its own behalf or that of a customer, protect the value of anticipated flows of income from exchange rate volatility. However, outright forwards are not the principal forward foreign exchange activity between banks. This is foreign exchange swap business. FX swaps are the simultaneous spot sale and forward purchase (or spot purchase and forward sale) of currencies and are extensively used for trading, matching and arbitrage purposes.

Foreign exchange transactions do not create assets and liabilities. They merely exchange an asset or liability in one currency for an asset or liability in another currency at an agreed rate of exchange. Until they come into value, forward exchange contracts are contingent assets and liabilities.

Dealing in the spot markets

Banks transact business on a principal-to-principal basis directly, through the intermediary of a broker or using one of the automated dealing services. To execute a spot deal in the market a dealer may telephone his counterpart at a market-making bank and ask for a price in, for example, sterling/US dollar. An exchange rate of £1 = $1.6155 - 1.6160 may be quoted. Sterling is the base currency and dollars the quoted currency. The exchange rate indicates how many dollars there are to the base currency, one pound sterling. The market maker normally quotes a two-way price. He stands ready to bid or offer up to some standard amount.

The last decimal place is a 'pip' or 'point'. In the quotation £1 = 1.6155 - 1.6160, each pip represents one hundredth of one US cent and the spread in this example is five pips. For a dollar/yen quotation, eg $1 = Y133.55 - 133.60, each pip is one hundredth of one yen. The spread is the difference between the two prices. Spreads quoted in the markets are, in real terms, small. With electronic broking, the spreads seen on dealing screens will be separated by one or two basis points, whereas rates on information vendor screens may show a spread of five basis points or more. These small spreads are indicative of normal market conditions. However, spreads frequently widen as market volatility increases and liquidity diminishes. In a highly volatile but thin market, spreads of 20,30,50 or 200 pips are not unknown. The spread does not represent a profit margin. This is only the case where the dealer is able to trade simultaneously for like amounts on his bid and offer sides. In the real world, the dealer is continuously trading in the market by opening, closing, building and unwinding positions. Rates of exchange are constantly moving and the bid and offered sides may move to a new trading range at any time. Although a trader may improve prices in relation to the market at any point in time, his ultimate success will largely depend on his ability to anticipate market movements correctly and to be able to run with, rather than against, the market trend over a period.

If one were to listen to a bank's dealer making prices in the market, it would bear little resemblance to the quotations illustrated above. Asked for a sterling/dollar price by another bank's dealer, the dealer would merely quote 55 - 60. He assumes his counterparty will be aware, firstly, which is his bid and offered side, and secondly, that the 'big figure' (ie the numbers before the points he quotes) is 1.61. In response to the quotation, the dealer may get a reply 'ten yours'. In this example, the amount 'ten' refers to sterling (the base currency) and means ten million pounds. 'Yours' means that the counterparty is giving (selling) sterling and taking (buying) dollars on the dealer's bid side. In this trade, using the quotation of £1 = $1.6155 - 60, dealer has bought £10,000,000 from and sold $16,155,000 to the counterparty. If the counterparty wished to deal in a round amount of a currency that has a relatively low unit value such as yen, the amount would most likely be in billions of yen. A billion yen is referred to as a 'yard' of yen.

Assuming that the caller wishes to deal, he will hit, that is accept, one side of the price. The dealer will note the deal in his position records and pass the details of the trade to the back office. Utilization against credit limits will be updated. Settlements staff will exchange confirmations to other banks by S.W.I.F.T. and confirm instructions for payments. Non-financial institutions may use FXMatch, an electronic confirmation system that has over 500 members. Nostro reconciliations staff will subsequently ensure that the respective currency amounts have been transferred into the designated accounts on the agreed value date.

Figure 14.1 shows a S.W.I.F.T. MT 300 confirmation sent by Bank A. Bank A has bought £100,000 at a rate of 1.6632 from Bank B, trade date 20 January 1998, value 22 January 1998. The deal is agreed by telephone.

Figure14.1 S.W.I.F.T. MT 300 Confirmation of spot foreign exchange transaction

Explanation	Field No	Format
Sender		S.W.I.F.T. Code Bank A
Receiver		S.W.I.F.T. Code Bank B
Message Type		300
General Information	:15A	
Message Reference	:20	:REF1A
Type of Operation	:22A	:NEWT
Common Reference	:22	:S.W.I.F.T. Codes: Bank A/Ref/ Bank B
Transaction Details	:15B	:
Trade Date	:30T	:19980120
Value Date	:30V	:19980122
Exchange Rate	:36	:1,6632
Currency, Amount Bought	:32B	:GBP 100000,00
Receiving Agent	:57A	:S.W.I.F.T. Code, London correspondent of Bank A
Currency, Amount Sold	:33B	:USD 166320,00
Receiving Agent	:57A	:S.W.I.F.T. Code, New York correspondent of Bank B
Optional General Information	:15C	
Dealing method	:24D	:PHON

Source: Based on format from S.W.I.F.T. User Handbook, reproduced with permission

Bank B will send a S.W.I.F.T. MT 300 with matching details. Each bank will send a General Financial Institution Transfer (MT 202) for payment of the respective currencies. Notice to Receive messages may be sent and the transactions will be reported on S.W.I.F.T. Statement of Accounts/ Confirmation of Credits advices.

Electronic trading and automated matching systems

Dealing is conducted electronically either using conversational trading systems or using automated matching systems. The Reuters Monitor Dealing System 2000-1 for conversation-based dealing was introduced in 1981 and is used generally within the financial markets. However, it is automated matching systems that have fundamentally changed the nature of the foreign exchange spot market and have significantly reduced the role of voice brokers.

There are two automated matching systems, EBS and Reuters Dealing 2000-2. The services provide anonymous electronic matching of spot foreign exchange orders. Both services started in the early 1990s with Reuters building its existing franchise and EBS being a response by the industry to the potential monopoly position of Reuters. EBS is a partnership owned by 14 major foreign exchange banks and has joined forces with the Minex Corporation in Japan. By 1998, EBS had some 700 bank subscribers using 2500 workstations around the world trading in 19 currency pairs. Some 43% of the overall spot broking market in London is done through EBS. Over 50% of spot broking in Singapore and Tokyo is undertaken using EBS and Minex. At July 1998, the Reuters Dealing 2000-2 system had 5,500 dealing users trading over 40 currency pairs in over 30 countries. The average deal size of Reuters tends to be smaller than with EBS, reflecting the size of institution using each service.

Subscribers enter their bid or offer and the size of deal they will do at this rate into the system. The system will automatically match counterparties provided there is mutual credit. Credit limits are keyed into the system before trading and are modified as deals are done. A record of the most recent deals (currency pair and rate) scrolls on dealers' screens. Deal sizes transacted tend to be in the $1m - $5m range, which makes it an ideal way for smaller banks to execute trades. Previously small banks wishing to buy or sell would approach the large banks who would provide liquidity while taking a profit. Because of the transparency of the system - the amount, size and rate of the latest deals are posted on screens throughout the system - the spreads on trading have reduced significantly. These systems cannot cover the whole of the market but only a specified number of currency pairs. All the settlement details are pre-advised between the participants for each currency pair.

In August 1997, Reuters introduced limited automated forward foreign exchange dealing in dollar/D-Mark for periods up to twelve months. A problem that this raises is limit setting. In spot dealing, it is relatively easy to agree a system for setting limits. Banks usually apply straightforward dollar values to define the amount banks are willing to trade with a particular counterparty. However, no two banks are likely to handle the allocation of forward credit limits in the same way. Reuters has a system of soft matching, which allows banks to give a simple yes or no credit indication for each participating bank.

Will automated matching systems replace voice brokers? Automated matching systems have many advantages. Pricing is transparent. The systems check credit availability before matching orders. They can support 24-hour trading and so make it very easy for Far East centres to access European time zones. Once the technology is set up, transaction costs are cheap. There is automatic position keeping and exchange of confirmations, which enhances risk monitoring and audit trails. There is a lower risk of error and no need for 'points', which occur with voice broking where voice brokers find themselves committed to one side of a trade but have lost the matching counterparty. There is no obligation on users to reciprocate quotations and automated matching systems are impartial.

The disadvantages of automated matching systems are that the number of currency pairs traded is narrow and liquidity is low in many of the pairs. Deals can be transacted only in round amounts. Automated matching systems may be slower than brokers in volatile markets. They fragment the spot market, which reduces overall liquidity. There is no exchange of information as with brokers which helps dealers build up a picture of market sentiment and acts as a means for price discovery for non-standard deals. Unlike brokers, automated matching systems cannot offer name switches that are used by voice brokers to add liquidity to the market. Whilst automation generally reduces costs, it does so by exploiting economies of scale. Whilst small banks are gaining the most from automated matching systems, they may find themselves squeezed out of the market at some future time because only large banks have the resources for large scale technological changes.

Voice brokers have retrenched and are investing in technology to speed up the processing of transactions so that there is not such a discrepancy with electronic systems. They have also diversified into other market sectors.

Risks in foreign exchange dealing

Foreign exchange open and mismatch position exposures (transaction exposure)

It is normal practice to segregate management and control of dealing positions from those relating to the bank's own internal, structural or hedging requirements. Each will be subject to separate measurement and accounting procedures. Management and reporting of overall foreign exchange exposure is covered in chapter 3.

Open positions are the extent to which a dealer is long or short, on his own account, of particular currencies and on which an exchange risk is run. A dealer who sells £10 million and buys $16 million is said to be short of sterling and long of dollars. If the position is closed out by the end of the day, the dealer will say his position is 'square'. The open position includes both spot transactions and forward commitments. The risk is that exchange rates will have moved adversely before the trades are matched or closed out. Dealers must adhere to their end-of-day and any intra-day open position limits. These will be set by management and will reflect the volatility and liquidity of the currency, the bank's attitude to risk, the dealer's experience and the bank's overall foreign exchange exposure position. Practice may be to give dealers autonomy to run their books as they wish intra-day but to allow only small overnight open position limits.

The extent of potential losses is kept within defined parameters by 'stop-loss' limits.

Should the open position be loss making beyond the defined limit, the dealer will be obliged to report this to management. A decision can then be taken as to whether to close out the positions and crystallize losses.

It is normal practice for overall foreign exchange exposure in all currencies to be measured in terms of the base or home currency unit. Being long in a currency, in accounting terms, represents a short position in terms of the base currency. For internal control purposes, the exposure should be measured as the aggregate of the base currency equivalent of all foreign currency positions both long and short. Although it may happen in practice, it is incorrect to base the measurement on the *net* base currency equivalent of the long and short currency positions, with cross currency positions perceived to compensate each other.

Forward or not-in-value commitments arise from forward foreign exchange dealing. For example, if an outright sale of dollars against the purchase of sterling for value in one month's time has been agreed and not covered, the dealer is short of dollars and long of sterling, one month forward. One way to unwind forward deals is to borrow or lend the respective currencies up to the value dates of the forward maturities.

Potential losses or profits can be calculated using current interest rates for the respective currency. This is why these exposures are usually monitored within the interest rate mismatch ladders of the bank. Mismatch limits are set by management to allow dealing in these forward commitments.

Counterparty risk

Limits will be set for each counterparty for the maximum daytime settlement risk that the bank is prepared to accept for current and spot settlement days and for each future value date, taking into account any netting agreements that are in place. A daytime exposure limit will be approved for each counterparty. The risk of forward deals is that, if the counterparty is liquidated, the deal will have to be replaced at current market rates. Before computers, limits may have been expressed, inadequately, at a notional rate, often 10% or 20% of the principal amount of the forward deal for deals up to 12 months with no adjustment as deals reached maturity. Systems are now available where limits take into account the mark-to-market value of forward deals, credit ratings, the period remaining, and the volatility of the currency pairs that have been traded. Limits administration officers will be on call to confirm limit availability to trading staff during the dealing day

Settlement risk

The Bank for International Settlements addressed the issue of settlement risk in foreign exchange transactions in a report dated March 1996. Traditionally, settlement risk had been considered a daytime exposure of a bank to the risk that the counterparty would fail to deliver the bought currency when the sold currency had been paid away. The collapse of Bankhaus Herstatt in 1974 first highlighted this risk. The banking license for this bank was withdrawn after it had received payments in D-Marks but before its dollar payments had been processed in New York. The BIS report highlights that operational issues mean that settlement risk is more than just an intraday problem. Indeed the time from issuing payment instructions to confirmation that the counter-payment has been received can easily stretch up to five days if weekends and public holidays are taken into account.

The report identifies three stages of settlement risk:

- Revocable: the trade commits the bank but the payment

instruction for the sold currency has not been issued or can be cancelled unilaterally.

- Irrevocable: a bank's payment instruction for the sold currency cannot be cancelled unilaterally either because the payment has been processed or because the counterparty's consent is needed.

- Uncertain: banks do not reconcile their corresponding receipts until the day after the value date. They do not know whether they have received bought currencies with finality until the reconciliation process has taken place.

The report advocates action by individual banks, industry groups and central banks. Actions which individual banks can take to protect themselves include the following:

- Improve their awareness of FX settlement risk, its measurement and risk control.

- Ensure careful release of payment instructions. Achieving this has been made more difficult by the introduction of straight through processing.

- Require better services from correspondents in turn-round time for payments and in monitoring and reporting receipts.

- Sign bilateral netting agreements such as the International Foreign Exchange Master Agreement (IFEMA) issued by the British Bankers' Association, and implement systems to put these agreements into effect.

Netting systems

Several netting systems have been set up by groups of banks. The principal ones are described below.

FXNET

FXNET was set up in 1986 by a consortium of large foreign exchange trading banks. It is an automated service for handling the netting of spot and forward contracts on a bilateral basis. The procedure for netting is as follows.

The counterparty to a deal is identified as a netting counterparty when a deal is passed to the back office for processing and individual/

gross processing is suspended. The deal details are forwarded to the FXNET system in S.W.I.F.T. MT300 format for matching. Computer links between back office systems and FXNET mean that deal capture is automated and there is no need to re-key deals. FXNET matches and confirms each individual deal with each counterparty. Net positions may be viewed real time within FXNET.

At the cut-off time, agreed bilaterally between the banks, net positions are exchanged automatically for each currency with the counterparties. There is no need to swap instructions between the counterparties. Net payment messages MT202/210 are produced by FXNET and sent to the back office. These allow nostro positions to be reconciled by the respective back offices and payment instructions to be sent via SWIFT. Statements of deals forming the net position are advised using MT950 messages to assist in reconciling general ledger entries. Once the cut-off time has passed, FXNET continues to control the generation of payment instructions for the FXNET counterparties but on an individual deal basis.

At the end of 1997 there were over 60 users of FXNET, the system being used in eight countries and netting taking place in over 40 currencies. Net settlement amounts show a reduction of over 50 per cent of gross amounts and the number of payments is reduced by over 80 per cent.

S.W.I.F.T. Accord

The S.W.I.F.T. Accord system was originally designed to provide confirmation matching facilities between counterparties that were members of S.W.I.F.T. It has been extended to calculate bilateral positions between pairs of counterparties that have entered into binding legal agreements with each other. The resultant net positions that are calculated enable net payments to be made in settlement. This provides a simple netting facility based on standard S.W.I.F.T. technology.

ECHO

Exchange Clearing House Limited (ECHO) provides multi-lateral netting of spot and forward contracts between participants on a global basis. A multi-lateral clearing system must have such a clearing house at its centre as the common legal counterparty for all foreign exchange contracts arranged between the users of the system. On each value date,

ECHO settles the net position, which is paid to or received from each of its users in each currency. ECHO reduces the settlement exposure to a maximum of one day through the use of structured settlement procedures and a payment versus payment approach. This reduces back office, message and nostro charges and simplifies reconciliation. The system has been accepted by most central banks as eligible for reduction in capital adequacy requirements.

Trades between users must be reported within two hours of execution. Confirmations are exchanged bilaterally using S.W.I.F.T. MT300 messages by counterparties and copied to the S.W.I.F.T. Accord confirmation matching system. This confirms matched trades to ECHO. There are two cut-off times for the settlement procedure. Net positions are advised by 06:30 Central European Time (CET) the day preceding the settlement day. This allows users to reconcile their records and execute trades to eliminate ECHO margin requirements and settlement exposures with other ECHO users. No further trades are allowed after the final cut-off time of 14:00 CET on that day. Instructions to pay away on behalf of a user are not made until all payments from the previous day from that user have been received with finality. Receipts are monitored in three time zones. If there are failures to pay in the Far East or European time zones, payments due to that user in time zones with later opening hours can be withheld. However, ECHO does not withhold payments if the failure to pay is for purely technical reasons.

ECHO reduces credit risks during the life of a forward contract and not just on settlement. If a user defaults, gains and losses on forward contracts are netted even when their currencies and value dates are different. A single net present value is established for the defaulting party, representing the profit or loss incurred in replacing its forward book. Losses are apportioned among the users concerned.

ECHO has recently joined with Continuous Linked Settlement Systems (CLSS), a similar group of banks that had developed the competing Multinet system, which ECHO has now superseded. This means that most major foreign exchange user banks are now part of the same multilateral netting initiative. CLSS aims to develop a real time payment versus payment foreign exchange settlement system, which it hopes will be launched within the next few years.

Spot and forward foreign exchange calculations

Spot foreign exchange rates

The following is an exchange rate for US dollars against sterling:

£1 = (bid) $1.6155 - (offer) $1.6160

Sterling is the base currency. Dollars are the counter currency or the quoted currency and the dollar rate is the variable in the exchange rate quotation. The rate quoted indicates that the market maker is willing to buy sterling (sell dollars) at the bid price of 1.6155. The market maker is willing to sell sterling (buy dollars) at the offer rate 1.6160.

If a dealer is buying an amount in the base currency, eg £1,000,000, he will *multiply* the amount by the exchange rate to obtain the quoted currency amount. Using the above rate, and on the basis that he has been approached for a price, the dealer will sell $1,615,500 at 1.6155. If a dealer is buying an amount in the quoted currency, eg $1,000,000, he will *divide* this by the exchange rate, and buy £619,195.05 at 1.6150.

The full set of quotations may be tabulated as follows:

Dealer buys	£1,000,000.00	Dealer sells	£1,000,000.00
Rate £1 = $	1.6155	Multiply	1.6160
Dealer sells	$1,615,500.00	Dealer buys	$1,616,000.00

Dealer sells	$1,000,000.00	Dealer buys	$1,000,000.00
Rate £1 = $	1.6155	Divide	1.6160
Dealer buys	£619,003.40	Dealer sells	£618,811.88

The method of quotation above is known as an indirect quotation, where there are variable amounts of the quoted currency against the domestic currency. International practice is, generally, to use indirect quotations, subject to the conventions outlined below. A direct quotation is easily calculated as the reciprocal of the indirect rate. Note that the order of the rates needs to be reversed to give the correct buying and selling rates:

Indirect rate	£1 = $1.6155	£1 = $1.6160
Direct (reciprocal) rate	$1 = £0.6190	$1 = £0.6188

Market practice to determine which is the base currency (before the introduction of the euro) is as follows:

- Sterling is the base currency if it is one of the currencies, except against the euro.

- The Irish punt is the base currency in an exchange rate, except against sterling and the euro.

- The ECU (while still a currency) is the base currency in an exchange rate, except against sterling and Irish punt.

- Australian and New Zealand dollars are the base currency, except against the above currencies.

- The US dollar is the base currency except against sterling or the above. (The basis of trading against the euro has still to be decided at the time of writing)

- D-Mark is the base currency except against the above.

Where the quoted currency has less than 20 units per unit of base currency (eg French francs to the US dollar), rates are quoted to four decimal places. Quotations for sterling and the US dollar against Japanese yen are to two decimal places.

Cross rates

A cross rate is an exchange rate that is calculated from two other rates. Most trading is against the US dollar and exchange rates involving two currencies, neither of which is the US dollar, are referred to as cross rates. Swiss franc/yen is a cross rate which can be calculated from $/SFr and $/yen rates. The method of calculation depends on whether the currency rates in the calculation are both indirect (or both direct) *or* one rate is direct and one indirect.

(i) Both indirect or reciprocal. You are given two rates against the dollar, eg

$1	=	SFr	1.5000 - 1.5010
			X
$1	=	Yen	130.00 - 130.10

As a dealer, you want to calculate a SFr/yen exchange rate. SFr will be the base currency. To calculate the rate at which you will buy SFr, (left hand side of the cross rate), select the rates quoted by other banks at which you are able to close out the trade, by selling SFr and buying yen.

- Sell SFr in the market versus $ - use other bank's offer rate of 1.5010

- Buy yen in the market versus $ - use other bank's bid rate of 130.00

The rule is to *divide* by the new base currency i.e.

$$\text{SFr1} = \frac{\text{Y130.00}}{\text{SFr1.5010}} = \quad 86.609$$

To calculate the rate at which you, as dealer, will sell SFr, select the rates at which you are able to buy SFr v dollars and sell yen v dollars, and *divide* by the new base currency.

$$\text{SFr1} = \frac{\text{Y130.10}}{\text{SFr1.5000}} = \quad 86.733$$

The full cross rate is: SFr1 = Y86.609 - 86.733

(ii) Where one currency is quoted directly and the other indirectly, the rule is to multiply the two bid and the two offered rates. In the following example, the cross rate for sterling/South African rand is calculated from sterling/dollar and dollar/rand rates.

£1 = $	1.6000 - 1.6010
	X X
$1 = R	5.0000 - 5.0010
Cross rate £/R	8.0000 - 8.0066

Outright forward foreign exchange calculation

Dealers are able to quote exchange rates for value on a future date. Quotations for forward rates are based on the spot rate minus a premium or plus a discount. The forward premium or discount is determined according to the interest rates for the respective currencies and period. Rates for same day value or 'tom' will also need to be adjusted to take account of interest rates between the deal and spot value dates.

Where interest rates for the base currency are higher than interest rates for the quoted currency, the quoted currency will be at a premium. You receive or pay fewer units of that currency on the future date. Where interest rates for the base currency are lower than interest rates for the quoted currency, the quoted currency will be at a discount. You receive or pay more units of that currency at the forward date.

A forward rate is sought by a client who wishes to buy dollars/sell sterling in one month's time. Dollar interest rates are lower than those of the base currency, sterling. The dealer can buy the dollars now and invest them for one month and borrow sterling to settle the spot trade. In one month's time he will give the dollars from the deposit to the client and use the client's sterling to repay his sterling loan. The dealer will earn less interest and will charge the 'loss' to the client by giving fewer dollars, which are therefore sold at a premium. The dealer sets the forward rate using the spot rate minus the premium.

There is more than one way to calculate the premium or discount. In the following example, the assumption is made that $1,000,000 is sold by the dealer for value in 30 day's time. Spot is £1 = $1.5995 - 1.6005. The dollar one month rate is 5.5 per cent (bid) and sterling 7 per cent (offer). The steps are, using the mid spot rate:

Spot value

Borrow:	£625,000 at 7.0%, interest £3,595.89, total £628,595.89
FX:	Sell £625,000, buy $1,000,000 at £1 = $1.6000
Invest :	$1,000,000 at 5.5%, interest $4,583.33, total $1,004,583.33
Forward rate:	Forward value of $ $\dfrac{1,004,583.33}{628,595.89}$ = 1.5981 Forward value of £
Forward points:	$1.6000 less $1.5981 = -0.0019 (19 points premium).

The figures can be expressed in tabular form:

	Sterling		US dollars
Today	Borrow 625,000.00 ↓	Spot rate = 1.6000 = $\dfrac{1,000,000.00}{625,000.00}$	Invest 1,000,000.00 ↓
	Add interest 3595.89 ↓		Add interest 4,583.33 ↓
At maturity	628,595.89	Forward rate = 1.5981 = $\dfrac{1,004,583.33}{628,595.89}$	1,004,583.33

The following formula can be used for calculating the forward rate.

Spot rate x [1 + (Days x counter currency interest rate/36500 or 36000)]
            [1 + (Days x base currency interest rate   /36500 or 36000)]

1.6   x   [1 + (30 x 5.5/36000)]   =   1.6 x   1.0045833   =   1.5981
             [1 + (30 x 7.0/36500)]   1.0057534

The following formula can be used for calculating the forward points.

Spot rate x [1+((Days x counter currency interest rate/36500 or 36000)-1)]
            [1+((Days x base currency interest rate   /36500 or 36000)   )]

1.6 x [1 + (30 x 7.0/356000 -1)] = 1.6 x (1.0057534 -1) = -0.0019
       [1 + (30 x 5.5/36000   )]   (1.0045833   )

Assuming the pips for the offered side of the forward quote are 0.0011, the two-way outright rate is:

	1.6000 - 1.6010
deduct premium	0.0019 - 0.0011
	1.5981 - 1.5999

The higher points on the left hand side are an indication that the quoted currency is at a premium. When calculating cross and forward rates, the spread will be wider than for the rates used in the calculation. If the spread has narrowed, the calculation is incorrect.

Foreign exchange swaps

Although the above example shows how forward rates may be calculated, it is not representative of how dealers would cover an outright forward deal in practice. The set of transactions is more complex. To cover a forward dollar sale for a market amount, the dealer would most likely:

• Buy the dollars spot.

• Undertake a swap transaction to

  - Sell dollars/buy sterling spot.

- Buy dollars/sell sterling forward.

• The spot dollar sale/sterling purchase will be incorporated and managed in the bank's spot position book.

• At maturity, the dollars bought through the swap will be given to the client while the sterling sold will be received from the client.

In tabular form:

Value spot	Buy $	Cash market	Sell £
Value spot	Sell $	Swap - spot leg	Buy £
Value forward	Buy $	Swap - forward leg	Sell £
Value forward	Sell $ to client	Outright	Buy £ from client

Swaps are the most common use of forwards. In considering swaps:

• The exact spot rate used does not have a material effect on the calculation, but it needs to be a market rate. Frequently the mid-rate is used. For client related transactions, it is usual to use the same side of the spot rate as is used for the forward points, eg right hand side of the spot rate and right hand side of the forward points.

• When forward dealers agree a swap, it is normal practice in the interbank markets for the amount of the base currency to remain constant. A euro/£ swap for euro10m implies that the spot and forward euro amounts are the same and that the sterling amounts are different. If this is not the case, there is a mismatch, which is taken into account in the trader's spot position.

• Dealers trade forward points in the market.

Example

Having received a quoted swap price of 96 - 100 forward points, the forward dealer buys and sells euro 10,000,000 against sterling (sells and buys sterling). The 'rising' points indicate that sterling interest rates are higher than interest rates for the euro, the base currency. Spot is set at euro = £0.7500. The dealer is selling euro forward and buying sterling forward at 100 points discount (right hand side of the forward points). The payment flows for the dealer to record are:

Spot	Receive euro 10,000,000	0.7500	Pay £7,500,000
Discount		+0.0100	
Forward	Pay euro 10,000,000	0.7600	Receive £7,600,000

Examples of the use of swaps for trading and arbitrage purposes are given in other chapters. Interest arbitrage swaps, to enable money market dealers to access a currency where the deposit market is not liquid, or to swap surpluses into another currency to obtain better returns are covered in chapter 13. Hedged acceptance credits are covered in chapter 15 and commercial paper arbitrage in chapter 17.

SAFEs

SAFEs are Synthetic Agreements for Forward Exchange. Banks that trade actively in forward foreign exchange will naturally find that they have mismatched positions in different forward periods, for example, being overbought in yen against dollars in three months but oversold yen against dollars in six months. Rather than transact separate swaps against spot, it is more efficient for a bank to undertake a forward/forward swap, analogous to a FRA, between the three months and the six months period. When concluding a SAFE transaction, the counterparties agree a swap price for the forward/forward period. The settlement date is at the start of the contract period. One party will pay the other a settlement amount based on the difference between the agreed swap price and the actual swap price on the settlement date.

Master terms for SAFEs have been published by the British Bankers' Association. These terms define the settlement sum, payable in the secondary currency, under a SAFE transaction.

Non-deliverable forwards

A further variant on forward foreign exchange is the Non-Deliverable Forward or NDF. Whereas conventional forward deals are settled by full exchange of the principal amounts, NDFs (as their name implies) do not involve full exchange of the principal amounts. Instead, the parties settle the difference between the agreed rate and the spot rate at maturity, settlement always taking place in US dollars.

For example, a customer wishing to hedge the US dollar value of a future receipt in Indian rupees could enter into an NDF contract with his bank as follows. The bank agrees to buy, notionally, from the customer the sum of Rs40m in exchange for $1m, the maturity being in three months' time. On the maturity date, the spot rate for Rs/$ is 50.00. The customer sells his Rs40m in the spot market (this does not have to be done with the same bank as the NDF) and receives $800,000. He also settles his NDF contract and receives a settlement amount calculated as:

$$\frac{\text{Notional Principal}}{\text{Agreed Rate}} - \frac{\text{Notional Principal}}{\text{Spot Rate at Maturity}} = \frac{40,000,000}{40} - \frac{40,000,000}{50}$$
$$= \$200,000$$

The customer's aggregate receipts under his spot sale and NDF settlement are thus equivalent to the $1m targeted originally. Note that if the spot rate had moved to, say, 30.00 at maturity, the customer would owe a US dollar settlement sum to the bank.

NDFs are of value to customers who wish to hedge their exposures to currencies where there is no liquid market in outright forwards. As settlement is always for the net amount and in US dollars, banks may be more willing to enter into NDFs than outrights because of the lesser credit and country exposure. There may also be restrictive regulations that prevent the development of a full forward foreign exchange market but do not prevent banks' activities in offshore NDF markets.

Banks will look to cover positions arising from customer NDFs as much as possible by matching deals within certain tolerances. Where this is not possible, they may hedge with a combination of spot deals and government securities positions. Both these methods of covering are far from perfect and so dealing spreads in NDFs tend to be wide.

15 Bank bills

Eligible bank bills are one of the instruments in which the Bank of England conducts its daily open market operations. These are bills of exchange as defined under the Bills of Exchange Act 1881. Similar types of instrument ("Bankers' Acceptances") exist in many countries.

Bills of exchange and acceptance credit facilities

Bills of exchange have long been in use for settling debts for cross border and inland trade. By 1882, their use was so widespread in England that an Act was passed, the Bills of Exchange Act 1882. A Bill of Exchange is defined as:

> *An unconditional order in writing from one person or company (the drawer) to another, requiring the person or company to whom it is addressed (the drawee) to pay a specified sum of money on demand (sight bill) or at a fixed or determinable future date (term bill) to or to the order of a specified person or to the bearer.*

Bank bills comprise those bills that are drawn by commercial enterprises and accepted by a bank. A bank's acceptance is evidenced by its signing the face of the bill and indicating clearly the place and the date on which it will be paid. The acceptance is an unconditional undertaking by the bank to make payment to subsequent holders of the bill, for which it charges an acceptance commission.

Bank bills are term bills. The purpose of drawing bank bills is to obtain finance by creating an instrument (the accepted bill) which is readily marketable and which may be converted into cash by selling it on a discounted basis. The quality of the bank's name on the bill will determine its marketability and sometimes the relative discount. These are clean bills which have no documentation attached to them.

Trade bills are drawn by one company on another company. They may be sight or term bills and are used by the drawer to obtain a commitment of payment from his creditors. These bills may be accompanied by trade documents, as with documentary credits. They may be used to obtain finance from banks who are asked to negotiate the bills. This type of bill is not described further in this publication.

In order to be able to draw clean bills or acceptances on its bank, a company will arrange a limit with its bank known as an acceptance credit facility. The ability to draw bills is often an option in a revolving credit facility for Libor linked loans. By drawing eligible bills, companies can benefit from discount rates that may provide funds at rates lower than other forms of finance. This is because they are drawing negotiable instruments, which are eligible to be rediscounted at the Bank of England.

The accepting bank will invariably discount the accepted bill. With the closure of the discount house market, the ability for companies to take the bills elsewhere to be discounted has disappeared. At maturity a new bill is often drawn, the discounted proceeds of which will cover most of the amount due on the maturing bill. The customer needs then only pay the discount, plus acceptance commission, on each new drawing as the facility rolls on. Acceptance commission can vary between 7.5 basis points and one per cent per annum, or more, depending on the type of customer and its credit standing. The acceptance obligation has a risk asset weighting of 100 per cent for capital adequacy purposes on a bank's balance sheet.

The eligible bill market

In 1981, new monetary control arrangements placed more emphasis on bills as the means by which the Bank of England regulated the supply of cash to the banking system. This gave rise to a need to increase the supply of eligible bills. The number of banks whose bills were eligible for rediscount at the Bank of England was increased to around 170 at that time. Bill finance became very popular with the amount of bills outstanding in the market becoming so large that it was referred to as the 'Bill Mountain'. The spread between bill discount rates and Libor interest rates was wide, up 70 basis points, making bills a very attractive form of finance for companies and providing arbitrage opportunities.

The importance of eligible bills in the Bank of England's daily operations has lessened in the 1990s but bills are still an important element of banks' holdings of liquid assets. With the introduction of repo in the Bank's daily money market operations in March 1997, the use of eligible bills has become just one of the options available to the Bank of England in its daily operations. The number of banks whose bills are eligible for rediscount at the Bank of England has reduced to around 120 in 1998. The difference between discount rates and Libor is now much smaller at around 20 basis points, depending of the term of the bill and market conditions. The volume of bills outstanding at the beginning of 1998 was about £21 billion. In 1981, the discount houses were the primary intermediaries with the Bank of England in the discount market. This role gradually reduced and following the March 1997 changes, the number of discount houses has fallen further.

Eligible paper is said to be discountable at the finest rates and to qualify as such must meet the following criteria:

- It must be accepted by a bank whose bills are eligible for discount at the Bank of England.
- It must be drawn in sterling, although the underlying trade invoice may be in currency.
- It must have a tenor not in excess of 187 days.
- The underlying transaction must be self-liquidating and trade related.
- It must be a properly executed bill of exchange, payable in the UK and claused in a manner which indicates clearly the underlying trade for which it was drawn.

The underlying trade may be:

- Imports and exports of goods, merchanting and third party trade, provided the trade is cross border and does not relate solely to trade in just one country abroad. Inland trade within the UK may be financed by way of eligible bills.
- Financing of stocks where the proceeds from them can be expected to be received within six months.
- Hire purchase and leasing where the bills are drawn against identifiable receivables.

- Services already provided for which an unconditional obligation to pay has been established.

The Bank may call for evidence of the trade or services. All eligible paper must identify the nature of the transactions and examples of clausing are as follows:

- Covering the export of motor vehicles.
- In consideration of sale of speciality chemicals.
- Against leasing receivables.

Some drawers have questioned whether the disclosure of this information on bills, which is divulged to third parties when a bill is discounted, is revealing confidential information. The clausing should, however, be of such a general nature that this is not a material risk. A drawer cannot require the accepting bank to hold the bills in its own portfolio as investment paper rather than discounting them.

Since the Finance Act 1984, holding and finance companies within a group have been able to draw bills in respect of trade undertaken by other companies in the same group.

The following types of bills would not be considered eligible:

- Bills drawn for a tenor of longer than 187 days. This applies irrespective of the remaining maturity of the bills.
- Bills whose drawer and acceptor have a shareholding link ('pig on pork' bills).
- Bills drawn by one bank on another bank. This will not exclude banks drawing bills on eligible banks to cover the provision of hire purchase or leasing credit where the bills are drawn against identifiable receivables.
- Bills drawn for foreign inland finance or for services not yet provided.
- Bills drawn in respect of capital goods. Only the last six month's instalment can be financed by an eligible bill.

The general conditions which must be satisfied by eligible banks and by any bank wishing to become an eligible institution are:

- The bank must have a broadly based and substantial acceptance business in the United Kingdom.

- Its acceptances must command the finest rates in the market.

- In the case of foreign owned institutions, British banks must enjoy reciprocal opportunities in the foreign owners' domestic market.

The Bank of England does not impose any direct upper limit for monetary control purposes on the volume of acceptance business written by eligible banks. It does, however, set internal limits on the holdings within its own portfolio of an individual acceptor's paper. This is a normal prudential concern to limit its exposure to individual counterparties, in order to contain the problems that would arise if an eligible acceptor ran into difficulties. This limit is related to the accepting bank's capital and to the proportion of the bank's global business that is conducted in the UK. If the Bank of England's holdings of an individual acceptor's bills approached the limit, the Bank would discuss the situation with the acceptor concerned. When Barings Bank ran into difficulties in 1996, its bills were among the first of its liabilities to be repaid.

Eligible banks undertake to maintain a continuing commitment to the acceptance market. There are limits on the minimum acceptance business that banks must undertake in terms of volume and counterparties in order to remain eligible. Banks should maintain a broadly based acceptance book, which should average of at least £15 million and at no time fall below £10 million.

The primary market

A company will approach the corporate dealing desk of its bank and seek quotations for accepting and discounting bills. Trading will take place before 12:00 am for same day value but can be done for value 'tom' or 'spot'. The minimum period for drawing bills is seven days but the yield benefit over Libor loans is usually only seen for one, two and three month bills. The cost of six month bills is usually the same as the cash market because there is no liquidity in the bill market for this period. The discount is paid at the beginning of the period, rather than at the end, as is interest. There is a cost in paying the discount early, which must be quantified, by converting the discount to a yield basis, in order to compare it to a cash advance. Subject to the notice of drawdown being given, drawings by way of acceptances under a syndicated loan will usually have the discount rate set using a 10:30 am fixing. Discount rates may be quoted in fractions or decimals.

Once the discount rate and the amount of discount are agreed, the details are recorded and passed to the bill dealer and the back office. The bill dealer will either rediscount the bills or retain them in his liquidity portfolio. The settlements office will arrange for the discounted proceeds to be paid to the customer's account with the bank or via the CHAPS system and for a confirmation of the deal to be sent to the customer.

Eligible bills are usually drawn in amounts up to £1,000,000 and then in multiples of £1,000,000 up to £5,000,000. They cannot be split once issued. Bills up to £1,000,000 do not need to be drawn in round amounts. Some companies ask for bills to be 'grossed-up' so that the proceeds they receive are a round figure. The minimum deal size is £500,000 if the finest discount rates are to given. £5,000,000 bills were not used until the opening of the Central Moneymarket Office, where most bills are now lodged after acceptance, whether or not they have been rediscounted.

As bills are normally made payable to the order of 'ourselves', they must be endorsed on the reverse of the bill as evidence of negotiation. Signed inchoate bills are usually lodged with the bank that has agreed to make the acceptance facility available and are usually numbered for audit purposes. The amount and clausing may be completed in advance or left for the bank to add when bills are drawn under the facility. The bank will add the date and maturity of the bill and the acceptance will be signed by authorised signatories of the bank. Where the company drawing the bill is located in London, it may arrange to deliver bills each time bills are accepted. Where the company is located outside the UK, it may provide a Power of Attorney allowing the accepting bank to draw bills on its behalf.

Figure 15.1 Bill Format - Clean Eligible Bill, Face and Reverse for Endorsement

```
Accepted  1st December 19xx    No      1020              1st December 19xx
Payable at                                    £   5,000,000
National Westminster Bank PLC At/on_____2nd March 19xx_____Pay this Sole of
                                                                      Exchange
10 Lombard Street              to the order of_____ourselves_____.
London  EC1 1CB                Amount in words  five million pounds  .
                               For value against import of wood products
For                                            and charge same to account
National Westminster Bank PLC To:                          for and on behalf of
                               National Westminster Bank PLC    EDFG PLC
                               10 Lombard Street     _____
Authorised signatories         London EC1 1CB        _____
```

Reverse of bill

```
                    for and on behalf of
                    EDFG PLC


                    _____
                    _____
```

Figure 15.2 Letter Confirmation of Acceptance and Discount

Bank name and address	Date	Ref
EDFG Ltd City Road, London		
Confirmation of Sterling acceptance and discount		
Face Value	£10,000,000	
Period	01.12.98-02.03.99 (91days)	
Discount Rate (incl. 0.1875% commission)	7.125%	
Discount	£177, 736.99	
Net Proceeds	£9,822,363.01	
Bills Nos. 1020 and 1021 have been used for this transaction. Net Proceeds have been credited to your account at Barbican Branch.		

The secondary market

The bank dealer has the option of holding and funding bills, rediscounting them in the market or using them in repo operations. When bills are traded between banks, prices are now quoted in decimals. Banks hold bills as part of their liquidity portfolios, but those the bank has accepted itself will not quality for regulatory or liquidity risk purposes. This is because, if a bank has liquidity difficulties, it is unlikely it will be able to sell its own paper. This is why banks sell bills they have accepted and purchase bills accepted by other banks. Banks can 'swap' packages of bills with each other in order to obtain appropriate liquid instruments. Where two banks have accepted bills under the same syndicated loan facilities, it is very easy for them to swap bills that are matching in all respects.

Other bill markets

There is a market in ineligible bank bills in London. The rates will be more deeply discounted than eligible bills and will equate to cash rates. Trade bills are ineligible bills.

Bill finance is used in many other countries including the USA, Canada, France, Japan and Australia, each having its own regulations and market practices. Bills in these countries are used to varying degrees in the daily money market operations by the respective central banking authority.

Calculations

Discount and net proceeds

When a discount basis applies, the sum specified on the bill, the face value, is payable at maturity to the holder of the bill. The discount of sterling bills is calculated on the basis of the actual number of days elapsed and a 365 day year. The formula for calculating the discount on a sterling bill is:

$$\text{Discount} = \frac{\text{face value x rate x period}}{365 \times 100}$$

Example: A three month bill for £1,000,000 nominal is discounted for 91 days at 7.875% per annum. The discount is:

$$\frac{£1,000,000.00 \times 7.875 \times 91}{365 \times 100} = £19,633.56$$

The proceeds from discounting the bill are £1,000,000.00 less the discount £19,633.56, ie, £980,366.44.

This answer can be obtained directly as follows:

$$£1,000,000 \times (1 - (7.875 \times 91/36500))$$

$$= \quad £1,000,000 \times \quad (0.98036644) \quad = £980,366.44$$

Yield

Having done the above calculation, the simplest way to calculate the yield is to multiply the discount rate by the face value of the bill and divide by the proceeds, as follows:

$$\text{Yield} = \text{discount rate} \times \frac{\text{face value}}{\text{net proceeds}}$$

$$7.875\% \quad \times \frac{1,000,000.00}{980,366.44} \quad = 8.0327\%$$

Or use the formula:

$$\frac{\text{discount rate}}{1 - \left(\frac{\text{discount rate x days}}{36500}\right)} = \frac{7.875}{1 - \left(\frac{7.875 \times 91}{36500}\right)} = 8.0327\%$$

Grossing up a bill

When a company wishes to receive a certain sum at the outset, the required proceeds must be grossed-up to determine the face value of the bill. To receive £1,000,000 proceeds now on a 91 day bill at 7.875% discount, the calculation is:

$$\text{Grossed-up amount} \quad = \quad \frac{1{,}000{,}000}{1 - \frac{(7.875 \times 91)}{36500}} = £1{,}020{,}026.76$$

Hedged acceptance credits

When there is a sufficiently large difference between discount and cash rates, companies are able to raise currency borrowing through bill arbitrage. An example is as follows. A company that is able to issue sterling bills requires US dollars 8 million for 59 days. It can issue bills at 7.25 per cent. The spot foreign exchange rate is £1 = $1.6000 and the forward points are 45 points premium. The cost of US dollars in the cash market is 5.625 per cent.

The process is:

(a)   Calculate the proceeds required from the sterling bill.
$8,000,000/1.6000   =   £5,000,000.00

(b)   Gross up the proceeds to find the face value of the bill at maturity.
$$\text{Grossed up bill} \quad = \quad \frac{£5{,}000{,}000.00}{1 - (7.25 \times 59/36500)} = £5{,}059{,}290.73$$

(c)   Using the forward rate, calculate the dollars repayable by the company at maturity:
Forward rate   = 1.6000 less 0.0045   =   1.5955
Forward dollar amount = £5,059,290.73/1.5955 = $8,072,098.36

(d)   Calculate the cost of dollars:
$$\text{Effective cost of \$} \quad = \quad \frac{\$72{,}098.36 \quad \times 36000}{\$8{,}000{,}000.00 \times 59} \quad = \quad 5.4990\,\%$$

Expressed in tabular form:

	Sterling		US dollars
Today	Receive bill proceeds 5,000,000.00 →	Sell for dollars at 1.6000 →	Receive 8,000,000.00
	Discount 59,290.73 ↓		
At maturity	Redeem bill ↓ 5,059,290.73 ←	Purchase sterling at 1.5955 ←	Dollars required 8,072,098.36

The cost of raising US dollars is over 12 basis points cheaper through the hedged acceptances in this example. The bank can offer this service as a package to companies, taking the mismatch in the dollar amounts of the swap into the bank's book. Larger companies may wish to arrange the sterling bill and forward swap elements separately, seeking the most competitive quotes for each element from their panel of banks.

16 Certificates of deposit

Origins and definitions

Certificates of Deposit (CDs) were first issued in 1961 by commercial banks in the USA. Before this, US banks had issued registered, non-negotiable certificates of deposit, which had limited appeal. The incentive for introducing a negotiable instrument was Federal Reserve Regulation Q which limited the interest rates that banks could offer on time and savings deposits. As interest rates in the money markets rose above Regulation Q levels, banks lost deposits to non-banks such as money market funds, which were not subject to this regulation. Deposits of $100,000 or more and with a minimum tenor or maturity of 14 days were exempt from Regulation Q, but investors managing overnight and short term funds needed liquidity. Negotiable CDs provided the mechanism for the holder to have liquidity by being able to sell holdings of CDs in a secondary market. The first issues of CDs in London were made in 1966 in US dollars.

CDs are negotiable instruments in bearer form, issued by banks (and building societies in the UK). CDs are transferable without endorsement, title passes on delivery and there is no contingent liability after the sale. With a fixed interest rate CD, the issuer certifies that a specified sum will be paid on a particular future date (the maturity date) on stated terms. With a floating rate CD (FRCD), the issuer certifies that a specified sum has been deposited with it at a rate of interest which may vary throughout the life of the CD. Interest is payable for each of the stated relevant interim periods between issue and maturity at a stated margin above or below a specified interest rate index for the relevant interest period. Discount CDs and zero-coupon CDs carry no stated interest rate but state that, at maturity, the CDs will be redeemed at its face value.

Tap issues, sometimes referred to as straight CDs, are made by an issuing bank when it wishes to tap the market directly to raise funds or is approached by investors with specific amounts to invest. Most issues of CDs in the London market are short term tap issues with maturities up to three months as the banking equivalent of commercial paper.

Tranche CDs are rarely, if ever, issued nowadays. These issues had the features of bonds and medium term notes. They were block issues, which were placed privately by a security house or houses. This may have been a single offering with the CDs being sold at the outset to investors or a 'renegotiable' CD issue. Investors in this type of CD bought individual three or six month CDs without being committed to re-invest for the remaining term of the original agreement. Unsold CDs were taken up by the securities house(s) that had underwritten the issue.

CD markets are established in many countries in the domestic currency of the country, for example, the USA, (including Yankee CDs issued by foreign banks in New York), Canada, France, the Netherlands, Denmark, Norway, Japan, Hong Kong, Singapore, Japan and Australia). International markets have developed in Paris, Luxembourg and Asian markets, principally in US dollars, but the main market for CD issues in non-domestic currencies is London.

History and development of the London CD Market

The first tap issue of fixed rate bearer US dollar CDs in the London market was made in May 1966. This was the first new money market instrument in London for almost 75 years. A secondary market started in that year. In 1967, the maturity range for US dollar CDs was established at a maximum of five years with the launching of the first tap and tranche issues. The Finance Act of 1968 made provision for the issue of sterling CDs by banks in the UK, for periods from three months to five years, without the deduction of withholding tax. The first issue was made in October of that year. The FRCD market was first opened in 1977 with tap and tranche issues being made with maturities of three years. During the 1980s and 1990s, CDs began to be issued in other currencies where the banking authorities for the currency gave their permission.

The Finance Act 1983 allowed building societies to issue sterling CDs with maturities up to 12 months. In 1987, following the Building Societies Act 1986, building societies were able to issue in any approved currency with maturities up to five years but issues in currencies have to be swapped into sterling. In the main, only building societies with assets of more than £1 billion issue CDs.

Issuing and trading in London CDs conform to and are regulated in accordance with:

- The Bank of England's notice dated 1 November 1996. Previous notices were dated 1986 and 1989.

- The British Bankers' Association's (BBA's) 'London Market Guidelines for CDs' issued in November 1996 which incorporates the minimum standards for 'London Good Delivery'. Earlier BBA booklets on CDs were dated 1984 and 1990.

- The Financial Services Act 1986 (FSA). CDs are included in the generic term 'debenture' in the FSA for the purpose of listing them as investments. Secondary market dealings in CDs (and, in practice, primary market dealings) are regulated by the FSA as 'investment business'. CDs will be regulated by the Financial Services Authority under the proposed Financial Services Act.

- The London Code of Conduct which sets out best practice for trading in CDs, including the requirements relating to 'wholesale counterparties'.

'London Good Delivery' means the security printing and delivery in the primary or secondary markets of CDs which must conform at the time of issue to all the relevant conditions laid down in the BBA guidelines and Bank of England's notice. Good Delivery obliges the depositor or investor to settle the transaction in accordance with current market practice.

Notice issued by the Bank of England, 1 November 1996

The notice covers the topics dealt with in the following paragraphs.

Deposit taking in the UK

Institutions authorised to take deposits in the UK, including the issuance of CDs, are institutions authorised either under the Banking Act 1987 or the Building Societies Act 1986, and European institutions as defined in the regulations implementing the Second Banking Co-ordination Directive.

London CDs

London CDs are issued subject to standard terms and conditions. Homogeneity at the primary issuing stage helps to ensure an orderly CD market. It reduces the scope for investor confusion about the nature of the instruments being traded. London CDs are:

- issued by authorised institutions, as defined above;
- issued and payable in the United Kingdom;
- designed to trade primarily in London.

Characteristics

London CDs are governed by English law and have the following characteristics:

Currency denomination. At July 1998, London CDs are denominated in fourteen currencies: sterling, US$, Canadian, Australian and New Zealand dollars, Yen, SDRs, ECU, Swiss francs, Danish krone, Norwegian and Swedish krona, French francs and Italian lire. An issuer should give advance notice to the Bank if it intends to issue London CDs in any other currency. The approval of the regulatory authorities of the country of the currency may be needed. London CDs will be issued in euros when the European single currency is operative.

Maturity. By market convention, CDs are short term instruments with a maturity of up to five years. Some overseas regulatory authorities may restrict the maximum term of CDs issued in their currency. Issues with an initial maturity of over five years would be subject to withholding tax on interest payments, which effectively precludes such issues. There is now no minimum maturity for London CDs.

Minimum Denomination. London CDs are issued with a minimum denomination of not less than £100,000 or its foreign currency equivalent to ensure that they comply with the definition of a wholesale instrument under the FSA 1986.

Interest basis. London CDs may carry interest at a fixed or variable rate or may be issued at a discount.

Early repayment option

London CDs may incorporate put or call options provided that the following apply:

- The terms of the option are clear to the initial and any subsequent holder of the CD.

- The means by which a holder will be informed if the issuer proposes to exercise a call option or the procedure to be used if the holder wishes to exercise a put option are clear.

- The home supervisory authorities of the issuing institution are content.

Guarantee

London CDs may be issued under a guarantee where the guarantor (as well as the issuer) is itself an institution in the UK authorised itself to issue CDs in the UK, or is a European authorised institution which is eligible to issue guarantees in the UK.

Notification of first issues of London CDs

Any institution contemplating its first issue of London CDs should inform the Bank of England in advance.

CDs purchased by issuers

Institutions may not make a false market in their own CDs, but may purchase them before maturity in particular circumstances where this would assist the maintenance of an orderly market. Prior consultation is required with the Bank where own name paper is purchased as a matter of deliberate policy.

Non-London CDs

The Bank expects authorised institutions that wish to issue CDs intended for trading primarily in London only to issue London CDs. On rare occasions, non-London CDs have been issued by institutions which are not themselves eligible to issue London CDs but which are nevertheless intended primarily for the London market. Non-London CDs must:

- be clearly labelled 'non-London' on the face of the certificate and all related documentation;

- satisfy the BBA's standards for London Good Delivery;

- not infringe the provisions of the Banking Act 1987;

- make clear the location of the issuing branch, where the interest and redemption proceeds will be paid and whether a UK issuing/paying agent is employed.

Statistical reporting

Institutions within the UK banking sector should report all their CD outstandings and all CDs held by them to the Bank. If a reporting institution holds CDs that it has itself issued, these should be excluded from both sides of its balance sheet. Issues of sterling CDs, net of holdings of sterling CDs issued by other UK banking sector institutions, are classified as eligible liabilities.

The London Market

The primary market

Issues of CDs by an institution to a depositor take place in the primary market. Issuers of foreign currency CDs should be aware of any requirements of the relevant home authorities for the currency in question before proceeding with an issue. Issuers considering making issues in currencies that are not already traded in London should give the Bank of England and the BBA advance notice before making an issue. The BBA is informed so that it may determine appropriate denominations.

Banks wishing to issue CDs will approach counterparties direct or through brokers with details of the period and amount they wish to issue. Investors wishing to purchase CDs will ask a bank or building society, direct or through a broker, where they will issue, indicating the period and amount they wish to invest. If the terms are acceptable the trade will be agreed. The denominations to be issued will be agreed. For sterling and euro issues, CMO numbers are exchanged. For currency issues, the investor will advise who will collect the CDs. Investors who do not maintain a CMO account or secure facilities will need to arrange for a settlement agent to take the CDs on their CMO account or collect the CDs against payment. Sterling CDs are dealt before 12:00 noon for same day value. Currency CDs are normally dealt for spot value but US and Canadian dollar CDs can be dealt for next day or same day value.

Fixed rate interest bearing CDs are issued at par with interest accruing on the actual number of days elapsed, based on a 365 day year for sterling and a 360 day year for other currencies, including the euro. On issues of one year or less, interest is paid at maturity. On issues between one year and five years, interest is normally paid annually. Where the period, at the time of issue, is more than one year but not an exact number of years, the stub period typically falls at the end of the life of the CD. On FRCDs, interest is paid monthly, quarterly, or half-yearly or with such frequency as may be specified on the CD. Interim interest payments on fixed rate and FRCDs are annotated on the reverse of CDs when the interim payments are made. If there is a discrepancy in the information on the face and the reverse of the CD, the information on the face takes precedence. Interest and discount rates are increasingly expressed in decimal form. However, sterling CDs are currently still dealt and quoted in fractions up to 1/64th of one per cent.

In the broker/dealer market, detailed information on CDs should not be offered on an unsolicited basis but only against a firm interest. It is assumed that any request in this market for specific details (eg the issuer's name, coupon or maturity date) on prices quoted on a generic basis, indicates a willingness to trade at that price.

CDs must not mature on non-business days. If, between the date of issue and the date of maturity, or the next interest payment date, a particular day is designated a non-business day, interest payments are calculated and paid for value on the next business day common to the appropriate business centres. If the date falls in a new calendar month, however, the revised date will be the immediately preceding business day common to the appropriate centres.

In the primary market, it is normal practice for the buyer to collect currency CDs. Payments for all CD transactions should be settled in a recognised clearing system. A letter of undertaking, confirming the recipient's intention to pay may be requested by the seller's agent, prior to release of the CDs to the buyer's agent.

Figure 16.1   Collection letter following issue of primary CDs

To NewBank plc	From Theta Bank plc
	Date: 18.01.99
	Value date: 20.01.99

Please release to our messenger the under-mentioned financial instruments:

Instrument type: CD   Currency: US$ Face value: US$50,000,000
Rate: 5.25%   Issue date: 22.01.99   Maturity date: 20.02.99

In consideration of your so releasing the above mentioned financial instrument we hereby undertake to pay:

Value: 22.01.99   Consideration amount: US$ 50,000,000
Payment to/for account of Gensoc New York, account NewBank plc London

Authorised signature

The secondary market

A CD is distinguished from a fixed term deposit with a bank by its negotiability in the secondary market. The secondary market consists of market makers (banks, investment houses and brokers) who regularly quote buying and selling yields and prices for CDs to investors. This market provides the holders of CDs with liquidity prior to the maturity date and enables them to have a wide choice of issuer names and maturities. It is normal practice for sellers to deliver currency CDs for secondary market transactions.

First Chicago Clearing Centre (FCCC) and First National Bank of Boston in London operate clearing centres and custody services for CDs and other short and medium term instruments. FCCC is the Issuing and Paying Agent (IPA) for about half of CD issues in London and is the agent for clearing of most CDs traded in the secondary market.

Format of CDs in the London Market

At the time of issue, all CDs must include the following:

- the full name and address of the issuing institution, and where applicable, the paying agents office where the CD must be presented for payment;
- the date of issue;

- the maturity date;
- the amount deposited, or, in the case of a discount CD, the amount payable at maturity;
- that the instrument is a CD;
- for interest bearing CDs, the rate of interest and frequency of interest payments for CDs with an original maturity of over one year;
- for FRCDs, the formula for calculating the rate of interest and the source of the rate fixing.

FRCD rate fixings are usually derived from screen based data provided by recognised information vendors. Less typically, they may be fixed from the average of the quotations of a number of reference banks. The rates are normally set using 11:00 am Libor rates for same day value in the case of sterling CDs and two business days prior to the start of the next interest period for foreign currency CDs.

CDs should carry no further clausing or qualifications, for example, events of default, as might be carried on other types of issues. CDs may be issued in one of four formats:

- in dematerialised form;
- in definitive form, including standard definitive and open standard definitive formats;
- in global form;
- in plain paper form.

Dematerialisation

Since September 1994, London CDs in sterling have been eligible to be lodged and transferred within the Central Moneymarket Office (CMO) in dematerialised form. The vast majority of sterling CD lodgements are now dematerialised. CMO members will have executed the CMO Deed of Covenant. By this means, they have accepted that rights conferred in respect of the issue and transfer of dematerialsied CDs by computerised book entry equate to those conferred by the Bills of Exchange Act 1882 in respect of the issue and transfer of physical instruments.

CMO cannot accommodate interim interest payments and so cannot handle CDs with maturities of over one year but such issues are rare.

CDs issued in euro in London will also be in dematerialised form and lodged at the CMO.

If a transfer were to entail CDs leaving the CMO, they must be exchanged, within the CMO's controlled environment, for definitive, security printed instruments provided by the CMO member who originally lodged the CDs.

Definitive CDs

Definitive CDs are security printed by an established security printer to the prescribed minimum London Good Delivery Standards. The only items to be added on issue are the issue and the maturity dates, interest rate and two authorised signatures. A specimen standard definitive CD is shown in Figure 16.2.

Standard definitive CDs leave certain features to be printed by an issuing and paying agent (IPA) or by an issuer. Such CDs are produced in two stages:

- The security printer produces blanks incorporating a number of security features, which are then delivered to the IPA.

- The IPA or issuer prints the rest of the CD immediately before use adding the issuer's name, the issue and maturity dates, the rate of interest where applicable, facsimile signatures and denomination numbers.

IPAs must obtain the approval of the BBA before producing CDs in this manner. The growth of the use of IPAs is due to the streamlining of settlements functions. The outsourcing of the back office functions of holding and issuing paper is more cost effective than for individual banks to complete these procedures in-house. Definitive and Standard Definitive CDs above prescribed minimum amounts are pre-printed with the denomination and currency.

Open standard definitive CDs are not preprinted with one of the prescribed denominations and may be held for issues of small denominations of between £100,000 and £250,000 or the currency denomination specified by the BBA. The words 'less than', followed by the currency and maximum amount appropriate to the currency must be printed on the face of the CD, eg 'less than US $250,000'.

Global CDs

Where primary and secondary market settlement of CDs takes place through the Euroclear system or Cedel Bank, CDs may be issued in global form. A global CD is a single, non-security printed document and, as such, is not required to conform to the requirements of the London Good Delivery Standards. A global CD represents a single issue of CDs which together are fungible and are issued with the same issue date and maturity dates and the same interest rate, interest amount and interest payment date or dates. At issue, a global CD is deposited with a common depository for the Euroclear system or Cedel Bank. All primary and secondary movements of respective interests in global CDs take place within these clearing systems. In order to issue global CDs, the issuer must:

- Meet the eligibility criteria of the Euroclear system or Cedel Bank.

- Enter into a Deed of Covenant. In so doing, the issuer states that the records of Euroclear or Cedel Bank are prima facie evidence of beneficial ownership.

- Ensure that a sufficient stock of definitive CDs is available to enable global CDs to be exchanged at any time for definitive CDs. If an issue is exchanged, the entire issue represented by the global CD must be so exchanged.

Plain paper CDs

Depositories and clearing systems may hold and transfer plain paper CDs in any currency subject to definitive certificates being issued if the CDs leave these systems. Plain paper CDs must carry a suitable form of protective wording rendering them invalid outside the depository or clearing system in which they are held, such as 'THIS CERTIFICATE IS VALID ONLY WHEN STAMPED BY (THE DEPOSITORY) WITH AN IDENTIFIER NUMBER'. A Deed of Covenant needs to be executed by the issuer of dematerialised and plain paper CDs in favour of subsequent holders. In practice, plain paper CDs are rarely used because the other formats are used efficiently.

Security

The bearer nature of many CDs renders them particularly prone to risks of forgery and fraud which was one of the reasons for the creation of the CMO in 1990. All movements of CDs should be closely monitored

Figure 16.2   Specimen Fixed Rate US$ 500,000 Definitive Certificate of Deposit

Front

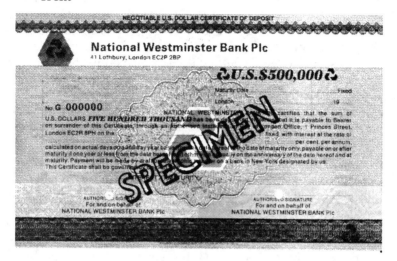

Back

and supporting documentation and systems should have built-in controls. CDs should be held only by banks or other financial institutions which have both well-controlled security arrangements required to protect holders of CDs against such dangers as fraud, forgery and theft. Printing of CDs must adhere to the minimum London Good Delivery Standards. Issuing institutions, or their appointed agents, must be prepared to verify any of their own issues of CDs during normal banking hours. In particular, they should be prepared to verify the authenticity of discount CDs with an original maturity of over one year. The form of verification should be placed on the certificate itself (front or back) and read: 'This document, as presented, if due today, would be paid today.' This will be dated and signed by two authorised signatories on behalf of the issuing institution.

Each CD should have a unique serial number and two character serial designators. Blank, completed and cancelled CDs should be handled only by authorised members of staff in secure areas and kept in a secure vault. Full records should be kept of all CDs, whether delivered, cancelled or held in incomplete form. A CD which has matured, or which has in some way been spoiled prior to issue, for example through being torn or because a mistake has been made, must be cancelled in the following way:

- the face of the CD must be clearly marked 'cancelled' in indelible ink;
- the top right hand quarter of the CD must be punched with a hole not less than five millimetres in diameter.

Minimum London Good Delivery Standards

The London Good Delivery Standards for definitive CDs cover the type of paper used, the printing process, issue procedures and approved currency denominations. All definitive CDs must be printed by an established high security printer.

The paper should be solvent sensitive, with watermarks, non-fluorescent and of a standard size, eight inches wide by five inches deep. Printing must incorporate pastel litho colours, solvent or aqueous sensitive inks, rainbowed litho and fine line duplex printing, a latent image and a high security engraved intaglio border. Features that will change when the CD is photocopied or scanned and which are only visible through a red filter must be included.

On issue, additional information added by IPAs must be at least as resistant to alteration as that produced by an established security printer. When certificates are completed manually, they must be handwritten in indelible ink or typed using an indelible ribbon. Spaces are lined out or filled with symbols (not numbers). Correctible ribbons should not be used. At the time of delivery, CDs must be signed by two authorised signatures in indelible ink. Where an agent issues the CD, these may be signatures of the agent and the issuer's signatures may be in facsimile.

Recommended checking procedures include checking the paper for watermarks and latent images and using a red filter and ultra-violet light to check otherwise invisible and fluorescent features. CDs should be checked that they have been completed correctly and that there are no alterations.

Issues of CDs for large trades will be made up of a series of pre-printed CDs and where necessary open CDs for minimum amounts of £100,000 and multiples of £10,000, or the nearest currency equivalents. CDs for sterling, US dollar or euro 5 million may not be readily negotiable in the secondary market. Issuers must split CDs when requested to do so. Requests for splitting must be made by 12:00 noon for sterling CDs and earlier deadlines may apply to other currencies. Approved denominations are given in Figure 16.3, including those for the euro.

Figure 16.3   BBA approved currency denominations for London CDs

'000s units of currency	£, $, euro	Yen	C$, A$, NZ$, SFr, SDR, Ecu	NKr, DKr, SKr
Open CDs less than Pre-printed	250 250 500 1,000 5,000	25,000 25,000 50,000 100,000 250,000 500,000	250 250 500 1,000	1,000 1,000 5,000 10,000

Source: British Bankers Association. Some of the smaller currency denominations will not be possible where currency fluctuations take their value below £100,000. French francs and Italian lire are omitted because CDs in euro will replace these currencies.

Funding considerations for banks

CDs are a useful source of short term funds for banks at rates close to or slightly below money market rates. As an issuer, a bank may build up substantial amount of issued CDs as part of its funding strategy. However, the issuing bank seeking to obtain funds for its lending operations can rely on successfully accessing the CD market only so long as the market remains in existence and there remains investor demand for the issuing bank's paper. If, for instance, other rated debt issued by the bank is significantly down-graded by the rating agencies, investor demand could be reduced or evaporate.

CDs should ideally be used for short term funding purposes but at volumes that do not make it vulnerable to downturns in confidence in the investment community. Even in a stable market, an issuer must guard against over issuing paper, particularly in clusters around particular maturity dates. Once an institution's paper begins to stick for a particular maturity, it can affect the marketability of all but the shortest maturities and can also impact on both the price and ability to make further issues.

On the asset side of a bank's balance sheet, investments or trading portfolios of other banks' CDs may be held. In normal market conditions, CDs issued by top quality banks will be liquefiable in the secondary market. All the same, a portfolio of short term CDs held for liquidity purposes should be well diversified by issuer name and maturity. In a doomsday scenario, it is questionable whether any leading bank's obligations will find favour with investors. In such circumstances, it is doubtful if even the very best names could be sustained as an alternative to government securities. CDs would then be illiquid until their maturity date. A liquidity portfolio of CDs should also be planned to yield a steady cash flow from natural maturities as well as being available for sale. It is also important that banks include CD purchases when considering their overall credit exposure to bank counterparties. Holding of CDs will utilise available limits.

Calculations

In the primary market, interest bearing CDs have interest calculated on the same basis as money market deposits. Discount CDs are quoted on a discount to yield basis in the same way as commercial paper for which calculation is explained in Chapter 17. In the secondary market, CDs are traded at a premium or at a discount, which is determined by current market rates.

Sale of a CD with an original maturity of up to one year

CD rates quoted in the Financial Times are for secondary market transactions. A £1,000,000 CD, issued with an original maturity of 91 days at 7.25%, is sold after 40 days when the secondary market dealer was quoting 7.00% - 7.125%. The right hand side of the quotation, 7.125%, is used because that is the rate the seller has to pay for the funds for the remaining period. There are two ways of calculating the sale proceeds.

(a) The seller will receive the maturity proceeds of the CD, discounted to present day value:

$$\text{Maturity amount} = £1,000,000 \times \frac{7.25 \times 91}{100 \times 365} = £1,018,075.34$$

Discounted to NPV:

$$£1,018,075.34 \times \frac{1}{1 + (7.125 \times 51/36500)} = £1,008,039.82$$

(b) The formula for the calculation is:

$$\text{Proceeds} = \text{Face amount} \times \frac{(\text{rate at time of issue} \times \text{tenor in days}) + 36500 \text{ or } 36000}{(\text{quoted yield on sale} \times \text{days to run}) + 36500 \text{ or } 36000}$$

Using the above example:

$$\text{Proceeds} = £1,000,000 \times \frac{(7.25 \times 91) + 36500}{(7.125 \times 51) + 36500} = \frac{37,159.75}{36,863.375} = £1,008,039.82$$

Yield calculation

The investor received £8,039.82 for holding the CD for 40 days. In yield terms, this is:

$$\text{Yield} = \frac{\text{Income earned} \times 36500 \text{ or } 36000}{\text{Face amount} \times \text{days investment held}}$$

$$\text{Yield} = \frac{£8,039.82 \times 36500}{£1,000,000 \times 40} = 7.3363 \%$$

Expressed another way:

$$\text{Yield} = \frac{\text{Income received}}{\text{Face amount} \times \frac{\text{days held}}{365}} = \frac{8,039.82}{£1,000,000 \times \frac{40}{365}} = 7.3363\%$$

Fixed rate CDs with an original maturity of over one year

For this type of CD, the sale proceeds are calculated by the repeated discounting of the proceeds at maturity and the successive annual interest payments. For example, a CD for $5,000,000 is issued for five years at 6.52% and sold after two years and 40 days at 6.38%. The annual payments still to be made before maturity are:

Year 3	$ 330,527.78	interest only
Year 4 (leap year)	$ 331,433.33	
Year 5	$ 5,330,527.78	includes repayment of interest

Starting at the final maturity, discount the sum payable at 6.38%:

$$\$5,330,527.78 \times \frac{1}{1 + (6.38 \times 365/36000)} = \$5,006,666.03$$

Discount $5,006,666.03 plus $ 331,433.34 interest, total $5,338,099.37 to be discounted for the fourth year (366 days) at 6.38%:

$$\$5,338,099.37 \times \frac{1}{1 + (6.38 \times 366/36000)} = \$5.012,943.17$$

Discount $5.012,943.17 plus $330,527.78 interest, total $5,343,470.95 to be discounted for the remainder of the third year (325 days) at 6.38%:

$$\$5,343,470.95 \times \frac{1}{1 + (6.38 \times 325/36000)} = 5,052,463.11$$
Net proceeds

Floating rate CDs

FRCDs are traded on the basis of price (rather than yield), by reference to a par price of 100, plus accrued interest for the actual days elapsed to the settlement date.

$$\text{Proceeds} = \frac{\text{Principal} \times \text{Dealing Price}}{100} + \frac{\text{Principal} \times \text{Interest rate of CD} \times \text{No of days since last interest period}}{36500 \text{ or } 36000}$$

For example, an FRCD for $ 10,000,000 with a current rate of 6% is traded at 100.14 for settlement 150 days after the last interest payment date of a 180 day interest period. Proceeds are as follows:

$$\frac{\$10,000,000 \times 100.14}{100} \quad = \quad \$10,014,000.00$$

$$+ \quad \frac{\$10,000,000 \times 150 \times 6.00}{36000} \quad = \quad \underline{\$\quad250,000.00}$$

$$\text{Proceeds} \quad = \quad \$10,264,000.00$$

Yield to the seller: $\dfrac{\$264,000.00 \times 36000}{\$10,000,000 \times 150} \quad = \quad 6.3360\%$

17 Commercial paper

Commercial paper (CP) is a type of short term unsecured promissory note issued in bearer form under programmes, mainly by corporates, but also by financial institutions and sovereign borrowers. CP has become a highly flexible addition to the choice of short term instruments available to borrowers and professional investors.

The benefits of CP to issuers are lower funding costs and the diversification of funding sources. However, if an issuer is to obtain the best terms of issue, it needs to access the market on an on-going basis in order to keep its name before investors. The cost of issues will be compared to the costs of raising funds from other sources of finance such as acceptances.

For investing institutions, better returns can be obtained than from other short term investments with the return reflecting the credit rating of the CP programme. CP is a form of disintermediation whereby funds are raised directly from investors rather than banks. The investors are financial institutions, banks, investment companies and other companies. The London CP market is restricted to professional investors.

Origins and the USCP market

Commercial paper originated in the US early in the twentieth century as a means for corporations, who were unable to borrow on competitive terms from local banks, to tap non-bank sources of funds. Banks are also issuers of CP in the US. At the end of 1997, there was around $940,000 million of USCP outstanding. Features of USCP are:

- Maturities of paper are permitted from 1 to 270 days. The maximum maturity, along with the requirement that CP is to be used for working capital purposes, is necessary to avoid the need for registration with the Securities and Exchange

Commission (SEC). Most issues have an original maturity of 30 days or less.

- A credit rating and a CP backup line from a bank or banks are essential requirements.

- Major issuers such as General Motors Acceptance Corporation issue directly rather than using dealers to distribute their paper.

- Settlement is almost always for same day value but some issuers will look to issue value spot in order to link issuance with foreign exchange swaps or to make comparisons with eurocommercial paper.

- Issuers may arrange issue and payment through the Depository Trust Company in New York.

Euronotes and ECP

Euronotes were the first form of eurocommercial paper (ECP), with a market starting in London in the late 1970s. Euronotes, mainly in US dollars, were distributed using a structured timetable. Banks were asked to bid for paper, indicating what margin they would buy paper at above a specified fixing, ie Libor. There would be an 11:00 am rate fixing on the bids that were accepted.

The cumbersome method of distribution of euronotes left much of the paper in the hands of banks. It was replaced in the early eighties by the US system of dealers who place euro-commercial paper with investors. The interest rate payable on ECP is governed by the issuer's credit rating in relation to a bench mark rate, eg Libor or Libid. At the end of 1996, more than $170,000 million ECP was outstanding.

Sterling commercial paper (SCP)

The issue of SCP was first permitted in May 1987 under the Bank of England's notice dated 27 April 1987. Further notices were issued in 1989 and 1990 widening the range of potential issuers and lowering the minimum issue amount. In its latest notice dated 18 March 1997, the Bank revised the range of issuers and the conditions for the issue of CP in the London market. SCP and ECP are now usually documented under a single programme. At the end of 1997, there was around £8,000 million SCP outstanding.

Other CP markets

CP has been introduced into many other countries where appropriate facilitating legislation has been passed. The issue of CP in any currency is subject to the regulations of the central bank of the country of the currency and these are varied and frequently restrictive. Whilst London is the centre of the ECP market, all issues are subject to the national regulations for the currency.

Commercial paper in the London Market

The remainder of this chapter relates to the market in London for ECP and SCP (together, CP). The latest notice from the Bank of England covers: who can issue CP; the conditions for issuing CP; and UK taxation matters. Under the Banking Act 1987, only banks (authorised institutions) can take deposits and, in the absence of specific guidance to the contrary, the issue of CP could be construed as taking deposits. The Bank of England's notice sets the arrangements under which commercial paper can be issued as exempt transactions.

The Bank's notice covers sterling and other currency denominated CP that is issued and payable in the UK. If other currency denominated CP is issued or payable in its country of origin, it will be subject to the national regulations of that country.

Qualifying issuers

The following institutions and companies are authorised to issue CP:

- Banks authorised under the Banking Act 1987 and European Economic Area authorised institutions making use of the 'passport' provisions of the Second Banking Co-ordination Directive. In practice banks normally issue certificates of deposit rather than CP.
- Entities exempt under Schedule 2 of the Banking Act 1987, these being principally central banks, building societies, insurance companies, local authorities and supra-national financial organisations. Building Societies are allowed to issue CP in currency provided that they swap the currency proceeds immediately into sterling.
- Companies incorporated in the UK or overseas that have net assets of at least £25 million and have shares or debt securities listed on the London Stock Exchange (LSE).

- Companies which have shares or debt securities listed on an EEA exchange and have provided to the LSE the listing particulars or prospectus relating to those shares or debt securities. This is more restrictive than before when the issuer could be listed on any recognised exchange, including exchanges outside the EEA.

- Overseas governments and overseas public authorities whose debt securities are traded or listed on the LSE, an EEA exchange or other approved stock exchange.

- Issuers whose commercial paper is guaranteed by any of the above qualifying issuers of CP.

Conditions for issuing CP

Form

CP may be issued in bearer or registered form. In practice it is usually in bearer form. It may be issued in global or definitive form (ie security printed physical securities). Where in global form, it must be made clear to the first and subsequent purchaser whether definitives will be made available, and if so, within what period of time. This must be stated in any documents relating to the issue. Definitive notes may only be available if there were an event of default.

Description

Any physical document of title must give the name of the issuer and any guarantor and carry a statement that it is commercial paper issued under an exemption from the Banking Act 1987 in respect of the taking of deposits. Where the issues embrace unusual features, these should be reflected in the title of the security.

Maturity

CP must be redeemed before the first anniversary of the date of issue but there is now no minimum maturity. Issues may be 1 - 364 days.

Currency denominations

Issues of CP in the UK are permitted in any currency (but subject to national regulations for the currency).

Minimum redemption amount

CP must be issued and transferable thereafter in minimum amounts of £100,000 or its currency equivalent. The minimum deal size is unlikely to be less than £1,000,000 and the average deal size is over £5,000,000.

Put and call options

Issues of CP may carry put or call options exercisable at any time during their life.

Repurchase of paper by issuers before maturity

This should not be done in a manner that creates a misleading impression about the market in the paper.

Monitoring

Issuers must advise the Bank at the commencement and at any extension of any CP programme where deposits are accepted in the UK, giving details of:

- the maximum amount they propose to issue;
- maturity;
- currency denominations;
- guarantor details;
- the issuer's qualification to issue;
- the intended use of funds.

Issues and redemptions of SCP must be reported to the Bank of England within one week of the end of each calendar month.

Investment regulation affecting CP

Managing, advising and dealing in CP constitutes investment business under the Financial Services Act 1986 (FSA). Intermediaries should be authorised under the FSA; exempted by virtue of Section 43 of the FSAct; or be investment firms carrying on business in the UK under an Investment Services Directive Passport. The market is restricted to professional or wholesale counterparties and the selling restrictions will be outlined in the information memorandum.

Interest and tax

CP is usually issued at a discount. Interest bearing CP will have interest paid at maturity without deduction of tax. Discount or interest paid is allowable against tax and interest received is taxable.

Arranging a CP programme

Factors issuers should consider when arranging a programme are:

- *The size of the programme.* Programme sizes range from $100 million to $ 10 billion. Since CP is uncommitted, programme ceilings should be set at levels that give the issuer flexibility for working capital and acquisition purposes. Otherwise, there should be a mechanism for increasing the programme by a straightforward side letter, from the issuer to the dealers, with the delivery of conditions precedent.

- *Currencies.* With deregulation by many central banks to allow the use of their currencies for ECP issuance, new investor sectors are available and greater flexibility can be built into programmes. The market offering the best advantage at the time can be accessed and the proceeds swapped to obtain the desired currency.

- *Denomination of the Notes.* There are no set denominations but issuers may specify the denominations to be issued of, say, £500,000 and £1,000,000, US$500,000 and US$1,000,000 and the nearest equivalent for other currencies. Global notes will represent a specified number of notes in these denominations.

- *Issuing entity.* The choice is complicated by legal, tax and regulatory requirements.

- *Choice of arranger, dealers and issuing and paying agent (IPA).*

- *Credit rating and back up lines, documentation, and costs.*

Role of the programme arranger

It is possible for a borrower to set up its own programme or make changes to a programme itself, but in practice most borrowers choose to work with a major CP dealer. This is in order to ensure co-ordination of all parties involved and to receive advice on market practice for matters such as regulations, dealing practice and publicity. Arrangers are accountable for the timetable and expenses for setting up the programme.

Technically, the role of the arranger ceases once a programme is signed. Although programmes are open-ended, they may need to be updated or amended after a number of years and the information memorandum should be updated annually. The original arranger is well placed to undertake these functions.

Role of and selection of dealers

The dealer handles the distribution of the paper on behalf of the issuer. For small programmes, a single dealer may suffice but this is not recommended, since issuers will benefit from obtaining competitive quotes. There may be up to four or five dealers for larger programmes. Criteria for the selection of dealers are: their performance and service including placement, pricing, foreign exchange execution and market commentary; their market position; their credit rating, because the dealer may become a swap counterparty; their related product delivery and the importance of existing relationships.

CP dealers always act as principals. This is so whether they are persuading issuers to issue in order to fill orders from investors or buying paper unconditionally from the issuer. This may be done with the objective of selling it to end-investors when the opportunity arises, but funding it in the meantime.

Credit rating

The use of credit ratings is a prerequisite in almost all CP markets. The real use of ratings began in the USCP market following the failure in 1970 of Penn Central with $82 million of CP outstanding. At that time, investors relied on name recognition as the principal criterion for issuer selection. Now, even though buyers of CP must make their own credit assessment, much reliance is placed on the independent commercial rating agencies to establish the creditworthiness of borrowers. Although the SCP market started without the need for borrowers to be rated, this is not the case now.

The prevalence of a rating system has enabled an easy price-tiering to be effected in the market, with prices being set in relation to Libor or Libid. Credit enhancement is possible through guarantees or letters of credit from highly rated parent companies or banks to enable an issuer to obtain the finest CP rates. Committed undrawn back-up lines from banks are a prerequisite to obtaining a rating. These lines provide last-line-of-defence assurance that issuers will be able to repay maturing CP even if market liquidity is tight at the time. The two major agencies are Standard and Poor's and Moody's. Their short-term rating definitions are:

Standard & Poor's	Moody's	
A1(+)	P1	Strong/superior ability for timely repayment
A2	P2	Satisfactory/strong capacity for timely repayment
A3	P3	Adequate/acceptable capacity for timely repayment
B/C/D	Not prime	Speculative/Doubtful/in default

Further details on the activities of rating agencies are contained in chapter 18.

Documentation

The *Information Memorandum* for circulation to potential investors will include:

- disclaimers on credit risks;
- summary of terms and conditions of issuance;
- financial information on the issuer and any guarantor;
- selling restrictions;
- specimen note/global note;
- a list of programme participants.

The *Dealer agreement* will include:

- details of the programme and the issue of notes;
- representations and warranties, covenants and agreements and conditions precedent by the issuer;
- obligations of the dealers;
- termination rights and conditions;
- appointment of additional dealers;
- law, communications, amendments and counterparts.

The *Issuing and Paying Agency Agreement* will set out the duties and responsibilities of the IPA selected for the issue.

Global notes evidence a tranche of paper and do not need to be security printed. A deed of covenant is necessary when global notes are issued. Definitive notes must conform to 'London Good Delivery' standards, which are outlined in chapter 16.

Costs

The costs of setting up a programme will include legal, documentation, publicity, printing, arrangement fees for back-up lines and initial rating agency costs. For accounting purposes, these can be spread over the life of the programme. How significant they are will depend on the average outstandings. Ongoing expenses will include annual commitment fees on back-up lines, IPA costs for custody, issuance, and payment and annual charges of the rating agencies. The latter can be in excess of $20,000 annually.

Issuing CP, role of the IPA and settling CP transactions

Issuing CP

On an on-going basis dealers will discuss with the issuer what demand there is for paper, providing advice on the most attractive amounts and maturities to offer. If the issuer finds the advice acceptable he will invite the dealer to bid for the paper, but the dealer is under no obligation to buy.

The issuer may seek competitive quotes, asking dealers to bid for a tranche of notes he plans to issue and accepting the lowest yield. Dealers may be prepared to buy paper and warehouse it until investors can be found.

Currency CP is usually dealt for spot value, as is sterling where deals are to be cleared through Euroclear or Cedel or the deal is linked to a foreign exchange swap. Otherwise, sterling issues are likely to be for same day value.

Role of the issuing and paying agent (IPA)

Once the issuer has agreed with the dealer that CP will be issued, he instructs the issuing agent to prepare the appropriate global note or definitive notes. Where global notes are issued, they will be deposited with a common depository acting for the Euroclear and Cedel systems.

Definitive notes must be authenticated by the appropriate number of authorised signatories. The issuing agent makes the notes available for collection by the buyer against an undertaking to make payment. If the note is in sterling, payment will be through the CHAPS system. The Central Money Market Office has not been used for lodging SCP for practical and legal reasons. A working party is seeking to make lodgement at the CMO acceptable from 1999.

On maturity of the CP, the issuer pays the maturity value to the paying agent and this is released to investors, through Euroclear or Cedel where the clearing houses are used. For definitive notes, the holder presents the notes to the paying agent who checks their validity. If acceptable, the holder is paid the maturity value and the notes are cancelled. Cancelled notes are then either returned to the issuer or destroyed.

There is no real secondary market in CP in London and dealers prefer to find end investors who will hold the notes to maturity. However, dealers may be prepared to buy back paper before maturity in order to provide investors with liquidity.

Yield and Arbitrage Calculations

Commercial paper is quoted on a 'discount to yield' basis. The rate quoted is a yield.

The calculation for discounting sterling commercial paper is as follows:

$$\frac{\text{Nominal amount}}{1 + \frac{(\text{Days x Yield})}{36500 \text{ or } 36000}} = \text{Purchase consideration}$$

If SCP with a face value of £5,000,000 and 90 days to run is sold to yield 7.23%, the purchase consideration is:

$$\frac{£5,000,000}{1 + \frac{(90 \times 7.23)}{36500}} = £4,912,424.26$$

Foreign exchange swaps are used in conjunction with CP issues. Issuers can raise CP in one currency and swap the proceeds into a desired currency. Investors can swap the currency they have to invest and purchase CP denominated in another currency to obtain a higher return. An example of CP arbitrage follows.

A fund manager has about euro 9,000,00 to invest for 14 days and is looking for a better return than the euro bid of 4.98%. He can invest in US dollar ECP yielding 5.25%. Spot is euro1.000 = $1.1000, forward points are par - .0001 discount. The CP dealer will use the rates to calculate whether it is worthwhile for the investor to swap into US dollar ECP. This involves the fund manager selling and buying euro (buying and selling dollars, right hand side of the forward rate), but making the calculations as follows:

(a) Discount the CP as follows:

$$1 + \frac{\$10,000,000}{\left(\dfrac{5.25 \times 14}{100 \times 360}\right)} = \$9,979,624.93$$

(b) Calculate amount of euro to be invested
$9,979,624.93/1.1 = $ euro 9,072,386.30.

(c) Calculate forward rate (1.1001) and forward euro amount
($10,000,000/1.1001 = euro 9,090,082.72).

(d) Calculate return in euro and yield
$$= \frac{\text{euro } 17,696.42 \times 36000}{\text{euro } 9,072,386.30 \times 14} = 5.0158\,\%$$

Expressed in tabular form:

	Euro		US dollars
Today	Invest 9,072,386.30 →	Buy dollars at 1.1000 →	Purchase CP 9,979,624.93 ↓ Add discount 20,375.07 ↓
At maturity	Receive 9,090,082.72	← Sell for euro at 1.1001	Receive 10,000,000.00

Although a marginally better return is achieved, it may not be considered enough to make the swap worthwhile. Another consideration of the investor is that the forward exchange contract is a commitment, which reduces the flexibility that would normally be available from purchasing commercial paper.

PART FOUR

Debt Capital Markets

18 Eurobonds and international capital debt markets

A bond is a debt instrument issued in bearer or registered form. It constitutes a commitment by the issuer:

- to pay a specified sum or sums of money to the holder at a predetermined date or dates;
- to pay interest to the holder at stated intervals either at a fixed rate agreed at the outset or on a floating rate basis often at a margin over a given benchmark, ie Libor or an agreed index, eg the FTSE index or gold.

The international debt markets are often thought of in terms of eurobonds only. Whilst the eurobond sector is the most visible, it is only one of the methods of capital finance and only one of the options for investors and there are many active domestic markets. Banks regularly access these markets to raise capital and are also active in them as lead managers, advisers, traders, market makers and investors.

Domestic debt issues

A domestic debt issue is one that an issuer raises within its own country and is denominated in its own country's currency. For example, an American company raising US dollars in New York is a totally domestic issue. Domestic issues invariably have a greater attraction to investors resident in the country of issue than investors from elsewhere since most domestic securities are subject to withholding tax. Foreign investors may not be willing or able to take advantage of double taxation agreements which may exist between their own and the issuer's country, for example, because of the delay in reimbursement of the amount withheld. Domestic issues, therefore, are usually placed mainly with investors of the issuer's country.

The largest and most developed domestic market is in the United States. It is expected that the European bond markets will expand considerably following EMU and in time may equal the US markets in terms of size, trading volume, liquidity and innovation. Investors will have a far bigger domestic market, whereas before they were likely to be restricted to their own national market. A shift is taking place in these markets from government to corporate issues, which mirrors the US markets.

Domestic issues are sometimes in registered (as opposed to bearer) form and regulations may require them to be issued without any premium or discount to the face value of the bond. A feature of some markets is the requirement by the central bank for issuers to submit to a queue procedure. This is to prevent an oversupply of issues at any one time with the monetary authorities establishing an orderly market through a calendar for new issues. The Bank of England's approach is less formal but the Bank must be pre-advised of new issues in sterling.

Foreign bonds

A foreign bond is one issued by a borrower on a foreign capital market with the securities denominated in the currency of that market, usually in registered form.

Examples are:

- Yankee bonds. A UK company raising US dollar debt in the USA is a foreign debt issue and is known as a Yankee bond. This is a deep and liquid market. Issuers have to comply with the requirements of the Securities and Exchange Commission (SEC).

- Samurai bonds. Issues in the yen public markets by foreign borrowers in Tokyo.

Brady bonds are bonds that were introduced following the proposal of US Treasury Secretary Nicholas Brady in 1989. They are a form of refinancing for countries' sovereign or bank debt. When a nation is unable to maintain its current payment schedule, it may make an exchange into Brady bonds. These are usually guaranteed by US Treasury zero coupon bonds which the nation purchases to back the bonds that are in default. The benefit to investors is that there is an active secondary market in these bonds whereas the previous holdings were illiquid. Originally used principally by Latin American countries, many Brady bonds are now being repaid as these countries' financial positions have improved.

Eurobonds

Eurobonds are fully negotiable, mostly interest bearing, unsecured securities. The definition of a eurobond given in an EU Directive is that it is a transferable security which:

- is to be underwritten and distributed by a syndicate at least two of the members of which have their registered offices in different States;
- is offered on a significant scale in one or more States other than that of the issuer's registered office;
- may be subscribed for or initially acquired only through a credit or financial institution.

The bonds are placed with investors internationally and this may exclude nationals resident in the country of the currency of issue. Interest is paid without deduction of tax. If withholding tax were applied to payment in a particular currency, it would effectively terminate any meaningful activity in bonds in that currency. This was recognised by the EU, which has given the following reason for exempting eurobonds from withholding tax:

> 'Interest on eurobonds is not subject to withholding tax in most Member States. If it were, the effect would be either that major European companies would be placed at a disadvantage compared to their US and Japanese competitors or that Community issuers would set up subsidiaries in third countries to float their bonds and thereby escape tax. Community investors would be likely to follow them. In both cases, harm would be done to Europe as a major financial centre.'

However, at the time of writing, the EU has proposed to apply withholding tax on EU Community issues, in any currency, held by individuals within the Community. Issuers usually agree to gross up payments of interest in the event of withholding tax being imposed.

They will include a call option to allow for repayment of the bond in these circumstances.

Eurobonds normally raise a single amount of funds on issue for the issuer. They may be issued at a discount or at a premium to the par value. They can be issued in the most favourable market at the time of issue with the proceeds of the issue being swapped to provide the issuer with his desired currency and interest basis. Originally the bonds were physical certificates (definitives) issued in bearer form with no register of holders and with ownership passing on delivery to the purchaser. Now global notes only are likely to be issued with individual holder's interests being recorded by the clearing houses. Because eurobonds tap an international investor base, larger and more frequent issues are possible than in domestic markets.

There are strict prohibitions on the sale of eurobonds in the primary market to US citizens until a 40-day lock-up period from the date of issue of the bonds has elapsed. If bonds are to be sold to US residents earlier than this, the issue will need to be registered with the SEC. One reason issuers choose the euromarket route is to avoid such registration with the SEC which is time consuming and onerous. The sale of eurobonds to UK investors is restricted, under the Financial Services Act 1986 and the Public Offers of Securities Regulations 1995, to professional investors such as banks and financial institutions. Similar restrictions restricting sale of eurobonds in the primary market to professional investors are found in other countries. Eurobonds are listed on one or more stock exchanges. However very few bonds are ever traded on them, being traded instead on over-the-counter markets.

Eurobonds and foreign bonds are known collectively as international bonds. Issues denominated in sterling, whether from a UK issuer or foreign issuer in the UK, which are marketed in bearer form to investors in the UK and elsewhere are now arranged and distributed as eurobonds.

Global bonds

A global bond (not to be confused with a global note) is an international issue placed at the same time in the eurobond and one or more domestic markets with securities fungible between the markets. The process of offering bonds simultaneously in the USA, Europe and the Far East allows issuers to place the paper at the best possible price. Global bonds usually combine the features of US foreign bonds and eurobonds. The issuer has to register its intended offering with the SEC in New York. The benefit to issuers is that a single world price is established for these bonds whereas yield differentials may be seen if separate issues are made in the separate markets.

Private placements

The time and expense involved in making public issues may sometimes be avoided by using private placements. These are issues to single investors or groups of investors rather than in the open market. They permit issuers and investors to match specific interests in terms of currency, maturity, covenants and any special features. Because of their specific nature and legal restrictions on trading, privately placed securities tend to be held by the original investor until maturity and can be highly structured deals.

In the United States, Rule 144a of the US securities regulations allows the issue of securities to qualified institutional buyers without the issue documentation needing to be registered with the SEC. Such issues can only be placed privately with, and traded by, large investing institutions. Yankee bonds may be issued under Rule 144a. Illiquidity may lead to slightly higher pricing than would otherwise be available for public issues.

The eurobond market

History of the eurobond market

The first eurobond was issued in 1963 by the Italian motorway construction company, Autostrade and the lead manager was SG Warburg. The issue was for $15 million. Eurobond issues in that year totalled 13 in number and the equivalent of $147 million in amount. These were large transactions at the time. They were innovative issues where British merchant banks took advantage of their experience in the securities market, their placing power and the growth of the eurocurrency market. Innovation continues to be one of the key features of the growth in the eurobond market as variations to issue types are sought to appeal to specific groups of investors. However, the ability to issue at any time still depends on favourable conditions and the availability of windows when investors are willing to purchase bonds or enter into swaps. Landmarks have included the following:

- By type of issue
  - 1970, the first dollar floating rate note issue;
  - 1975, the first pre-priced deal;
  - 1979, the first currency swap related issue and the first convertible issue;
  - 1980, the first issue with debt warrants;
  - 1981, the first zero coupon bond;
  - 1984, the first perpetual floating rate note;
  - 1989, the first global bond by the World Bank for $1.5 billion;
  - 1997, the first euro-fungible bonds.

- By major currency
  - 1963, issues in USD, D-mark and European Unit of Account (EUA, precursor of the ECU);
  - 1965, Dutch guilder;
  - 1967, French francs;
  - 1972, sterling;
  - 1981, Ecus;
  - 1998, euros.

In 1997, there were 2,813 eurobond issues with a value of US$671 billion. Over 52 per cent of these issues were in US dollars, over 23 per cent in currencies which will form the euro and over 9 per cent in sterling (Source: ISMA). However, statistics are now usually given in broader categories because the distinction between types of issue is no longer clear-cut and it is easy to double-count issues. For example, global bonds usually comprise a foreign and a eurobond issue.

In 1997, there were 4,043 international bond issues totaling $872 billion. Approximately 74 per cent of these issues were fixed rate (72 per cent by value), 19 per cent FRNs (21 per cent by value) and 6 per cent convertibles (Source: IFR). The proportion of international bonds denominated in US dollars was higher in 1997 than in other recent years. International bonds denominated in US dollars accounted for approximately 44 per cent of new issues in 1997.

Issuers, investors and lead managers

Issues of eurobonds are made by banks and financial institutions, supra-national bodies such as the World Bank, governments and government agencies, corporates and special purpose vehicle companies. Broadly speaking, about one half of new issues are made by financial institutions, one quarter by government bodies and one quarter by corporates although the distribution varies from year to year. Significant proportions of new issues are now securitisations (up to 40 per cent) which are explained in Chapter 21, and bonds issued under medium term note programmes, which are discussed in Chapter 20.

Most issues in the early years were sold on a retail basis to groups of private investors, wealthy individuals looking for attractive investment opportunities whose primary concern is to maintain the value of their capital. In the 1980s, institutional investors became major players, resulting in larger issues and bigger average sizes, and they now dominate the market. These investors can be international bond funds, pension funds, insurance companies, government agencies, commercial banks and central banks.

London is the centre of the eurobond market but this is a truly international market and, in the league tables of lead managers or book runners for issues, it is American and European investment houses which now dominate. The relative position of investment houses in the league tables for new issues is still scrutinised by the market because higher positions give better chances of winning new mandates, and greater income.

Features of eurobond issues

The usual range of issue size is $150 million to $500 million though larger issues are frequently made by governments and supranational issuers. The lower limit is dictated, among other factors by the costs of issue. Floating rate notes can be much larger and longer term because the interest rate risk for investors is much lower. A number of FRN issues over $5 billion have been made.

Up to the 1970s, issues frequently had ten to fifteen year terms. Since then, the usual term of eurobonds has been five to ten years and longer terms are only seen if market conditions are favourable. Issues for shorter periods are not unusual. There is an occasional market for longer issues by financial institutions. It is now usual for such issues to have call and step up features. In step up issues, the spread over the base cost payable increases significantly after a defined period, such as five or ten years. Some centenary bonds with 100-year maturities were issued by Far Eastern borrowers in 1996.

Eurobonds have been issued in over 35 currencies although the market in some currencies is very limited and issues infrequent. The main currencies of issue are US dollars, which has always accounted for the largest percentage of new issues, those which will make up the euro (mainly D-Marks and ECU), sterling and Yen. Bond issues in emerging market currencies are made infrequently, as market conditions allow. In 1997 these included the Argentine peso and Philippine peso. For the more exotic currencies, the opportunities for issues and finding suitable swap counterparties are often infrequent. Global bond issues have been made in most major currencies. The authorities for some currencies apply restrictions on who can lead manage issues or on the minimum maturity or denomination of the bonds.

In 1997, bonds known as parallel bonds were issued and documented so that they are converted into euros when the single currency is introduced in January 1999. Issues are being made with tranches in D-marks, Dutch guilders and/or French francs with the tranches being fungible after 1999. That is, they will be considered as one bond and the tranches will be interchangeable. They carry identical characteristics (coupon and maturity), allowing them to be merged into a single tranche after redenomination. In 1998, issues are being made in euro. The first annual interest payment will not be payable until after the scheduled start date for the single currency.

Fixed rate eurobonds pay interest annually. A bond of £10,000 with a coupon of 9.625 per cent will pay annual coupons of £962.50 per annum. The interest is called the coupon because the printed bonds (in the past and where they are still issued) have coupons attached. The coupons, which have the details of paying agents on the reverse, are clipped and presented to a paying agent to claim the interest payments. Interest on floating rate issues is paid according to the terms of each issue with the basis of the rate fixings needing to be defined. The denominations of individual bonds within an issue may range from $1,000, for retail investors, to $100,000 to meet the needs of institutional investors.

It is increasingly common for issues to remain in the form of a global note without definitive bearer bonds being printed. A global note represents the entire principal amount of the issue. It is held by a third party, called a common depositary, on behalf of the clearing systems who keep book entry interests of the holders of individual bonds. Definitive bonds will usually only be issued in the event of a specific request by the investor, a default by the issuer or the clearing systems ceasing to carry on business.

Bonds denominated in euro

Existing issues in European currencies that join the euro may be re-denominated, that is, converted to euros. All of the participating member states will redenominate government debt upon the introduction of the euro, but not many private sector issuers are expected to redenominate outstanding issues. Bonds may also be renominalised, meaning a change in the minimum nominal denominations of bonds. For example, a French franc 10,000 bond may, upon conversion, be equivalent to euro 560.666751, which could be renominalised to euro 560.67 or even euro 560. Renominalisation may require cash payments to bondholders where rounding down occurs. Market participants have agreed that:

- Redenomination should only occur on an interest payment date.
- Redenomination is at the issuer's option, does not require the bondholders' consent, but requires 30 days' notice.
- If a bond is redenominated, it should be renominalised and the market conventions for the euro should be adopted going forward.
- Redenomination and renominalisation are easiest if notes are held in permanent global form. Most issues outstanding to date have provided for a permanent global note. The practicalities of renominalisation of definitive notes have yet to be worked out at the time of writing and are likely to be onerous.
- Interest payable on the interest payment date on which the bonds are redenominated should be payable in the original currency.
- Redenomination and renominalisation should be to the nearest eurocent, which does away with the need to pay away odd amounts if a higher denomination were chosen.

Where bonds are linked to swaps or other derivative products, renominalisation and the adoption of market conventions for the euro could cause problems. An element of mismatching could be introduced into previously fully hedged transactions and will affect the cash flows of deals.

Types of issues

Fixed rate issues

These are the most common type of issue. They are issued at or close to their face value. The advantage of fixed rate bonds to the issuer is that its financing costs are certain for the life of the bond. The disadvantages are that issue costs are heavy and the time of issue may depend on market conditions, not the issuer's preference. This is really the only mode of issuance available to corporates. However, if they require floating rate exposure, they can swap the proceeds of fixed rate issues.

The advantages of fixed rate bonds to the investor are that he obtains a certain rate of return and normally has the ability to sell his holding in the secondary market before maturity of the bond.

Step-up and step-down bonds allow for increases or decreases in coupon rates during the life of the bond. Deep discount bonds, convertibles and bonds with warrants are types of fixed rate issues.

Partly paid issues

It is possible for bonds to be issued on a partly paid basis with, say 50 per cent of the bond payable by the investor at the outset with one or more subsequent installments. The investor may derive a gearing benefit initially since interest is payable on the full principal amount of the issue. It also means that the price volatility of the bonds in the secondary market is proportionately greater until the bond is fully paid. If the investor fails to honour subsequent calls then his holding is forfeit.

Deep discount and zero coupon bonds

Deep discount and zero coupon bonds are issued at a price well below the par or face value of the bond. The investor receives the par value at maturity, which means that his return is partly, or wholly capital gain. This type of bond is of interest to issuers who do not wish to make interest payments during the life of a bond, but may still be able to claim the annual capital increase as the equivalent of interest payments.

There are advantages for investors. The bonds will appeal to individuals whose income tax rates are higher than their capital gains tax marginal rate. The bonds are in effect fixed rate bonds and offer protection against falling interest rates, with the effective re-investment rate of coupons being fixed.

The disadvantage to the investor is that the bonds are subject to much greater price volatility in the secondary market. This is because the capital value has to reflect interest rate changes for the whole of the life of the bond. They are, therefore, more attractive to speculative investors.

Convertibles

Convertible bonds are equity-linked bonds. That is, the bonds are exchangeable into equity on predetermined terms. They give an option to buy equity and the cost to the investor is that he accepts coupons on the bonds that are lower than current interest rates at the time of issue. The conversion price is usually set at a premium of between 10 per cent and 25 per cent over the price of the equity at the time the convertible is issued. The currency of the shares need not be the same as the currency of the bond, nor need the shares be those of the issuer.

The attractions to issuers are that lower coupons can be set on the bonds and if the bonds are converted, it is the equivalent to a rights issue without the costs. Convertibles are often issued when it is difficult to raise equity directly due to market conditions.

The benefit to an investor is that he has the potential to make a capital gain if the share price rises in line with expectations, without exposure to a share price fall if he held the equity. If the bonds are converted, any accrued interest on the bond is lost. The timing of the next dividend payment on the shares also needs to be taken into account in assessing the profitability of conversion.

With warrants

A bond with warrants attached gives the holder of the warrant the option to acquire another asset at a predetermined price. When bonds are issued with a warrant attached, a lower coupon on the bond is compensated for by the potential benefits conveyed by the warrant. The warrant can be, and generally is, detached and sold separately. The asset may be equity, another bond, currency or a commodity such as gold. The warrants are usually only exercisable at defined times or for a defined period. A bond issued with warrants can be traded in three ways, as a cum-warrant, ex-warrant (where the warrant has been stripped from the host bond) and as the warrant itself. Ex-warrant bonds tend to be illiquid because they have below market coupons but otherwise will trade as normal bonds. Warrants can be issued 'naked', without bonds.

The benefits to the issuer are that investors will pay a premium to acquire the warrant and that the warrants can be for any asset that the issuer holds and is willing to dispose of, or for the issue of additional debt at a predetermined rate.

The benefits to investors are that the bond is repaid at maturity, or can be sold in the secondary market, and the warrant is a highly leveraged option with the potential for capital gain. However, warrants expire without value if they are not exercised before the expiry date thereby generating a loss.

Calls and puts

A call option gives the issuer the right to redeem a bond before its stated maturity date, at or within set dates. An issuer may consider issuing a call option when fixed rate bonds can only be issued at high interest rates, in order to allow refinancing if rates fall later. The bonds would be redeemed at a premium in this event. A put option gives the investor the right to early repayment of the bond if certain conditions are met, at or within set times. Usually both calls and puts can only be exercised after a period of time specified by the regulatory authority responsible.

Dual currency bonds

In dual currency bonds, an issue is made in one currency, say Swiss francs, with redemption in another currency, say, US dollars, at an exchange rate fixed when the issue is launched. The issuer chooses in which currency he will pay interest. Investors whose assets are in the currency of repayment can avoid exchange risks on their investment. Borrowers can issue in low interest currencies and repay the bond in a currency where they will have assets available at the maturity of the bond. Issuers should, however, not be misled into accepting a liability to repay in a currency where they have no natural cash flow simply because the interest rate looks attractive. The coupon rate on dual currency bonds is usually higher than that on comparable straight eurobond issues. The redemption amount is usually favourable to the investor compared to the spot rate of exchange at the time of issue. The currency aspect of these bonds is similar to long dated forward foreign exchange contracts. However, interim interest payments are made rather than the interest differentials being incorporated into the forward price.

Floating rate notes

Floating rate notes (FRNs) are instruments where the interest rate is reset at regular intervals according to predetermined conditions. This will normally be the same interval throughout the life of the notes, the most common periods being three and six months with a margin set in relation to Libor. Borrowers who seek a term commitment of funds yet feel that interest rates are too high for a fixed interest coupon may consider a floating rate note issue. FRNs are used by banks to raise capital either because issues can broadly match assets held or because they want exposure to floating rates. The interest rate payable on the borrowing will be brought into line with current market rates applicable usually to the three or six month Libor rates for the currency concerned. Notification will be issued in a format similar to that shown in Figure 18.1. FRNs provide investors with a higher rate of return than they could expect to receive from a bank deposit over the same interest period. FRNs are likely to be preferred to fixed rate bonds by issuers when interest rates are high and volatile.

Figure 18.1 Example notice of FRN rate re-fixing

LONDON BUILDING SOCIETY
£200,000,000 Floating Rate Notes due 2005
For the interest period 30 November 1998 to 28 February 1999, the Notes will carry a Rate of Interest of 7.90% per annum with interest amounts of £194.79 per £10,000 principal and £1,947.95 per £100,000 principal, payable on 28 February 1999.

Bank AB   Agent Bank

The first FRN issue in the eurobond market was launched in 1970. For a short period in the early 1980s it was the fastest growing capital market. However, problems arose with perpetual FRNs that had no stated maturity date. This was because of an excess of large issues by banks who were raising long term capital by issuing subordinated bonds, but in effect paying short term rates. Banks were also large holders of FRNs when the rules on banks' capital were changed in late 1984. Holdings in other banks' subordinated debt had to be deducted from their own capital base. There was a rapid contraction of the market and collapse in liquidity and many issues still trade below their par value. FRNs have accounted for approximately 20 per cent of new eurobond issues in recent years. They have been made mainly by banks, sovereign and supranational borrowers. Banks continue to raise subordinated debt in this manner for capital adequacy purposes through selective issues and not through the 'jumbo' issues which typified the 1980s. Most floating rate note issues are made in US dollars but issues are also made in D-marks and sterling.

Floating rate notes can be issued incorporating caps and/or floors (maximum and minimum rates payable). Reverse FRNs are issues where the interest rate is set at a fixed rate less the applicable Libor for the current interest period. A drop lock issue converts into a fixed rate issue if the reference rate falls below a certain trigger point.

Repayment

The majority of bonds are now issued with repayment in one sum at the stated maturity, known as a bullet repayment. This is because investors attach a high importance to the duration of their investments, being the time-weighted average of the present value of cash flows, expressed as a proportion of the price or term of years. Staggered redemption could be in the form of a note purchase programme. Repurchases in the open market are likely to be made when the market is weak.

The role of rating agencies

A credit rating by one of the credit rating agencies for a new issue, though not a regulatory requirement, is now essential in order to obtain a good reception from investors. Many investment funds are restricted by their own rules to investing in debt with a particular rating. A good rating will appeal to a wider set of investors and so help the issuer obtain the best terms for his debt. A poor debt rating, on the other hand, can damage not only a bank's ability to issue debt but also the terms on which it deals in the interbank market and the willingness of counterparties to enter into longer term derivative business.

There are several rating agencies, the major ones being Standard and Poor's (S & P), Moody's Investors Service, Fitch IBCA and Thomson BankWatch. The latter two specialise in ratings for banks. The purpose of a rating for a bond issue is to indicate the likelihood of a particular issue not being repaid in full when it falls due for redemption. Strictly speaking, a rating applies to an issue, not an issuer, and so will take into account the individual characteristics of each bond (such as the degree of subordination). Whilst each issuer can, therefore, have several different ratings for its different issues, the ratings on senior, unsubordinated debt are usually taken as reflecting the relative standing of the issuer itself.

For bank issuers, ratings are published following examination of a bank's published accounts and in-depth discussions with the bank's management. The agencies charge issuers for the privilege of obtaining a rating on their securities but the added marketability that ratings provide is a sufficient advantage to outweigh the fee for most issuers. Factors likely to be considered by a rating agency for a bank issue will include:

- *Quantitative factors.* Asset quality (spread of portfolio, bad debt experience, etc); capital adequacy; profitability and liquidity.

- *Qualitative factors.* The quality of the issuer's management; business franchise; hidden strengths and reserves; hidden weaknesses and overvalued assets; government ownership and support or support of a major shareholder.

- The environment in which the company operates, including the strength of the main economies where its main businesses are located; political and regulatory regimes; the strength of the banking industry locally and globally.

Specifically, the following information will enable the rating agencies to make their evaluation:

- A comprehensive description of the organisation and

management structure of the bank, its management policies and performance.

- The issuer's operating efficiency, relative market position and relative country risk.

- Detailed accounting statements for the last five years for the bank and major subsidiaries reflecting revenues by asset origin or fee type; details of expense items by type; major assets and liability classes; and details of reserve provisions and accounting policies followed.

- The liability structure of the bank including the stability and diversity of fund sources both domestically and internationally; an understanding of the bank's liquidity policy and management; the liquidity aspects of its investment portfolio; balance sheet liquidity requirements and the liquidity afforded by external resources available to the bank.

- Interest rate exposure policies and management and control of the related risks.

- Exposures resulting from foreign exchange trading and other activities.

- Projections, including assumptions, for the next five years.

Particular attention is paid to the quality of a bank's loan portfolio. The agency will wish to know:

- details reflecting distribution geographically and by industry and market sector;

- the nature of the largest borrowers;

- lending policy and loan administration practices, particularly as they relate to externally imposed constraints and regulatory activities. Historical loss experience; write-off policies and practices; credit controls; collection procedures.

When published, ratings tend to follow a letter code with "triple-A" representing the lowest risk. The rating codes used by the main agencies are shown in Figure 18.2. Categories down to BBB/Baa are often referred to as 'investment grade' and many funds will not purchase bonds with lower ratings. Note that the ratings between AA/Aa and B can be further sub-divided by the use of suffixes, +/- for Standard & Poor's and 1/2/3 for Moody's.

Figure 18.2		Rating Categories
S & P	**Moody's**	**Interpretation**
AAA	Aaa	Ability to repay principal and interest on a timely basis is extremely high
AA	Aa	Very strong ability to pay interest and principal on a timely basis
A	A	Very strong, but more susceptible to changes in circumstance
BBB	Baa	An acceptable capacity to repay principal and interest
BB	Ba	There are significant uncertainties that could affect the ability to adequately service the debt obligations
B	B	Adverse developments could negatively affect the payment of principal
CCC	Caa	A high likelihood of default
CC	Ca	Highly speculative, may be in default
D	D	In default

The ratings in Figure 18.2 are those used to categorise long-term debt issues. The agencies' short term debt ratings were described in Chapter 17.

19 The primary and secondary market for eurobond issues

The primary market

Issuance of eurobonds can be divided into four phases: origination, syndication, placement or distribution and closing.

Origination

It is important for potential fund-raisers to have an ongoing policy of examining their debt requirements. When issuing for the first time, issuers will consult their advisers on their needs in terms of the type of debt instrument, amount, currency, maturity and interest rate structure of the potential borrowing. They will consult potential lead managers about market conditions and the structure the lead manager can offer. They will also have preliminary conversations with the rating agencies who will make an assessment of the rating for the issue. The purpose of ratings, requirements of the rating agencies and the way ratings are set are discussed fully in chapter 18. Banks issuing eurobonds need to consider how a eurobond issue will meet their requirements for funding, capital raising and investment.

The lead manager or bookrunner's role is to advise on:

- interest rate trends which might affect the cost of funding;
- the timing of the issue;
- the performance of recent bond issues;
- investor appetite and the demand for particular types of bonds;
- the possibilities for using swaps;
- the probable cost of funds, bearing in mind the rating the issue will be given;

- documentation of the issue.

Once an issuer is content with the outline terms offered, he will appoint a lead manager for the issue. The lead manager will, together with the issuer, select the other parties involved and will take responsibility for production of the documentation. He will also be responsible for ensuring that 'due diligence' has been observed in the provision of details by the issuer and on the issue. Other key parties to be appointed or included at this stage are:

- Paying agents. One or more paying agents will be nominated to provide representation in the key financial centres. A principal paying agent will be nominated. These agents are responsible for payments made to investors in respect of principal and interest, and notices.

- Trustee or fiscal agent to represent the interests of bondholders in monitoring administrative and substantive aspects of the issue.

- The issuer's accountants and auditors to advise on tax and accountancy aspects and to certify the financial data as revealed in the issue prospectus.

- Legal advisers to advise on all legal aspects.

- Printers to prepare the prospectus and agreements and a recognised security printer to prepare bonds in definitive form.

- The listing agent to arrange for the issue to be listed on the desired exchange(s). This role is generally undertaken by the lead manager.

The time it takes to bring an issue to the market will depend on whether the issuer is a new or regular issuer. If an issuer has a draft offering circular and documentation in place, perhaps under a medium term note programme, the issue can be made very quickly, whereas a stand-alone issue can take about a month to document.

Syndication and distribution

Once a mandate has been secured, the lead manager will recruit other investment houses to assist in the underwriting of the issue usually with the agreement of the issuer. The purpose of syndication is to spread the underwriting risk by committing to purchase unsold bonds.

If the issuer is a new borrower, is relatively unknown in the euromarkets, or is proposing an unusual structure for the bond, it may be necessary to undertake a programme of investor education by circulating information to or visiting potential investors. A series of presentations in various locations is known as a 'roadshow'.

Under the process of syndication, the lead manager or book-runner arranges for the launch of the issue. Invitations to potential syndicate members to underwrite the issue will first be made and accepted by telephone. Formal invitations, which are contracts, will then be made by fax, telex or PC-to-PC software such as Bondware BookRunner for acceptance of allotted commitments. If the price of the issue has been pre-set, which is usual, the lead manager will announce allotments within one working day of the launch.

Participating houses may be termed co-lead managers or co-managers depending on the extent of their agreement to underwrite the deal, their ability to add features to its structure (eg swaps) and their contribution to its distribution. The manager group will maintain contact with potential investors so that they can assess likely future demand and trade the issue in the grey market. The formal invitation will include:

- a list of the managers and their underwriting commitments;
- details of commissions;
- the timetable for the issue;
- a summary of the terms and conditions of the bond;
- details of the managers' allotments and payment instructions;
- the deadline and wording for acceptance;
- the wording for the Power of Attorney to enable the Lead Manager to sign the Subscription Agreement.

Signing will be within two to three weeks with closing and payment usually within one month of the formal invitation being made. An example of the wording for an invitation to join a FRN issue is given in Figure 19.1.

Figure 19.1   Invitation to join a bond syndicate

(appears at end of chapter)

As soon as an issue is launched, a grey market (effectively secondary market trading or trading on an if, as and when issued basis) is likely to develop. This is trading in bonds that have not yet been issued. Banks not invited into a particular issue can deal in this way and those who were involved can sell bonds if needed. Grey market prices are available on screen services and through brokers allowing investors to check that they are not being offered bonds at a higher price by one institution than by another.

The lead manager should try to ensure an orderly market in the new issues it has arranged though stabilisation in the grey market. It supports the price by actively trading the issue in the market. This process is undertaken under International Primary Markets Association rules. The managers in the issue must agree to stabilisation and the bookrunner must maintain a separate account of stabilisation transactions. The costs, within limits, can be passed onto the managers although they are usually assumed by the stabilising manager itself and this will be set out in the invitation.

Closing

Issuance is completed on the closing date. On this date, the syndicate pays the issuer for the bonds underwritten and interest starts to accrue on the bond. The issuer delivers a global note into the custody of a clearing house with the ownership being assigned to individual investors by book entry transfer. Each issue will have a unique ISIN (International Securities Identification Number) assigned to it by the clearing house.

Coupon rates

What rate of interest or coupon rate should an issuer pay? The benchmark is the rate at which government securities for the same currency and term would be issued. The rate the issuer will have to pay will be a number of basis points more than the benchmark rate to reflect the credit rating of the issuer and the stability of the market at the time of issue. There is a strong correlation between credit ratings, the type of bond and the interest rates and commissions payable for a new issue. Volatile markets will increase the spread over the relevant government security.

An example of the coupon and commissions payable on a new five year eurobond issued during 1997 is:

Fixed rate issue rated AA/Aa

Currency, amount, term	$750 million, five years
Coupon	14 bp over 5 year US Treasuries
Management commission	0.875% Underwriting fees 0.125%
Selling commissions	0.875% Praecipuum Nil

A praecipuum is a front end fee for the lead manager. Selling fees are often passed on to investors to encourage them to buy bonds in the issue. In calculating the overall cost, issuers will need to take into account whether the issue is made at a premium or a discount and, in addition to the above fees, all legal, printing, listing, rating, trustee and paying agency fees. These costs may be amortised over the life of the issue in order to determine the true annual cost.

Pricing

Eurobonds were originally issued on an open-priced basis. Investors were only offered indicative terms during distribution, which could take up to 14 days. When the price was fixed, allotment took place on the following day when the documentation was signed. This system allowed the syndicate to test investor demand and vary the indicative terms. This became unacceptable to issuers who might end up paying a significantly higher coupon when rates moved upwards. Pre-priced bought deals were introduced in 1975. Their fixed terms mean that investors can assess opportunities for portfolio switches earlier and swaps can be assessed and exploited more easily.

The fixed price re-offer method of issue was introduced in 1989 and is now the principal pricing method. This is still a pre-priced deal but is a much tighter structure. Smaller management groups are used and the timetable for issue is shorter. The co-managers agree not to re-offer the bond at less than the price fixed by the bookrunner until the syndicate is broken by the bookrunner. The bookrunner will not break the syndicate until the issue has been placed with investors.

This means that co-managers will not dump bonds in the grey market as had happened previously and has resulted in issues being priced and fees set more realistically. However, it increases the risk of an issue being cancelled due to *force majeure*, as happened during the Gulf War.

Listing

Eurobonds are listed on stock exchanges, frequently in London and/or

Luxembourg for three reasons:

- for UK issuers to qualify for the quoted eurobond exemption, allowing payments to be made without deduction of tax;
- investors may only be permitted to invest in listed securities;
- to generate greater confidence in the paper.

The listing documents to be provided in London include:

- three copies of the offering circular (draft copies followed up by approved copies);
- draft formal notice for publication by the Stock Exchange setting out brief details of the issue;
- draft non-applicables letter (explaining non-compliance with Offering Circular content requirement);
- Schedule 3B (application for listing);
- Schedule 4B (Listing agent's declaration);
- a copy of the issuer's resolution authorising the issue.

Documentation

The following documents will be prepared:

- The *Offering Circular*. The purpose is to provide detailed information on the issue and the issuer. It is a standard requirement for the stock exchange listing. It will be dispatched to the managers to be used to promote the issue.
- The *Subscription Agreement*, between the issuer and the management group. This covers the managers' commitment to subscribe for the bonds at the issue price, the issuer's commitment to issue them, commissions and fees payable, the terms of the issue and representations and warranties by the issuer as to the accuracy of the information provided.
- The *Agreement Among Managers* sets out the responsibilities of the lead manager and managers between themselves for underwriting, allotment of bonds and fees. This agreement is rarely produced as a separate document but as an industry standard version is deemed to have been entered into at the same time as the Subscription Agreement.

- The *Trust Deed* which constitutes the bonds and establishes the terms under which the trustee will act on behalf of the bondholders.

- The *Paying Agency Agreement* between the issuer and the nominated paying agents, outlining their responsibilities for timely payments.

- The *global note* or bonds representing evidence of the debt owed by the issuer to the investor and including the terms of issue.

- Legal opinion, and accountants' letter of comfort confirming the accuracy of the financial information provided by the issuer.

The terms of a public eurobond issue will be set out in the trust deed and will also be printed on the global note. They will cover:

- *Status of the bonds.* The bonds usually rank *pari passu* or equal, in terms of legal protection for the investor, with previous indebtedness of a similar type of the issuer.

- *A statement* of the form and denomination of the bonds.

- *Subordination.* Bank issues must be subordinated to count as capital for regulatory purposes. In the event of the winding up of the issuer, the holders of subordinated paper should not expect to receive payment from the liquidator until all the senior claims and ordinary creditors have been satisfied in full. There may be several tiers of subordination.

- *Negative pledge.* A negative pledge is an undertaking by the borrower that he will not offer security to investors in further bond issues without offering similar security to existing bondholders. UK bank issues ranking as capital must not contain a negative pledge or cross default clause which could accelerate payment.

- *Interest.* Floating rate notes will include definitions of interest periods, interest determination dates and how rates are determined.

- *Redemption.* For bullet repayment issues, the notes will be redeemed at a specific date in the future. If there is a sinking fund or a note purchase agreement, the redemption clause will include the details.

- *Payments.* How investors can obtain payment of interest and redemption proceeds.
- *Taxation.* Payments will normally be paid without deduction of withholding tax.
- *Prescription.* The coupons and bonds normally become void unless presented for payment within six and 12 years from the due dates respectively.
- *Events of default/enforcement of rights.* Non-payment of interest or principal and appointment of a receiver are the key events of default. If they occur, the trustees have the right to take proceedings against the issuer on behalf of the bondholders.
- *Details of replacement* in the event of theft or loss of the bonds.
- *Notices.* Where notices relating to interest rate fixings for FRNs and redemption will be published.
- *Meetings of Bondholders.* How they will be convened.
- *Changes to terms and conditions.* Allowable or where bondholder approval is needed.
- *Further issues.* Normally allowed without consent of the bondholders for this issue.
- *Governing Law.*

International Primary Markets Association

The primary market is overseen by the International Primary Markets Association (IPMA) which was formed in 1984. Its objectives are to promote the interests of lead managers of new issues of debt instruments in the international capital markets. IPMA issues recommendations on the methods and manner of issues and documentation. It has no formal powers but makes recommendations that are usually acceptable to all. These include the following:

- the need for lead managers to provide documentation at least one day before signing;
- limits on the deduction of fees for stabilisation;

- minimum information in new issue invitations;
- ban on sham co-managements;
- minimum allotment amounts;
- penalties for late payment of fees;
- arrangements for custody of global notes.

IPMA introduced a computerised information system linking members that enables details of new issues to be sent and responded to on an on-line basis.

The secondary market

All trading after the closing of a eurobond issue takes place in the secondary market. This is an over-the-counter market, with bid and offer quotes, in which transactions are negotiated with market makers who use the services of inter-dealer brokers. Brokers act as principals and they do not take positions of their own. Trading between professional counterparties is by telephone, with systems such as Reuters 3000 used as a database of outstanding bond issues.

International Securities Markets Association

The International Securities Markets Association (ISMA) was formed in 1969 to act as a self-regulatory body to promote stability in the secondary market. The expansion of the market at that time had caused many failed trades. ISMA has its headquarters in Basle. It has established rules for trading and settlement and provides conciliation and arbitration services. An important rule concerns deliverability of stock. If a seller cannot deliver a security within 21 days of the value date of a transaction, the buyer gives the seller 14 days notice in which to complete the transaction, failing which ISMA nominates a firm to buy the securities at the best rate available in the open market. ISMA produces a weekly handbook of eurobond prices and maintains an electronic database of bond prices.

Some of the essential features of secondary market trading, under ISMA rules, are:

- Normal settlement takes place on the third business day after the dealing day (T + 3), or as agreed by both parties.

- Prices are quoted in decimals as a percentage of par of 100.

- Accrued interest is added to the purchase price quoted for the period from the last interest period to the value date. For fixed rate bonds, this is calculated assuming a year of 12 months of 30 days (30/360 bond basis). This means that January and February are both deemed to have 30 days if the whole interest for these months is accrued. For fixed rate issues in euro, ISMA has endorsed an actual/actual day count basis.

Prices of bonds in the secondary market fluctuate in response to the above but particularly to changes in interest rates and in market conditions. Prices vary around par of 100. In simple terms, if interest rates were 11 per cent, a 10 per cent coupon stock would stand at a price below par; if interest rates were 9 per cent, the stock would stand at above par.

TRAX

TRAX is the trade matching and confirmation system that is subscribed to by ISMA members worldwide. TRAX matches buy and sell orders by market participants, providing the means for traders to quickly and accurately confirm trades. The system requires both counterparties to a trade to input the trade details within stipulated times of the trade agreed. The information required is: trade date and time; settlement date; counterparty; type of security; quantity; price; and any special conditions. The TRAX computer will search for a matching instruction from the counterparty. The system provides a mechanism to subsequently amend or cancel unmatched orders and to evaluate all trades through a reconciliation function. The status of advised trades can be monitored in real time. TRAX is used in the UK for the mandatory reporting of trades under the Financial Services Act. The system has brought efficiency, transparency and security to secondary eurobond trading.

Liquidity

Liquidity is a measure of the ease with which purchases and sales can be transacted. This depends on market conditions, which may be influenced by external events. Large issues of $1 billion or more and issued by supra-nationals such as the World Bank, or an OECD sovereign state, are highly liquid and are regularly traded throughout their life on very tight bid/offer margins. They provide benchmarks along the yield curve for the market that serve as measures of relative value for less liquid transactions.

In spite of the overall size of the market, there are few individual issues of a size that can provide liquidity. Many new issues are targeted at specific investors. The lack of standardisation and the multitude of issues mean that eurobonds cannot be traded in the same way as government bonds, which are near commodities in terms of the size and structure of the instruments. Liquidity in eurobond issues is variable and is affected by the following factors:

- The continued creditworthiness of the issuer.

- The maintaining of the (investment grade) rating of the issuer.

- The size and currency of the original issue; the larger the issue and the more common the currency, the more liquid the secondary market is likely to be.

- Securities houses being willing to make two way prices. For small issues, even the lead manager may stop making a market in the bonds after a short time.

- Straight issues are more marketable than issues with additional features or complex structures ('bells and whistles').

- Most secondary market trading takes place during the first three months of the life of the bond.

- During the last years of an issue, bonds become locked into portfolios and often rarely trade.

- If interest rates fall or rise greatly, liquidity may be lost. Investors will not be willing to pay large premiums when interest rates fall (the price of the bond is high) or sell holdings which involve a capital loss when rates have risen.

- Market sentiment affects liquidity, as did the crisis in the Far East at the end of 1997.

The clearing houses

The existence of two clearing houses, Euroclear and Cedel Bank, facilitates the back office functions for settlement of many types of bonds and short term paper. Euroclear was created in 1968 by Morgan Guaranty Trust Company and is located in Brussels. In 1972, it was sold to 120 banks and now has around 2500 participants. Although initially designed for settling eurobond transactions, Euroclear now also settles transactions in debt securities and/or equities from 32 domestic markets through direct or indirect links with local clearing systems. More than 100,000 different securities are now accepted including eurobonds, domestic and corporate bonds, equities, warrants, CP, CDs and government securities. Cedel Bank was established in 1970 in Luxembourg and has over 100 shareholders. In 1997, some $52,845 billion trades (for many types of securities and financial instruments) were settled through these houses.

The functions of the clearing houses are to provide:

- Electronic, book entry transfer of ownership of securities through delivery versus payment settlement. This involves trade validation and matching, reporting and statements services and money transfer facilities.

- Custody services which eliminate the physical delivery of securities. These are immobilised in common depositaries.

- Securities borrowing and lending services.

Messages to and from the clearing houses may be communicated using S.W.I.F.T., telex or mail or to Euroclear using EUCLID, its proprietary communication system. Systems within the clearing houses match settlement instructions received from participants and effect payments and deliveries of securities over participants' cash and custody accounts. Matching instructions must be received from both counterparties before the settlement process can proceed. All trades must identify the serial number of the issue of securities (ISIN number), which was assigned during the primary distribution of the issue, as well as the securities account numbers of the parties making the trade. There is an electronic bridge between Euroclear and Cedel Bank with transactions being netted out at the end of the day and the necessary transfers made between the systems.

Custody related services include administration of interest, dividend and redemption payments, assistance with recovery of tax withheld and exercise of warrants and options. Virtually all new issues for internationally traded securities are closed and issued on a same day against payment basis through the clearing systems.

Securities borrowing and lending services are designed to improve the efficiency of securities settlement and increase market liquidity. Lenders are mainly institutions that are not active traders. Lenders earn fees on securities lent but can specify which securities they wish to make available for this purpose and they have the right to recall securities lent. Borrowers are usually active traders who need securities to avoid trade fails. They may be automatic borrowers, where the clearing centre identifies borrowing needs or they may choose the specific issues they need to borrow. The clearing houses are increasing their roles as the agent in tri-party repo deals and in managing the collateral for these deals.

Instructions to Euroclear need to be given on the previous day and settlement is processed in two overnight batches. Limited same day processing is available for same day value with completion at the end of the day. Euroclear will introduce real time same day matching and settlement, in addition to the batch processing.

Calculations

The calculations explained below are current yield, calculation of the price of a eurobond in the secondary market and the proceeds of a sale of bonds in the secondary market.

Current yield

A bond purchased at a price of 97.5, having a coupon of 12 per cent, will give a current yield of 12.3 per cent, calculated as follows:

$$\text{Coupon} \times \frac{100}{\text{Net Price}} = \text{Current yield} \qquad 12 \times \frac{100}{97.5} = 12.3\%$$

Price of a eurobond with annual coupon

The example shows how the price of a three year eurobond with a coupon of 9 per cent which yields 8 per cent is calculated. First, the cashflows are determined. These are normally depicted as follows:

		Redemption value
Coupon 9%	Coupon 9%	+ Coupon 109%
↑	↑	↑
↓ Year 1	Year 2	Year 3

Price now?

Each cashflow is discounted by the yield to maturity, 8%.

$$\frac{\text{Coupon}}{(1 + \text{yield}/100)} + \frac{\text{Coupon}}{(1 + \text{yield}/100)^2} + \frac{\text{Coupon} + \text{Face value}}{(1 + \text{yield}/100)^3} = \text{Price}$$

$$\frac{9}{(1 + 8/100)} + \frac{9}{(1 + 8/100)^2} + \frac{109}{(1 + 8/100)^3} = \text{Price}$$

$$8.333 \quad + \quad 7.716 \quad + \quad 86.527 \qquad = 102.58$$

This calculation shows the principle involved. The calculations become more complex as more years, semi-annual interest payments and the fact that most trades do not conveniently have a value date on the anniversary of a bond issue are taken into account. Most calculations first require discounting for part of a year to the next coupon date. Bond dealers will use PCs or programmable calculators to calculate secondary market prices.

Proceeds of sale of eurobonds in the secondary market

Twenty bonds each with a nominal value of $100,000 are sold at 98.28, trade date 20 October, value date 23 October. The last coupon of 7.5 per cent was paid on 23 January. The proceeds are the price plus accrued interest:

Principal $2,000,000 x 98.28/100   = $ 1,965,600.00
Accrued interest for 9 months of 30 days
$2,000,000 \times \dfrac{270 \times 7.5}{36000}$ = $ 112,500.00
Total proceeds   = $ 2,078,100.00

Figure 19.1   *Invitation to join a bond syndicate*

To ...*Investment Bank*   8 January 1999
From WestBank International PLC (WBI)
WestBank International PLC
Pounds Sterling GBP 200,000,000
Floating Rate Note due 2004 ('the Notes')

1 Invitation
Further to our telephone conversation earlier, on behalf of the issuer, WBI and
ALCO Bank N.V., each as a joint-lead manager, are pleased to confirm to you
our invitation to join the management group for the above-mentioned issue
as a co-lead manager with an underwriting commitment of pounds sterling
10,000,000 on the terms and conditions set out below.

Underwriting commitment (pounds sterling)

WBI	70,000,000
ALCO Bank NV	70,000,000
...Investment Bank	10,000,000
...Investment Bank	10,000,000
...Investment Bank	10,000,000
...Investment Bank	10,000,000
...Investment Bank	10,000,000
...Investment Bank	10,000,000
Total	200,000,000

Commissions: Total commissions will be 0.15 per cent of the principal
amount of the notes divided as follows:
Combined management and underwriting commission   : 0.10 per cent
Selling commission   : 0.05 per cent

Share of management and underwriting commission: the combined
management and underwriting commission will be divided among the
managers in proportion to their respective underwriting commitments. There
will be no adjustment of the commission for stabilisation profits or losses or
unreimbursed expenses.

Proposed timetable:

Thursday 7 Jan 1999	Issue launched, allotments finalised.
Friday 8 Jan 1999	Invitation and allotment telex despatched.
Monday 11 Jan 1999	Formal acceptance of invitations and allotments by managers to be received by 17.00 London time.
..(to be advised)..1999	Signing of the subscription agreement.
Friday 5 Feb 1999	Payment, delivery and closing.

2. Summary of the terms and conditions of the Notes

Issuer:	WestBank International plc
Principal Amount:	Pounds sterling 200,000,000
Final Maturity:	5 February, 2004
Coupon:	3 month Libor plus a margin of 0.0625 per cent per annum payable quarterly in arrear on 5 May, August, November and February commencing on 5 May 1999 on an actual/365/366 day basis, subject to adjustment in accordance with the modified following business day convention.
Issue Price:	99.84 per cent of the aggregate principal amount of the Notes.
Form, Denomination:	Subject to 'Delivery of the Notes', below, the Notes will be issued in bearer form only. Notes will be issued in denominations of pounds sterling 10,000 and pounds sterling 100,000.
Status of the Notes:	The Notes will constitute direct, unconditional, unsubordinated and unsecured obligations of the issuer and will rank without preference among themselves and at least pari passu with all other creditors of the issuer, save those whose claims are preferred by any bankruptcy, insolvency, or other similar laws of general application.
Taxation:	Payments by the issuer in respect of the Notes will be made without deduction for, or on account of, any present or future taxes in the United Kingdom, except as required by law. In the event that such taxes are imposed, the issuer will, subject to customary exceptions, pay additional amounts so that the net amount received by the Noteholders after such withholding or deduction shall equal the full amount of principal and interest which otherwise would have been receivable in respect of the Notes, all as more fully described in the Offering Circular.
Tax Redemption:	The Notes may be redeemed in whole but not in part, at the option of the issuer, on any interest payment date, at their principal amount plus accrued interest if, as a result of certain changes in the laws or regulations of the United Kingdom, the issuer becomes obliged to pay additional amounts, all as more fully set out in the Offering Circular.
Cross Default:	None

Negative Pledge:	None
Rating of Notes:	The Notes, on issue, are expected to be rated A1/A+ by Standard and Poors and Fitch IBCA.
Listing:	Application will be made to list the Notes on the Luxembourg Stock Exchange.
Governing Law:	English law
Delivery of the Notes:	The Notes will initially be represented by a Temporary Global Note without coupons, which will be deposited with a common depositary on behalf of Cedel Bank and Euroclear on or about 5 February 1999 and will be exchangeable on or after a date (the 'Exchange Date') which is expected to be 18 March 1999 for interest in a permanent Global Note. Definitive Notes will not be issued except in limited circumstances set out in the Temporary Global Note.
Further issues:	The issuer may from time to time, without consent of Noteholders, create and issue further notes ranking pari passu in all respects which shall be consolidated and form a single series with the outstanding Notes.
Selling Restrictions:	As more fully set out in the Subscription Agreement and the Offering Circular.
United States:	Not 144A eligible.
United Kingdom:	You are required to agree that [1] you have not offered or sold and you will not offer or sell any Notes to persons in the United Kingdom prior to the expiry of a period of six months from the issue date, except to persons whose ordinary activities involve them in acquiring, holding, managing or disposing of investments (as principal or agent) for the purposes of their business or otherwise in circumstances which have not resulted in and will not result in an offer to the public in the United Kingdom within the meaning of the Public Offers of Securities Regulations 1995 or the Financial Services Act 1986. [2] You have complied with and will comply with all applicable provisions of the Financial Services Act 1986 with respect to anything done by you in relation to the Notes in, from and otherwise involving the United Kingdom; and [3] You have only issued or passed on and will only issue and pass on in the United Kingdom any document received by you in connection with the issue of the Notes to a person who is of a kind

described in article 11 (3) of the Financial Securities Act 1986 (Investment Advertisements) (Exemptions) Order 1996, or is a person to whom the document may otherwise be lawfully be issued or passed on.

Stabilisation:	FSA/IPMA - WBI is stabilisation manager.
Agreement among Managers:	IPMA version 1
Force Majeure:	IPMA clause 2 (modified to be expressed as being after consultation with the issuer if practicable).
Notes ISIN number:	XS0094040153
Notes common code:	9404015

3 Allotment

On behalf of the issuer, subject to signature of the Subscription Agreement, we hereby allot to you:

Pounds sterling 10,000,000 principal amount of the Notes on the terms hereof and of the Subscription Agreement and the Final Offering Circular to be dated the signing date. Payment for the Notes must be made in pounds sterling at the rate of £ 9,969.00 for each £10,000 Principal Amount of the Notes (representing the issue price of 99.84 per cent of the Notes less the selling commission of 0.05 per cent, and less the combined management and underwriting commission of 0.10 per cent of the Principal Amount. Receipt of and payment for your allotment will be executed as provided below on 5 February 1999. We are implementing the 'Delivery against Payment' settlement procedures as recommended by I.S.M.A. Delivery of your allotment will be executed by way of a book entry clearance against payment in either Euroclear or Cedel Bank. We will notify you separately of the manner in which payment is to be made.

Upon delivery of the Temporary Global Note to the Common Depositary your account with Euroclear and/or Cedel Bank will be credited with your allotment against receipt of your payment.

4 Acceptance of Invitation and Allotment

Please confirm your formal acceptance of this invitation and underwriting commitment above to WBI by 17.00 hours London time on Monday 11 January 1999 in the form set out below.

Quote: To   WestBank International PLC
            From

                    WestBank International PLC
        £ 200,000,000 Floating Rate Note due 2004 ('the Notes')

We confirm our acceptance of your invitation to join the management Group for the above mentioned issue and our allotment of £10,000,000 of Notes on

the terms set out in your invitation telex of Friday 8 January 1999.
We wish to appear as (insert legal name) for all legal purposes and as (insert publicity name) in all publicity related to the transaction.

5 <u>Signing and Power of Attorney</u>
Following acceptance of this invitation, please send a copy of your Power of Attorney in the following form, for the execution of the Agreements, before the signing date to be advised.

<u>Power of Attorney</u>
WestBank International PLC
<u>£ 200,000,000 Floating Rate Note due 2004 ('the Notes')</u>

We, (name if institution) hereby appoint …….. or …….. or any authorised officer of Westbank International PLC severally as our Attorney and Agent, to approve the final form of and execute and deliver on our behalf the Subscription Agreement in relation to the above issue, and generally to execute such other documents and to do and perform any other act or deed necessary or deemed desirable in connection herewith by the said Attorneys, or any of them. We hereby agree to ratify and confirm all things which the said Attorneys shall lawfully do or cause to be done by virtue thereof. This Power of Attorney shall be irrevocable for 30 days from the date hereof.
For _____ By _____ Date _____

20 The euro medium-term note market

Whereas eurobond issues normally raise a single large amount, medium term notes are sold in smaller tranches either on a continuous basis or in response to investor demand. Investors are able to specify an amount, a rate, a maturity profile and repayment structure that is then proposed by dealers to issuers where pre-arranged programmes are in place. The financings resemble small eurobond issues (which they sometimes are) but the method of distribution resembles that of commercial paper.

The market in medium term notes (MTNs) originated in the 1970's in the USA. Domestic dollar MTNs were sold to investors on a best efforts basis through dealers, usually in registered and book entry form without delivery of physical certificates.

The EMTN market

The euro-medium term note (EMTN) market originated in London in 1986 when the US dollar was the dominant currency and issuers were encouraged to offer paper on a continuous basis. This is now a mature market in London. EMTNs have been issued in over 40 currencies. Each of these is subject to compliance with the regulations of the central bank of the country whose currency is issued. Otherwise, issuers have flexibility in the frequency, amount, currency and structure of individual issues under their programmes.

Notes can be for periods as short as one month or can range up to 30 years but are usually issued for periods between eighteen months and five to ten years. Individual notes are usually between $1m and $20m or the equivalent in other currencies.

Programmes

Prospective issuers are canvassed by investment houses to arrange programmes, which can take up to three months to arrange. The matters that need to be considered by potential issuers are the size and currency of the programme, the types of issues that might be made and the issuing pattern that will be adopted.

EMTN programmes are typically for amounts between one or two billion US dollars, or the equivalent in another currency. However, smaller and larger programme sizes are regularly seen. Potential issuers need to assess the correct size of the programme. If a programme is larger than necessary, it may give the impression of over-extending borrowing and therefore send the wrong signals to potential investors. If it is too low, this might indicate a lack of proposed issuance or may require the administrative burden of updates once the limit is breached. The level should be set to cover at least two years' of the issuer's requirements.

Multi-currency programmes are always to be recommended and issuers should specify the currencies where they expect to see any issuance in the Offering Circular. However, subject to regulatory controls, any currency can be issued with prior consent between the dealer and issuer. To give the greatest flexibility, the possible structures of individual note issues should be set out in the Offering Circular. The following types of issue may be included, though any type of new and innovative structure can be issued with prior agreement between the dealer and issuer, subject to regulatory controls for the currency:

- Fixed and floating rate notes; reverse floating rate notes.
- Capped and collared notes; discount and zero coupon notes.
- Dual currency notes, optional dual currency notes.
- Index linked notes; commodity and equity linked notes.

The issuing patterns seen in EMTN programmes differ widely. The dealer's role is to match the requirements of investors and issuers, which may be achieved utilising the derivatives markets. The majority of EMTN issues are swapped to achieve issuers' and investors' objectives. Alternatives open to an issuer are:

- To continuously post aggressive rates for a wide range of maturities and be willing to issue in any reasonable size upon request.
- Not to post rates, but to give dealers advance notice of funding

requirements and be receptive to finely priced offers of funding.

- To circulate periodically to its dealers a list of forthcoming issuing requirements, accepting the most attractive bid on each issuing date.
- To respond to 'reverse enquiry' where the investors specify the terms and timing of a transaction.
- Use its EMTN programme as a vehicle for public bond issues.

The benefit of issuing eurobonds under EMTN programmes is that much of the preparation (appointment of trustees, etc) has already been done. The issue of an Offering Circular, produced from that on file, and underwriting and placement of the notes are the main tasks.

The arranger

The arranger's roles are to deal with the administration when a programme is set up and to ensure appropriate and timely liaison between the parties involved in the programme. Once appointed, the arranger will, among other things:

- Agree and monitor a timetable for the documentation.
- Negotiate and circulate draft documentation between the parties and arrange the signing of documentation.
- Advise on the selection of dealers.
- Provide advice on regulatory matters.
- Act as Listing Agent for the listing of the programme.
- Liaise with legal advisers, stock exchange(s) and printers.
- Monitor cost controls for setting up the programme.
- Ensure due diligence has been observed in the provision of details by the issuer.

The issuer will need to update the programme annually, renewing listings and updating the Offering Circular. New dealers may be added and existing ones deleted and the size of the programme may be increased. An issuer should consider annually the performance of dealers, pricing objectives and results, operating procedures, regulatory changes and funding requirements for the year ahead.

Dealer group

A dealer's role is to approach the issuer with various funding opportunities that will satisfy the borrowing targets that have been set. Choosing an appropriate dealer group, in terms of size, expertise and geographic spread, is important to the success of the programme. For most programmes, a group of between three and six houses will be used, depending on the programme size and funding demands. When assessing potential dealers, an issuer should consider:

- Credit ratings, since the dealer's house may be a swap counterparty for some issues.
- Market position. The house must have appropriate technical expertise and distribution capabilities.
- Currency and geographic diversity. A dealer may be chosen for its strengths in certain currencies or geographic area.

Relationship banks and banks that have performed well in other programmes will be on the proposed dealer list.

Paying agents

In a multi-currency programme, one or more paying agents will be appointed. The Principal Paying Agent's responsibilities are to ensure that:

- The Pricing Supplement prepared for each trade is properly drawn up.
- The note is issued into the appropriate clearing system and issuer is paid.
- Subsequent coupon payments and principal repayments are carried out in a timely fashion.
- All necessary reporting requirements are carried out for each particular currency regime.

Documentation

The principal documents for a programme are:

- *The Offering Circular.* This sets out the terms and conditions of the notes which will eventually be issued under the programme and the financial information and general business description of the issuer.

- *Dealers' agreement.* This will set out the mechanics of issuance and will contain:
    - The representations and warranties and undertakings to be given by the issuer, any guarantor and dealers.
    - The conditions precedent which must be satisfied before any issuance takes place.
    - Pro-forma examples of Pricing Supplements required for trades.

    It may also include:
    - A pro-forma syndication agreement that may be used for public syndicated issues.
    - A pro-forma Dealer Accession Letter for use when employing dealers not named on the programme, when the 'reverse enquiry' facility is operated.
- *The Trust Deed* as for eurobond issues.
- *Settlement Procedures Memorandum.* This sets out the operational procedures of all parties who are involved in completing a trade from initiation to settlement.
- *Listing Documents* as for eurobond issues.
- *Notifications* to the central banks of currencies in which issues are to be made.
- *Legal opinion* that the documentation is valid and binding.
- *Auditors' comfort letter* covering the period since the last audited accounts.
- *Issuer's resolution* authorising the establishment of the programme and the signing of the documentation.
- A *Pricing Supplement*, such as that illustrated in Figure 20.1, to record the terms of each note issue.

Figure 20.1   Specimen Pricing Supplement for Y1,000,000,000 Note

(appears at end of chapter)

Issuance procedure

Once the programme is in place, dealers who have identified an issuing opportunity will contact issuers. After an initial telephone conversation, the process is generally that:

- The dealer faxes an indicative terms sheet to the issuer with all the terms of the proposed trade, including how the funding level will be achieved if swaps are proposed.

- If the terms are satisfactory, telephone consent is given to the dealer to execute the trade. This 'working mandate' is given to the dealer for a specific period of time in order that the dealer can close a deal with an investor(s) on a timely basis.

- Once the trade is completed a final terms sheet confirming the details of the trade is faxed to the issuer, together with any swap confirmation.

- Both parties will confirm the trade with the Principal Paying Agent who will arrange for a Pricing Supplement setting out the terms of the trade to be sent and for issuance of the note(s). A global note will normally be issued for each tranche, which will be delivered into one of the clearing systems.

- The Paying Agent will submit the Pricing Supplement to the respective stock exchange if that tranche is to be listed under the listing approval granted for the programme.

The Bank of England's requirements for debt securities

The Bank of England's notice dated 18 March 1997 covers issues of commercial paper and debt securities of one year or over. Issuing CP and MTNs is similar to the taking of deposits. Since deposit taking is only allowed by institutions authorised or exempted under the Banking Act 1987, the notice sets out how exemptions from the Act apply to CP and MTNs. The term 'Medium Term Note' is not used as the notice covers all debt securities arranged and issued in London, and refers to them as commercial paper (less than one year, see chapter 17), shorter term debt (one to three years), and longer term debt securities (three to five years). Debt securities, including issues in currencies other than sterling (but subject to national regulations for the currency) can be issued by:

- Authorised institutions, european authorised institutions and building societies, without restriction.

- Any company can issue listed debt securities. Where the original maturity is three years or over, there is no minimum denomination requirement. Where it is below three years, the minimum denomination is £100,000.

- Those companies which have net assets of £25 million or more can issue unlisted debt securities provided that they have a minimum denomination of £100,000 and the issuer has shares or debt listed on the LSE or an EEA exchange.

- Overseas governments and overseas public authorities can issue unlisted debt securities if they are listed on the LSE or an approved overseas stock exchange.

There is no maximum maturity for these exempt issues. This used to be five years. Issues of sterling denominated paper with a maturity of over one year are subject to the Bank's lead management regime. Overseas firms may arrange or lead manage issues only where UK firms have reciprocal opportunities in the respective overseas centre. The Bank of England requires prior notice of the inclusion of a sterling option in an EMTN programme. Sterling tranches must be reported on a monthly basis, usually by the Paying Agent.

The secondary market

A secondary market exists in EMTNs. However, the market relies mainly on the commitment of dealers to make a market in notes where they act as dealers, to back-up their continuing involvement in the programme. Market practice is similar to that for conventional eurobonds. Dealing houses need the ability to unwind swaps and repackage structured notes.

Figure 20.1   Specimen Pricing Supplement for
Y1,000,000,000 Note

Series No:	313
Tranche No:	1

Medium Term Note Programme
Issue of
Yen 1,000,000,000
Fixed Rate Step-up Notes due 25 November 2002

This Pricing Supplement (as referred to in the Information Memorandum in relation to the above Programme) relates to the Series of Notes referred to above. The particulars to be specified in relation to such Series are as follows:

Issuer:	
Relevant Dealer:	
Syndicated:	No
Currency:	Japanese Yen (JPY)
Principal Amount of Series:	JPY 1,000,000,000
If to form a single Series with existing Series, Series No:	Not Applicable
Issue Date:	25 November 1997
Issue Price:	100.25
Commissions:	0.250 per cent
Form of Notes:	Temporary Global Note exchangeable for Permanent Global Note
Denomination(s):	JPY 100,000,000
Interest:	**Interest Payment Dates**: Each 25 February, 25 May, 25 August and 25 November, from and including 25 February 1998 to and including 25 November 2002, subject to adjustment in accordance with the Modified Business Day Convention. **Interest Rates** From and including 25 November 1997 to but excluding 25 November 1998: 1.00 per annum, which equates to JPY 250,000 per denomination. From and including 25 November 1998 to but excluding 25 November 1999: 1.32 per annum, which equates to JPY 330,000 per denomination. From and including 25 November 1999 to but excluding 25 November 2000: 1.64 per annum,

	which equates to JPY 410,000 per denomination. From and including 25 November 2000 to but excluding 25 November 2001: 1.96 per annum, which equates to JPY 490,000 per denomination. From and including 25 November 2001 to but excluding 25 November 2002: 2.28 per annum, which equates to JPY 570,000 per denomination. **Calculation Base**: 30/360 **Business Day Convention**: Modified Following **Business Centres**: Tokyo and London
Redemption:	25 November 2002, subject to adjustment in accordance with the Modified Following Business Day Convention.
Redemption Amount:	JPY 1,000,000,000
Optional Early Redemption Date:	**Call Dates**: Each 25 February, 25 May, 25 August and 25 November from and including 25 November 1998 to and including 25 August 2002, subject to adjustment in accordance with the Modified Business Day Convention. **Call Option Period**: Up to 5 Business Days Prior to each Call Date. **Business Centre**: Tokyo and London
Optional Early Redemption (Put):	Not Applicable
Redemption Amount following an event of Default:	JPY 1,000,000,000
Taxation:	Not applicable
Listing:	No
Stabilisation:	Not applicable
ISIN:	
Common Code:	
Common Depositary:	
Other Relevant Terms and Conditions:	Not Applicable
Any Additional Selling Restrictions:	For the purposes of the issue of the Notes, the reference in paragraph 3 of Schedule 2 to the Second Amended Dealer Agreement to 'Article 11(3) of the Financial Services Act 1986 (Investment Advertisements)(Exemptions) Order 1995' shall be read as a reference to Article 11(3) of the Financial Services Act 1986 (Investment Advertisements) (Exemptions) Order 1996, as amended.

CONFIRMED

_____
Authorised Signatory

Date

21 Securitisation and loan transfers

Loan or asset transfers are the means by which banks move assets off their balance sheets to third parties. Securitisation involves the additional step of issuing tradable paper against such assets.

Asset securitisation

Banks and financial organisations have long been active in this process of transferring loans and assets, whether in whole or in part, and in issuing securities backed by these assets. The source of interest and principal payments on these securities is based on the cash flows of the assets rather than that of a specified borrower. The term securitisation is defined as follows:

- The pooling and packaging of a group of homogenous loans, receivables or financial assets.
- The sale of these packages to investors in the form of securities, frequently through issues of floating rate notes (FRNs) and through special purpose vehicle companies (SPVs).
- The securities are collateralised by the underlying assets and their associated income.

Securitisation is a process through which illiquid assets are transformed into a more liquid and manageable form and distributed to a broad range of investors through the capital markets. The packaging typically involves the transfer of the underlying assets to the investment vehicle without recourse to the original owner (the originator or seller). Securitisation techniques are now used in all major markets and the largest market is in the US. London is the next largest market.

Issues of securities, backed by, amongst other things, property, car loans, credit card receivables, corporate loans and student loans have been made but the largest proportion of issues relate to residential mortgages and property. Banks manage the structure of their balance sheets either as the issuer or purchaser of securities. As issuers, banks can securitise a pool of otherwise illiquid assets to remove them from their balance sheets. As purchasers, they are able to rebalance the exposure of their loan portfolios in favour of a particular type of business. Securities issued by the SPV may be FRNs, fixed rate bonds or commercial paper. The characteristics of issues will be determined primarily by the characteristics of the assets to be securitised. The process of arranging an issue of FRNs and bonds is as described in chapter 19.

Origins: mortgage-backed securities (MBS) in the US

These markets originated in the United States in the early 1970s. The original form of mortgage-backed security was the 'pass through'. Under this structure, the original lender grouped together a pool of individual mortgages and sold them to an intermediary, perhaps a trust, which raised finance through the sale of securities to investors. During the life of the loans, all payments of principal and interest, less any servicing fees, were 'passed through' the intermediary, with a specified time lag to allow time for administration, to the end investors. The effect of this was that investors received a proportionate share of the cash flows as if they had lent to the mortgagors themselves. This applied not only to scheduled interest and principal payments but also to unscheduled early repayments and any losses as a result of default in the underlying loan pool. Most of the mortgages were fixed rate with an original term of over 20 years and early repayment rights. A fall in interest rates would lead to a proportion of the underlying loans being prepaid since borrowers could refinance their loans more cheaply. A number of models have been developed to predict the repayment patterns depending on the age of the mortgages and levels of interest rates. However, the uncertainty of cash flows of pass through securitisations is a deterrent to many investors who will consider other types of mortgage backed security.

Collateralised Mortgage Obligations (CMOs) were developed using a variety of structures to enhance the predictability of cashflows for investors. The payment flows are paid to SPVs, sometimes through trust companies. The securities are structured, having tranches with different payment and risk characteristics to satisfy differing investor preferences. For example, repayments may be applied to tranche A securities before tranche B, with tranche B investors receiving a higher return in exchange for the greater risk. Tranches may be designed to have reasonably certain cash flows whilst other tranches will absorb excess prepayments. Asset-backed securities are now normally structured in this manner.

The best known issuers of mortgage-backed securities in the US are the various government agencies, for example, the Government National Mortgage Association (GNMA or 'Ginnie Mae') and the Federal National Mortgage Association (FNMA or Fannie Mae). The US market in all types of asset-backed securities is very deep and liquid with a variety of different structures available to financial institutions and banks to use in their balance sheet management or trading activities.

Development of the securitisation market in the UK

The UK securitisation market has suffered many false dawns but since 1996 it has witnessed sustained growth in volumes. The traditional mainstay of the UK market was the residential mortgage backed securities market. However, following the onset of the housing recession in the early 1990s, the market has widened to include privatisations, project finance and the sale of low-yielding corporate assets by a number of banks.

In 1997 there were a number of large transactions with issuance amounts in excess of £1 billion. Characteristics of the growth of the UK market in recent years have been:

- The use of securitisations linked to the Private Finance Initiative introduced by the last Conservative Government. This has included the sale of portfolios by the government using securitisation techniques rather than funded state sector entities. Examples of this type of transaction include: the Autolink M6 road transaction (£138.8m), where future payments will be made from shadow road tolls payable by the Government; Health Management (Carlisle) PLC (£75.8m), a securitisation of lease receivables on a hospital; Finance for Residential Social Housing PLC (£961.3m), to finance a portfolio of housing association loans sold by the Government;

and Annington Finance Ltd No. 4 PLC (£3.14bn), in respect of the sale of the married quarters estate of the armed forces.

- The use of securitisation in corporate acquisition. The Aire Valley Finance issue of £979m represented the largest residential mortgage transaction in the UK to date. It securitised mortgages acquired by the Bradford and Bingley Building Society through its acquisition of Mortgage Express.

- The emergence of the corporate loan securitisation market, widely known as collateralised loan obligations (CLOs), has acted as a spur to a number of banks looking to increase capital returns and release capital tied up to support low margin lending. These securitisations also enable banks to meet their capital adequacy requirements and pursue strategic initiatives and such as acquisitions and share repurchase. NatWest's Rose (Repeat Offering Securitisation Entity) No. 1 funding in 1996 represented the first corporate loan securitisation structured specifically to remove low earning, investment grade loans from the bank's balance sheet. This was followed in 1997 by Rose 2, a US$5.5bn corporate loan securitisation. Both issues had several tranches of debt securities. By May 1998, approximately US$40bn worth of corporate loan securitisations have been undertaken globally. Many market commentators predict that CLOs will become the largest asset class for securitisations.

Features of mortgage-backed and credit card securitisations and CLOs

Most mortgage-backed securities in the UK have been issued on a floating rate basis, with coupons linked to Libor, to match broadly the floating rate basis of the underlying assets. Where UK banks have offered fixed rate mortgages, they have tended to use swaps or direct bond issues to match the interest rate risk rather than resort to securitisation. With floating rate issues, the rate of early repayment is not likely to be affected by changes in interest rates for these loans. The originator may be obliged to 'top up' the pool of mortgages in the early years of the issue, substituting new mortgages for those that repay early. This means that there will be no unexpected prepayments of the securities in the early years. Similarly, there may be an option for the issuer to 'mop up' any remaining mortgages if the outstanding balances are reduced to relatively small amounts of the original balance after, say, 15 years. A residential mortgage securitisation needs to be at least £150 million to warrant the costs involved. If mortgages with an average value of £50,000 are securitised, a securitisation issue needs, say, 3,000 mortgages to be viable.

Credit cards permit borrowers to vary the drawn amount of their credit facility within an agreed limit. Repayment is at the borrower's discretion subject to minimum amounts per payment. Securitisation of such receivables involves issuing notes of a fixed amount and term against assets of a fluctuating amount and indefinite maturity. There is a need to insulate investors from the effects of the fluctuating balances. This is achieved by assigning shares in the receivables to the investors and to the originating bank. The amount assigned to the noteholders stays fixed at the amount of their funding whilst the amount assigned to the bank rises and falls as borrowers make drawings and repayments.

Schemes will have a revolving period and an amortising period. During the revolving period, the investors will receive their share of interest but their share of principal will be re-invested in the pool. During the amortisation period, the investors' share of principal repayments is used to redeem the securities. Receivables outstanding at the end of the scheme will need to be refinanced by another scheme or taken back by the original bank. The regulatory authorities will only allow these schemes if the quality of the assets has not deteriorated and the originator has adequate liquidity both during and on refinancing the securitisation.

There are three types of CLOs. First, there is the true sale where loans are sold to the SPV and bondholders have title or a senior secured interest in the collateral loans. This is the most secure structure and it isolates the bonds from any downgrade of the issuing bank. Second, there is the quasi-sale, where loans or sub-participations are transferred to a trust. Here the bondholders in the SPV do not necessarily have a first lien on the assets being securitised. This implies that the rating of the issuer will act as a cap on the bonds since the bank still controls the collateral. The NatWest Rose deals are structured on this basis. Third, Credit Linked Notes (CLN) can be issued. Under this structure, the issuer does not transfer the loans to the SPV. The SPV purchases CLNs from the issuing bank, which are obligations on the bank to pay interest and principal on specific reference credits, subject to the non-default of these credits. CLNs are described in more detail in Chapter 29.

Benefits of securitisation

The main benefit from asset securitisation for banks is that it enables them to pass on the risks of lending to other parties, thus freeing their balance sheets from these assets and the related capital costs. This can be a deliberate strategy to move away from traditional bank lending in order to concentrate of the business they know best, generating the assets through sales, but not funding them. The rating of asset-backed securities is often higher than that of the originator who, through securitisations, is able to tap funding sources to which it may not normally have access.

Securitisation can help a bank in its asset and liability management. First, it offers a bank that is heavily exposed to a particular region or economic sector the ability to transfer part of its portfolio. It can purchase other types of ABS with the proceeds, thus achieving a more diversified portfolio. Second, interest rate risk can be reduced by passing it on to investors. A bank, wishing to extend its lending but not having funds of adequate maturity, can avoid a maturity mismatch by securitising new loans.

Banks engaging in one or more of the securitisation roles, such as originator, servicer, trustee, enhancer or investor, can increase and diversify their sources of fee and interest income. The yield on the pooled assets should be greater than the coupon on the securities and more than cover the costs of securitisation. Any surplus at the end of the life of the securitisation accrues to the owners of the SPV.

Securitisation can also have benefits for borrowers. Securitisation generally helps to improve the liquidity of credit markets and can increase the availability of credit to borrowers and may allow them to obtain funds at lower cost.

The benefit of securitisation for investors is that it provides a broader range of investment opportunities. Asset pools are often divided into separate tranches with different maturities and risk characteristics that are targetted to different investor preferences. Asset backed securities typically offer a yield premium over other debt instruments with similar ratings. They offer a greater degree of protection because the risk is spread over many underlying loans. Securitisation provides investors with the opportunity to participate in other markets, such as retail markets, which it would be difficult for them to lend to directly.

Risks of securitisation

The main risk that a bank may face in a securitisation is that a true sale may not be achieved. The selling bank may then be forced to recognise some or all of the losses if the assets cease to perform. A true sale would not be achieved if there were any obligation to repurchase or exchange any of the assets; if an investor can have recourse to put back assets to the selling bank; or if the seller had to account for interest and principal payments on the assets sold. For a true sale to be achieved, the selling bank must have no ownership or management control of the SPV that owns the pooled assets. There must be no requirement to consolidate the SPV, which must not contain the selling bank's name.

There is a potential conflict of interest if a bank originates, sells, underwrites and services an asset-backed security. A bank that has originated and transferred assets may be exposed to moral pressure to repurchase the securities if the assets cease to perform. After having completed a securitisation, the seller does not disappear but usually exercises other functions in the process. Investors are aware of the identity of the provider of the assets backing the securities and they could, at least morally, cause pressure to be put on the seller to support the securitisation scheme. The seller may be inclined to do so in order to protect its name. Regulatory authorities therefore impose conditions to maintain the segregation of functions and responsibilities.

A further concern of regulators is that banks may sell their best assets and thereby increase the average risk in their remaining portfolio. Investor demand for high quality assets may encourage this tendency. An ongoing securitisation programme needs a growing loan portfolio and this may lead to a bank lowering its credit quality in order to generate the necessary volume of loans. In practice, banks that have securitised large amounts of loans do not show evidence of lower asset quality. Banks do, in any case, have a need to maintain asset quality for reputational and rating agency purposes.

Because the payment pattern of the assets cannot be predicted exactly at the outset, there will remain some liquidity and interest rate risks that need to be addressed at the outset and during the life of the securitisation. Payments of interest and principal into the pool are held by the trustee until they are due to be paid out to the investors. FRNs, being Libor linked, typically make repayments quarterly and bonds usually make annual payments. If there is a large unexpected inflow, the trustee may be unable to invest these funds at a high enough interest rate to cover the interest payable to investors.

There may be a Guaranteed Investment Contract in place between the trustee and the bank, which guarantees, for a fee, to meet the necessary rate of interest on funds deposited.

The risks for banks acting as a servicer are principally operational, comparable to those of an agent bank in a syndicated loan. However, the number of loans in the portfolio and the different parties involved mean that there are higher risks of malfunction for which the servicer might become liable. Servicers need to engage adequate personnel, equipment and technology to process these transactions in order to minimise these operational risks. While all banking activity entails operational and legal risk, these are greater in securitisations because of their complexity. The securitisation process, if not carried out prudently, can leave risks with the originating bank without allocating capital to them.

Credit enhancement

The securities issued will be rated by one of the rating agencies and will reflect the nature of the underlying assets rather than the credit of the originator. Credit enhancement is used to obtain a higher rating and therefore a lower coupon on the issue of securities.

Asset backed securities usually pay a higher rate of interest than securities of equivalent term. This reflects not only the potential volatility of prepayment rates but also the fact that investors are taking direct credit risk on the underlying borrowers. The level of risk investors assume depends on the strength of the asset pool and the credit enhancements. To determine the appropriate enhancement, the estimated credit risk in the pooled assets is assessed together with its historical loss profile. Usually this results in an enhancement that covers, by a multiple of several times, the historical default rates of the underlying assets. Regulatory authorities require that credit enhancements are undertaken at the initiation of schemes; are disclosed in any offering circular; and are documented separately.

The most common forms of credit enhancement are senior-subordinated debt structures; irrevocable letters of credit; over-collateralisation; spread accounts; and cash collateral accounts. Different forms of enhancement may be combined in any securitisation. The simplest form of enhancement is a recourse arrangement providing the buyer of the assets with the right to receive payment from an enhancer or guarantor for the first losses sustained by the scheme. This shifts the credit risk fully to the guarantor and a bank providing this facility will be required to deduct the amount of the facility from its capital.

An irrevocable letter of credit may be issued by a third party bank to cover the portion of the assets normally equal to the estimated loss profile and is often subordinated to the other enhancements. Non-bank insurance companies have been active in the UK by providing third-party insurance against the first portion of debt default.

Where the enhancement is provided by a senior-subordinated structure at least two classes of securities are issued. The senior tranche has a prior claim on all cash flows from the underlying assets. Losses will accrue first to the junior or subordinated securities up to the amount of this particular class. If, for example, an issue consists of 90 per cent senior and 10 per cent subordinated securities, the holders of the subordinated securities will carry the first losses up to 10 per cent of the assets of the scheme.

Over-collateralisation means that the value of the underlying assets in the pool exceeds the amount of the securities issued. In such schemes the excess collateral must be maintained at a level sufficient to provide the agreed amount of credit enhancement. If the value declines below that level the enhancer must fill the gap with new collateral

A spread account is a deposit typically built up from the spread between the interest paid on the pooled assets and the lower interest paid on the securities issued. The servicer, instead of passing the spread back to the originator, passes on all the funds collected to the trustee where they are accumulated up to the level required for the credit enhancement. After reaching this level, all future spread earnings can be passed back to the originator. To provide for early losses the originator normally has to deposit funds in the spread account in advance. The account is used to cover any losses on the pooled assets. Any balance left over in the spread account when the securities are redeemed reverts to the originator.

A cash collateral account is a deposit equal to the credit enhancement, which is held for the benefit of investors in the securities. The balance available will be used if losses occur. Cash advances may be made to this cash account by the originator or a third-party lender.

Methods of transfer

There are three ways to transfer financial assets. These are novation, assignment and sub-participation. The method of transfer determines the risks assumed by buyers and sellers and the treatment by the Financial Services Authority (FSA) for capital adequacy purposes.

Novation

This is the only way of effectively transferring both rights and obligations. The existing loans are cancelled and a new agreement substitutes all the original rights and obligations for new ones. The main difficulty with this technique is that it requires the consent of all the parties to the original loan. For capital adequacy purposes, a transfer through novation will be regarded as a clean transfer by the FSA. The loans will be excluded from the seller's risk asset ratio and included in the buyer's.

Legal and equitable assignments

Under English law, a lender may assign his rights under a loan agreement to a third party, ie his rights to interest and principal payments. A loan agreement may impose restrictions on assignability and in these cases a buyer could have difficulty enforcing an assignment against a seller. In any event, a buyer cannot gain greater rights than the seller.

A legal assignment passes all the legal and beneficial rights in a loan to the assignee. It must be in writing, be absolute, cover the whole of the loan and will be completed by notice in writing to the borrower. An equitable assignment covers only beneficial rights, not legal rights, and in consequence a buyer may not be able to proceed directly against a borrower. It will be in writing, cover the whole loan and may be completed by notice to the borrower.

Assignments notified to the borrower can achieve an effective transfer of the seller's rights and the remedies available to him to enforce those rights. These rights may be impaired by any right of set-off that exist between the borrower and the seller. When notice is given, the borrower may make payments direct to the buyer. Notice prevents the seller and borrower from varying the terms of the underlying contract. The seller retains any outstanding obligations, for example, to advance further funds. For capital adequacy purposes, transfers by assignment notified to the borrower will be regarded as a clean transfer, provided that the buyer has taken reasonable precautions to ensure that his rights are not impaired. A minimum requirement is a warranty from the seller that no rights of set off exist between the seller and the borrower.

With silent assignments, where the borrower is not notified of the assignment, there may be additional risks. For the buyer, this is because the absence of notice to the borrower removes some of the legal protection he would otherwise have. For the seller, this is because, as lender of record, he will remain subject to requests to reschedule or re-negotiate the loan. For capital adequacy purposes, a transfer through silent assignment will usually be regarded as a clean transfer by the FSA. However, the seller must recognize that he remains the lender of record and will be the focal point for pressure from the borrower to advance further funds and for rescheduling or renegotiating the loan. The volume of individual loans sold on a silent assignment basis must be subject to appropriate internal controls. The FSA may disregard a transfer by silent assignment in calculating the risk asset ratio of the seller if it is not satisfied on the above.

To cover the practical difficulty of obtaining consent, most loans are now structured to facilitate transfer. Essentially, all the parties agree in advance that all or part of the loan can be transferred.

Sub-participation

A sub-participation is a separate legal agreement from the underlying loan, creating a debtor-creditor relationship between the buyer and seller. It does not transfer any rights or obligations from the seller to the buyer. It is an entirely separate funding arrangement under which the buyer places funds with the seller, with no recourse to the borrower. The loan itself is not transferred. This is the most common securitisation technique, particularly for the transfer of loan assets by banks.

The buyer assumes a credit exposure on both the underlying borrower and the seller because it is reliant on the latter to pass through payments received from the borrower.

For capital adequacy purposes, when a loan is funded via a sub-participation, the FSA will recognise the transfer of credit risk by excluding it from the original lender's risk asset ratio. It will include it in the sub-participant's as a claim on the underlying borrower.

Conditions for all securitisations

The following conditions, common to all securitisations, must be satisfied for banks to be able to exclude assets from their risk asset ratios:

- The transfer does not contravene the terms and conditions of the underlying loan agreement.

- The seller has no residual beneficial interest in the loan and the buyer has no formal recourse to the seller for losses.

- The seller can demonstrate that it has given notice to the buyer that it is under no obligation to repurchase the loan nor support any losses suffered by the buyer. The buyer may retain an option to repurchase the loan providing it remains fully performing.

- The buyer and not the seller would be subject to any rescheduled or re-negotiated terms.

- Where payments are routed through the seller, he is under no obligation to remit funds to the buyer unless and until they are received from the borrower.

The origination and structure of asset-backed securities

Packaging asset securitisations is a long and costly business. The process can take up to 18 months to complete. The first stage will be carried out internally and will include:

- Creating a securitisation committee, which will include members of Treasury, Finance, Credit, Loan administration, Audit and Systems.

- Reviewing the documentation for all assets it is proposed to securitise. It has been standard practice for a long time to include transferability clauses in asset documentation.

- Creating the SPV and appointing internal and external auditors.
- Considering the requirements of the rating agencies.
- Reviewing data management and management information systems.

SPVs are thinly capitalised and must be independent of the originator and the servicing agent. Where the originator buys subordinated debt in the SPV, the FSA's requirement is that this is deducted from the bank's capital. The next stage in a securitisation includes:

- The preparation of legal documentation.
- Selection of a lead manager with the necessary distribution capabilities for the bond or FRN issue.
- Obtaining a liquidity facility for the SPV to meet any temporary cash shortfalls and approving arrangements for reinvesting short term surpluses at market rates.
- Consideration of credit enhancements needed for the rating process and the final selection of assets to be securitised.

The role of service agents

When assets are securitised, the selling institution will most likely retain the role of service agent to administer the loans. The FSA requires that the following conditions be met to ensure that a service agent's role is not seen as being more than that of agent.

- Records must be available to satisfy auditors that the terms of the scheme protect it from any liability to the investors, save where it is proved to be negligent.
- Any offering circulated should contain a highly visible and unequivocal statement that the servicing agent does not stand behind the issue and will not make good any losses in the portfolio.
- The servicing agent may not own any share capital in the SPV

for the scheme nor have any proprietary interest or control in the company.

- The Board of the SPV must be independent of the servicing agent, although the latter may have one director representing it.

- The name of the SPV must not include the name of the servicing agent or imply any connection with it.

- The servicing agent must not bear any of the recurring costs of the scheme. However, at the outset of the scheme, it may make a one off contribution to enhance the creditworthiness of the issue. It may lend on a long term subordinated basis to the SPV provided the debt is repayable only on the winding up of the scheme. These must be disclosed in any offering circular.

- The service agent may not bear any losses arising from the effect of interest rate changes, except for unintended temporary losses. The servicing agent may enter into interest rate swaps at market rates with the vehicle.

- A servicing agent may not provide temporary finance to cover shortfalls arising from delayed payments or non-performance of the loans it administers.

Loan transfers

Banks frequently sell corporate loans or loan fixtures to other lenders by way of sub-participation. The sub-participation agreement will state that the buying institution has made its own independent credit assessment on the borrower and is not relying on the seller. The selling bank will receive a deposit from the buyer to fund the individual loan.

When banks transfer undrawn commitments to other banks, the commitment will be excluded from the selling bank's risk asset ratio only when the transfer is by novation or assignment with a formal acknowledgment from the borrower. The seller will otherwise have to record a risk asset weighting against the purchasing bank (a 20 per cent risk asset weighting for OECD banks), to reflect the fact that the buyer is relied on to provide funding in the event of drawdown by the borrower.

22 Government securities

Government securities are the main way governments finance the gap between their expenditure and tax revenue, including servicing existing debt interest and repayment commitments. They are IOUs with a promise to pay interest on due dates and the principal amounts at maturity.

Sterling Treasury bills

The first UK Treasury bills were issued in 1877. The bills are bearer instruments issued on a discount basis through a weekly tender and are redeemed at their face value at maturity. Although the tenor can be one, two or six months, bills are usually issued for 91 days. The denominations are £5,000, £10,000, £25,000, £50,000, £100,000, £250,000, £500,000, £1,000,000, £5,000,000 and £10,000,000. Although issues are still available in paper form, most issues are immobilised within the Central Moneymarket Office in dematerialised form. The Bank of England (the Bank) is responsible for issuing UK Treasury bills.

The primary market

The method of issuing sterling Treasury bills was last modified in May 1995. The volume of bills to be issued is announced on a Friday, for allocation following receipt of bids at 12:30 pm on the following Friday. The major participants in the market may make their bids by phone. Bids may be made by fax by 12:20 pm or directly over the counter at the Bank of England. When bidding by telephone, the only details bidders need to specify are the name of the organisation, the price bid, the total value of the bid and the tenor (term) of the bills. Separate bids must be made for bills of different tenors. Bids must be for a minimum of £50,000, made in multiples of £5,000 and are irrevocable. The Bank's record will prevail in the event of a dispute or misunderstanding. Following changes by the Bank of England to its operations in the sterling money markets in March 1997, Treasury bill issues are no longer underwritten.

The results of the tender are announced between 1:15 pm and 1:30 pm with successful applicants being contacted by the Bank who will ask:

- the date they wish the bills to be issued, which will be on a delivery versus payment basis on a day of the applicant's choice in the following week;
- the denominations required;
- whether the bills are to be issued into the CMO and if so the account name and participant number.

Successful bidders will confirm these details by fax by 2:00 pm and letters of allotment will be available from the Bank by 3:00 pm.

Bids are made on a price basis to three decimal places, eg a price of 98.200, which for a 91-day bill is a discount rate of 7.2198 per cent and yield of 7.3521 per cent. Bills are allocated in full to bidders at the highest price (so paying the lowest rate of interest) until the tender is sold. Successful bidders pay the price they bid with bills, therefore, being sold at different prices. Details of the tender are published in the format of figure 22.1.

Figure 22.1   Specimen result of Bank of England Treasury bill tender

```
Bank of England    Treasury bill tender,    Friday 5 June 1998
91 Day bills
Applied for Stg 620m
Average date of discount 7.2198%
Allotment price 98.200
All bids at this price allotted in full
Next week on offer - Stg 100 mn 91 day bills
```

Source: Reuters' screen BOE/MONEYOPS5

Calculations: A bid of £98.200 represents a discount rate of 7.2187 per cent and yield of 7.3521 per cent, calculated as follows:

Discount $\dfrac{(100 - 98.200) \times 365}{(100 \times 91)}$ =   7.2198%

Yield $\dfrac{(100 - 98.200)}{98.200} \times \dfrac{365}{91}$ =   7.3521%

Following changes by the Bank to its operations in the sterling money markets in March 1997, the level of the weekly issue has often been at the low level of £100 million and the total amount of bills outstanding was around £1,300 million at June 1998. The small amount of bills available means that the prices bid are high (yields are low) because of demand from institutions. This level of issuance is not a permanent feature and may increase in future periods. There is a market in 'hots', that is bills not yet issued but which will be available the following week.

Secondary market trading

Bills can be sold before their maturity date in the secondary market as bills are held by banks for liquidity purposes and used by the Bank in its daily money market operations. However, the secondary market is not liquid. Any bills that are made available tend to be bought for inclusion in portfolios and held to maturity. Rates in the secondary market are quoted on a discount basis.

Gilts

Gilts is the term used to describe medium to long term debt securities issued and guaranteed by the UK government. Gilts have a history dating back over 400 years. They are registered securities issued with fixed redemption dates for various periods up to 30 years. UK gilts have now largely been immobilised and the transfer of ownership is carried out by computer book entry at the Central Gilts Office (CGO). Since 1966, it has been possible to hold gilts in Euroclear or Cedel Bank. Gilt coupons are paid net of withholding tax unless the holder requests gross payments, which is now possible without restriction. Gilts are listed on the London Stock Exchange. Each gilt stock has a 12 digit ISIN that incorporates the SEDOL (Stock Exchange Daily Official List) number for UK securities.

The United Kingdom Debt Management Office (DMO) assumed

responsibility for the UK Government's debt programme in April 1998. It is responsible for issuing gilts and for monitoring secondary market trading.

There are a number of types of gilts in issue. The main types are Treasury, Exchequer, Convertible and index-linked. All new issues are Treasury issues. Exchequer issues have not been made for several years. Convertible stocks are issued at one coupon but on a given date are convertible at the option of the holder into a different interest rate and maturity date and all current stocks of this type have been converted. Index-linked gilts were first issued in 1981. Both coupons and redemption value are linked to the UK retail price index. Some issues are double dated, eg 2004-2008. Such gilts have a call option, which can be exercised by the government on three month's notice between the relevant dates. Some undated stocks, such as War Loan 3.5 per cent, are still in existence.

At December 1997, there were approximately £280 billion gilts outstanding. There were 43 fixed rate stocks in issue: 16 short-dated gilts with remaining lives up to five years; 22 medium-dated gilts where maturity is between five and 15 years and five long-dated gilts whose maturity is over 15 years. There were also 12 index-linked stocks and six undated stocks. Fixed rate issues account for over 80 per cent of issues, index-linked for 16 per cent and floating rate note issues for 3 per cent. The largest current issue is the 8 per cent Treasury 2021 with £16.5 billion outstanding and this is one of the benchmark issues. The current policy is to increase the size of issues to create benchmark issues along the yield curve. There are now around 20 issues of over £5 billion.

From November 1998, interest will accrue and be payable based on an 'actual/actual' or the actual number of days elapsed over 365 or 366 days. Previously interest was paid semi-annually on an actual/365 day basis. This meant that there were two equal coupons for 182.5 days each per annum. The FRNs pay interest quarterly.

Investors' holdings of gilts in 1996 were as follows: Life assurers 33 per cent, pension funds 22 per cent, overseas holders 19 per cent, banks and building societies 10 per cent, other financial institutions 11 per cent and the remainder, including retail, 5 per cent.

The primary market

Until 1986, issues of stock were made to investors who applied for advertised or unsold issues through jobbers (now called market makers). This method became inefficient and liable to manipulations since the new issue market was in the hands of two large jobbers. In 1986, the market was opened up and 27 institutions became market makers. Their number is now reduced to 16. These are Gilt-edged Market Makers (GEMMs). GEMMs are committed to make two-way prices on a continuous basis in all trading conditions, in return for which they have a closer dealing relationship with the DMO and a privileged position in auctions.

Primary dealers in government securities markets are specialist intermediaries between the authorities and the market. Their role is to ensure the efficiency of the primary market and the depth and liquidity of the secondary market. Their obligations usually consist of supporting auctions and guaranteeing liquidity in the secondary market. GEMMs are required to make continuous two-way prices at which they stand committed to deal. Unusually, they are required to make prices for the whole range of government securities, not just for leading stocks. The privileges of GEMMs are:

- The ability to put in late bids at auctions and to submit bids by telephone.
- Exclusive rights to bid for certain issues such as tap issues.
- Exemption from the usual requirement to submit payment at the time of bidding.
- Exclusive access to inter-dealer brokers for secondary market trading.
- The ability to borrow short term from the DMO and to obtain stock on repo.

Conventional gilts are issued by auction. Index-linked gilts are issued through the tap mechanism but auctions of index-linked stock started in 1998. One of the weaknesses of the gilts market until the mid-1990s was the unpredictability of new issues. There is now a calendar for auctions of issues of conventional gilts. The calendar is announced in advance each year, although it may be subject to revision as the government's funding requirements change. Calendars allow for market participants to plan ahead. They allow primary dealers to market issues to their customers and they allow overseas investors who may not be closely focussed on the market to arrange currency transfers. Details of the auction are given one week in advance. When a single stock is offered, auctions take place on the third Wednesday of the month of issue. Dual auctions, for the sale of two stocks with different maturities, take place on the third Tuesday and Thursday of the month. Only seven auctions are planned in the fiscal year 1998/9 due to the falling Central Government Borrowing Requirement.

Bids, on a price basis (and in decimals from November 1998), are submitted by 10:30 am on the auction date. Results are published by 11:15 am. Bids can be made on a competitive basis or a non-competitive basis. Competitive bids must be for a minimum amount of £500,000 and in multiples of £100,000 up to £1 million and in multiples of £1 million thereafter. Competitive bids are met at the yield bid until the issue is sold. A proportion of the issue, say up to 20 per cent of an issue, is reserved for non-competitive bids of not less than £1,000 and not more than £500,000. These are issued at the average allotted price of successful bids and are scaled down if oversubscribed. GEMMs are allowed to make more bids in the final minutes of the auction and to increase their non-competitive bids, up to a total of 0.5 per cent of the stock on offer.

Fixed rate gilt issues are usually made initially in blocks ranging from £1.5 to £3 billion. To be successful, an issue is expected to be oversubscribed and the 'cover ratio' is carefully monitored by all parties. The 'tail' is also monitored. The tail is the difference in yield between the highest successful bid and the average successful bid. The size of the gilt is often increased at later dates by re-openings either through auctions or unscheduled, opportunistic funding (taps or taplets). These techniques help create liquid benchmark issues. The DMO takes a pro-active approach to determining the availability and price of tap sales.

Although there is no maximum limit on the amount dealers can bid for, the issue process is monitored by the DMO to ensure that a participant, or number of participants in collusion, does not corner the market. Competition between primary dealers enhances the price formation process.

GEMMs are not required to put funds up with their bids but all other participants must prepay. Because of this, and the primary market-makers privileged bidding position, most bids are channelled through primary dealers. Primary dealers must choose whether or not to trust their clients or to seek prepayment from them. Settlement is on the following business day. Issues are usually made below par (at less than £100 per £100 of stock), although they are repayable at par.

There is a market in 'when-issued' gilts, which is a form of grey market. This is permitted from the time of the confirmation of the specific stock to be auctioned until the results of the auction are announced, currently over a period of seven to nine days. This market is principally used by GEMMs to go short of stock before it is available.

Sale by auction is the technique used by most governments to sell debt to the non-state sector. The technique is market-oriented and transparent. The sale of securities is announced in advance. Purchasers declare their price on a competitive basis and by the same deadline. Most governments conduct auctions of securities on a sealed bid and bid-price basis. Sealed bid systems, which include bids made by phone or electronically, do not reveal information to bidders during the auction process itself. In a bid-price auction, each successful bidder pays the price he bids. In a common price system, all the securities are allocated at the lowest yield, or highest price. There are risks in using auctions. There may be insufficient bids to cover the amount the government wishes to sell and the bids may be below the price the government wishes to accept. The market will be aware of any adverse results of auctions.

Secondary market trading

Average daily turnover for gilts, excluding repo, was £7.8 billion in 1996/1997. From November 1998 prices in the secondary market will be quoted in decimals, the previous 'tick' size for trading being 1/32nd (where a price of 100 - 08 was 100 8/32nds). Dealing spreads will depend on the terms and duration of the particular issue. Gilts may be purchased in nominal value increments of one penny. Settlement is normally for the working day following the trade but may be agreed for settlement at a later date. Cash trades for same day value between clients with a CGO account must be agreed by 2:00 pm on that business day. A specimen confirmation for a secondary market purchase is given in figure 22.2.

Figure 22.2   Specimen contract confirmation for purchase of gilts

```
TO              NEWBANK CAPITAL MARKETS  ATTN...
FROM            GENCREDIT GILT-EDGED DIVISION

TRADE REF       :040872
TRADE DATE      :26 JAN  99        TIME     : 18.12
VALUE DATE      :29 JAN  99
STOCK REF       :10015             ISIN     : GB0008881541


WE CONFIRM OUR PURCHASE FROM YOU AS PRINCIPALS
SUBJECT TO THE REGULATIONS OF THE LONDON STOCK EXCHANGE.
GBP 500000 UK TREASURY 8.00000% 07-DEC-15
AT 120.78125
                                             603,906.25
ACCRUED INTEREST 53 DAYS                        5,808.22
TOTAL CONSIDERATION
                                   GBP     609,714.47


DELIVERY AND PAYMENT:              PLEASE DELIVER THE BONDS
                                   TO OUR CGO ACCOUNT 8952
                                   AGAINST PAYMENT
```

Inter dealer brokers (IDBs) are wholesale brokers intermediating only between GEMMs for purchases, sales and switches of stock. They operate screen-based systems linking GEMMs, which display firm two-way prices. Deals are executed on a matched book basis. They are transacted on an anonymous basis between GEMMs to avoid any distortion of the market.

Since 1996, a 'shop window' has operated with details of the amounts of stock in official portfolios available for resale or switching given on screen pages. The amounts on offer are no higher than £100 million and the DMO responds to bids rather than actively offering stock.

Gilt strips

Gilt stripping has been officially allowed since December 1997. It is a technique that can be applied to any bond but is most frequently used for government securities because they are issued in adequate volume to make the process viable.

Strip is an acronym for the 'Separate Trading of Registered Interest and Principal'. Stripping is the process of separating a standard coupon-bearing bond into its constituent interest and principal payments. These can then be held or traded as zero coupon instruments. For example, a five year bond can be separated into 11 zero coupon bonds, one from the principal amount and ten from the semi-annual coupon payments. Coupon payments due, say six, 12 and 18 months after issue would, if the underlying bond were stripped, become six, 12 and 18 month zero coupon bonds. The cash flows on the bundle of zero coupon strips, which can be traded separately, would be identical to the cash flows on the original unstripped bond. The process can be done in reverse to reconstitute a gilt into its original form.

Gilt coupon and principal strips created through the official gilts strip facility remain direct obligations of the UK government. They are registered securities in their own right and are held at the CGO in book entry form. They cannot be held outside the CGO.

There are no restrictions on who may invest in gilt strips unless investors are subject to their own restrictions on how funds may be invested. Through investing in strips, an investor can in principle achieve a desired pattern of cash flows more easily. Long term savings institutions may be interested in higher duration assets which stripping will make available, allowing liabilities to be more easily matched without reinvestment risk.

The total nominal amount of strippable stock in December 1997 was around £80 billion. This is made up of eight stock issues maturing between 2000 and 2021. All these stocks have common interest payment dates of 7 June and 7 December so that the coupons are interchangeable for trading purposes. They are not, however, fungible. The minimum strippable unit permitted is £10,000, which is increased in multiples of £10,000. The minimum displayed bid and offer amount on an IDB screen will be £1 million. Each strip is allocated an ISIN. Strips can be used in repo or as collateral in the same way as unstripped gilts.

The Central Gilts Office

The CGO system was first introduced in 1986 to provide electronic book-entry settlement with assured payments in the gilts market. The service was used for Stock Exchange transactions only until December 1986 when membership was opened to all participants in the gilt-edged market. The system was upgraded on 10 November 1997 in order to introduce new features that will:

- Facilitate the stripping and reconstitution of gilts.
- Allow back offices to process repos more effectively.
- Effect automatic reporting to the Financial Services Authority and the London Stock Exchange.
- Make membership and account management more flexible so increasing the scope for investors to hold gilts in dematerialised form.
- Allow better control by settlement banks of their exposure to CGO members for which they act, reducing any residual risk in the settlement process.

The upgrade includes multi-currency software, specifically to provide dual currency functionality from 1 January 1999. This will enable the CGO to handle transactions in euro or sterling denominated securities. If the decision is taken for the UK to join EMU, then the CGO will revert to a single currency system at the date of entry. The base currency of the system would be the euro and any outstanding sterling considerations in the system on that date would be converted.

A future development will be to allow dividend and redemption payments to be made direct to CGO members' cash memorandum accounts, rather than outside the system as at present. Gilts currently go ex-dividend seven working days before the dividend payment date. Elimination of the ex-dividend period for gilts held in the CGO system has been recommended, but not yet implemented. A five working day ex-dividend period for gilts held outside the CGO or on the National Savings Stock Register will be implemented.

Participation in the CGO service

There are two methods of participation in the CGO service:

- *Direct membership.* A direct member has a book entry account in the CGO in his own name and inputs and receives deliveries via a terminal. A direct member arranges for a settlement bank to make and receive assured payments on his behalf for stock transferred to or from any other member of the service.
- *Indirect participation.* Settlement is conducted on behalf of

indirect participants by a nominee which is itself a direct member of the service. These arrangements facilitate a broad membership at low cost.

CGO accounts

All CGO members have accounts within the CGO system in which records of their stock balances are held. The balances on these accounts constitute *prima facie* evidence of title to stock. Details of member-to-member deliveries between CGO accounts are notified to the Registrar who continues to maintain the stock registers, which constitute the prime record of legal title. The balance on each CGO account has three components: balance available; quantity earmarked for delivery; and quantity reserved as physical collateral.

When Delivery By Value (DBV) instructions are given for the transfer of stock, CGO selects stock to be delivered from members' CGO accounts. When stock denominated in euro becomes available, the CGO system will not discriminate stock on grounds of currency alone. If a member does not want his euro securities to be delivered, it is proposed that these stocks can be flagged to exclude euro issues from DBVs. If members do not wish to accept euro denominated securities, it is proposed they will have the ability to accept these securities at their discretion.

Cash memorandum accounts (CMA)

On the introduction of the euro, members wishing to use the dual currency functionality would require a euro CMA in addition to the sterling CMA. The account would be linked to the sterling debit cap to control payments out of the CMA. When calculating the headroom available under the debit cap, the system would take into account debits and credits posted in both currencies. The sterling/euro exchange rate would be that which applied at the close of business on the previous day.

Book entry transfer

The CGO service is based on the concept of book entry transfer. This allows transactions in securities between CGO members to be settled without stock transfer forms (STFs), stock certificates or paper payments. Movement of stock is dependent on both the seller having sufficient stock available on his CGO account and the taker positively accepting the offered delivery through the terminal connection. An irrevocable payment instruction is generated simultaneously (but in the opposite direction to) the movement of the stock between accounts in the CGO. Once stock is credited to a taker's CGO account, it is immediately available for onward delivery. STFs are still required where delivery is being made to or from a party who is not a CGO member or participant.

Assured payments

The assured payments arrangements are based upon the following principles:

- The settlement banks have given an unconditional undertaking that, at the moment the CGO transfers stock from the CGO account of a seller, the buyer's settlement bank takes on an irrevocable commitment to effect payment the same day to the seller's settlement account. The CGO system ensures that stock can only move off a CGO account to another CGO account against this irrevocable payment commitment.

- The settlement bank's exposure arising from its irrevocable commitment to make payment can be covered by a charge given in its favour by the buyer over stock held on the buyer's CGO account and over monies receivable by the buyer for any stock transferred out of his CGO account.

Each CGO member must nominate a single account at one of the settlement banks over which the net payment of that member for completed transactions with all other members is passed. A further account in euro may be needed from 1999. Settlement takes place towards the end of each business day across bank accounts at the Bank of England. The CGO produces schedules for each settlement bank that set out the final net payment positions, to enable the banks to make the relevant postings. The banks have a 'treasurer's membership' with the CGO which enables them to enquire during the day on the net payment positions of their CGO member customers' accounts. At the close of business they can enquire on the value of stock held by their customers, excluding stock held for collateral. This is not a real time settlement system, the implementation of which is still being considered

Reference prices and consideration checking

The CGO system ensures that the consideration and payment amounts equate, within a defined range, to the value of the stock being transferred. Reference prices are held within the CGO system for all securities. These are determined each afternoon by the Government broker and are based on the middle market price of each stock, adjusted to include the effect of accrued interest and rounded up or down to the nearest whole number. Prices are applied to each transaction on the following business day. Where the consideration falls outside the wider of two bands, deliveries are initially blocked.

Stock delivery

Delivery between CGO members

A delivery of stock between two CGO members (a member-to member delivery) is effected by the giver of stock inputting the relevant details of the delivery into his terminal. Once authorised by the giver, the delivery is added to the giver's stock queue. The offer of stock is displayed to the taker for acceptance. Once authorised and accepted, the stock is debited from the giver's CGO account and credited to the taker's CGO account and a payment instruction is created.

Inward deliveries

Where a CGO member is to receive stock from outside the CGO system, a Stock Transfer Form (STF) must be lodged at the CGO. The CGO credits the stock to the member's account and it is immediately available for onward delivery.

Outward deliveries

A delivery from a CGO member to a non-CGO member is effected by the member lodging an executed STF at the CGO for enfacement (enfacement shows that stock is attached and therefore represents good delivery in the market). The delivery is added to the member's stock queue. Payments for inward and outward deliveries must be made outside the CGO system.

Stock queues

All deliveries are entered into a stock queue where they remain until sufficient stock to meet them is available on the member's account. Delivery will be made in the order stock is inputted unless the member exercises control over the sequence of stock released. Stock is apportioned by the CGO system up to 1:30 pm when a system of 'circles processing' completes deliveries and payments.

Transaction referencing

Each offer of stock within the CGO system has a transaction reference consisting of three digits plus an alphabetical code. This is unique for each day, security, type of transaction and CGO member and must be recorded on stock transfer and withdrawal consent forms.

Stock loans

Deliveries between CGO members in satisfaction of stock loans, or their return, are in book entry form. The CGO system does not distinguish stock loans from any other delivery. The consideration amount may be calculated from the reference price for the stock and a payment instruction is created to move money in the opposite direction. When the reference price of a stock changes, margin payment adjustments may be needed in respect of the revaluation (the stock lent is constant). These calculations are made by the parties concerned and any payment is effected outside the CGO system.

Collateral

Stock may be used to provide collateral in either book entry or physical form. Book entry collateral may be delivered using the normal member to member delivery or through the DBV. The CGO system does not distinguish collateral from any other delivery and as the reference price of stock changes the amount of stock held as collateral may need to be increased or decreased (the cash loan is constant). Collateral may be provided on an overnight basis between 2:00 pm and 3:00 pm after the completion of apportionment and circles processing. The system selects the stocks to be used for delivery by value, using securities with the earliest maturity first. The stock delivery and assured payment are reversed at 10:00 am the following business morning.

New issues

New issues may be credited direct to a member's CGO account or allotment letters for new issues may be lodged. The stock may then be delivered in book entry form in the same way as stock that is registered.

Registration

Each evening the CGO provides the Registrar with details of that day's settled deliveries that have been effected through the CGO system and require registration. There is a daily reconciliation of balances between the CGO accounts and the Registrar.

UK Government ecu/euro Treasury Bills

The first UK Ecu Treasury bill issue was made in October 1988 with the proceeds of these bills being added to the UK's foreign exchange reserves. Euro Treasury bills are now being issued. Bills are issued on a discount basis with tenors of one, three and six months. Denominations are Ecu/euro 10,000, 100,000, 1 million and 10 million. They are issued primarily as global bills and held by the Bank of England as common depository for Euroclear and Cedel Bank clearing systems. Definitive bills are available if requested. They are not held in the CMO. The discount is calculated on the basis of a 360 day year. A Global Treasury Bill is illustrated in figure 22.3.

The primary market

Bills are issued on a bid-yield basis with tenders being made on the second Tuesday of each month. A tender notice is published by the Bank a week in advance with bids to be submitted by 10:30 am on the day of the tender. In 1998, the pattern of issue was for Ecu 200 million to be offered with one month maturity, Ecu 500 million with three month maturity and Ecu 300 million with six month maturity, a total of Ecu 1 billion. Bids are for a minimum amount of Ecu/euro 500,000, with higher amounts being in multiples of Ecu/euro 100,000. Value is two working days later. The cost of funds to the Bank is below Ecu/euro Libid and the funds raised are placed in the Ecu/euro markets.

Figure 22.3   UK Government Global Euro Treasury Bill

(appears at end of chapter)

Secondary market trading

A number of institutions have undertaken to act as market makers in Ecu/euro Treasury bills. They also support the tender. The Bank of England contributes to liquidity by standing ready to buy bills from market makers and by providing repo facilities.

UK Government euro Treasury Note programme

UK Government euro Treasury notes are issued under a programme for which the latest information memorandum was issued on 13 January 1998. Notes are interest bearing. Denominations are euro 1,000, 10,000, 100,000, and 1 million. Global notes are deposited at the Bank of England as the common depository for Euroclear and Cedel Bank clearing systems but are available as definitive certificates. They are not held in the CGO. Interest is calculated on an actual/actual basis. Notes are free from withholding tax.

Practice is normally to make an issue of euro 1 billion in the first month of the year with further quarterly fungible tranches of the same issue of euro 500 million. Bills are issued by tender on a bid-yield basis. The tender is on the third Tuesday of the respective month. A tender notice is published by the Bank a week in advance with bids to be submitted by 10:30 am on the day of the tender. Bids are for a minimum amount of euro 500,000, with higher amounts being in multiples of euro 100,000. Value is usually seven calendar days after the initial tender and three working days after tenders for subsequent tranches. The rate on the initial tranche each year is set at the highest accepted yield bid, rounded down to the nearest ¼ per cent. Thus, the three year note issued in January 1998 has a coupon of 4.25 per cent. The coupon applicable to further issues in this series remains unchanged but adjustments are made to the price paid for tranches to reflect the yields bid.

US government securities

The US treasury market is the largest and most liquid government bond market in the world and developments in it are watched closely by other government bond issuers. All US Treasury bills, notes and bonds are available only in book-entry form on the national safe-keeping and transfer system run by the twelve Federal Reserve Banks. The size and frequency of issues give rise to secondary markets in these instruments of immense depth.

US Treasury bills (T-bills) are short term bearer securities issued at a discount with maturities of three, six or 12 months through the Federal Reserve Bank of New York. Auctions of 91 and 182 day bills take place weekly and auctions of year bills monthly. The discount is based on actual days over a 360 day year.

Treasury Notes are securities with maturities from two to 10 years. Two year notes are auctioned monthly and five and ten year notes quarterly. Treasury Bonds are long term securities with original maturities of 30 years and are auctioned semi-annually in February and August. These issue patterns change over time to reflect the US government's borrowing requirements. Bids are on a yield basis through primary dealers who underwrite issues. Notes and bonds pay semi-annual coupons on an actual/actual basis. The tick size for US Government securities is 1/32nd. In the early 1980s, US government securities were stripped into zero-coupon bonds by investment banks. They were given titles such as CATs (Certificates for Accrual on Treasury Securities) and TIGRs (Treasury Investment Growth Receipts). The US Treasury offered facilities for Strips in 1984 and these are now an integral part of US Government debt.

US Treasury Inflation-indexed Notes were first issued by auction in 1997. This adds to the existing index-linked markets, which now exist in 15 countries. Index-linked bonds widen the choice of investment for those wishing to hedge real interest rate exposure and to exploit real yield differentials between markets.

Figure 22.3   *UK Government Global Euro Treasury Bill*

Global Treasury Bill

Due...............

Issued under the Treasury Bills Act 1877 and the National Loans Act 1968.

[000000]

Euro............

London, ...[Date]

This Global Treasury Bill entitles the bearer to Payment of ....
euro out of the National Loans Fund on ....
[Date] on surrender of this Global Treasury Bill to the Bank of England,
subject to and in accordance with the Treasury Bills Regulations 1968 as
amended.

On any business day (as defined in the Treasury Bills Regulations 1968 as
amended) on or after the Issue Date stated above upon surrender or
presentation of this Global Treasury Bill to the Bank of England, this Global
Treasury Bill shall be exchanged by the Bank of England without charge in
whole or in part for definitive Treasury Bills in the form prescribed by the
Treasury Bills Regulations 1968 as amended and in the denominations
permitted thereunder and requested by the bearer. Upon exchange of a part
of this Global Treasury Bill for definitive Treasury Bills, the portion of the
principal amount hereof so exchanged shall be endorsed by the Bank of
England on the Schedule hereto, whereupon the principal amount of this
Global Treasury Bill shall be reduced for all purposes by the amount so
exchanged and endorsed.

.............euro.........

Secretary to the Treasury

[000000]

SCHEDULE
EXCHANGES FOR DEFINITIVE BILLS

The following exchanges of a part of this Global Treasury Bill for Definitive Treasury Bills have been made:

Date made	Part of face amount of this Global Treasury Bill exchanged for definitive Treasury Bills	Remaining face amount of this Global Treasury Bill following such exchange	Notation made by the Bank of England
....	....	....	....
....	....	....	....
....	....	....	....
....	....	....	....
....	....	....	....
....	....	....	....
....	....	....	....
....	....	....	....
....	....	....	....
....	....	....	....
....	....	....	....
....	....	....	....
....	....	....	....
....	....	....	....
....	....	....	....
....	....	....	....
....	....	....	....
....	....	....	....
....	....	....	....

23 Repo markets

Financial institutions continuously buy and sell securities of all descriptions, including government bonds and bills, domestic and international bonds. Bonds are often purchased before the cash to fund them has been obtained. On subsequent days, further transactions will change the portfolio and any borrowing needs will be different. These institutions frequently seek to borrow cash overnight in the wholesale markets to fund their holdings of securities. Banks and other financial institutions are unwilling to lend the large amounts of money required even overnight because of the credit risk and they may want to charge commercial rates rather than interbank rates for any funds lent. If the investments were to be used as security or collateral, a bank would be more willing to lend at market rates. To take this one step further, a lending bank could buy the investments to give it full title to them. It could agree simultaneously to sell them back on the following day. This is how repo markets work. Repo is short term collateralised money market lending.

Because of the way central banks operate in the money markets, commercial banks often find, in their daily money market operations, that there is a shortage of funds in the market. The central banks will step in to relieve these shortages by providing liquidity. They too have the same concerns over lending unsecured so assistance to the market is frequently provided via repo. The market originated for this purpose in the United States and is used daily by the Federal Reserve for money market intervention. Repo has been used widely in this way by central banks in Europe. It will be the principal method used by the European System of Central Banks in the daily money market operations and to control short term interest rates.

The repo markets in the United States are probably the largest money market and are deep and liquid. Repo markets are used extensively in

Japan, Canada, Australia and European countries but real growth in London only started in the early 1990s. London is now a major centre for cross-border international repo, which is conducted in a wide range of currencies and securities.

It was only in January 1996 that the Bank of England opened up trading in repo using gilt-edged stock. Previously, this activity was restricted to Gilt-edged Market Makers and the now defunct Stock Exchange Money Brokers. The Bank of England now uses repo in its daily money market operations as well as the outright purchase of bills.

Anyone with a portfolio of acceptable securities can use them as collateral for short term funding. What constitutes acceptable securities depends on market practice in the centre concerned. It is estimated that, in Europe, over 50 per cent of repo uses government securities and over 25 per cent uses eurobonds as collateral. Repos may be used to suit the precise maturity needs of the seller from overnight up to one year with many deals being rolled over on a daily basis.

Repo

A repo is a combination of two simultaneous transactions in a single contract. It is an arrangement whereby a financial institution sells securities to a third party for immediate payment with a commitment to repurchase the assets after a stated time or in the event of a particular contingency. It is an irrevocable commitment. The sale and repurchase are executed at prices that yield an agreed rate of return on the funds lent. The loan is, in effect, repaid with interest at maturity against return of the securities.

Reverse repo

This is the same transaction but from the stand-point of the lender of funds. It is a contract under which a holder of cash agrees to purchase securities and simultaneously agrees to resell them at an agreed price after a stated time or in the event of a particular contingency.

Trades initiated by the holders of securities are said to be stock driven. Trades initiated by holders of funds are said to be cash driven. An easy way of remembering who is doing what to whom is to recall that you 'reverse in' the securities (and lend out the money). The movement of securities and funds is illustrated as follows:

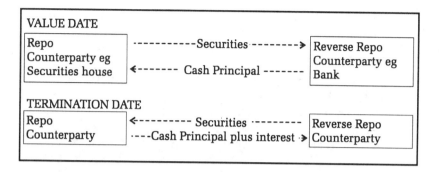

Specials

All securities are issued in defined quantities. When there are securities which, for any reason, are in short supply and are sought after in the repo market, holders are able to take in cash on which they pay a low rate of interest to the repo buyer, so earning extra profit when the funds are reinvested in the market. The rate of interest paid can even be negative. If investment houses corner the market in an issue of securities, it means that they can dictate the repo rate to houses that are short of the issue.

In the gilt repo market, placing and receiving funds against gilts where the gilts to be received are not specified is known as general collateral and delivery is by value. Where a market participant requires a particular gilt, this is called a specific repo. When the stock is in short supply and the repo rate diverges by more than 10 basis point from the prevailing general collateral rate, the gilt trade becomes 'special'.

Documentation

The type of repo covered above is known as classic repo. Classic repo is evidenced under a written agreement that contractually links the two legs of the transaction. Standard documentation is based on Global Master Repurchase Agreements produced by the Public Securities Association (PSA) in the USA and the International Securities Market Association. A Master Agreement between two counterparties will covers the usual representations and warranties, default, tax and payment clauses. Individual transactions are added as annexes to the Master Agreement.

Features of repo that will be incorporated in the documentation are as follows:

- How securities are to be delivered.
- A margin in excess of the loan amount may be required as collateral margin.
- The buyer has the right to mark to market the valuation of the securities each day during the life of the repo, revaluing the securities at current market prices. He can call for additional securities as collateral margin if the value of the securities falls to or below a certain value. The borrower of cash can call for securities to be returned if their value rises above a higher trigger amount.
- Substitution rights may be granted. The borrower who has sold securities may call for them back at any time during the repo provided he substitutes securities of equal market value. He may do this any number of times during the life of the repo.
- The lender may sell back equivalent securities, that is, bonds from the same issue as those purchased but not the same serial numbers as those received as collateral. Cash payments relating to different transactions may be netted, as may securities deliveries provided they are of the same issue.
- Interest accrued on the securities during the term of the repo belongs to the counterparty selling and repurchasing them. The buyer undertakes to pass any coupon received to the seller as soon as it is received.

Benefits and uses of repo

The benefits and uses of repo for the holders of securities, as a means of borrowing cash are summarised as follows. Because repos are collateralised, often with government securities that are regarded as default risk free, the cost of finance (cost of carry) is reduced, particularly for institutions without direct access to the interbank deposit markets. Long positions in bonds and gilts can be financed, whether they are held for investment, risk taking or arbitrage purposes. A trading house may purchase bonds in a new issue and finance the purchase by means of a repo until the bonds are sold. With a normal positive yield curve, the return on the holding of the long term instruments is higher than the cost of short term repo finance. Because repo involves a temporary exchange, it allows investors access to cash without having to liquidate securities they are holding at what could be unattractive market prices.

If a security provided as collateral is 'special', then interest payable on the funds received can be substantially lower than normal rates giving an enhanced yield of reinvestment of the funds. Because the collateral must be issued by creditworthy names, the creditworthiness of the holder of securities may be lower (but it must still be acceptable).

The benefits of reverse repo for the lenders of cash are that reverse repo offers a secure, collateralised use of funds. This reduces credit risks and the use of credit lines significantly. Capital adequacy costs may be reduced if the institution is subject to a capital regime such as the Capital Adequacy Directive, which applies a capital charge only to any shortfall between the mark-to-market value of the collateral and cash loan. Reverse repo also offers an opportunity for institutions to sell or go short of securities that are reversed in temporarily. One reason for doing this is that a dealer may feel that prices of the securities are likely to fall.

Operations

Individual transactions are agreed by telephone, using the Bloomberg dealing system, directly or via a broker and subsequently documented by an exchange of confirmation. The key factors to be agreed by the dealers are:

- the trade date, the purchase date and the repurchase date;
- the price at which the securities are to be repoed;
- the currency and amount lent and the repo rate.

The confirmation will identify:

- the counterparties;
- the securities purchased (with their identifying ISIN numbers);
- the buyer's margin for provision of additional collateral (if called for);
- the seller's margin for return of excess collateral (if called for);
- settlement details for delivery of the securities and payment;

• whether the transaction forms part of and is subject to a global master agreement.

The seller transacting a repo usually delivers the securities via a clearing house on a delivery versus payment basis (DVP) or delivery by value (DBV). This may require physical delivery or use the electronic book entry settlement of a clearing house such as Cedel Bank or Euroclear or the CGO for gilts. Dealing times need to take into account the cut-off times for delivery of securities. A hold-in-custody repo, where the securities remain with the selling bank, imposes an additional risk on the buyer that the securities may be pledged elsewhere and so is not normal practice.

Figure 23.1   Fax confirmation for reverse repo transaction

```
                                                      20 JAN 1999
TO :     NEWBANK CAPITAL MARKETS  LDN  ATTN UK GILT SETTLEMEN
FROM   : COMBANK AG LONDON BRANCH

WE SHOULD LIKE TO CONFIRM THE FOLLOWING REPO WITH
YOURSELVES.
CONTRACT DATE              :20 JAN 1999
PURCHASED                  :UKTREASURYSTOCK  7.5% 07/12/06
                            ISIN   GB0009998302
NOMINAL AMOUNT             :              5,250,000
CONTRACTUAL CURRENCY  :GBP
BUYER                      :COMBANK AG
SELLER                     :NEWBANK CAPITAL MARKETS LDN
PURCHASE PRICE             :100.62
TOTAL PURCHASE PRICE   :            5,282,550.00
FINANCING RATE             :6.05%
REPURCHASE DATE            :21 JAN 1999
REPURCHASE AMOUNT      :            5,283,425.58

BUYER'S SETTLEMENT DETAILS:   MIDBANK SECURITIES SERVICES
                              CGO ACCT 8787  ACCOUNT
                              COMBANK AG LONDON NO.856228
SELLER'S SETTLEMENT DETAILS:   NEWBANK LONDON CGO 9125

THIS CONFIRMATION IS ISSUED IN ACCORDANCE WITH THE RULES OF
THE INTERNATIONAL SECURITIES MARKET ASSOCIATION.   NO OTHER
FORM OF CONFIRMATION WILL BE ISSUED.
```

Tri-party repo

A tri-party repo is a repo in which an independent agent (bank or clearing house such as Cedel Bank or Euroclear) oversees standard two party repo transactions. An agreement is signed between the three counterparties which details the terms of dealing, including the criteria which the collateral needs to meet, eg 20 per cent of the collateral must be AAA rated, debt of issuers in certain countries may be excluded. A tri-party repo transaction, from the point of view of the cash lender, has the following stages:

- The lender agrees the terms of the repo (principal, rate, term etc) directly with the counterparty.

- The lender pays the principal to the intermediary.

- The counterparty gives collateral to the intermediary. The collateral will consist of a number of different stocks meeting the criteria of the legal dealing agreement.

- When the intermediary has received and checked the collateral, it pays the counterparty.

- The intermediary retains possession of the collateral, and performs all required margining on behalf of the lender.

- On maturity of the deal, the counterparty repays the principal plus interest to the intermediary, who checks the settlement, passes the funds on to the lender and returns the collateral. Charges for the administration of the collateral are for the account of the borrower of funds.

The gilt repo market

Before January 1996, repo in gilts was restricted to Gilt Edged Market Makers and Stock Exchange Money Brokers. Repo was not practical also because gilts were paid after deduction of withholding tax. These restrictions were eased in 1996 and now there are no restrictions on counterparties for trading gilt repo. To qualify for gross interest, gilts had to be maintained in designated accounts at the CGO (known as 'star' accounts). From April 1998, there are no restrictions for payment of gross interest. The Bank of England's objectives were:

- To increase the demand for gilts, particularly from overseas investors, and enhance the liquidity of the gilts market since it provides a method of financing holdings.

- To seek benefits from the closer integration of the sterling money and gilts markets.
- To reduce the volatility of short term interest rates which had been a feature of the sterling money market.
- To bring the UK more into line with European practice.

Gilt repo had been used to a limited extent between 1994 and 1997 by the Bank of England in its daily operations to provide liquidity to the sterling money markets. There was a fortnightly round for 21 or 35 day repos with settlement on the day following the offer. Since March 1997, gilt repo is the main means of providing daily liquidity to the sterling market. The volume of gilt repo outstanding in the gilt repo market at February 1997 was £71 billion.

The Gilt Repo Legal Agreement

The legal documentation drafted by the Bank of England for use between participants is based on the PSA/ISMA Global Master Repurchase Agreement for gross-paying securities with supplemental terms to fit the characteristics of repos in gilts. Besides the legal clauses, the agreement provides for:

- The absolute transfer of title to the securities being repoed.
- Re-margining during the life of a repo contract, or for a contract to be closed out and repriced.
- Close out and set off of all contracts in the event of default.
- The use of a series of DBV transactions (securities delivered by value rather than by individual security), until either party wishes to end or amend the transaction.

The Gilt Repo Code of Conduct

The code applies to all activities in gilt repo by all participants: Market professionals, principals, brokers and end users. The key elements of the code are:

- General market standards should be maintained in respect of confidentiality; being responsible for the actions of staff; acting with due skill, care and diligence; and ensuring fair treatment where conflicts of interest cannot be avoided.

- Before entering into a gilt repo transaction, and regularly thereafter, participants should review all legal, credit, systems and procedural matters relating to gilt repos to ensure that trading is adequately controlled and understood.
- New clients should be made aware of the code.
- Participants should be clear whether the capacity in which their counterparty is acting is as principal, agent or broker.
- Gilt repo transactions should be subject to a legal agreement between the two participants. Particular attention should be given to the effectiveness of any legal agreement proposed with a non-UK incorporated counterparty.
- Margin should be called for whenever a counterparty has a mark to market exposure which is considered material.
- Taking delivery of securities and margin directly or via a third party can reduce potential credit risk. Those leaving securities in the custody of their counterparty (a hold-in-custody repo) should consider their counterparty's creditworthiness, systems and control procedures.
- Before declaring an event of default, counterparties should consider whether the event is real or technical, should close out positions at fair market value and should do so without unnecessarily disrupting the market.
- Confirmations should be sent out on the same day and checked on a timely basis. Special consideration should be given to stock events such as ex-dividend dates, conversion option arising during the life of the repo.

Initial margins

The Bank of England specifies the margin it requires for gilt repo transacted in its daily operations in the sterling money market. These are percentages of the purchase price. The trigger ratios when top-up gilts will be called for and when a margin return may be requested are given in brackets.

Gilts with a residual maturity of up to five years	101.5%	(101%/102%)

| Gilts with a residual maturity greater than five years | 102.5% | (102%/103%) |
| Non sterling debt issued by HM government | 103.5% | (103%/104%) |

So, for an amount of £10,000,000, the Bank will only lend £9,756,097.56 (10,000,000 x 100/102.5) where the gilts have a residual maturity of over five years.

Margins are negotiable in repo trading between banks. On overnight and short dated trades, there may be no margin requirement.

Calculations

Stock driven gilt repo

Amount and security	£ 10,000,000.00, Treasury 6% 2004 (Coupon date 54 days earlier)
Term	30 days, 5 April to 5 May
Clean price	95.00
Repo rate	6.25%

The all in or dirty price, including accrued interest is:

Nominal x clean price	£10m x 95.00/100	= £ 9,500,000.00
accrued interest	£10m x 54 x 6.00/36500	= £ 88,767.12
Consideration or purchase price		£ 9,588,767.12

(The dirty price, quoted to two decimal places, would be 95.89 per £100 stock)

Stages to the trade are:

£10,000,000 of stock at agreed consideration of	£ 9,588,767.12
Repo interest £ 9,588,767.12 x 30 x 6.25/36500	£ 49,257.37
At termination £10,000,000 of stock returned for	£ 9,638,024.49

Cash driven gilt repo

Where the trade is cash driven, the cash consideration is likely to be a round amount and the amount of stock to be passed over at the dirty price will be an odd amount. This does not matter since gilts can be delivered to 1p of nominal stock. The amount of stock needed for a cash driven trade of £10,000,000 where the dirty price is 95.89 would be calculated as follows:

Value of gilts $\quad=\quad \dfrac{£10,000,000.00}{95.89 \times 100} \quad=\quad £10,428,616.12$

Interest at maturity on a loan of £10,000,000 for 30 days at 6.25 per cent would be £51,369.86.

Sell/buy back and stock lending
Sell and buy back

The sell and buy back (or buy/sell) is the simplest but least common form of repo. It involves the outright sale of securities for value on the near date with an outright purchase on the forward date. There are two transactions rather than just one repo transaction. There is no formal documentation between the counterparties except for the confirmation. Accrued interest belongs to the buyer of the securities and this is reflected in the payment calculations with the purchaser earning a money market rate of return. Any interest or coupon payments during the term of the buy/sell will belong to the purchaser.

Stock lending

Stock lending involves a transfer of securities or shares for a temporary period in exchange for collateral, which may be other securities or cash. It does not involve a sale and repurchase but is used by investment houses that need to acquire ownership of a particular bond or security because of a failed trade or deliberately taken short positions. The borrower is required to deliver collateral (other acceptable securities) to the securities lender and to pay a fee for the use of the borrowed securities. Although there is transfer of title (including any voting rights), the benefits of ownership, including dividend and coupon payments, remain with the lender. There is a legal obligation on the borrower to make the lender whole by passing back any payments or distributions received. Daily marking to market is undertaken and additional collateral must be provided to make up shortfalls in valuation.

The securities and stocks lent are typically held by investors such as insurance and pension companies who hold long term investments with global custodians or clearing houses. The clearing house asks holders of securities if the investors are willing for their holdings to be used for stock lending purposes. The permission given may allow the investments to be lent without reference or may require the specific permission of the investor for each transaction. This allows the investors to earn incremental income on otherwise dormant assets, which can be used to offset custody fees. The volume outstanding in one sector of this market, gilt stock lending, at February 1996 was £21 billion.

PART FIVE

Derivatives

24 Markets in derivative instruments

Derivatives have been the financial phenomenon of the 1990s. Their name comes from the fact that their value is derived from that of some other underlying financial instrument, the derivative contract relating to some aspect such as forward pricing, optional delivery, leveraged returns and so on. Their growth began as a response to the volatility in the financial markets in the 1980s coupled with deregulation in the major countries. The principal markets that are the subject of this section are forward rate agreements, financial futures and options, interest rate and currency swaps and credit derivatives. These markets do not work in isolation of each other or of the markets in the underlying financial commodities. This is aptly illustrated by the name of one of the products, a swaption, or option on a swap.

Derivatives are traded over-the-counter on a principal to principal basis or are traded in centralised meeting places known as exchanges, with automated screen trading becoming a feature of futures markets. It is estimated that outstandings in the over-the-counter (OTC) markets have grown from $500 billion in 1985 to about $ 4 trillion in 1991 and then to over $30 trillion in 1997. More than two thirds of these trades are interest rate swaps. Trading in derivatives often exceeds transactions in the markets for the underlying instruments or currencies.

Users of derivatives comprise banks, securities firms and other financial institutions, companies and investors who are in the markets to hedge risks, to manipulate funding and investment and to trade for profit. Several factors underpin the growth of these markets. It is often cheaper to trade in derivatives than in the underlying commodities, stock or currencies from which they are derived. More sophisticated methods are being devised for pricing and managing the risks. Restrictions on the use of derivatives have been eased and, for banks, the capital adequacy weightings under the Basle rules can be lighter for derivatives than for assets that appear on their balance sheets.

The main benefit of derivatives is that they allow banks to unbundle the various risk elements of a transaction into constituent parts and to hedge each exposure separately. Thus, for example, a fixed rate loan can be hedged by borrowing short term money and taking out an interest rate swap thus separating interest rate and maturity considerations. This facilitates a transfer of risk from one institution to another in accordance with their appetite for different kinds of risk. Insurance companies, for example, have an appetite for long term fixed rate investments but are unwilling to take the credit risk implied in commercial lending. If banks take the credit risk, the insurance company may well, via a swap, be prepared to take the interest rate risk.

This ability to unbundle also enables banks to produce more complex structures of lending propositions (combining different currencies, providing optional termination dates, etc) so as to provide a better match for customers' needs. Uncertain customer exposures, such as those arising when tendering in foreign currencies, can be hedged with options.

A greater range of funding opportunities can now be accessed, both in short term and long term markets, with the ultimate currency and rate structure of the issue being determined by swap transactions.

The efficiency of arbitrage processes is also increased when there is a variety of cheap, straightforward instruments available that carry limited credit risk. Off balance sheet instruments also enable banks to diversify and enhance their income streams by earning fees and commissions with limited use of capital.

OTC and exchange traded contracts

It is useful to consider why both over the counter and exchange traded derivatives exist. Each type of trading has its own advantages and disadvantages, which can be summarised as follows:

Advantages of OTC trading

- Flexibility. Market makers are prepared to deal in contract sizes that can be tailor-made to counterparties' requirements.
- Quotations are likely to be available for a broader spread of currencies and time periods.

- Initial and maintenance margins are not mandatory but may be agreed by negotiation.
- No transactions fees are payable other than brokerage, and that may be avoided if dealing principal to principal.
- Quotations may be obtained and deals transacted outside of the limited trading hours of an exchange.
- Corporate customers frequently prefer to trade directly with their bank rather than through a broker.

Disadvantages of OTC trading

- Lack of transparency compared to exchange traded contracts where traded prices are public information.
- Lack of standardisation means that it can be difficult to unwind a position in a non-standard period or amount. Sometimes the only alternative is to return to the original counterparty. Standardised contracts are less likely to be the subject of error in negotiation and their terms and conditions are subject to the regulations of an exchange.
- Positions opened and closed with two different counterparties will involve both legs running to maturity, using up credit lines and regulatory capital. Exchange traded contracts usually extinguish all remaining liability once offsetting contracts are dealt.

Risk management

However, assessing the risks in these markets is not easy, either for an institution's management or for the regulatory authorities. A special working party to investigate these risks was established by the Governors of the Central Banks of the Group of 10 Countries in 1991 under the chairmanship of Larry Promisel of the US Federal Reserve Board. Their report concluded that:

'The development of new financial instruments and strategies has provided the financial sector with better opportunities to manage risks and enhance returns. These developments, however, also confront institutions active in wholesale markets with significant new challenges in risk management.'

The growth of these markets has generated a much greater volume and a much more complex set of interrelationships within the financial community than existed before. The level of bilateral settlements between banks has also escalated. It is not immediately obvious what exact exposures exist since the value of many of the new products varies with market prices and consequently cannot be known with certainty in advance. It also requires constant vigilance to ensure that the exposure does not get out of control. The valuation of complex products is a specialised activity and it is probable that only a few people in the organisation understand it. Senior management may not be sufficiently well informed as to the true nature of the risks to make a considered judgement and may become reliant on the specialists who have a vested interest in promoting their own case. They may also simply get it wrong.

New products often require specially designed systems to process them. Care needs to be taken to see that they are properly designed and tested. Derivatives are often highly leveraged constructions and a small movement in the price of the underlying instrument may trigger a large change in the price of the derivative with high possible losses on open positions.

The interpretation of company balance sheets has been obscured by the off-balance sheet nature of the new instruments such that it is now harder to discern the health of a company from its financial statements.

Banks may become reliant on new markets to handle a large part of their risk management. Given their relative youth, the continued liquidity and legal status of the markets should not be taken for granted. Regulatory authorities have also expressed concern that the unbundling of risks has meant that individual market prices now react much faster to news and may develop positive feedback so as to precipitate unjustifiably sharp price movements.

Group of Thirty global derivatives study

In 1993, the Group of Thirty (a Committee of regulators, academics and practitioners) published a study on best practice for derivatives users. Their recommendations are summarised below. Many of these are of general applicability and their relevance is not limited to the field of derivatives. Indeed, a number of the points are referred to in Chapter 5 above. Nevertheless, they bear repeating here.

The role of senior management

Dealers and end users should use derivatives in a manner consistent with the overall risk management and capital policies approved by their boards of directors. These policies should be reviewed as business and market circumstances change. Policies governing derivatives use should be clearly defined, including the purposes for which these transactions are to be undertaken. Senior management should approve procedures and controls to implement these policies, and management at all levels should enforce them.

Marking to market

Dealers should mark their derivatives positions to market for risk management purposes, on at least a daily basis.

Market valuation methods

Derivatives portfolios of dealers should be valued based on mid-market levels less specific adjustments, or on appropriate bid or offer levels. Mid-market valuation adjustments should allow for expected future costs such as unearned credit spread, close-out costs, investing and funding costs, and administrative costs.

Identifying revenue sources

Dealers should measure the components of revenue regularly and in sufficient detail to understand the sources of risk.

Measuring market risk

Dealers should use a consistent measure to calculate daily the market risk of their derivatives positions and compare it to market risk limits. The group recommends using value at risk techniques allowing for absolute price or rate change (delta); convexity (gamma); volatility (vega); time decay (theta); basis or correlation; and discount rate (rho). The 'greeks' are explained in Chapter 28.

Stress simulations

Dealers should regularly perform simulations to determine how their portfolios would perform under stress conditions.

Investing and funding forecasts
Dealers should periodically forecast the cash investing and funding requirements arising from their derivatives portfolios.

Independent market risk management
Dealers should have a market risk management function, with clear independence and authority, to ensure that the following responsibilities are carried out:

- The development of risk limit policies and the monitoring of transactions and positions for adherence to these policies.

- The design of stress scenarios to measure the impact of market conditions, however improbable, that might cause market gaps, volatility swings, or disruptions of major relationships, or might reduce liquidity in the face of unfavourable market linkages, concentrated market making, or credit exhaustion.

- The design of revenue reports quantifying the contribution of various risk components, and of market-risk measures such as value at risk.

- The monitoring of variance between the actual volatility of portfolio value and that predicted by the measure of market risk.

- The review and approval of pricing models and valuation systems used by front and back office personnel, and the development of reconciliation procedures if different systems are used.

Practices by end users
As appropriate to the nature, size and complexity of their derivatives activities, end users should adopt the same valuation and market-risk management practices that are recommended for dealers.

Measuring credit exposure
Dealers and end users should measure credit exposure on derivatives in two ways: current exposure, which is the replacement cost of derivatives transactions, that is, their market value; and potential exposure, which is an estimate of the future replacement cost of derivatives transactions. This is explained more fully later in this Chapter.

Aggregating credit exposures

Credit exposures on derivatives, and all other credit exposures to a counterparty, should be aggregated taking into consideration enforceable netting arrangements. Credit exposures should be calculated regularly and compared to credit limits.

Independent credit risk management

Dealers and end users should have a credit risk management function with clear independence and authority, and with analytical capabilities in derivatives, responsible for:

• Approving credit exposure measurement standards.

• Setting credit limits and monitoring their use.

• Reviewing credits and concentrations of credit risk.

• Reviewing and monitoring risk-reduction arrangements.

Master agreements

Dealers and end users are encouraged to use one master agreement as widely as possible with each counterparty to document existing and future derivatives transactions, including foreign-exchange forwards and options. Master agreements should provide for payments netting and close-out netting, using a full two-way payments approach.

Credit enhancement

Dealers and end users should assess both the benefits and costs of credit enhancement and related risk-reduction arrangements. Where it is proposed that credit downgrades would trigger early termination or collateral requirements, participants should carefully consider their own capacity and that of their counterparties to meet the potentially substantial funding needs that might result.

Promoting enforceability

Dealers and end users should work together on a continuing basis to identify and recommend solutions for issues of legal enforceability, both within and across jurisdictions, as activities evolve and new types of transactions are developed.

Professional expertise

Dealers and end users must ensure that their derivatives activities are undertaken by professionals in sufficient number and with the appropriate experience, skill levels, and degrees of specialisation.

Systems
Dealers and end users must ensure that adequate systems for data capture, processing, settlement and management reporting are in place. Dealers should have risk management systems that measure the risks incurred in their derivatives activities including market and credit risks.

Authority
Management of dealers and end users should designate who is authorised to commit their institutions to derivatives transactions.

Accounting practices
International harmonisation of accounting standards for derivatives is desirable. Pending the adoption of harmonised standards, the following accounting practices are recommended:

- Dealers should account for derivatives transactions by marking them to market, taking changes in value to income each period.
- Amounts due to and from counterparties should only be offset when there is a legal right to set off or when enforceable netting arrangements are in place.

Disclosures
Financial statements of dealers and end users should contain sufficient information about their use of derivatives to provide an understanding of the purposes for which transactions are undertaken, the extent of the transactions, the degree of risk involved, and the manner of accounting for them.

Recognising netting
Regulators and supervisors should recognise the benefits of netting arrangements to the full extent that they are enforceable and encourage their use by reflecting these arrangements in capital adequacy standards.

Legal and regulatory uncertainties
Legislators, regulators and supervisors, including central banks, should work in collaboration with dealers and end users to identify and remove any remaining legal and regulatory uncertainties.

Tax treatment

Legislators and tax authorities are encouraged to review and, where appropriate, amend tax laws and regulations that disadvantage the use of derivatives in risk-management strategies.

Accounting standards

Accounting standards-setting bodies in each country should, as a matter of priority, provide comprehensive guidance on accounting and reporting of transactions in financial instruments, including derivatives and should work toward international harmonisation of standards on this subject.

Customer suitability

There have been several well publicised cases in recent years (and a great many more not so well reported) where customers have claimed that they were misled by derivatives salesmen into doing deals that subsequently caused heavy losses. Whilst the customers concerned may not always have been as ignorant as they later claimed, it is certainly wise for banks involved in the derivatives business to ensure that the products which they sell are appropriate for the customers concerned. Derivatives products involving hidden currency options or highly leveraged payoffs in the event of specific, low probability events can be constructed so as to offer corporate treasurers an apparently attractive borrowing rate in return for their taking on extra risks. It is questionable whether such practices are ever justified. Even in those cases where a valid reason exists, the bank selling the derivative should take care to ensure that their counterparty understands and acknowledges the risks being accepted. Written explanations of the structure of complex deals are often provided to ensure full understanding.

Derivative traders should remember that whilst they have the ability to create weird and wonderful structures, that does not necessarily make them suitable for sale. Likewise, they should remember that low probability events do sometimes occur and structures relying on their non-occurrence are dangerous. It is no use selling a deal to a customer if that customer is subsequently harmed by it, possibly to the extent of being unable to complete the contract and very probably with resulting damage to the reputation of the bank.

Credit risks

Special mention should be made of the nature of credit exposure where derivatives are concerned. Unlike loans, where the principal amount outstanding is almost certainly the dominant consideration, the value of a derivative product is usually dependent mainly on market rates, which can fluctuate from day to day. The credit risk against counterparties is therefore composed of two parts:

- The likelihood of the counterparty failing to meet their obligations within the terms of the agreement.

- The market related cost incurred in replacing the counterparty if they should default.

Derivatives are often contracts-for-difference, that is, the parties settle the difference between the value of the derivative and an agreed price or rate rather than exchanging the full principal amounts. This limits the credit risk although there is, of course, a delivery risk on payment dates.

At the outset, the credit risk cannot be known with certainty and limits against counterparties will be assessed having regard to the following factors:

- whether fixed or floating rate interest is to be received;

- whether foreign exchange exposure needs to be included;

- the term or maturity of the contract;

- the level of volatility of interest rates in the currency or currencies of the deal.

The risk is more difficult to assess than cash based lending because the risk is market-contingent. That is to say that the risk is primarily dependent on the extent that interest and exchange rates move as time elapses. These movements may be adverse but need not be. If rates move such that the bank owes the counterparty money, the bank will not be harmed if the counterparty defaults. At the inception of the deal, though, the bank has no way of knowing whether it will owe or be owed money by the time the contract reaches maturity.

It is normal to evaluate the risk by considering the replacement cost. For example, an interest rate swap may be written for £100,000,000 for five years where the writer is to receive floating rate interest (six month

Libor) against fixed annual payments of 10 per cent pa. The counterparty defaults after one year and current fixed rates for four-year swaps are 11.00-10.95%. Assuming the bank had covered the original contract, it will look to be a payer under a replacement swap at 11 per cent in order to protect the Libor receipts. It will suffer a loss equal to the present value of £1,000,000 (one per cent) for each of the remaining four years of the swap.

A simple approach to putting a figure on the likely replacement cost is to express it as a percentage of the notional principal amount. Usually, a matrix of risk weightings, taking the above factors into account, is produced allowing pricing and risk to be determined speedily during negotiations for deals. Such rules of thumb may, in the case of very active derivatives traders, be backed up by more complex analyses of potential changes in exposure as rates move. Between frequent counterparties, the level of exposure may depend on the relative movements of a mix of different currencies and interest rates. The estimation process may then take into account a range of volatilities and correlations between them.

Some banks also use stress tests, revaluing their whole portfolios on the assumption of a major movement in rates so as to identify pockets of high risk. There is, however, no certain way to determine what the future will bring forth and so there will always remain a subjective element in estimating the credit exposure of derivatives.

Credit exposure on derivatives can be controlled to some extent by trading out of positions in the (rather limited) secondary market. If a counterparty has a swap on its book that it wishes to cancel, for example, there are three routes open to it.

(i)   Swap sale or novation. It is possible under swap documentation to assign a deal to another counterparty. This would be for a cash consideration either paid or received representing the difference in fixed rates for the remaining term, discounted to present day value. The original counterparty will need to be satisfied with the credit of the new counterparty before giving permission for the assignment.

(ii)   Cancellation by the original counterparties for cash settlement.

(iii)   Netting. Under the provisions of the International Swaps and Derivatives Association master agreement, the sum payable in the event of a default by a particular counterparty would be the net amount due under all outstanding deals between the two parties and not the gross amount owing. Whilst this agreement appears to have legal force as regards US banks, its status elsewhere is open to question. Informal netting can be achieved by calling for collateralisation of exposures when they exceed a certain pre-agreed level.

25 Forward rate agreement markets

Forward Rate Agreement (FRA) markets are over-the-counter markets and so are found in all major financial centres. They were first traded in London around 1983. Market makers in FRAs provide users with an alternative method of hedging risks associated with movements in interest rates. FRAs effectively replaced forward/forward deposits because they overcame the inefficiencies of that product, which are explained later in this chapter. They are also similar in effect to interest rate futures but perhaps more flexible in terms of the currencies and periods available.

The notional amounts traded per deal are relatively large with wholesale deals being around minimum $5,000,000 or the equivalent in other currencies. FRAs are, therefore, traded principally between banks, although the market is being accessed increasingly by commercial clients with banks warehousing smaller deals until they can be covered in market size.

Definition

Forward Rate Agreements are a means of hedging against future movements in interest rates on future loans and deposits. A period, currency and rate of interest are agreed by the counterparties in respect of a notional loan or deposit amount. Payment of a settlement sum on a discounted basis will be made on the first day of the notional loan or deposit period. There is no obligation on either party to borrow or lend the principal amount. Although the FRA itself is a contractual obligation, it is entirely separate from any underlying loan or deposit.

Banks sell FRAs at their offer rate to buyers who wish to protect themselves against rising interest rates. The buyer will receive a settlement sum if rates rise above the contract rate, but will pay out if rates fall. Similarly, banks will buy FRAs at their bid rate from sellers who wish to protect themselves against falling rates. The seller will receive a settlement sum if rates fall, but will pay out if rates rise. Banks may trade to match orders or on a speculative basis.

Interbank Forward Rate Agreements in the London market are dealt under FRABBA terms. These were first published in August 1985 by the British Bankers' Association (BBA) in association with the Foreign Exchange and Currency Deposit Brokers' Association. They have been updated several times since.

A typical transaction

A typical transaction would be for a bank to sell a three months versus six months FRA (referred to as 3v6) on the following terms:

Agreement date	3 February
Contract Currency	US dollars
Contract Amount	10,000,000
Contract Period	5 May - 5 August
Fixing Date	3 May
Settlement Date	5 May
Maturity Date	5 August
Contract Rate	10% pa

If the interest settlement rate on the fixing date is 11 per cent, then a *settlement sum* of $24,856.80 will be payable by the bank to the *buyer*. The words in italics are defined terms under FRABBA terms. The calculation of the settlement sum is explained later in this Chapter. For contracts transacted in London in sterling, the fixing date and settlement date will be the same, in this case 3 May.

When completing the transaction the dealer will need to ascertain the following information, recording the relevant information on his dealing ticket:

- The counterparty and whether a credit limit is in place;
- Whether the deal is a purchase or sale;
- The currency, amount, fixing date, settlement date and maturity date;

- The price or rate;
- The broker involved, if any;
- Whether the deal is on FRABBA terms or any variations to FRABBA terms are agreed;
- Payment instructions for settlement of any amount due on the settlement date;
- Whether the counterparty is a listed institution, an existing or a new wholesale counterparty with the appropriate verbal warning being given in the latter case.

Periods and quotations

The standard contract periods dealt are three, six, nine and twelve month fixture periods with the standard fixing dates being one, two, three, six, nine and twelve months in the future. Quotes can be made for irregular contract periods, eg one, three or five months but liquidity for such periods is thin. Liquidity in 12v24 month FRAs is good as the second half of two year interest rate swaps can be 'stripped out' (matched) in this way. FRABBA terms gives the settlement calculation for deals with a contract period of over twelve months but the market for such deals is extremely thin, if non-existent.

The most common periods traded are those with a three month gap between dates, ie 1v4, 3v6, 6v9 months and so on. 12v24 months is a standard period and US dollar FRAs may also be quoted in relation to futures contract dates, for example with June to June being quoted as a 2v14 FRA in April and a 1v13 in May.

Spreads between offer and bid rates quoted by dealers will be around four or five basis points for standard periods and settlement dates but much wider for odd or broken dates. Indicative rates are quoted by brokers on Reuters information screens in the manner shown in Figure 25.1. This shows US dollar FRAs, with a spread of 4 basis points being seen.

Figure 25.1   Typical quotation screen for US dollar FRAs

1 v 4	5.78 – 82	1 v 7	5.78 – 82	12 v 18	6.05 – 09
2 v 5	5.77 – 81	2 v 8	5.76 – 80	18 v 24	6.30 – 34
3 v 6	5.72 – 76	3 v 9	5.75 – 79	12 v 24	6.27 – 31
4 v 7	5.69 – 73	4 v 10	5.73 – 77		
5 v 8	5.66 – 70	5 v 11	5.74 – 78	IMM	
6 v 9	5.68 – 72	6 v 12	5.77 - 81	1 v 13	5.87 –91
9 v 12	5.77 - 81			4 v 16	5.92 – 96

Having quoted and traded, the dealer has the option of covering his exposure by:

- transacting an opposite FRA in the market;

- using the forward/forward deposit, foreign exchange swap, financial futures or options markets to hedge his position;

- deliberately maintaining an open position because of his expectations on interest rate movements.

Currencies, amounts and settlement rates

When FRABBA terms were introduced in 1985, the BBA arranged for 11 o'clock fixings in five major currencies to be calculated and advised via Telerate for twelve fixture periods, from one month maturity through to twelve months. The number of currencies traded has now greatly expanded, but it will be reduced again with the launch of the euro. The key to establishing an FRA market is to find an acceptable method of establishing an interest settlement rate, which could include a selling bank's own Libor fixing. The BBA publish daily BBA Interest Settlement Rates (BBAISRs), the procedures for setting them were stated in Chapter 13.

An investor who sells a FRA must take into account that when investing funds on the Fixing Date, the bid rate he is able to obtain will not be at a set spread below the Libor fix. A buyer wishing to fix the cost of his liabilities may find a variation between the BBAISR and the basis on which the margin on his loan is set.

Because payments and the potential for profit relate only to net movements in interest rates, it is only possible to offer the finest rates for deals of, say, the equivalent of US dollars 10,000,000 for 1v4 month or of US dollars 5,000,000 for 1v7 month FRAs. Smaller deals would be uneconomic.

Pricing

FRA rates are determined by supply and demand but will bear a close relationship to forward/forward deposit rates for arbitrage reasons. As an example, let us calculate the implied forward rate (IFR) for a sterling 1v4 month FRA. A flat yield curve is assumed and mid-market rates used, where the funds would be borrowed by the dealer for four months (122 days) and reinvested for one month (31 days), both at 10 per cent pa. The implied forward rate is calculated as follows:

$$\text{IFR} = \left(\frac{1 + (\text{Borrowing Rate} \times \text{Period})}{1 + (\text{Reinvestment Rate} \times \text{Period})} - 1 \right) \times \frac{365}{\text{Forward Period}}$$

$$= \left(\frac{1 + (10/100 \times 122/365)}{1 + (10/100 \times 31/365)} - 1 \right) \times \frac{365}{91}$$

$$= 9.916\%$$

From the mid market rate, the dealer will establish his offer and bid rates at, say, 9.94 - 9.89. The dealer's position and his view on future rate movements will influence his prices.

Note that the cash market in forward/forward deposits has never been very active for the following reasons:

- use of the cash markets involves increased settlement risks;
- credit lines are used when funds are reinvested with counterparties;
- the bank's balance sheet is used with consequent capital adequacy implications;
- dealing spreads may be wide because other bank's rates are used;
- any positions taken would be difficult to unwind.

Where there is a significantly positive yield curve in deposit rates, the implied forward rate will be higher than the underlying cash market rate for the period concerned. Where the yield curve is negative, the IFR will be lower than the cash market rate. Where there is a flat yield curve, the IFR will also be lower than the cash rate solely because of the compounding effect of reinvesting the interest that will be received, after 31 days in the example.

You can check this by calculating the implied forward rate using the formula and periods above with the following rates:

Bid rate (31 days)	Offer rate (122 days)	IFR
9.75	10.25	10.33
10.25	9.75	9.50

There are no premium or margin requirements for FRAs.

Settlement Calculation

Taking the details of the transaction outlined earlier in the Chapter, the settlement sum is the one per cent movement on US dollars 10,000,000 for 92 days:

$$\frac{\$10{,}000{,}000 \times 1 \times 92}{100 \times 360} = \$25{,}555.56$$

The sum of $25,555.56 needs to be discounted to present value using the settlement rate of 11 per cent since it is paid 92 days before interest would be settled on the notional loan the FRA represents, ie:

$$\$25{,}555.56 \times \frac{1}{1 + \left(\frac{11 \times 92}{100 \times 360}\right)} = \$24{,}856.80$$

The settlement formula in FRABBA Terms, for contract periods of up to one year, incorporates the two steps above, as follows:

Where the BBA Interest Settlement Rate (L) is greater than the Contract Rate (R):

$$\frac{(L\text{-}R) \times \text{Days in Contract Period (D)} \times \text{Contract Amount (A)}}{(365 \text{ or } 360 \times 100) + (L \times D)}$$

Where R is higher than L:

$$\frac{(R\text{-}L) \times D \times A}{(365 \text{ or } 360 \times 100) + (L \times D)}$$

The calculation of the Settlement Amount using the figures from the example is:

$$\frac{(11 - 10) \times 92 \times \$10,000,000}{360 \times 100 + (11 \times 92)} = \$24,856.80$$

Documentation - FRABBA terms

FRABBA terms, published by the British Bankers' Association, are the standard terms on which FRAs are dealt between banks in the London market.

FRABBA terms were devised to bring uniformity to the documentation for FRAs. When FRAs were first traded, banks dealt on the basis of individual documentation for each deal or relied solely on telex confirmations for transactions. When published, FRABBA terms became normal market practice for interbank transactions. Banks are, of course, free to deal on other terms if they wish, but are under an obligation to make clear to would-be counterparties any variation from FRABBA terms. Market makers may elect to quote to commercial customers and to banks abroad on FRABBA terms.

Under FRABBA, legally binding contracts are established at the point when the parties agree terms. This is most often by telephone or by telex. FRABBA terms provide for an exchange of confirmations both on the agreement and the settlement dates. However, these confirmations only evidence the particulars of an already established contract and do not constitute the contract itself.

The Recommended Terms and Conditions form the legal basis on which FRAs are transacted. Included in this section are clauses covering representations and warranties, settlement, payment, cancellation, events of default, indemnity on default, rights of parties and governing law. Under the representations and warranties, each party warrants to the other that it has full power and authority to enter into the FRA, that the obligations assumed by it under the FRA are legal and valid and that all payments will be made without deduction of tax.

FRABBA terms may be used as the basis for dealing with companies but will be varied to include conditions precedent (eg board resolutions, legal opinions and an acknowledgement that FRAs are to be used for hedging purposes and not for speculation). Representations and warranties and events of default are likely to be more comprehensive and specific operational points may be included.

26 Interest rate and currency swaps markets

Interest rate and currency swaps are over-the-counter, off-balance sheet products separate from contractual balance sheet obligations. They should not be confused with the spot against forward or interest arbitrage swaps discussed in Chapter 14.

The currency swap market was the first of the two to develop and had its origins in the back-to-back or parallel loans that were previously used to manage currency assets and liabilities. The market first emerged in the mid-1960s and remained fairly small until the 1980s. The interest rate swap market emerged at that time and swaps have grown to the extent that there were over US$ 22 trillion outstandings in mid-1997. Swaps have become one of the main methods by which participants in the market can manage balance sheet assets and liabilities and interest and exchange rate exposures.

The swap market today is a commodity-type market in the major currencies with a large number of market makers quoting prices for a wide range of maturities. The markets have developed to the extent that any stream of cash flows can be transformed into virtually any other stream, no matter what currency or basis is used or required, through interest rate and currency swaps.

Reasons for using swaps

Financial institutions and companies need the ability to structure their liability bases using a broad spectrum of sources at the most economic cost together with the ability to reverse previously arranged fixed rate funding to a floating rate basis or vice versa.

Swaps can be used by companies and financial institutions who have the size and credit rating to access the bond markets but who may not be able to issue on the most favourable terms or in the desired currency. By accessing the bond markets where they are able to obtain the best terms, issuers are able, through separate but contemporaneous swap transactions, to obtain cheaper funds and the desired liability mix for their business.

Although no figures are available, it is estimated that, at times, up to 80 per cent of new issues are swapped on behalf of issuers into another currency or interest basis. Swaps can also be used to reverse previously agreed structures without disturbing underlying commitments.

It is neither advisable nor usually possible for financial institutions and companies to use the bond markets continuously to obtain the mix of fixed and floating funds in the variety of currencies needed to fund their businesses. In addition, sectors of the bond markets may be closed to issuers for the following reasons:

- Credit and country risks. Names that are readily acceptable in the short term money markets may not be so attractive to the longer term capital debt markets. Where a particular name, or a group of names from the same country, taps an international capital market, the market's appetite for that issuer or country may quickly dry up and premiums be placed on future issues.

- Anomalies in ability to raise funds in different financial centres. A triple-A rated US corporation may have little difficulty in raising funds from the US capital markets but funds may not be so readily available from capital markets outside of the US where its name may not be so well known.

- Differentials between pricing of bank credits and capital debt. Bank floating rate funds may, according to the perceived credit risk of a company, be available within a range of 1/8th per cent to 1 per cent p.a. over Libor, whereas capital debt markets may discriminate by up to 2 per cent.

- Liquidity. A lack of liquidity within a particular sector of the market may mean that issues cannot be made on the desired basis. There is also an absence of liquid secondary markets for amending or restructuring various forms of liabilities without refinancing through further market entry.

Swaps developed from the existence of these anomalies in the financial markets with the result that issuers now use the markets where they obtain the best terms and then through swaps convert the price advantage gained into advantageous rates in other currencies or interest bases.

Other companies who are not able to issue bonds can obtain the desired liability mix through swaps. However, the days when banks would match counterparties as a broker for a fee or would stand as guarantor between two counterparties have passed. As the swap market developed it became impractical to match counterparties with equal and opposite requirements. Now an intermediary will quote for one side of a swap upon request and maintain a portfolio of swaps.

When commercial clients wish to access fixed rate term loans but are unable or unwilling to use swaps, banks themselves are likely to match such loans by means of interest rate swaps, funding the loan on short term fixtures.

Interest rate swaps

Interest rate swaps are agreements by which two parties agree to pay each other interest on a notional amount over a defined period but calculated according to a different interest basis. In a simple example, one party would agree to pay interest calculated on a fixed rate basis, often annually, over the life of the deal and the counterparty would agree to pay interest, say, six monthly on a floating rate basis with the floating rate refixed every six months for the life of the deal.

Although the most common type of interest rate swap is the fixed to floating swap, there are a number of variations on this theme, some of which are described later in the chapter. Figure 26.1 illustrates the payments expected under a sterling interest rate swap of fixed rate against 3 months Libor. Bank A and Bank B agree that for a predetermined period, say 3 years, they will exchange the implied interest payments on a notional sum of, say, £50 million. Bank B will pay a fixed rate that will be set according to market conditions at commencement, say 8 per cent. Bank A will pay whatever is 3 months Libor, this rate resetting every three months. Thus, if 3 month Libor for a particular period is 10 per cent, Bank A will pay to Bank B the equivalent of 10 per cent interest on £50 million whilst in exchange

Bank B will pay to Bank A the equivalent of 8 per cent interest on the same sum. If, in the next period, Libor falls to 6 per cent, Bank A will pay a sum equivalent to interest on £50m at 6 per cent whilst Bank B will continue to pay the fixed rate of 8 per cent.

Figure 26.1 Interest rate swap

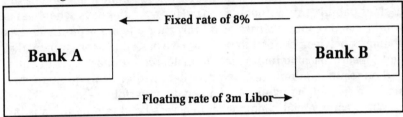

Note that:

- The principal amount employed is a notional amount only used to calculate the relevant interest payments. No movement of principal takes place.

- As no funds are lent or borrowed, the transactions are regarded as off-balance sheet. There may not be an underlying asset or liability.

- When interest payments coincide, parties usually agree to net payments.

Availability

Swap transactions in the interbank market can be arranged in all major currencies in amounts of $1m to $100m or the currency equivalent, though interbank deals are usually between $10m and $25m. Periods can range from one year to 25 years though two to ten year deals are the usual range and counterparty credit risk concerns can limit appetite to a maximum of five years. Brokers have a significant role in matching banks' needs.

Price quotations

Indication rates for interest rate swaps are available via brokers' screens. Figure 26.2 shows a typical broker's screen for interest rate swap quotations. Four major currencies are shown with quotes for annual periods from 2 to 10 years. Spreads vary between 1 and 4 basis points, which will reflect the liquidity of the currency and period concerned. The annotations beneath each currency code reflect the rate calculation basis, which varies with national conventions. All reflect a floating rate of 6 month Libor but the fixed side is calculated on different bases. For dollars, AMM means "annual money market" ie actual/360; D-mark is quoted on the annual bond 30/360 convention; sterling and yen are based on semi-annual bond, actual/365. Note that the sterling rates in this example show a negatively sloped yield curve.

Figure 26.2 Typical broker's screen

	USD 6m v AMM	DEM 6m v An Bond	GBP 6m v SA Bond	JPY 6m v SA Bond
2	5.87 – 5.88	4.17 – 4.20	7.58 – 7.61	0.74 – 0.76
3	5.90 – 5.92	4.34 – 4.37	7.31 – 7.34	0.92 – 0.94
4	5.93 – 5.95	4.49 – 4.52	7.09 – 7.13	1.12 – 1.14
5	5.95 – 5.96	4.62 – 4.65	6.91 – 6.95	1.29 – 1.31
6	5.96 – 5.98	4.72 – 4.75	6.74 – 6.78	1.46 – 1.48
7	5.98 – 6.00	4.84 – 4.87	6.62 – 6.65	1.61 – 1.63
8	6.00 – 6.02	4.91 – 4.94	6.53 – 6.57	1.74 – 1.76
9	6.01 – 6.03	4.99 – 5.02	6.43 – 6.47	1.85 – 1.87
10	6.02 – 6.04	5.05 – 5.08	6.39 – 6.43	1.96 – 1.98

These rates would be those that an interbank dealer would expect to pay or receive. A fixed rate payer for a five year dollar swap would expect to pay 5.96 per cent in this example, that being the intermediary's offer price. A commercial client will pay a higher rate which will include credit risk and some profit for the bank. A fixed rate receiver would expect to receive 5.95 per cent, the intermediary's bid price, less any credit risk and profit element. The floating rate payments are normally based on a flat or unadjusted reference rate, with the dealer's turn being taken through a margin on the fixed rates.

Swaps against 3 month Libor rather than 6 month Libor are quite common. Banks would probably quote fixed rates that were more or less identical on an annual basis to those for swaps against 6 month Libor, but adjusted for the payment frequency.

Cash flows relating to the fixed rate side of the swap can be established at the outset, as can the first floating payment. A company using a swap to convert a floating rate loan into a fixed rate liability must ensure that the Libor fixings are on the same basis for both the loan and the swap. Rate fixings a few days apart, or even ones based on quotes from a different panel of banks, can lead to significant cost differences, given the large nominal size of many swap transactions.

Variants of interest rate swaps

Forward start and cash flow swaps

It is possible to agree a swap that starts at a future date but with the rate set now. To protect their return, dealers may buy or sell government bonds or similar instruments, holding them until the start date, or use futures or a shorter term swap to fill the gap. The net cost of holding the matching asset will be reflected in the price of the swap. Swaps may be of increasing amounts during their life but are more frequently amortised to match a counterparty's commitments and cash flows.

Zero coupon swaps

In this structure one counterparty agrees to pay (or receive) Libor. The other counterparty will not receive (make) the fixed rate payments until the end of the swap when a lump sum will be paid representing the fixed flows. The lump sum will be the future value of the fixed rate payments so that the receiver avoids the reinvestment risks.

Swaptions

For payment of a premium, banks may write options on swaps. These are known as swaptions. The buyer has the right but not the obligation to assume a position in the swap at some time in the future. A 'Receiver' swaption gives the buyer the right to receive a fixed rate and a 'Payer' swaption is the right to pay fixed. The basis of pricing and risks of swaptions are similar to other financial options, which are discussed in chapter 28.

Basis swaps

Basis swaps involve the exchange of two floating rate interest streams. This can make sense where banks have assets linked to one particular rate index (say, base rate or prime) but liabilities linked to another (say, interbank Libor). By entering into a prime/Libor swap, they can match the rate profile of both assets and liabilities.

Another example of a basis swap is the overnight indexed swap, which exchanges Libor against the average overnight rate during a specific period. Given the volatility of overnight rates, it is important to have a reliable benchmark measure to use as the standard for such a swap. In the UK, the benchmark used is the Sterling Overnight Indexed Average (SONIA) which is calculated by the Wholesale Market Brokers' Association as the average rate on all sterling deposits of more than £5m made through the top seven London money brokers before 3pm each day.

Asset swaps

Whereas the description of swaps so far has been in relation to liability swaps, an equally important segment of the market is asset swaps. Financial institutions that have funds to invest may not be able to find bonds or other assets that meet their investment preferences. Using swaps, these institutions can transform their assets to give them the desired portfolio.

Another technique is for investment houses to purchase bonds that are trading at a high discount in the market, because they do not meet investors' criteria in their original form, and transform them into more easily saleable commodities. One application of this was seen when the UK government US dollar floating rate notes issued in 1986 were swapped to produce synthetic US dollar gilt-edged bonds. Another application is the purchase of low coupon bonds with warrants where the warrants have been stripped, so that the bonds trade at a deep discount. It is possible to transform the capital gain to be realised over the remaining life of these bonds into an annual return for investors in line with current market rates.

Hedging alternatives

Interest rate swaps are just one of the ways that a bank or its customers can protect against interest rate movements. Futures, FRAs, caps and floors provide alternatives. The availability of alternatives adds to market liquidity particularly in the period up to two years where FRAs and futures are usually traded.

The swap would have a fixed rate covering the whole period. Strips of FRAs or futures would be purchased at current market rates. Whilst the rates for these would all be known at the start, the rates could be different for each period, reflecting the shape of the yield curve. For FRAs, futures and caps, the first period will be covered in the cash market with only the subsequent periods being covered by the off-balance sheet products. Although the cash flows are different for each instrument, the effective rate over the whole period will be similar. If not, dealers will arbitrage between the markets.

To summarise with an example, if a borrower wishes to fix his interest costs for a twelve month period from 2 January, he could borrow in the cash market for the whole period or borrow on three month rollovers, paying a margin if appropriate, and cover the exposure for each quarter as shown in Figure 26.3. Note that with a one year swap it is likely that only one fixed rate payment will be made (at the end) against quarterly floating rate receipts.

Figure 26.3 **Alternative interest rate hedging strategies**

Period	Swap	FRA	Futures	Cap
Q1		Rate fixed in cash market	Rate fixed in cash market	Pay premium : Rate fixed in cash market
Q2	Receive floating rate	3v6	March contracts	Receive payment if fixing is over strike price
Q3		6v9	June contracts	
Q4	Make fixed payment at end	9v12	Sep contracts	

The credit limit to be marked against the counterparty that is fixing its interest costs is least with the cap, once the premium has been paid. Futures require profits and losses to be settled daily after being marked-to-market, thus minimising the credit risk. Counterparty credit limits will be established for the other instruments.

Currency swaps

The term currency swap is used to describe an agreement between two parties to buy specific amounts of foreign currency from each other on a spot basis and to sell the same amounts of foreign currency to each other on an agreed future date. An identical rate of exchange is established at the commencement of the deal and used to establish the payment flows at both the beginning and end of the swap. In the period up to maturity, each party makes interest payments on the currency it has received to the other party. The exchange rate used is normally the spot rate of exchange prevailing when the agreement is arranged.

Interest on the two currencies can be calculated:

- on a fixed rate basis for both currencies (fixed-fixed);
- on a floating rate basis for both currencies (floating-floating);
- on a fixed rate for one of the currencies and on a floating rate for the other (fixed-floating).

Figure 26.4 illustrates the cash flows under a fixed sterling / floating US dollars currency swap. Bank A agrees to pay a floating rate of 6 month Libor on a principal of $150 million whilst in exchange Bank B will pay a fixed rate of 8 per cent on a sterling amount of £100 million. The current exchange rate is £1 = $1.5.

Figures 26.4a/b/c Currency swap

(i)   At commencement

(ii) During the life

(iii) At maturity

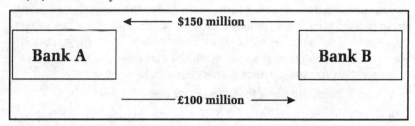

It should be noted that:

- Exchange of the currencies at the commencement of the swap is optional between the counterparties if it is based on the current market rate.

- An exchange of principal amounts takes place at maturity, the rate of exchange being the same as that used at the start of the deal.

- In view of the fact that interest payments accrue in different currencies, they are paid in full and netting does not take place.

Example

A European company wishing to make an investment in Japan may not be well enough known to obtain funds on favourable terms in the Japanese domestic markets. The company can however raise funds on favourable terms in one of the european capital markets. The company would borrow where it found rates most favourable, say in sterling. It would then enter into a sterling/yen currency swap, matching the interest rate basis as appropriate. The bank advising the company on its funding issue would very probably also arrange the currency swap.

In the past, a Japanese counterparty would have been sought who could issue a bond in the Japanese markets but who required liabilities in the currency that the european company can raise on favourable terms. Both companies would then make issues in their market of comparative advantage. Intermediaries would not necessarily seek to match the counterparties in this way now but may manage positions on a portfolio basis. The currency swaps market is, however, more reliant on the issue of bonds as underlying funding than the interest rate swaps market.

In this example there would be an initial exchange of currency. Servicing of the swap interest payments by the european company would be from its earnings in Japan.

Availability

Currency swaps can be arranged for most currency pairs, including many exotic currencies provided that exchange control regulations permit. The size of currency swaps tends to be larger than for interest rate swaps, with a minimum of $5 million or equivalent. The risk on currency swaps is higher which tends to limit maturities to a maximum of ten years.

Documentation

The International Swaps and Derivatives Association (ISDA), has taken a lead in developing standard documentation for derivatives transactions. They have produced model documents, including detailed definitions of terms, which are intended for use in relation to all types of OTC derivative transaction. Regular counterparties will complete a Master Agreement between themselves which defines the basic terms under which they will trade. Each transaction is then evidenced by an exchange of confirmations, which detail the specific terms of that deal.

ISDA produces several model Master Agreements, the most general being the Multicurrency – Cross Border agreement. This will include details of the following items as agreed between the parties:

- Events of default, which may include bankruptcy, misrepresentation, breach of the agreement, failure to pay or deliver on time or cross-default relating to other agreements.
- Termination events, which apart from default may include changes in law, tax or merger of one of the parties.
- Rights and calculations applicable in the event of termination.
- Provisions relating to withholding tax.
- Netting arrangements.
- Applicable definitions.
- Governing law.

A Schedule appended to the Master Agreement will specify which branches and offices of the two parties are covered by the agreement; who will act as calculation agent; and other items of detail.

Confirmations will include details specific to each trade. For an interest rate swap, the following items would be amongst those included:

- Notional amount and currency.
- Dates;
  - trade date, ie when the deal is done.
  - effective date, ie the value date at the start of the deal.
  - termination date, ie the final maturity.
- Fixed rate side;
  - fixed rate payer.
  - the rate applicable.
  - day count convention.
  - payment dates.
- Floating rate side;
  - floating rate payer.
  - floating rate index and spread, if any.
  - rate payable for the initial period.
  - day count convention.
  - payment frequency and reset dates.
- Business day convention (see below).
- Details of accounts to which payments should be made.

Similar items would be included for other types of OTC derivative with amendments as appropriate. For example, with a currency swap the initial and final exchange amounts would be stated whilst for interest rate options details of cap or floor rate and european or american exercise would be included.

One point of detail that it is important to remember is that derivative transactions often run for several years and their regular cycle of payments can be disrupted when a normal payment date falls on what is a non-business day because of weekends or public holidays. Agreements will specify how this is to be handled. There are three main conventions:

- Preceding day, where payments are made on the business day immediately preceding the usual date.

- Following day, where payments take place on the next business day.

- Modified following business day, where payments take place on the next business day unless it falls into a different calendar month, in which case the preceding business day is used. This is the most common option.

Differences in the payment calendar can lead to timing mismatches with hedges that are undertaken in other instruments and care needs to be taken in setting these up.

Managing a swap portfolio

When transacting an individual swap, an active swap trader will rarely seek to find an exactly matching counterparty immediately. Instead, the swap book will be managed on a portfolio basis with the aggregate interest rate and currency exposure being calculated and hedged as a whole rather than on a deal by deal basis. This increases the dealer's ability to quote two way prices to customers in varying sizes and dates whilst covering his position with deals in standard market periods and amounts.

The principle underlying portfolio management of swap books is that of discounted cash flow. At the inception of a five year swap, for example, the expected payments/receipts from the fixed rate side of the deal are known with certainty for the whole life of the transaction whilst the floating rate side will reset to a known index every three or six months. It is therefore possible, at any time in the life of the swap, to apply current market rates to the known cash flows and discount them to present value. The sensitivity of this present value to movements in interest rates in general or to the shape of the yield curve can then be calculated. There may be a variety of deals that could be undertaken in order to provide a hedge for this sensitivity, perhaps using futures or bonds in addition to other swaps, and the portfolio manager can select whatever is the most appropriate at the time, taking into account relative cost and whatever limits are in place.

Most swap portfolios are run on a closely matched basis with little outright interest rate or currency risk being taken. The aggregate limit on this risk may be expressed in conventional mismatch ladder terms or, more commonly, in terms of a duration constraint perhaps expressed in terms of the sensitivity of the book to movements of one basis point in interest rates (the present value of a basis point or PVBP approach). In addition to outright rate exposure, however, a swap portfolio is also exposed to changes in the slope of the yield curve (a combination of three and five year swaps is, for example, a good hedge for a four year swap but not perfect) and also to changes in the spread between swap rates and rates on hedging instruments such as bonds. Such exposures should only be incurred within specified limits but may be a source of trading profits for a skilled trader.

In some banks, the valuation of swap portfolios for accounting purposes is also based on a present value approach with profits and losses being determined by regular marking-to-market. In this case, a proportion of the calculated profits should be set aside as a provision against possible future credit losses. Although the general standard of counterparty in the swaps markets is high, there are occasional defaults that prevent banks from realising the value they had expected from swap transactions.

27 Financial futures markets

In the last century, those involved in the production and distribution of commodities and raw materials realised the risks posed to their businesses by price fluctuations. Trading in commodity futures in centralised market places enabled them to minimise these risks.

The development of financial futures was stimulated by the collapse of the Bretton Woods Agreement, which in 1948 had fixed the value of developed nations' currencies in terms of gold. During the 1960s, however, the economies of these nations advanced at different rates, bringing the agreement under considerable pressure. When currencies were floated in 1972, and so allowed to move freely against each other, both exchange rates and interest rates began to fluctuate.

Organisations handling finances on a large scale now became exposed to potentially damaging rate movements. Financial futures markets were pioneered in Chicago from 1972, drawing on the experiences developed in the commodity markets and being co-located with them. Financial futures have become one of the established ways for organisations to minimise financial risks.

Financial futures trading in exchange rate contracts commenced with the opening of the International Monetary Market (IMM), a subsidiary of the Chicago Mercantile Exchange (CME) in May 1972. Futures in interest rate contracts were first traded on the Chicago Board of Trade Exchange (CBOT) in October 1975, with futures on share indices being introduced in 1981 on the Index and Options Market (IOM), also a subsidiary of the CME.

During the 1980s and 1990s exchanges have been established in Europe and the Far East. The London International Financial Futures and Options Exchange (Liffe) opened for business in September 1982. Liffe remains Europe's premier futures exchange although it has been challenged by the Marche à Terme International de France (Matif) based in Paris and Frankfurt's Deutsche Terminbörse (DTB). Financial futures markets are now established in many countries, although the depth of trading in some local markets can be rather thin.

Practices and procedures and contract specifications are not consistent between exchanges. In this chapter we will use the exchanges in Chicago (CME, IMM and CBOT) and London (Liffe) as primary examples.

The futures exchanges

The Futures Exchanges are responsible for the membership, organisation and trading rules of the exchange. Their common objectives are to maintain financially sound, orderly, competitive and supervised markets.

Exchanges are normally subject to surveillance by official bodies. Liffe is registered as a Recognised Investment Exchange under EU rules. In the United States, futures contracts may only be traded on a Board of Trade exchange approved by the Commodities Futures Trading Commission (CFTC), which was established in 1974 to supervise and regulate all futures markets operating in the USA.

Functions of the exchanges

Each exchange and/or its supervisory body will:

- establish trading, accounting and recording standards, procedures and practices with which all or specific members are expected to comply;

- regularly review the financial integrity and status of each member;

- have audit and investigation departments, together with other supervisory committees to examine members activities and records;

- hold authority to introduce stringent disciplinary procedures, including the right to suspend, expel and withdraw membership should market makers abuse the privileged position afforded to them, disrupt the orderly conduct of the markets, fail to comply with accounting and other rules of the exchange or fail to meet the financial criteria of the exchange,

its clearing house or its supervisory body;
- establish confirmation procedures.

Membership of an exchange and trading authority

Membership of an exchange is achieved by the purchase of a seat, or the purchase of a licence to a seat on that exchange. Although the number of seats on any one exchange is limited, they are transferable and may be leased on some exchanges from non-trading members. The purchase or lease of a seat will be subject to the purchaser or lessee satisfying the qualification requirements and financial criteria of the exchange. One seat on the exchange will only permit the deployment of one floor member or screen trading station. Floor members are the only persons authorised to trade on the floor of the exchange.

Membership of an exchange does not always automatically provide trading authority and members may have to apply specifically for floor membership to be able to undertake business on the floor of the exchange. A demonstration of expertise including a period of assessment or other form of examination by the exchange is also common practice for all floor personnel.

Floor members may be brokers employed by commission broking firms executing orders for clients or traders on their own account (known as 'locals').

Some exchanges also provide restricted trading membership, which will permit trading in one or a limited number of specified contracts on the exchange. Bonding requirements for individual floor members are not unusual in the United States.

Trading arrangements

(i) Open outcry systems

Futures exchanges are, traditionally, central meeting places that provide facilities for their authorised members to buy and sell futures contracts by 'open outcry'. Open outcry is exactly what its name implies. Traders in designated 'pits' make known the prices at which they are prepared to deal by shouting out their bids and offers, supplemented by hand signals. Trading is conducted face to face, with all prices being instantly available to all participants in the markets.

The trading rules of each exchange will clearly define the manner of trading on that exchange. Access to the trading floor is normally tightly controlled, being restricted to floor members and exchange officials, together with their respective, but often limited, number of employees.

On the floor of an exchange the trading of each separate contract is undertaken in a pit designated by the exchange for that purpose. Trading may normally take place only within the area designated and only during such trading periods for that contract as defined by the exchange. The contract specification will include details of the times during which contracts are traded on the exchange. The opening and closing of each period of trading are normally signified by the sounding of a bell.

The floor broker must execute the order by open outcry, that is he must make either a bid or an offer aloud in the pit so that all other traders have an equal opportunity to hear and accept, or he must be the first to respond to another trader's bid or offer. Bids and offers are only valid if accepted immediately, if not accepted they lapse and a new bid or offer must be made.

The purpose of these requirements is to ensure that:

- a common market place exists for all orders in each futures contract;
- the prices in each futures contract are determined competitively;
- all trades are focused into the market place;
- access is allowed to the market for all orders.

Pit observers are employed by the exchange to ensure that the trading rules are adhered to and to relay information on trading prices. These prices are made available to all parties either on the price quotation boards of the exchange itself or on screens from quote information vendors.

(ii) Screen-based trading

Electronic trading systems are now available in some centres where trades can be transacted using prices quoted on screens from dealers' offices. For example, trading on the DTB is wholly screen-based. In June 1992 CBOT's and CME's after hours screen trading system, Globex, became live. As with most screen trading systems, Globex is an order matching system and does not attempt to simulate pit trading. Terminals installed at member firms offices allow world wide access to futures trading. Matif was the first European exchange to establish direct trading links with Globex though other exchanges are negotiating to establish formal links.

At the time of writing, there is considerable debate as to whether Liffe should abandon the open outcry system and adopt screen based trading. The latter can be attractive in that systems can operate for long hours (virtually round the clock in some cases); are convenient (being based around terminals located in traders' offices); are less prone to errors (in theory at least); and can be cheaper (as they do not require expensive floor traders). On the other hand, open outcry is more transparent, with all brokers aware of who is bidding for what contracts at what price, and is less prone to technology breakdowns which have been a problem with some of the screen-based systems.

Futures contracts

Financial futures contracts are binding agreements to buy or sell standard quantities of specified financial instruments or commodities at prices agreed at the time of the deal, for delivery at specified times in the future. They are not used for buying and selling the financial instruments themselves but in the expectation of generating gains or covering losses on the forward value of the instruments. This is achieved by buying or selling contracts and selling or buying offsetting contracts before their maturity, rather than waiting for a delivery day. Only a very small percentage of futures contracts are left open until the specified delivery day.

Financial futures are available in the following underlying commodities:

- Interest Rate Contracts: Interbank Deposits. Fixed Income Instruments.
- Foreign Exchange (Currency).
- Stock Exchange Indices.

When contracts are allowed to run through to their final delivery day, many are settled on a cash basis which means that only gains and losses are paid over. The margin system (described below) means that most of the profits and losses will already have been received or paid daily during the period the contracts are held and only a final adjustment on the delivery day will be made. Government bond futures usually require actual delivery of the underlying bonds.

The survival of trading in contracts depends on the number of lots traded on a continuing basis and the liquidity which traders and hedgers bring to the markets. It is not unusual for new contracts to be added and trading in illiquid ones suspended. When launching new contracts where there is little natural liquidity, exchanges may appoint commission brokers as designated brokers for the contract in order to encourage continuous liquidity. Designated brokers will undertake to make two-way prices in the contract to give potential users confidence that they will be able to trade in and out of their desired positions.

There was a move in the 1980s to make contracts fungible between exchanges. That is, it becomes possible to buy or sell the same contracts on more than one exchange. The Three Month Eurodollar contract and currency contracts on CME and Singapore Mercantile Exchange were successfully made fungible. Due to differences in contract specifications, technological and settlement difficulties and rivalry between exchanges, further progress in making contracts fungible was limited.

In the 1990s there has been renewed rivalry between exchanges, including the launch of competing contracts, which from the point of view of the end user dilutes liquidity and may harm the process of price discovery. On the other hand, of course, competition keeps the cost of trading low.

Contract characteristics

Given the number of different futures contracts now offered on exchanges around the world, and the frequency with which they are revised, it would be impossible to give an authoritative listing of all the contracts with which traders may come into contact. To give a flavour of the typical terms, however, this section outlines the characteristics (as at the time of writing) of three typical contracts:

- Three Month Sterling Interest Rate Future on Liffe.
- US Treasury Bond on CBOT.
- D-Mark currency contract on IMM.

Three month sterling interest rate - Liffe

The contract is based on a three month sterling deposit, assumed to be for an exact quarter of a year in order to produce a standardised value for the notional interest payable.

Unit of trading:	£500,000
Delivery months:	March, June, September and December
Last trading day:	The third Wednesday of the delivery month
Delivery day:	First business day after the last trading day
Quotation:	100 *minus* the rate of interest.
Minimum price move:	0.01 or £12.50 (one 'tick').
Trading hours:	8.05 to 16.05
Contract standard:	Cash delivery based on the Exchange Delivery Settlement Price

Futures markets' convention for quoting short term interest rate contracts is to take the implied interest rate away from 100 so as to give a quasi-bond style of pricing. As interest rates fall, futures prices should rise and vice versa. Thus, for example, a futures price of 90.00 implies an interest rate of 10 per cent. The prices quoted by futures traders will reflect their views as to where interest rates are likely to be on the respective delivery date. They will also calculate the forward/forward rates embedded in the yield curve (see Chapter 25) and compare with existing FRA prices in order to identify arbitrage opportunities.

Note that whereas FRA dealers quote rates with possibly a four basis point spread between the bid and offer, just a one basis point spread is enough to divide buyers and sellers of futures contracts. As dealers in the separate markets will have different expectations on likely future movements in rates, there may be slight differences in the rates quoted in each market.

The Exchange Delivery Settlement Price is determined by reference to the British Bankers' Association's official Libor rate for three month sterling deposits at 11:00 am on the last trading day. There is no physical settlement of the contract, those that run to maturity being settled on a net cash basis. As profits and losses since inception are settled on a daily basis, this will only involve movements in the contract price since the previous day's close.

US Treasury Bond Future- CBOT

Unit of trading:	$100,000
Delivery months:	March, June, September and December
Last trading day:	Seven business days before the last day of the month

Delivery day:	On any business day during the delivery month at the seller's option
Quotation:	As a percentage of nominal value of $100
Minimum price move:	One tick = 1/32nd or $31.25 (100,000 x 0.01 x 0.3125)
Trading Hours:	7.20 to 14.00
Contract standard:	$100,000 nominal par value US Treasury Bond with 8% coupon

The contract standard relates to a notional bond bearing a coupon of 8 per cent. Actual bonds eligible for delivery must meet the following criteria:

- Any US Treasury Bond maturing at least 15 years from the first day of the delivery month date provided they are not callable. If they are callable, the earliest call date must be at least 15 years from the first day of the delivery month.
- Bonds must be delivered in multiples of $100,000 par value.
- Interest must be payable half-yearly.
- Bonds must be capable of transfer by means of the US Federal Reserve wire transfer system.

As the bonds will have various maturity dates beyond 15 years and various coupon rates, the invoice price on delivery is adjusted by a conversion factor system to produce an equivalent eight per cent yield. In addition to the invoiced settlement price, all accrued interest on delivered bonds will be invoiced and paid over.

Hedgers and arbitrageurs need to take account of the individual bonds' conversion factors in constructing their positions. This they will do by calculating hedge ratios, that is how many contracts need to be bought or sold to achieve as close a hedge as possible. It also makes it possible to be selective when delivery is required and find bonds that are 'cheapest to deliver'.

The price at which traders are willing to quote for T-Bond futures follows the usual principal of forward pricing taking into account the rate at which funds can be borrowed to finance the purchase of bonds until the delivery date, and allowing for interest accruals receivable.

D-Mark Currency Future - IMM

The D-Mark contract is likely to die away with the introduction of the euro but the principles of trading with currency futures will be the same whatever the underlying.

Unit of trading:	$ against DM125,000
Delivery months:	January, March, April, June, July, September, October and December
Last trading day:	Two business days before the third Wednesday of the delivery month
Delivery day:	Third Wednesday of the delivery month
Quotation:	$ per D-Mark
Trading Hours:	7.20 – 14.00
Minimum price move:	$0.0001 or $12.50 (125,000 x 0.0001)

Pricing is a function of forward foreign exchange rates, which are determined, primarily, by interest rates in the respective currencies as explained in Chapter 14.

Delivery requires the delivery of D-Mark by the short position holder, who has sold contracts, to a specified bank account in Germany against receipt of US dollars.

The exchange quotes all currency prices in 'American' terms, which is the reciprocal of the direct quote. An exchange rate of $1 = DM1.6 will give a futures price of 0.6250 (DM1 = $0.625).

The clearing house

An integral, but usually separate, function to the operations of the futures exchange is that of the clearing house. Each exchange appoints a clearing house through which all contracts traded on that exchange are cleared and registered. Clearing houses may be independent bodies, subsidiary or associate companies or be owned by all or some of the clearing members of an exchange. They are profit making organisations whose operations are conducted independently from the exchange. The clearing house for the CBOT is the Chicago Board of Trade Clearing Corporation, for the CME, the Chicago Mercantile Exchange Clearing Corporation and for Liffe it is the London Clearing House (LCH).

Members of the exchange who wish to become clearing members must make separate application for membership of the clearing house. The clearing house will only clear trades and have a direct relationship with its members. For trading and clearing purposes, membership is usually categorised according to the authority granted to:

- trade and clear contracts for its own account;
- trade and clear contracts on behalf of customers;
- whether trading and clearing can be delegated to, or be conducted on behalf of other members;
- 'locals' who will use the clearing services of members.

Members are required to pay a registration fee on each contract cleared and registered on their behalf by the clearing house.

Margins

Futures exchanges operate margin systems to protect against the danger that a member will be unable to meet trading losses. Such systems typically have several parts to them.

Initial margins

To secure the performance of each outstanding contract registered in the name of clearing members, the clearing house will require members to place initial (or original) margin with, or to the order of, the clearing house. These margins will be required on all net positions as reflected in the accounts of the clearing house. A clearing member's clients' positions and their own positions are required to be margined separately. Commission Brokers will collect margins from their clients to cover the net position of each client and may impose more stringent requirements than those of the clearing house so that they may hold margin moneys in excess of those they are required to place with the clearing house.

The levels at which these margins are established will be determined by the clearing house, in conjunction with the exchange and will be based on the assessed maximum movement that may be expected in market prices on any one day. Initial margins only constitute a relatively small percentage of the underlying contract value and are effectively collateral against day to day price movements.

Initial margins on short term interest rate contracts may be below one per cent of the value of the underlying, whereas for long term bond contracts, five per cent to ten per cent is not unusual. Should volatility of prices in the markets change, the clearing house has the right at its discretion to increase or decrease initial margin requirements which means that calls or repayments may be made in respect of existing open contracts.

Spread margins

Reduced levels of initial margin are frequently allowed for specific trades that a clearing house recognises as being acceptable as compensating positions against each other. These may include:

- Inter-delivery month spreads. These comprise 'spread' or 'straddle' positions where long positions in one delivery month are compensated by short positions in another delivery month of the same contract, for example September and December Swiss franc contracts. The current delivery month's contracts may be excluded from this concession.

- Inter-commodity spreads. This will provide for long positions in one contract to be offset by short positions in another contract on that exchange where it is perceived that a close correlation exists between price movements of various types of contract traded.

- Hedge Margins. These are available to recognised hedgers of cash market positions, subject to registration as a hedger with the clearing house.

Reduced inter-commodity and hedge margins are usual in the United States but not on european exchanges. Some United States exchanges require higher levels of margin for spot or current delivery month contracts.

Variation margins

Each contract is marked-to-market when the day's closing prices are established with contracts being settled-to-market early the following morning. This means that in addition to initial margins, profits and losses are received or paid on a daily basis by contract holders.

On Liffe, variation margins are additional to initial margins. In the United States any losses incurred can be offset against the initial margin until prescribed minimum maintenance levels are reached, at which point they must be restored to the initial margin requirement level.

The settlement of margins on a daily basis is fundamental to the working of futures exchanges. Should any member or client default on a margin call, their open positions will be liquidated and any losses made up from the initial margins deposited.

SPAN

With trading in futures and options contracts becoming more widespread and traders' portfolios consisting of a mixture of different instruments, the exchanges have come to adopt more complex models of the risks that traders may be running. These are designed to recognise the interrelationships in the way that the prices of individual contracts move. An example is the SPAN (Standard Portfolio Analysis of Risk) margining system, which was introduced by the Chicago Mercantile Exchange in 1988 and is now used by a number of exchanges. Its aim is to determine the largest loss that a portfolio might reasonably be expected to suffer from one day to the next. Exchanges and brokers can vary the assumptions and degree of confidence that they wish to apply in order to establish appropriate margin levels.

Each day, the SPAN office carries out a set of complex calculations on the sensitivity of futures and options prices to a specific set of risk scenarios and creates a risk parameter file, which is transmitted to users. Each contract will be tested against sixteen possible variations of price and volatility, defined appropriately for existing market conditions. These include two extreme assumptions designed to test the sensitivity of option positions to market shocks. The largest loss from the sixteen scenarios is taken as the Scanning Risk Charge for that commodity.

Further adjustments to portfolio risk are made in respect of month-to-month correlations within a contract and such cross-contract correlations as the exchanges may permit to be recognised. There are also special adjustments for contracts that are close to delivery. SPAN then outputs the calculated minimum margin requirement for the particular set of positions.

Settlement of margins

Each clearing house will prescribe the methods by which initial margin requirements can be satisfied. Initial and variation margins are usually calculated on the basis of each day's closing positions and collected from (or any excesses returned to) clearing members or contract holders early on the subsequent business day. Interest may be paid to contract holders when margin moneys deposited exceed agreed levels.

Trading and clearing practice and procedures

Commission brokers are the intermediary for their clients to participate on the exchange. Clients will give orders to their commission brokers whose dealing rooms are located outside the exchange. Transactions arranged for clients are on a principal to principal basis, with the commission broker being required to conduct his business in compliance with investor protection legislation. The commission broker will need to assess the creditworthiness of his clients, setting limits on the volume of contracts he will buy or sell on the client's behalf.

The typical sequence of order execution begins at a broker's office with a client placing an order to buy or sell. This is recorded on an order sheet, which is time stamped. Orders may be taken on the basis of execution at 'best' or to be executed at specific prices and within specific time frames (limit orders). For example, the order may be 'good all day at 90.00'.

If trading is by open outcry, then during trading hours the order is immediately conveyed to a floor member's booth where it is again recorded and time stamped on an order slip. The order is conveyed by the clerks to a floor broker, the commission broker's representative on the floor who buys and sells in the trading pit. Hand signals are often used to communicate orders to the floor broker. Larger clients may be able to call direct to the member's booth, by-passing the broker's office and speeding up the execution process.

Once the price has been agreed, the floor brokers must both fill out trading chits recording details of the contracts traded. Processing of the trades continues in two directions. The details on the trading chit, including the commodity, price, and number of lots bought or sold, the contract month, names of the buying and selling members and clearing members to be used are relayed by each of the parties to the deal to the clearing house for registration. Simultaneously, the contract details are recorded in the brokers' back offices. It is only when the clearing house is able to match both sides of the trade and confirm them via the screens to each broking house that the brokers are able to treat the deal as completed. However, the deal between the broker and client is contractually binding once the broker has advised that the order has been filled.

Any trades reported by buyers and sellers which are not matched or differ in detail, for example, trade size or trade price, will be rejected by the clearing house. It is then the responsibility of the floor members who executed the transactions to investigate and correct the trade and arrange for its resubmission to the clearing system. If the floor members are unable to resolve the issue, it will be referred to an exchange official who will, if necessary, instruct either one or both parties to close the deal in the pit for clearance and registration, pending resolution of the dispute. The adoption of electronic order matching systems clearly reduces the scope for errors (or 'out trades') substantially.

At the end of each business day the clearing house will provide each clearing member with a trading statement giving details of all accepted contracts which it has received in that member's name. The clearing member is required to verify the detail and confirm its acceptance within stipulated time periods, advising any contracts which are to be transferred to the account of another clearing member.

On receipt of the clearing member's acceptance of daily trades, the clearing house will register contracts and issue a registration certificate to each member. Once a contract is registered the clearing house will, subject to any restrictions in its rules, guarantee the fulfillment of all contracts by its clearing members. From the point of registration, the clearing house becomes principal with the broker who buys or sells each contract, releasing them from credit control considerations on each other. The guarantee comes into effect the morning after trades are concluded and is contingent on receipt of initial and variation margins by specified times.

Up to the point of registration, floor members have direct contractual relationships as principals with each other. The credit risk for this period is normally accepted on the basis of the exchange's frequent vetting of its members together with the other controls implemented to ensure performance. The credit risk then resides with the clearing house until such time as a position is closed or settled at maturity.

Processing of trades on screen-based trading systems follows the same lines, though completely electronically, with daily cut-off times being established for the issue of registration statements.

Users and uses of futures

Financial futures are used by hedgers, traders (speculators) and arbitrageurs. Hedgers are looking to protect themselves from adverse price movements in their financial assets or liabilities. Traders, who are essential for providing liquidity in the markets, are willing to take positions in the anticipation of profiting from price movements. 'Scalpers' trade rapidly during the day, hoping to make a small profit on each trade. Day traders aim to finish the day without an open position. Position traders aim to profit from positions built up and liquidated over a period of time. Arbitrageurs will look for inconsistencies in prices in different markets as the cash markets or the futures market move in advance of each other. The arbitrageur may take a position in the selected futures contract and an opposite position in the futures or cash market where the prices are out of line, in anticipation of the markets correcting themselves. Because of the existence of arbitrage, market prices will not drift far apart.

Hedging example - Short term interest rate futures

It is April. A bank has a US dollar floating rate note issue with six-monthly rate fixings, the next one being due in July. The bank's treasury believes that interest rates will rise in the meantime. A decision is made to hedge $50 million by selling eurodollar interest rate futures contracts. Since futures contracts are three, rather than six month duration, the bank must calculate how many futures contracts to sell, as follows:

$$\frac{US\$ \ 50,000,000 \times 184 \times 12}{360 \ \times \ 3} = 102.22 \text{ contracts}$$

That is, approximately double the number of three month futures contracts based on 90/360 days are needed to hedge a six month run of 184 days. September contracts are sold because these will mature after the rate fixing on the FRN, allowing the bank to close out the futures contract, hopefully crystallising a gain in the meantime. Assume the current futures price is 95.00, representing an interest rate of five per cent and the six-month LIBOR is 5 1/8th per cent.

On the rate fixing date in July, the six month Libor is fixed at 6 1/8th per cent and 102 September contracts are bought at 94.00 thus closing out the futures position. The outcome is as follows:

Cash Outcome	Interest	Futures hedge	
184 days @ 5 1/8	$1,309,722	102 contracts sold at	95.00
@ 6 1/8	$1,565,277	102 contracts bought at	94.00
Extra cost	$ 255,555	Profit 100 ticks x $25 x 102	$255,000

The bank has therefore locked almost exactly into current interest rates by undertaking the hedge. In the reality of daily business, the hedge is unlikely to match the cash position so precisely because of various factors comprising basis risk:

- The six month Libor may not increase to the same extent as three month Libor.

- The futures price is based on the implied forward rate and this will be different from the spot rate. Over time, however, the futures and spot rates will converge and be equal at the quarterly delivery dates.

- The standardised amounts and trading periods are unlikely to coincide with the hedger's exact requirements.

- The expectations of dealers in the cash and futures markets may cause the respective rates to diverge.

- It may not be possible to sell all the 102 contracts at exactly the same price.

- The costs of hedging and margin requirements have not been taken into account.

- Futures profits and losses are settled daily whereas the extra cost of the underlying borrowing will not be realised until its maturity.

Other hedging examples

(i)   Investment managers responsible for long term investment are vulnerable to falling interest rates if receipt of funds is anticipated on a future date. The purchase of government bond futures most closely resembling their projected portfolio can help minimise these risks.

(ii)   Treasurers responsible for currency positions can use currency contracts to protect against adverse movements in rates. As an illustration, if a treasurer has a known purchase of D-Marks to make against sale of US dollars, he can protect against the strengthening of the dollar as follows:

Current futures rate	DM1 = $0.6025 ($1 = DM1.6600)
For each contract bought	DM125,000 = $75,312.50

If the US dollar future strengthens to, say, 0.6061 ($1 = DM1.6500), for each futures contract sold, DM125,000 = $75,762.25. The movement is 36 ticks or $450.00 (36 x $12.5)

Providing the spot rate has moved to the same extent:

Loss on spot position	DM125,000 at 1.66 =	$75,301.20
	DM125,000 at 1.65 =	$75,757.76
	=	$ 456.37
Profit on futures for each contract	= US$	450.00

The difference in the two amounts is a rounding error introduced by the different method of quoting rates.

Advantages and disadvantages

The benefits of financial futures to hedgers are:

- They are off-balance sheet, providing a method of hedging exposures without delivery of the underlying commodity or financial instrument.
- Because contracts are standardised and traded on exchanges, they provide a fair pricing mechanism and there is no price discrimination between small and large trades.
- The costs of trading are low as are the levels of margins payable. Futures allow significant leverage, that is, the ability to cover large exposures by committing only a relatively low level of resources.
- Only minimum levels of credit facilities are used by participants in the markets.
- The credit risk between brokers is removed as the obligations are taken over by the clearing house, but note that this guarantee does not extend to dealings between brokers and their customers.
- Positions are revalued on a daily basis, providing an early warning mechanism if rates are moving contrary to expectations.

The disadvantages are:

- As contracts are for standard amounts and periods and have a restricted contract range compared to cash instruments, constructing hedges may be imprecise as well as being expensive to monitor and administer.
- Margin calls must be monitored daily as positions are marked to market, possibly involving the use of separate bank accounts with

overdraft arrangements and the need to provide margins in more than one currency with consequent cash flow considerations.

28 Financial options markets

Although currency, interest rate and stock options are among some of the most recent financial instruments, the antecedents of this type of contract can be traced back many years. A similar contract referred to as privileges was first traded on the Chicago Board of Trade in the 1860s and there are references to other contracts that could be recognised as options in ancient China.

Definitions

Financial option contracts are binding agreements between two parties which give one party the right, but not the obligation, to buy or sell an agreed quantity of a particular currency, financial instrument, futures contract, stock index or stock at an agreed price, on or before a predetermined expiry date. They are a means by which buyers can hedge financial exposures whilst at the same time retaining the benefit of favourable movements in rates and prices.

Options can be traded either by negotiation of terms between the two principals (over-the-counter or OTC options) or on recognised exchanges. An extensive jargon has developed to describe the features of options contracts. The following definitions apply to both OTC and exchange traded types.

Call options and put options

Call options provide the purchaser with the right to buy the underlying subject matter and put options provide the purchaser with the right to sell the underlying subject matter. The purchaser is also referred to as the holder and the seller as the writer or grantor.

Strike price, at-the-money, in-the-money, out-of-the-money

The price at which the option holder has the right to put or call the underlying subject matter is referred to as the strike or exercise price. The strike price is said to be at-the-money or at-the-market when the current market price of the commodity is the same as the strike price of the option.

If the immediate exercise of the option would result in the holder receiving a payment from the writer, the option is said to be in-the-money. A call option (right to buy) is in-the-money when the strike price is lower than the current market value. It is out-of-the-money when the strike price is higher than the current market value. Conversely, a put option (right to sell) is in-the-money when the strike price is higher than the current market value and out-of-the-money when the strike price is lower than the current market value.

Exercise and expiry dates

An option written on 'American terms' may be exercised on any business day up to and including the expiry date with delivery taking place when the option is exercised. An option on 'European terms' is exercisable at any time during the life of the option but delivery can only take place at the end of the period on the value date specified in the contract.

The expiry date is the last day on which the option may be exercised. The terms of the option will usually incorporate a specific time of expiration, which is the latest time on the expiry day that the grantor will accept notice of exercise. If an option contract is not exercised during the exercise period the option will be considered abandoned and the grantor is under no further obligation. The onus of exercising options technically lies with the holder but market practice is now for in-the-money contracts to be exercised automatically at expiry on behalf of holders.

Premium

The option buyer will pay the grantor a premium for the rights contained in the option. The buyer can never lose more than the premium and any fees paid in establishing the contract. Conversely, the seller's risk is open-ended unless hedging action is taken. The premium is payable up-front, when the option is written, except for some exchange traded options.

Intrinsic and time value

The intrinsic value of the option is the in-the-money value (if any) that could be realised on immediate exercise of the option. The time value is the part of the premium that is not intrinsic value. The premium on out-of-the-money contracts consists solely of time value. Even contracts that are out-of-the-money and so of no value if exercised today can still have considerable time value because of the possibility of their moving back into the money before expiry.

Example: Currency option - holder's perspective

An investor, with a future need to buy sterling/sell US dollars fears sterling will strengthen. He purchases a call option on £1,000,000 for three months at a strike price of £1 = $2.00, the current market price, at a premium of $0.05 per pound. The terms are:

Right to buy	£1,000,000
against delivery of	$2,000,000
for payment of premium of	$ 50,000
Time value	$ 50,000
Intrinsic value	Nil

If the current market value moves to £1 = $2.10 within the option period (sterling has strengthened), the investor will exercise the option. The overall cost of acquiring the sterling is then $2,050,000 (including the premium) rather than the current spot cost of $2,100,000, a saving of $50,000.

If Sterling weakens to £1 = $1.90, the investor will allow the option to lapse and will purchase the sterling in the market for a total cost of $1,950,000 (including option premium).

Other option strike prices could have been chosen. If an in-the-money strike price is agreed of £1 = $1.80, then the terms could be:

Right to buy	£1,000,000
against delivery of	$1,800,000
for payment of premium of, say	$ 205,000
Time value	$ 5,000
Intrinsic value	$ 200,000

Unless sterling weakened to £1 = $1.8000 or below, the investor could be expected to exercise the option in order to retrieve the intrinsic value.

If an out-of-the-money option strike price of £1 = $2.20 is agreed, the terms could be:

Right to buy	£ 1,000,000
against delivery of	$ 2,200,000
for payment of premium of, say	$ 2,000
Time value	$ 2,000
Intrinsic Value	Nil

The investor would be unlikely to exercise the option unless sterling strengthened higher than to £1 = $2.2000 although this contract has higher leverage for the investor because of the lower outlay.

Pricing

No one within any market can determine accurately the actual price for financial commodities in the future. The only factors that can be established with certainty are current prices and historic trends. Consequently a large element of the expertise used in pricing the premium value, and the hedging strategy for options, is based on assumptions and probability factors determined by current and historical data.

The option premium comprises both time value and intrinsic value. For most options time value is a function of four factors: period; current market versus the strike price; interest rates; and volatility (the major variable, which is discussed below). Current levels of supply and demand will also impact upon option prices. For example, if there were many purchasers of options but few grantors, the grantors' risk potential would increase as the opportunities to hedge sales with purchases would diminish. Premiums will therefore be lower in liquid markets.

Period

The longer the period an option has to run the greater the probability that the option will at some point during its life move into the money, or, if already in-the-money, increase its intrinsic value. Therefore longer dated options are generally more expensive than shorter dated ones.

If we say a one month option costs $1,000 then it would be logical to assume that a four month option costs $4,000 and a nine month contract costs $9,000. These are logical assumptions but in the case of options quite wrong. Experience (and statistical theory) has told option grantors that the relationship of cost to time for options works on an approximate square root relationship. So if a one month option costs $1,000 then a four month contract would cost $2,000 (two being the square root of four) and a nine month contract would cost $3,000 (three being the square root of nine). In practice the relationship would not be so exact.

In option pricing it is also necessary to consider the impact of the decreasing period of an option during its life. Accounting convention would tell us that this should be amortised on a straight line basis. However, again this is not the case, and experience shows option grantors that the actual movement of time value is small until the last 30 or so days of an option's life. For an option with 180 days to expiration, the passing of one day has far less impact than when only ten days are left. The time value decay curve is in fact a square root curve.

Current market price versus strike price

Generally speaking the nearer the strike price is to current market levels the greater is the uncertainty as to whether the option will expire in or out-of-the-money. The nearer the strike price is to the market, the higher the time value in the premium will be. Deep in-the-money and deep out-of-the-money options command very little time value because the future course of action of the holder is more predictable.

As an option moves into the money the premium obviously becomes more expensive as it commands both time and intrinsic value. Consequently, as leverage is one of the main advantages of using option, it becomes less attractive to buyers and for that reason a point will be reached where the premium is wholly intrinsic value. Out-of-the-money options may reach a point where there is only a very remote possibility of exercise and will be worthless.

Interest rates

The premium for an option is usually paid immediately. Therefore the premium has earning potential to the option grantor and represents a loss of potential income to the option holder. This is reflected as a discount in the option premium calculation and will be based on current levels of interest rates - the higher the interest rate, the larger the discount.

Volatility

With the exception of the possible exercise and delivery dates for American style options, each of the factors discussed above are determinable. Future volatility is not, and the assumptions, calculations and probability factors used in measuring its expected course are the secret of options pricing.

Volatility is the most arbitrary figure that goes into an option calculation and can vary from one grantor to another depending upon what assumptions that grantor uses to calculate volatility. The calculation would normally treat the more recent prices as having greater significance, as these will be perceived to be of more importance than movements of some months ago.

If perceived volatility is calculated and reflects a movement of, say four per cent over the last three months, then for a three month option the premium would take into account the possible repetition of that movement and provide for the fact that the movement may be greater. The more volatile the underlying commodity, the more the option will cost since it is more likely to acquire intrinsic value during its life.

The above are applications of the Black-Scholes formula devised in the 1970s by Fisher Black and Myron Scholes as a theoretical model for determining the fair value of option premiums and hedging strategies. Since it was designed originally for call options on individual equity stocks, the formula needs to be modified by users for other types of option and there is a growing set of variants of the basic model which have now been published in the academic literature. The mathematics of the various option formulas are beyond the scope of this publication.

Dealers also trade volatility itself rather than any actual movement in market prices. This involves, for example, buying two matching options, a call and a put, which exactly cancel each other out. One may give the right to buy sterling at 1.60 to the dollar in three months time, the other to sell at the same rate. Underlying market risk (delta risk) is neutralised. What remains is a play on volatility or gamma risk. If the volatility on which the premium were based rises from 5 per cent to 10 per cent, both the call and put options may be sold at a profit. If volatility does not rise but prices in the market move far enough, no matter in which direction, then one option could be exercised at a profit, leaving the other to expire. This type of trading is extremely specialised and should only be undertaken within strict dealer limits. If the volatility remains static or falls, the premium payments will be lost and the costs of carry of the premiums can be substantial.

Risk control and hedging

The risk management of options portfolios relies heavily on mathematical models that measure the sensitivity of the portfolio's value to changes in the various pricing factors. These factors have become known collectively as the 'Greeks', reflecting the mathematical symbols used in the formulas.

Delta risk

Option values are sensitive to moves in the value of the underlying rate or instrument. The only certain way to totally protect or hedge against these moves is to purchase an option that is identical in every way to the one that is written. In this case the only profit, if any, made would be from the bid/offer spread. The delta provides another way to hedge the option, although some risk remains.

The delta of an option gives a measure of what the change in the option's price should be when there is a change in the price of the underlying. This can be used to calculate the amount that should be bought or sold in the cash or futures market so that any unfavourable movement in the price of the underlying is offset by the profit made on the cash or futures.

The delta is also known as the hedge ratio since it reflects the sensitivity of the option price to a change in the price of the underlying. The value of the delta always lies between 0 and 1 for calls and 0 and -1 for puts.

An at-the-money-option will have a delta of approximately 0.5, representing a 50 per cent chance of exercise, since the market has an equal chance of rising or falling. If it moves out-of-the-money, it will have a delta closer to zero reflecting a lower probability of exercise whilst if it moves into-the-money delta will move away from zero.

Although a book of options could be completely delta hedged (delta neutral) there is still an element of risk since the mathematics of options pricing are such that any change in the price of the underlying causes a change in the delta. The rate at which the delta moves is known as the gamma. Gamma is highest when the option is at-the-money.

Further measures of risk are:

- Vega, which measures the impact on the option's premium of a change in volatility.

- Theta, which measures the impact of the passing of time on an option's value as expiry approaches.

- Rho, which measures the sensitivity to changes in interest rates.

Delta hedging strategy - example

Computer programs are used to calculate the hedge ratio. The following simplified example illustrates the basic assumption of hedging strategy although it would not be used in isolation of other factors and hedging techniques.

A dealer grants a three month at-the-money call option on £1,000,000 against US dollars at a strike price of 2.0000 for a premium of $50,000. The option is on American terms and can be exercised with delivery taking place at any time.

A 500 point strengthening of sterling to 2.0500 would absorb all the premium if the option is left naked or uncovered by the grantor since if the option is exercised, the sterling would have to be purchased by the grantor at a higher cost in US dollars.

The grantor could immediately purchase £1,000,000 at the spot rate of 2.0000, but this would leave him vulnerable to a weakening of sterling since the option would not then be exercised. If the rate moves to £1 = $1.9500, the cash position would have to be reversed with only $1,950,000 being realised from the sale of sterling, resulting in a loss of $50,000.

A third alternative would be for the grantor to hold a 50 per cent hedge. This means that the dealer will be able to absorb a 1,000 point movement in rates before the premium income is used up. Figure 28.1 illustrates further outcomes at expiry.

Figure 28.1   *Options hedging strategies: profit and loss*

Market price	Premium received	Loss on exercise	Profit/Loss on 50% hedge	Net Profit/Loss
2.1000	$50,000	($100,000)	$50,000	0
2.0500	$50,000	($50,000)	$25,000	$25,000
2.0000	$50,000	-	0	$50,000
1.9500	$50,000	-	($25,000)	$25,000
1.9000	$50,000	-	($50,000)	0

The hedge position can be adjusted as the option moves in- or out-of-the-money. Each change in hedge ratio will move the top and bottom of the profit and loss scale. A higher hedge ratio may be chosen where the option strike price is in-the-money and a lower hedge ratio for out-of-the-money contracts.

The reader should note that whilst the example above illustrates the principle of delta hedging for a single option, the reality of managing an options portfolio will be far more complicated. In this example, we assumed that the market moved uniformly in one direction or the other throughout the life of the option and no account was taken of the costs of hedging. In reality markets do not behave in a rational manner nor do they move consistently up or down. A perfect hedge is rarely available and even the most sophisticated programmes are often unable to provide against all eventualities. Large losses may result from unanticipated events and additional hedging costs. The real risk within an option programme is not where you are now but where you might be tomorrow should the unanticipated happen. These risks should be continuously quantified and controlled within the context of 'what if' scenarios.

Risk management of options according to the Greeks can never be more than approximate and is best suited to large option portfolios that contain many natural risk offsets within them.

Over the counter currency options

Over the counter options (OTCs) are established directly between the purchaser and grantor and are tailor-made to the purchaser's requirements. Options on almost all currencies against the US dollar are now available in the London interbank market, as are many crosses of sterling against major currencies.

Amounts traded can be up to $100 million for major currencies with typical periods being for three weeks to one year or, exceptionally, several years in major currencies.

Market practice

Market practice is generally governed by the International Currency Options Market (ICOM) Terms and Guide, issued by the British Bankers' Association in association with the Foreign Exchange Committee in New York and the Tokyo Market Practices Committee. ICOM terms incorporate a Master Agreement. Banks may enter into bilateral Master Agreements covering all options deals between them with the terms of each deal being evidenced by an exchange of confirmations. The Master Agreement and confirmations, sent preferably electronically, will constitute a single agreement.

There are two generally accepted methods of price quotation: premium and volatility. It is now very common for dealers to quote and trade the volatility only and, indeed, the BBA publishes daily benchmark levels of volatility for several major currency pairs including in-, at- and out-of-the money values. When dealing in terms of volatility, the counterparties agree on a figure expressed as a percentage per annum which, when combined with the spot rate, interest factors of the currency pair, the expiry date of the option and the strike price, is used to compute the premium.

Counterparties also need to agree upon:

- Option style (american or european);
- Call currency, put currency and amount;
- Expiration date, expiration time;
- Premium payment date, settlement date;
- Strike price.

An option may be settled with gross payments being made as for foreign exchange contracts. Where it is agreed between the parties that settlement of the in-the-money amount will be on a net basis, the intrinsic value to be paid over will be calculated as in the following example:

US dollar call/D-Mark put: contract amount $10,000,000 at strike $1 = DM 1.6.
Spot price for settlement purposes $1 = DM1.6850 *less* strike price $1 = DM1.60
equals DM 0.085 per $.
Net settlement sum = 0.085 x $10,000,000 = DM850,000.

The level of the spot price at the time of exercise is crucial to the
ultimate value of the net cash settlement. As the spot price used is
determined in good faith by the seller, the buyer should ascertain at the
outset how it will be fixed.

It is normal for there to be automatic exercise of options which are
in-the-money at the expiration time and have not been exercised by
notice of delivery, provided the in-the-money amount of the call or put
currency exceeds the strike price by one per cent.

Types of OTC currency option

The continuing extension of the market has given rise to more
sophisticated products being devised. An example is cylinder options,
which involve two options written simultaneously, the purchase of a
call and sale of a put at strike prices that reduce or eliminate the premium
payment by the holder. The writer will incorporate the two transactions
into his hedging portfolio. Other examples are:

- Average rate or Asian options, where the buyer can protect a
  series of currency flows over a period, perhaps a year, against
  exchange losses.

- Look-back options, which allow the holder to deal at the most
  favourable rate achieved during a specified period.

- Digital or binary options involve a fixed payoff if the option
  expires in-the-money no matter how far in-the-money it may
  be.

- Barrier options can be activated or extinguished by the price of
  the underlying touching a particular price at any time during
  its life, the value of the option thus being contingent not just
  on the price at expiry but also on the path of price movements
  during its life.

The pricing and hedging strategies for these types of option are more
complex for the writer and require a high level of confidence in the
mathematical models used.

Over the counter interest rate options

OTC interest rate options are used by borrowers and investors to set maximum interest rates they are willing to pay or to protect minimum returns on investments in return for paying premiums to writers.

Types and availability of OTC interest rate options

- Interest Rate Guarantees (IRGs) are short term contracts whereby the purchaser will be compensated should interest rates rise above or fall below the agreed contract rate, known as borrowers' and lenders' respectively. IRG quotations will be based on Forward Rate Agreement rates.

- Caps are agreements by the seller of the cap to protect the buyer's interest rate costs from rising above a specified level over a period of time for an up-front premium.

- Floors are agreements by the seller of the floor to protect the buyer's interest rate return from falling below a specified level for an agreed period of time. Interest rate caps and floors are effectively a series of IRGs.

- Collars are a combination of an interest rate cap and an interest rate floor. One party to the agreement will write the cap and one the floor to reduce or eliminate any premium payment.

OTC interest rate options can be written in most major currencies. Notional principal amounts can be between £500,000 and £100,000,000 or the currency equivalent. Interbank agreements are becoming increasingly commoditised and so tend towards larger size. Periods can range from three months to ten years.

Caps and floors can be created on many indices including Libor, base rate, commercial paper, Treasury bills, and certificates of deposit. The frequency of reset dates on which the level of interest rates is compared to the strike level to find out what payments need to be made, can be monthly, quarterly or six monthly but are usually quoted on a three month basis against three month Libor.

Examples
Borrower's IRG - £10,000,000

FRA Period	FRA Rate %	Premium - Strike Price at FRA rate	Premium - Strike Price at 25 bps out-of-the money
3v6 months	8.34	0.13 (£13,000)	0.06 (£6,000)

The premium is usually payable up front. A credit limit will need to be established for the buyer if payment of the premium is deferred.

If in three months time Libor is fixed at 9 per cent, the holder of the IRG purchased at the at-the-money strike price of 8.34 per cent will be compensated for the interest differential of 66 basis points, ie £16,454.79, assuming a 91 day interest period. Whether settlement is to be made at the rate fixing time on a discounted basis or at the end of the notional fixture will have been agreed by the parties at the outset. If Libor falls to 8 per cent, the buyer will allow the option to lapse. As with FRAs, IRGs are separate from the underlying debt obligation, which must be arranged separately by the holder.

Interest rate cap

A typical cap agreement could have the following terms:

Term of cap	: Three Years
Notional amount	: $10,000,000
Rate Fixing	: Quarterly
Strike level	: 7%
Payment	: Quarterly in arrears on an actual/360 day basis
Up front premium	: One per cent or $100,000

One feature to note in this example is that there will be eleven rate fixings. A loan in the cash market will be taken out by the buyer to cover the three month period from the start date. At the subsequent three monthly rate fixing dates the writer of the cap will compensate the buyer in any quarter where the three month Libor exceeds 7 per cent. If Libor is set at 8 per cent at the start of the second quarter, then, assuming this quarter is 92 days, a payment of $25,555.56 will be payable at the end of that quarter.

Indication cap and floor premiums are quoted on brokers' screens on Reuters and Telerate although it is now common for brokers to quote volatilities rather than the full premium.

Pricing of premiums and hedging strategies by writers are undertaken in a similar manner to that for currency options, taking into account the maturity, strike price, current market price, interest rates and above all volatility of the underlying. OTC interest rate options and option portfolios are likely to be hedged or partially hedged by writers using exchange traded interest rate futures and options.

OTC interest rate options may be evidenced solely by an exchange of confirmations but it is common for documentation to be based on ISDA terms, which are outlined in Chapter 26.

Exchange traded options

Exchange traded options are standardised and are quoted and traded on exchanges in a similar manner to futures contracts examined in Chapter 27. Procedures for trading are very similar to futures trading with the clearing house becoming the purchaser and grantor of contracts after registration.

Trading of options on exchanges is normally on American terms thus providing the holder with the right to exercise and take delivery at any time during the life of the contract. The underlying is usually a futures contract of the same exchange, the exercise of the option thus resulting in the holder obtaining a futures position. Where a purchaser does exercise, the clearing house assigns, at its discretion, notice of exercise to a clearing member with a short position in the same series and class as the option exercised. Consequently any short holder must be prepared to accept an assignment of exercise and make delivery at any time during the period for which the short position is held.

Options on each type of underlying subject matter are referred to as 'classes' of options. Within a class, all options that have the same expiry date are referred to as a 'series'.

Contract characteristics

The characteristics of two types of contract are outlined below to illustrate the workings of exchange traded options contracts.

- Traded option on short term interest rate futures contract - Liffe option on 3 month sterling futures

- Traded option on bond futures contract – CBOT T-Bond option

Liffe option on 3 month sterling interest rate future

Unit of trading	1 Sterling futures contract (£500,000)
Expiry months	March, June, September and December
Last trading day	Last trading day of the futures contract
Exercise/Expiry day	Exercise by 17:00 on any business day. Delivery on the first business day after the exercise day. Expiry at 12:30 on the last trading day.
Quotation	Multiples of 0.01 (ie 0.01%)
Minimum price move	0.01
Tick value	£12.50
Trading Hours	08.07 - 16.05

The contract standard is assignment of one Three Month Sterling futures contract for the delivery month at the exercise price. Exercise price intervals are at 0.25 (ie 0.25 per cent) eg 93.00, 93.25, 93.50.

When a new series is traded each quarter, 13 exercise prices are listed. Additional exercise prices are introduced on the business day after the futures contract settlement price is within 0.12 of the sixth highest or sixth lowest existing exercise price. The premium payable is collected on a margin basis rather than all being payable up front.

CBOT Option on US Treasury Bond Futures

Unit of Trading	One CBOT T-Bond futures contract
Expiry months	Front month of the current quarter plus the next three quarterly contracts.
Exercise	Exercise by 18:00 on any business day
Last trading day	12:00 on the last Friday that is at least five business days before the last business day of the month preceding the option contract month
Minimum price move	1/64 of a point
Tick value	$15.625
Trading hours	07.20 – 14.00

The exchange offers a front month option contract that exercises into a futures contract of the current quarter. For example, an October option relates to a December futures contract, as does a November contract. Where the month concerned is a normal futures quarter month, no monthly contract is listed. T-bond options cease trading in the month prior to delivery of the underlying futures contract.

29 Credit derivatives

The latest additions to the family of derivatives are those relating to an underlying credit exposure. The Bank of England defines credit derivatives as follows:

> *"Credit derivatives" is a basket term used to describe various swaps and option contracts designed to assume or lay off credit risk on loans and other assets, in return for either interest payments or payment of premium. The transfer of credit risk may be for the whole life of the asset or for a shorter period, and it may be a complete or a partial transfer of credit risk.*

They are a natural extension of the market for products that unbundle risk (such as interest rate swaps), allowing banks to transfer credit exposure in isolation from other forms of risk on any underlying transactions. Different banks use different terms to describe varieties of credit derivative but the following are the main types:

Total return swap

A Total Return Swap transfers the total economic performance of a reference asset, including all associated cash flows as well as capital appreciation or depreciation. The total return payer pays all contractual payments plus any price appreciation on the reference asset in return for a negotiated floating rate plus any depreciation on the reference asset. For example, Bank A may agree to a total return swap with Bank B linked to a bond issued by XYZ Corporation. The terms of the agreement might be such that Bank A receives periodic payments equal to any positive mark-to-market movements in the price of the bond (including any coupon payments) and in return makes payments to Bank B equal to any negative movements in the price together with

Libor plus a spread. Figure 29.1 illustrates these arrangements.

Figure 29.1   Total Return Swap

This effectively mimics the returns from actually holding the bond with funding from the interbank market and is economically similar to a repo transaction. The spread over Libor will be negotiated between the two counterparties and will reflect the fact that hedging the transaction may require use of balance sheet capacity, plus a profit margin. In this example, Bank B could hedge its position by buying the underlying bond in the market, using the Libor payments from Bank A to cover its funding costs. Changes in the value of the bond whilst it was held by Bank B would be exactly compensated by the payments due to or from Bank A, leaving the negotiated spread as Bank B's profit.

Note that the maturity of the derivative may be shorter than that of the bond to which it is referenced.

By being the total return payer, a bank can hedge existing credit risk. By being the total return receiver, a bank can take credit risk on names where it may have ample credit appetite but does not have the necessary direct contacts to originate by other means as much exposure as it might like to hold. This is an attractive structure for banks which are active traders in bonds and which may have a need, from time to time, to hedge the credit exposure on their inventory.

Credit default swaps/options

Under a default swap, the buyer of credit protection pays a fee (which can be one-off, as with an option, or periodically recurring similar to a swap) in return for the right to receive a conditional payment if a specified reference credit defaults. For example, Bank A might agree to pay (receive) a fee in return for which Bank B would undertake to make (receive) a payment if there is a defined act of default by the reference credit, XYZ Corporation. This is illustrated in Figure 29.2.

Figure 29.2   Credit Default Swap

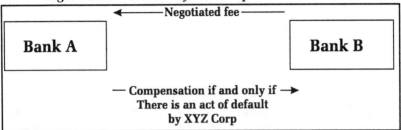

This is the most straightforward structure for a commercial bank looking to hedge or diversify its credit exposures. Economically, the transaction is very similar to a guarantee or risk participation. The key difference is that there is no necessity for either bank to have any other connection with XYZ Corp. As banks start to regard their credit portfolios as tradable, rather than the legacy of previous lending decisions, the ability to choose to take, increase or reduce credit exposure to any tradable name by means of credit derivatives will become more common.

Credit linked notes

This involves the issue - through a trust - of a note that is collateralised by a bond issue by XYZ Corporation. If no default by XYZ occurs, the note matures and is redeemed at par. If, though, XYZ defaults the note is redeemed a short time after the default at the recovery value of the underlying bond. Such notes have been structured so as to base the redemption value on the performance of a basket of bonds from various issuers with the payoff being contingent on default by any of the basket bonds or on default by a specific number of the bonds.

The credit linked note structure is also now being used as a kind of quasi-securitisation with the underlying assets of the trust being corporate receivables or a pool of bank loans. These pools can be revolving with the manager of the structure having the right to substitute loans into the pool under specified circumstances.

Credit linked notes have, to date, largely been set up by investment banks sometimes using their own loans as the underlying pool. A credit default swap (or set of credit default swaps) between the bank and the trust may also play a part in the structure, either as a means of getting credit risk exposure into the asset pool or as a means of providing some first loss protection. In the latter case, there is a clear economic similarity with the provision of a guarantee to a securitisation vehicle but the legal structure is different.

The Credit Derivatives market had reached a size of $170 billion by the end of 1997. In addition to these three structures, banks may also make use of securitisation approaches such as Collateralised Bond Obligations (CBOs) and Collateralised Loan Obligations (CLOs) to manage their credit exposure. CBOs and CLOs are described in Chapter 21.

Uses of credit derivatives

Credit Derivatives have developed as part of a growing recognition by banks that their credit portfolios need to be managed throughout their life and not simply left to run to maturity without further review. Changes in the quality of counterparties over time, together with the tendency for a few major counterparties to dominate a single bank's exposures have led to the development of interest in the application of techniques of portfolio management, initially used in equity fund management, to the control of bank credit portfolios. The details of this approach lie beyond the scope of this publication but it is relevant to note that the natural illiquidities of bank credits means that instruments such as credit derivatives, which permit the transfer of credit risk without changing the underlying contractual and relationship arrangements are virtually essential for the effective application of the approach.

By using credit derivatives, a bank can:

- Hedge excess exposures that the bank does not wish to have, and either cannot sell down or does not wish to be seen to be selling for relationship reasons.

- Free up lines so that the bank can pursue new, profitable business with its most active customers. This is very helpful in handling exposures to frequent counterparties for the Treasury's trading activities, which may build up to worrying large amounts and also fluctuate with market prices.

- Obtain exposure to non-relationship credits which the bank believes are favourably priced and which enhance the diversification of the overall book.

Documentation and regulation

There are a number of practical issues that need to be considered when structuring credit derivative transactions. In particular, the credit event that gives rise to a payment needs to be carefully defined. If the derivative is linked to a publicly traded bond, it will be clear when a default occurs and this will be a matter of common knowledge. With credit derivatives that are linked to bank loans, or credit exposure on other derivative products, an event of default may only be known to the bank itself and there may be reasons of client confidentiality that prevent the bank from calling on the cover that it has under the derivative.

Payments due upon the occurrence of a credit event also need to be defined in advance. Transactions may be structured such that the buyer of credit protection has the right to transfer the underlying asset to the seller so that the question of managing the work out of the defaulting asset becomes the seller's problem. If this is not the structure, then a means of defining the value of the default compensation is required. This could be 100 per cent of the asset's value although in practice few defaulting assets are worth nothing at all. There can also be legal issues in some jurisdictions if the compensation payments are not seen to be equivalent to the loss actually suffered by the hedging bank. A common structure is to link the compensation to prices that can be obtained in the market for defaulted debt a specified number of days after the credit event occurs. This gives a reasonably objective measure that can be demonstrated as fair to all parties.

It is also important to bear in mind the matching of maturities of a credit derivative and the underlying exposure. These are quite likely to differ if the derivative is, for convenience, linked to a public bond whilst the underlying exposure is a direct loan. Where the derivative matures before the underlying, the bank will be left with uncovered exposure at some time in the future. Regulators have been reluctant to recognise this as being a fully hedged position for purposes of exposure measurement. Where the derivative matures later than the underlying, the bank is paying for cover on an exposure it no longer has, which may be uneconomic.

The regulation of credit derivatives is a developing area and there are potential anomalies in the capital treatment of credit derivatives as compared to very similar traditional products such as guarantees.

ISDA credit swap confirmation

To date, the main users of credit derivatives have been the leading investment banks. ISDA has taken a lead in developing documentation and has produced a standard credit swap confirmation that can be used in conjunction with its Master Agreement.

In addition to the usual details such as trade date, counterparty details and business day convention that will be applied, a credit swap confirmation will also need to address the features described in the following paragraphs.

The reference entity and, where applicable, the reference obligation, must be clearly defined. Corporate group structures can be quite complicated, including many different legal entities all with similar names. It must be clear which one (or ones) are covered by the agreement. Likewise, where there is a reference obligation to which the terms of the swap are tied, this must be made absolutely explicit.

The events that can be considered as triggering a payment under the swap agreement may include the following:

- bankruptcy (under the terms of the governing law);
- merger, where the creditworthiness of the resulting merged entity is materially weaker than that of the original reference entity;
- cross acceleration or cross default, where an event triggers early payment or payment default on another obligation of the reference entity;
- downgrade, where a reduction in the external rating given to the reference obligation means that it falls below a pre-agreed level;
- failure to make payments when due;
- repudiation of its supposed obligations by the reference entity;

- restructuring of the reference entity's obligations such as to materially weaken the position of any interested party.

The confirmation will also define the level at which any credit events may be deemed to be material. This may relate either to the price of the reference obligation or to its spread. For example, it may specify that a ten per cent reduction in price following a credit event is evidence that such an event is material. This would clearly be more than might be expected due to normal market factors. If linked to spread, a 200 basis point rise in the spread over the benchmark rate might be considered a suitable materiality trigger. Details of the mechanism for obtaining these valuations will also be included.

Details for settlement of any payment upon a credit event will also be included. This is normally expected to be by cash payment based upon the price of the reference obligation a certain number of days after the credit event but may be by physical delivery of the reference obligation.

PART SIX

Other Treasury Operations

30 Principles of treasury accounting

The prodigious increase that has taken place in the number of financial instruments traded by banks has raised many issues for the accountancy profession. Regulators must, of necessity, rely to a large extent on a bank's published accounts, prepared in accordance with accepted accounting standards. Ensuring that these standards are adequate to reflect the true risks faced by banks when dealing in ever more complex instruments is indeed a challenge.

In the UK audited accounts are prepared in accordance with Generally Accepted Accounting Principles (GAAP) and in line with the EU Bank Accounts Directive. This chapter discusses some of the difficulties arising in respect of particular instruments and runs through some examples of the book-keeping procedures necessary to ensure that proper records are kept. Full details of accounting standards are beyond the scope of this book as are taxation issues.

International accounting standards

Through its own regulatory and/or professional accounting bodies, each country has established its own criteria for the presentation of financial statements and, in particular, disclosure requirements. For example, the United States has developed specific legal requirements in respect of the presentation and disclosure of the financial statements of US incorporated banks and bank holding companies. These are required to be prepared in accordance with the statements of the Financial Accounting Standards Board (FASB) and regulations of the Securities and Exchange Commission (SEC). In the United Kingdom, the EU Bank Accounts Directive applies as part of the harmonisation process. This resulted in new legislation prescribing the form and content of banks' financial reports, removing the option that previously existed of reporting in the same manner as non-banks.

Not only do banks in the UK now have industry specific legislation but they continue to be subject to the Companies Acts generally for regulations concerning consolidated accounts and for matters where banking companies are not specifically addressed. In addition, they are subject to the Financial Reporting Standards (FRSs) published by the Accounting Standards Board (ASB) and to the Statements of Standard Accounting Practice (SSAPs) published by its predecessor, the Accounting Standards Committee (ASC), and adopted by the ASB on its inception in 1991. Statements of Recommended Practice (SORPs) are also prepared by the ASB in conjunction with industry bodies such as the British Bankers Association.

Many countries, including the UK, follow closely the standards published by the International Accounting Standards Committee (IASC), which was established in 1973. It is controlled by a board comprising representatives of national accounting bodies and by a world-wide committee of financial analysts.

The objectives of the committee are:

- to form and publish, in the public interest, accounting standards to be observed in the presentation of financial statements and to permit their world-wide acceptance and observation;

- to work generally for the improvement and harmonisation of regulations, accounting standards and procedures relating to the presentation of financial statements.

Income recognition

A common area of difficulty in accounting for treasury products relates to the timing of income recognition. The main factors to consider are whether the transaction relates to a speculative trading position or general banking position and whether it constitutes a hedge. In general, banking book positions are accounted for on an accruals basis whereas trading positions are marked-to-market.

Hedging

Hedging transactions are those entered into to reduce the risk of loss arising from movements in interest rates, exchange rates and/or market prices inherent in existing assets, liabilities or positions or in future cash flows.

A hedge need not be perfect, but there must be a high degree of probability that it will eliminate a substantial part of the market risk that would otherwise be borne. It is not necessary for the transactions to be matched on a one-for-one basis. It is acceptable for a position, or part thereof, to be regarded as hedging a group of liabilities, assets and off balance sheet transactions. A position being hedged may include off balance sheet exposures, specific anticipated transactions or future cash flows expected to arise in the normal course of business.

There should be clearly defined procedures in place for identifying hedges and adequate evidence of the intention to hedge at the outset of a transaction or, in the case of an appropriation of a position as part of a hedge, at the time of transfer.

Any profit or loss arising from marking-to-market a position when it is first earmarked as part of a hedge should be taken to profit and loss account immediately. Positions removed from a hedge should be marked-to-market before transfer to a trading or investment portfolio and the profit or loss arising should be treated so as to match the flow of income or expenditure from the remaining assets or liabilities which had been hedged.

The valuation of the individual parts of an ongoing hedge must be consistent. That is, the accounting treatment of the hedge should match that of the position being hedged. The entire transaction may be valued at market rates or, if a loan or deposit is hedged, the appropriate treatment is likely to be cost.

Advances and deposits

Interest is generally brought into account on an accruals basis, provided that its collectability is not subject to significant doubt. Doubtful interest should be excluded from the profit and loss account. It may be necessary to continue to accrue entries to the customer's account in order to compute claims against him, although such interest will be carried to an "interest in suspense" account until such time as there is no longer any realistic prospect of recovering it.

Fees should be amortised over the expected life of the transaction.

Forward foreign exchange

Banks actively trading in the forward foreign exchange markets will ensure that their trading and speculative positions are marked-to-market on a regular basis, and the resultant profit or loss, discounted to net present value where appropriate, taken immediately to profit and loss account.

Forwards hedging loans or deposits will require any premiums or discounts to be amortised over the life of such balances, and for the results of deposit swaps to be similarly treated.

Financial futures

Futures are traded on recognised exchanges. Being tradable, with published closing prices, marking-to-market causes no problems. Variation margin payments and receipts during the life of the contract constitute assets and liabilities. Dealing commissions should be taken to profit and loss account on receipt or payment.

Options

For options forming part of a hedge, the general principles for hedges should be followed. The premium payable on such an option should be charged to profit and loss account in the period in which the results of the transaction, as a whole, are accounted for, which will necessitate spreading it in appropriate cases.

Where options are purchased or written as part of a trading portfolio they should be marked-to-market. Options written should not be valued by the writer in excess of the premium received and options purchased should not be valued by the purchaser at a negative amount.

Dealing commissions should be taken to profit and loss account as incurred, except those in relation to hedges, which should be spread to correspond with the treatment of the income resulting from the remainder of the hedge.

Swaps

The general hedging principles apply to swaps taken out to hedge existing income, expenditure, assets and liabilities. In particular, interest rate swaps should be accounted for by taking into account the net payment or receipt under the swap in determining the interest charged or credited to profit and loss account. Lump sum payments receivable or payable under such swaps should be time-apportioned over the life of the swap and, where such treatment might have a materially different impact, by taking account of the fact that the lump sum payments receivable or payable will generally be determined on a net present value basis.

Swaps entered into as part of a trading portfolio or for speculative purposes, should be marked-to-market by determining the net present value of future cash flows expected to arise under the swap at the current market interest rate. A zero coupon yield curve, constructed from the normal market curve using an appropriate arithmetical technique, would normally provide the best source for determining discount factors. A part of the net present value of anticipated future profits should be spread over the life of the transaction, having regard to all likely future costs and risks.

Fees earned or paid on the arrangement, or granting, of swaps entered into, other than for hedging purposes, should generally be taken or charged to profit and loss account as incurred.

Forward rate agreements

The general principles of hedging apply, with the net cash payable or receivable, as determined on the date when the contract crystallises, being spread over the relevant period. That is, interest is not spread from the date on which the contract is entered into to the date on which it settles, but on the period from the settlement date for the notional period thereafter. For example, if the agreement covers three month Libor from a future date, the payment or receipt will normally be spread over that three month period commencing on the appropriate forward date.

FRAs taken out as part of a trading portfolio, or for speculative purposes, should be marked-to-market by reference to the interest differential between the market rate and the rate implicit in the contract and the period remaining to the settlement date. If the sums are substantial, future cash flows should be discounted at current interest rates.

Securities

The treatment of securities positions will depend on the purposes for which they are taken and will distinguish between market making and dealing securities and investment securities.

A market marker is defined as one who quotes a regular two-way price with the aim of profiting primarily from the bid/offer spread and who maintains positions for that purpose. Dealing securities are holdings (or short positions) turned over relatively rapidly and may comprise, mainly, short term paper, often as part of liquidity management. Investment securities are bought for the longer term and turned over with far less frequency or may be held to maturity.

In general, securities should be marked-to-market with the exception of those identified as being held for the longer term. Unquoted securities are valued at directors' estimate of market value. That is a price that could reasonably have been achieved at the balance sheet date, after providing for the costs of sale. Prudential safeguards are recommended for the valuation of holdings which are larger than normal size, exceptional dealing positions and securities subject to, or part of, a hedge.

Investment securities may be valued on a basis of cost, with premiums and discounts on redeemable securities amortised to maturity, preferably on an actuarial basis. Provision should also be made for any diminution in value that is expected to be more than temporary.

In exceptional circumstances and with adequate authorisation and documentation, transfers between categories, at market value, are permissible, any resultant profit or loss passing through the profit and loss account.

The treatment of securities positions forming part of a hedge are dealt with above.

Sale and repurchase agreements

A sale and repurchase agreement (or repo) is, in practice, a secured deposit and a reverse repo is a secured loan. Accordingly, they are balance sheet items. For the transferor of the security, the assets remain in the balance sheet and the proceeds are shown as owed to the transferee. For the transferor the assets are excluded from the balance sheet but the cost is shown as owed by the transferor.

For a repo, the difference between the sale price and the repurchase price represents effectively interest and should consequently be time-apportioned over the life of the transaction.

Provisioning and reserves

Care must be taken to ensure proper valuation of assets and liabilities.

This should take into account possible future diminution of value owing in particular to credit losses but also to various other factors that may otherwise result in value being overstated.

Factors to consider would be the costs of executing closing transactions, future administrative costs, early termination risks and operational risks. Particular attention may be required where positions are held in markets that have limited liquidity and the position held is large in relation to what could be closed out quickly. Products that are valued in relation to a mathematical model, as is the case with some exotic options, should be valued on the basis of conservative assumptions.

When reviewing the size of reserves, equal focus should be placed on both under and over reserving. Accounts should aim to present a fair but not over-conservative view. Over reserving can lead to complacency.

Accounting for multiple currencies

Accounting systems are designed these days in a modular format. Individual transactions will be recorded, initially, in a treasury system that is likely to provide data on currency exposure, cash flow, maturity analysis and other data, current and forward, emanating at bargain level. This data will feed the main accounting, or general ledger, system which will generate controls over aggregate customer balances, nostro accounts and reconciliations thereof.

Assets acquired with foreign currency may be recorded on purchase in the base currency, a single currency system, either at the cost of the currency itself, the method most frequently adopted by non-banks, or by translating the currency to base currency at the rate of exchange applicable on settlement date.

Banks maintaining foreign currency positions will, in general, choose between a dual or multi-currency accounting system.

A dual system records the currency dealt in and the base currency equivalent in adjoining columns. The disadvantages of such a system are:

- Many transactions, such as loans and deposits, do not involve the base currency and it is necessary to create artificial base currency equivalents, which are meaningful only at the time of creation;

- On profit evaluation it is necessary to revalue the balance on every account to a new base currency amount;

- Unless revaluation occurs on the occasion of each new account transaction, the aggregate base currency balance on each account has no precise meaning;

- If one accepts that a customer's bank statement should represent an exact copy of his account in his banker's books, accurately recording his dealings with them, it will be appreciated that the system is incapable of producing such a statement. Either the document must be censored to omit the base currency or it will record a currency in which the customer may well have had no dealings.

The advantages of such a system are:

- The ability to monitor exposures for customers holding balances in more than one currency is enhanced.

- Treasury aggregate cash and liquidity positions may more readily be controlled.

A multi-currency accounting system, by comparison, requires the maintenance of a separate, self-contained, accounting system for each currency in which the bank or its customers maintain accounts.

The disadvantages of such a system are:

- The necessity to record all spot purchases and sales of currency in at least two sets of balances or, for cross-rate transactions not involving the base currency, three sets if the performance of each is to be measured against the base currency;

- The apparent complexity to those used only to dealing in their domestic currency;

- The difficulty of monitoring aggregate exposures for customers holding balances in a number of currencies.

The advantages of such a system are:

- The accounts accurately reflect transactions, such as loans and deposits conducted wholly in a foreign currency and no arbitrary translation to base currency is required;

- In the base currency books, only one total account in respect of each foreign currency dealt in needs to be revalued on the occasion of every profit evaluation;

- Settled spot positions for each currency are continuously available;

- Statements for loans and deposits accurately record customer dealings with the bank;

- A higher volume of transactions can usually be handled than with a dual system;

- Individual currency cash and liquidity positions may more readily be monitored;

- Whilst the predominant practice in a multi-currency system is to refer purchases and sales to the base currency, it is possible to provide a system, preferred by some treasury dealers, of initially referring all such transactions and performance measurement to the most prominent currency, ie the US dollar. However, it is essential to appreciate that the position risk relative to the true base currency will have to be catered for.

In the examples below, the multi-currency system has been used for illustrative purposes and sterling has been assumed to be the base currency.

Practical accounting

The accounting system will contain a general ledger for each currency dealt in, including the base currency to record spot (ie settled) transactions. At each revaluation date the currency Exchange Dealing Account will be translated at the current market rate of exchange, using, normally, for active traders, mid-market prices, and the appropriate Exchange Dealing Account in the base currency ledger will be adjusted to the current value by transfer to/from profit and loss account.

Forward transactions, and spot transactions which have not yet reached settlement date, will normally be kept either in a diarised format, or in a memorandum accounting system feeding the general ledgers only on settlement day.

The frequency of valuation will normally depend upon the nature of the accounting system employed. For manual systems, entries should be made no less frequently than each time internal profit and loss accounts are produced, normally monthly. Computer systems can be programmed to generate accounting entries each time a table of rates is input, which will normally be at the end of each day's trading.

The greater the frequency of calculation and accounting for profits, the sooner problems can be identified and, if necessary, rectified. Computers can be programmed to identify and reject deals that are erroneous or fraudulent, by recognising those that are done at rates varying, by more than a pre-determined margin, from the previous deals or from the input market rates. Such programs will also ensure that decimal points are not misplaced.

Market rates are obtained from an independent source. In most banks the rates used are an average of those quoted by a pre-determined group of leading banks as shown on their respective pages on the screens of the Reuters or Telerate services. For illiquid currencies or periods, brokers may be asked to supply estimated market rates.

The first example, below, shows the accounting entries and revaluation resulting from one spot purchase of US dollars for sterling. The second example, whilst omitting the detailed accounting entries, demonstrates the revaluation process for both spot and forward positions.

It also shows that the actual timing of the valuations will not affect the ultimate results and that it is not practicable to distinguish realised profits from unrealised profits.

EXAMPLE 1 - A purchase of $1 million for sterling at 1.785, value 2nd June

$ General Ledger

2nd June	Dr $ Nostro	$1,000,000.00
2nd June	Cr Exchange Dealing Account x (spot position account)	$1,000,000.00

£ General Ledger

2nd June	Dr $ Exchange Dealing Account	£560,224.09
2nd June	Cr £ Nostro	£560,224.09

In this example, had there been no other transactions, an end month revaluation, when the £/$ rate was 1.78, would result in the long $1 million position, having cost £560,224.09 being worth £561,797.75, a profit of £1,573.66. This would be recorded in the sterling general ledger, the resulting balances on which would be:

30th June	Dr $ Exchange Dealing Account	£561,797.75
2nd June	Cr £ Nostro	£560,224.09
30th June	Cr Foreign Exchange Profit and Loss Account	£1,573.66

If a balance sheet was required, the dollar general ledger balances would be translated, individually at the month end rate, and a consolidated balance sheet produced in which the Cr Exchange Dealing Account, translated from the dollar general ledger, would exactly equal and be cancelled against an equivalent Dr dollar Exchange Dealing Account from the sterling general ledger.

Thus the balances would initially comprise:

	Currency Equivalent	Sterling
Dollar General Ledger		
Dr $ Nostro	1,000,000	561,797.75
Cr Exchange Dealing Account	1,000,000	561,797.75
Sterling General Ledger		
Dr $ Exchange Dealing Account	-	561,797.75
Cr £ Nostro	-	560,224.09
Cr Foreign Exchange Profit and Loss Account	-	1,573.66

Leaving a balance sheet comprising:

Profit and Loss Account	1,573.66	$ Cash at Bank	561,797.75
Overdrawn £ Nostro	560,224.09		
	£561,797.75		£561,797.75

It should be appreciated that the "original cost" of spot foreign currency ceases to be of relevance to the treasurer almost instantly, consequently once a revaluation has been recorded it is never reversed and original cost is lost from view. Subsequent revaluations represent only adjustments to previous revaluations.

The reason that this simplistic transaction has been analysed in some detail is that any foreign exchange accounting problem, however complex, can always be resolved by returning to the basic principles.

EXAMPLE 2 - A series of purchases and sales of spot US dollars against sterling (shown in tabular form)

	Rate	$ - Long/(Short)	£ - Long/(Short)
2nd June	1.7850	1,000,000	(560,224.09)
2nd June	1.7855	1,000,000	(560,067.21)
2nd June	1.7845	(500,000)	280,190.53
2nd June	1.7849	250,000	(140,063.87)
2nd June	1.7848	(150,000)	84,043.03
		1,600,000	(896,121.61)

If revaluations are recorded at the end of the day and the closing rate is 1.78, the long spot position now has a value of £898,876.40. The net cost of various purchases and sales was £896,121.61, resulting in a profit of £2,754.79. This is entered into the bank's sterling general ledger. The dollar Exchange Dealing Account will have shown a debit of £896,121.61 and this will be increased to the revalued amount of £898,876.40 by:

| Dr | $ Exchange Dealing Account | £2,754.79 |
| Cr | Foreign Exchange Profit and Loss Account | £2,754.79 |

If no further transactions are undertaken by the end of the following day, 3rd June, when the closing rate is 1.7830, the long spot position of $1,600,000 will have changed in value to £897,363.99. Having written up the dollar Exchange Dealing Account by the above entry to £898,876.40, it must now be reduced by £1,512.41, the amount lost by holding $1,600,000 for one day, to the current value of £897,363.99 by:

| Dr | Foreign Exchange Profit and Loss Account | £1,512.41 |
| Cr | $ Exchange Dealing Account | £1,512.41 |

It will be appreciated that, if no profit had been recorded at the end of day trading on 2nd June, the value, by the end of the following day, would have increased by £1,242.38 over the original net book cost (£897,363.99 - £896,121.61), which is equivalent to the 2nd June recorded profit, £2,754.79 less the following days recorded loss £1,512.41. Therefore, the quantum of profit will be unaffected by the frequency with which it is recorded. Further, due to the volume of dealing and the fungibility of currency, no particular purchase can be identified with a particular sale. In an active dealing room the sequence in which deals are recorded may be fortuitous and thus the extent to which dealing profits are, or are not, "realised" cannot be precisely determined until a spot, or precisely matched forward, position reverts to zero.

To determine the results in each individual currency, it is necessary to maintain either a separate Foreign Exchange Profit and Loss Account for each currency or an analysis of a global account.

Forward valuations

Example 1 demonstrated the relationship between the Exchange Dealing Accounts, showing the position in each currency and the corresponding Exchange Dealing Accounts held in the base currency. Example 2 looked at a series of spot transactions. Had they been forward transactions entered into on 2nd March for three month settlement, they would be recorded in a diary outside the main accounting system. Thus, to incorporate the profits and losses in the intervening period, it is necessary to create a suspense account within the general ledger to which they may be passed until maturity.

In practice, the forward book will comprise a large number of purchases and sales maturing on various dates into the future. To determine profitability it is necessary to calculate the net position and the contracted net cost/proceeds for each currency for every future date and to value each such position at the market rate and to compare that value with the contracted price.

Unlike spot bargains, results are continually measured against original contract price that will, in any event, need to be maintained to enable settlement to be made on the due date.

The aggregate result, which may be analysed by individual currency, will be carried as a balance on the Forward Foreign Exchange Profit Suspense Account. As each revaluation is made the suspense account balance will be adjusted to the latest valuation, for an increase in profit or reduction in loss by:

> Dr   Forward Foreign Exchange Profit Suspense Account
> Cr   Foreign Exchange Profit and Loss Account

and vice versa for lower profits or higher losses.

As forward contracts reach maturity date, they automatically fall out of the valuation process and thus out of the suspense account, whereupon they end up, without further intervention, as part of the spot position in the general ledger.

As market rates are not published for every future date, those for each day are usually interpolated from the rates for standard market periods published on the screens by the major banks.

The balance of the Forward Foreign Exchange Profit Suspense Account will be included in the Balance Sheet, at accounting dates, with Other Assets or Other Liabilities, as appropriate.

Cross-rate Transactions

In order to measure performance of each currency against the base currency, even when dealing "on the cross", without the intervention of the base currency, it is necessary to assign a notional base currency rate to one of the currencies dealt in (normally the more active) and apply the base amount to both buying and selling Exchange Dealing Accounts in the sterling general ledger.

EXAMPLE 3 - A purchase of $ 1 million for DM @ 1.641 value 2nd June

	$ General Ledger	
2nd June	Dr $ Nostro	$ 1,000,000.00
2nd June	Cr Exchange Dealing Account	$ 1,000,000.00
	DM General Ledger	
2nd June	Dr Exchange Dealing Account	DM 1,641,000.00
2nd June	Cr DM Nostro	DM 1,641,000.00
	£ General Ledger	
2nd June	Dr $ Exchange Dealing Account	£560,224.09
2nd June	Cr DM Exchange Dealing Account	£560,224.09

From the foregoing the relationship between rates in various currencies and the opportunities for arbitrage can be seen. Using the same £/$ rate as in Example 1, the cross rate transaction results in a short DM position at an effective £/DM rate of 2.929 (ie DM 1,641,000/£560,224.09 or in exchange rate terms 1.641 x 1.785).

Swap deposits

Swap deposits, commonly known as interest arbitrage, is the term given to an inter-related series of transactions whereby, in its simplest form, one currency is borrowed for a fixed term, sold spot through the cross market, thereby being swapped into another currency which is lent for an identical fixed term. On the inception of the transaction, a forward cross-rate transaction is entered into for the maturity date of the loan and deposit, swapping the anticipated proceeds of the loan into the currency of the deposit so that the funds are available to make the repayment.

The main reasons for such a complex transaction are to enable a bank either to lend a currency that it is incapable of borrowing, possibly because of exchange controls, or to benefit from anomalies in differences between interest rates and forward exchange rates in different currencies.

Consideration of the relationship between spot and forward rates resulting from interest rate differentials is essential in such transactions. If the respective three month inter-bank rates for US dollars and the Danish krone are 4 per cent and 10.5 per cent, the differential of 6.5 per cent pa will result in a discount for the three month DKr/$ rate to the spot rate.

EXAMPLE 4 - A customer wishes to borrow DKr1 million for three months from 1st July to 1st October when the spot cross rate against the US dollar is 6.36. The bank will:

Borrow	$157,232.70	
Sell	$157,232.70	
Buy spot	DKr1,000,000.00	@ 6.36
Lend three months	DKr1,000,000.00	
Sell three months forward	DKr1,000,000.00	@ 6.44
Buy three months forward	$155,279.50	

Additionally, to crystallise profits in dollar terms, the bank will:

Sell its interest earnings forward

Sell three months forward	DKr26,833.33	@ 6.44
Buy three months forward	$4,166.67	

On 1st October:

The bank pays $157,232.70 + (157,232.70 x $\frac{4}{100}$ x $\frac{92)}{360}$

$= \$158,839.97$

The bank receives DKr1,000,000 (1,000,000 x $\frac{10.5}{100}$ x $\frac{92)}{360}$

$= \text{DKr}1,026,833.33$

which it has contracted to sell in
exchange for $155,279.50 + 4,166.67 $=$ \$159,446.17

making a profit on the transaction of $ 606.20

The forward cross rate could have been computed on the above information as follows:

DKr(1,000,000 x $\frac{10.5}{100}$ x $\frac{92)}{360}$ + 1,000,000 = 1,026,833.33

$(157,232.70 x $\frac{4}{100}$ x $\frac{92)}{360}$ + 157,232.70 = 158,839.97

If the latter is divided into the former a forward rate of 6.4645 gives a forward discount of 1045 points and any lower discount obtained will result in a profit. A point is defined as 0.01 per cent, that is, one in ten thousand.

The transactions in Example 4 constitute a hedge in which the ultimate out-turn is known in dollar terms when the deal is done. No movements in spot or forward exchange rates in the period from 1st July to 1st October will affect that result. Consequently, it is essential that the positions created are, as far as possible, eliminated from any valuation, and from dealing positions as they do not represent positions which the dealers are free to trade.

The positions resulting from the hedge in the example are:

Short spot $157,232.70

Long spot   DKr1,000,000.00

Short forward	DKr1,000,000.00 + 26,833.00
Long forward	$155,279.50 + 4,166.67

By earmarking the transactions as a hedge they can be segregated from the other open positions in the computer produced valuation and dealer information programs and eliminated from the former. In a non-computer environment, an approximate equivalent result can be obtained by earmarking only the forward leg, separating it in a unique hedge position account and valuing that position at the spot rate.

Additionally, by separately identifying the related US dollar deposit and Danish krone advance the relevant dealers can be put on notice that repayment funds have already been catered for.

The profitability of the deposit swap transaction would have been readily assessed before entering into the deals by use of a programmed arbitrage calculator, widely used in all modern dealing systems. However, it is a fairly straightforward exercise to calculate the profit manually. To achieve this, we need to know, as a minimum, the spot exchange rate and any *two* of the other rates applicable to the overall transaction (ie interest rate for the borrowed currency, interest rate for lending the derived currency and the forward exchange rate). With this information we can calculate a break-even point. To take the transaction in Example 4 above, let us assume that the uncertain factor was the interest rate for borrowing the US dollars.

The three months' forward exchange cover would be:

Sell DKr1,026,833.33 @ 6.44
Buy $159,446.17

The Danish krone asset is fully covered (ie maturing principal plus interest); the break-even rate to borrow dollars is 5.5086532 per cent pa, ie

$$\frac{2.213.47}{157,232.70} \times 100 \times \frac{360}{92}$$

If we can borrow dollars at a lower rate we are in profit. We borrowed the dollars at 4 per cent pa; our profit is 1.5086532 per cent pa, ie

$$157,232.70 \times \frac{1.5086532}{100} \times \frac{92}{360} = \$606.20 \text{ profit}$$

Currency loans and deposits

The taking of deposits and granting of loans in a foreign currency does not, of itself, give rise to a currency position. The earning of interest receivable and the funding of interest payable does, however, create an exchange position effect to which is given by raising an internal deal. The internal deal is required to record a pre-existing condition and not to create that condition. If the deal was not done, the exchange risk would remain but might be harder to recognise.

EXAMPLE 5 - a bank borrows $10,000,000 at 4 per cent for three months value 1st July, and lends $9,750,000 at 5.5 per cent for three months value 1st July.

When the transactions are entered into the books will record balances:

1st July	$ Deposit	10,000,000.00
	$ Loan	9,750,000.00
	$ Nostro	250,000.00

Following repayment the dollar general ledger will record the following:

1st October	$ interest paid	Dr 102,222.22
	$ interest received	Cr 137,041.67
	$ Nostro	Dr 34,819.45

The bank has no other dollar assets or liabilities. It has earned net interest of $34,819.45 which is held in its bank in New York, it thus holds a position of this amount which is not yet recorded as such, hence the necessity to create internal deals to correct the situation.

The dealers should be instructed to buy interest received of $137,041.67 and sell interest paid of $102,222.22 for settlement to the corresponding accounts in the sterling general ledger. Assuming a rate of 1.78 the dollar interest paid and received accounts will revert to nil and the dollar general ledger will carry the following balances:

Dr	$ Nostro	$ 34,819.45
Cr	Exchange Dealing Account	$ 34,819.45

and the sterling general ledger:

Dr	$ Exchange Dealing Account	£19,561.49

Dr	Currency interest paid	£57,428.21
Cr	Currency interest received	£76,989.70

The creation of the internal deals thus does no more than reflect what has actually occurred. In order to crystallise the bank's ultimate profit in sterling terms, the dealers would need to sell the position of $34,819.45 in the market (ie to third parties).

The net interest in the above example will have accrued over the period as follows:

July	$11,354.17
August	11,732.64
September	11,354.17
October	378.47
	$34,819.45

Alternative strategies would have been to buy all the interest forward on 1st July to hedge and crystallise the overall result of the loan and deposit book or to buy each month's net accrual at the close of each month, but in either event until a deal is effected with the market the ultimate result cannot be determined, and until then whichever strategy is adopted the only effect will be to vary the overall result as between net interest and spot foreign exchange profit.

31 Correspondent banking relationships

A variety of written and informal agreements with banking institutions abroad is essential to every bank that engages in international business. There are basically two ways by which these arrangements may be made. Correspondent banking relations may be established with other banks usually indigenous to the host country abroad. Such banks may offer reciprocal business despite the intense competition between banks for profitable business. The other course adopted is to channel the overseas business through a branch, subsidiary or affiliate organisation with appropriate representation in the overseas country.

The operating costs involved in providing many of the services involved are high and, in order to cover the overheads, there is considerable competition between banks within each major financial centre to attract the high volumes required to achieve optimum employment of expensive automated equipment and sophisticated systems.

Individual banks' philosophy in this context varies from total reliance on correspondent bank relations to total independence through an international branch and subsidiary network. By far the majority of international banks, however, use some of the required services provided by correspondent banks, even in centres where they do have representation, and rely totally on correspondent banks where no local representation has been established. Examples exist of mutual agreements between banks to specialise geographically, with all business enquiries in the bank's non-specialist region being referred to the partner. It is probable that multi-lateral alliances along similar lines will develop.

Reciprocity, quality and price of the services provided by the correspondent banks are the main criteria on which decisions to direct specific business are made. Although long-standing relationships tend to be an influence, the diminishing profitability of many banks has focused greater attention on the above three prime criteria.

Moreover, in order to satisfy customer demand for the widest range, highest quality, lowest price and most adaptable service, banks in an increasingly competitive environment are conscious of the need to be duly selective in their choice of correspondent banks. Indeed, customers often have firm ideas as to the choice of overseas correspondent for specific types of business and it is essential for banks to be able to cater for such 'directed business' if their customers' wishes are to be satisfied.

Agency agreements

The written agreements vary from simple documents setting out arrangements between two offices to provide international transfer services to the more detailed arrangements agreed between two major banking groups involving a wide range of services to be provided for the specified branches and subsidiaries. Increasingly, agreements will specify quantitative service standards that must be maintained by the correspondent in order to ensure proper service to the bank's own customers. These may include accreditation under the ISO 9002 standards.

The range of services

Many services carried out by one bank on behalf of another do not, necessarily, feature in agency agreement documents. Foreign exchange facilities, placing and stand-by lines are usually the subject of separate arrangements, which, like any credit facilities, selectively granted, will be carefully controlled and kept under constant review.

The initial correspondent relationship involves a discussion of the services the two banks (or their groups) can offer each other and the fees involved (where applicable). If any relationship is contemplated each bank and their involved branches and subsidiaries must be able to authenticate messages by mail, telex or electronic transfer systems purporting to have originated from the other bank. An exchange of authorised signatures and testing cyphers is, therefore, a fundamental requirement, whether or not any mutual account holding relationship is sought.

The list of services offered and sought by correspondent banks given below is by no means comprehensive. New technology gives rise to new systems and enhancements of existing services. Development and diversification of banking business in various countries and the creation of new markets continue to add to the list. Detailed breakdowns of trade related services such as documentary credit (opening, advising, confirming, transferring, amending, accepting, negotiating, paying) are not developed here since they are adequately covered by numerous textbooks on the subject of Finance of International Trade.

Subject to relevant current exchange control requirements services may be provided for facilities denominated in local currency and foreign currency.

The services are:

- Accounting and transfer facilities including cheque clearing, transmission of funds, settlement of international payment instructions and the maintenance of accounts in local currency and third country currencies.

- Trade related services involving the handling and processing of shipping documentation and contract guarantees, particularly collection and documentary credit services.

- Financial facilities including overdrafts, loans acceptances, various financial facilities provided by local branches and subsidiaries and syndications.

- Cash management facilities, automated balance reporting and vostro account investment schemes.

- Money market and treasury facilities including foreign exchange lines, placing lines, futures, options, interest rate swaps and currency swaps.

- Securities facilities including purchase and sale, custodian, clearing, registrar, paying and fiscal agency, underwriting, new issue management and advisory services.

- Travel services including foreign notes and coin, travelers' cheques, drafts, travelers' letters of credit, eurocheque encashment facilities, local drawing and cheque encashment facilities and local borrowing supported by bankers' guarantee.

- Commercial and economic advisory services including status reports, industry surveys and economic reports on countries and international matters and markets.

- Other facilities such as insurance, trustee and advisory services on mergers and acquisitions.

The most common services offered are documentary credits, foreign exchange, settlement services, clearing, collections and account facilities. The size and nature of the banking institution's business and its country of domicile will give rise to variations and other preferences. Although the services indicated in this paragraph are widely considered to be profitable, banks will usually seek reciprocal business as part of any agreement to use their correspondent's services.

Correspondent banks are not only customers but in the main are an essential corner stone to the provision of international banking services for all the other customers of the bank. It is essential, therefore, to maintain an efficient and cordial working relationship.

Quality of service has been cited earlier as one of the prime criteria a bank should seek in choosing its banking correspondents. Errors will be made from time to time no matter how efficient a banking operation may be and it is essential that errors, when made, are effectively and swiftly corrected; that the error rate itself is low; and that where loss has been incurred the bank responsible compensates without argument or delay. The quality of service can also be measured by the time taken to process operational transactions. In this context correspondents that offer the required services via electronic/automated/computerised systems are likely to be the most successful, always providing that the systems work properly and that the error rate is low. A mechanism should also exist for communicating advices of transactions that have been effected.

In order to maintain a good working relationship with correspondents mutual visits of well briefed account officers and senior managers are essential. The list of services offered can easily exceed 100, the principal ones being listed above. Account officers, when offering services to correspondent banks, will previously define which services the bank wishes to promote and be aware of the relative return to the bank, if any, likely to be achieved from each service. It is easy to give away someone else's money.

Index